FREDER

SPINOZA

HIS LIFE AND PHILOSOPHY

2006

JOSEPH RUIZ

Elibron Classics
www.elibron.com

CONTENTS

BENEDICTUS DE SPINOZA.

Cui natura, Deus, rerum cui cognitus ordo,
Hoc Spinosa statu conspiciendus erat.
Expressere viri faciem, sed pingere mentem
Zeuxidis artifices, non valuere manus.
Illa viget scriptis: illic sublimia tractat:
Hunc quicunque cupis noscere, scripta lege.

INTRODUCTION

THE purpose of this book is to put before English readers an account, fairly complete in itself and on a fairly adequate scale, of the life and philosophy of Spinoza. It aims, in the first instance, at being understood by those who have not made a special study of the subject; but I hope that it may also be not useless to some who already know Spinoza at first hand, and even to critical students of philosophy. In order to reconcile these objects as far as possible, I have thought it well to collect once for all in this introductory chapter a certain amount of critical and bibliographical matter, which the reader who is interested in it will thus find ready to his hand, while the less curious may with equal ease pass it over. I propose here, not to enter at large on the bibliography and literature of Spinoza, but to give sufficient indications to any one who desires to go further on his own account. This will involve some partial repetition of matters elsewhere touched upon in the course of the book. But I prefer repetition to obscurity.

First let me premise that a most useful, one may indeed say an indispensable, companion to anything like a critical study of Spinoza is Dr. A. van der Linde's *Benedictus Spinoza: Bibliografie* (the Hague, 1871). This is a classified catalogue of the literature of the subject, which, if not absolutely complete, is as complete down to its date as the learning and industry of one man could in the nature of things make it. While I am mentioning the work of a Dutch scholar, I may at the same time gratefully acknowledge my personal obligations to several members of the Spinoza Memorial Committee in the Netherlands for help and information freely given on various points. Herein I am specially bound to Dr. Betz, the Secretary of the Committee, Dr. Campbell, of the Royal Library at the Hague, and Professor Land, of Leyden.

What has to be said here may be distributed under the following heads: —

I. Editions and translations of Spinoza's works.

II. Authorities for Spinoza's life.

III. The early or controversial stage of Spinoza literature.

VI. Modern writings on Spinoza's philosophy as a whole.

V. Monographs and special discussions treating of parts (especially the *De Deo et Homine)* and particular aspects of Spinoza's work.

Dr. van der Linde's work is referred to as *Bibliogr.* simply. It brings us down, as I have said, to 1871. Much more has appeared since that time, as to which I can only call attention to the more important of the publications with which I have become acquainted. In some few particulars I am able to supplement Dr. van der Linde's information as to writings of earlier date.

I. THE WORKS OF SPINOZA

These, in the original order of publication, are as follows:—

1. Renati des Cartes Principiorum Philosophiæ pars I & II, more geometrico demonstratæ per Benedictum de Spinoza Amstelodamensem. Accesserunt ejusdem cogitata metaphysica, &c. Amsterdam, 1663.

2. Tractatus Theologico-politicus, continens dissertationes aliquot, quibus ostenditur libertatem philosophandi non tantum salva pietate et reipublicæ pace posse concedi: sed eandem nisi cum pace reipublicæ ipsaque pietate tolli non posse. Hamburg (really Amsterdam), 1670. Some notes of Spinoza's own to this treatise came to light later. See Bruder's preface, and Ed. Böhmer: Ben. de Sp. Tractatus de Deo et Homine &c. atque Adnotationes ad Tractatum Theologico-politicum. Halle, 1832.

3. B. d. S. Opera Posthuma. Amsterdam, 1677. The contents are:

  Ethica ordine geometrico demonstrata.

  Tractatus politicus.

  Tractatus de intellectus emendatione.

  Epistolæ doctorum quorundam virorum ad B. d. S. et auctoris responsiones.

  Compendium grammatices linguæ hebrææ.

4. (Tractatus de Iride.) Stelkonstige reeckening van den Regenboog. The Hague, 1687. *(Bibliogr.* no. 36.)

This work was long lost sight of and supposed to have perished. It was recovered and reprinted by Dr. van Vloten in his Supplementum (see below).

5. Letter of Spinoza to Dr. Lambert van Veldhuysen. 1844. Published by Prof. Tydeman, and given in ed. Bruder as Ep. 75. *(Bibliogr.* no. 35.)

6. Ad Benedicti de Spinoza opera quæ supersunt omnia supplementum. Amsterdam, 1862.

By Dr. J. van Vloten. Uniform with Bruder's ed. (see below), so as to make a supplementary volume to it. Contains Spinoza's early *Essay on God and Man,* the *Treatise on the Rainbow,* and some letters and parts of letters not before published.

7. In 1705 two letters written in Dutch by Spinoza, and including a paragraph not given in the Opera Posthuma, appeared in a periodical called *Boekzaal der Geleerde Werrelt.* They seem to have been forgotten till Prof. Land quite recently lighted upon them: see his paper reprinted from the proceedings of the Dutch Academy of Sciences, 'Over de eerste uitgaven der brieven van Spinoza,' Amsterdam, 1879; and Appendix C to this book.

8. Letter of Spinoza to Dr. Meyer of Aug. 3, 1663. French translation given by Saisset, *Œuvres de Spinoza,* iii. 458. The original is printed for the first time in this book (Appendix C). This letter might conveniently be cited as *Ep.* xxix. *a.*

Three collected editions of Spinoza's works have been published: by Paulus (Jena, 1802, 2 vols.), Gfrörer (Stuttgart, 1830), and Bruder (Leipzig, 1843-6, 3 vols.). Full titles and particulars in *Bibliogr.* 38, 39, 41. The edition by Paulus is still useful to the student, as all the authorities then known for the life of Spinoza are conveniently brought together in the *Collectanea* at the end of vol. ii. Unfortunately the text is by no means free from misprints; and more unfortunately this edition seems to have been used to print from in both Gfrörer's and Bruder's, and some serious errors, though not all, thus remain uncorrected. I have noted the following in the *Ethics:* —

Part I, Prop. 22: 'Quicquid ex *aliquo* Dei attribute,' &c. So *Opp. Posth.,* as the sense requires. All the modern editions give *alio.*

Part 3, Prop. 21, Demonst.: 'Deinde quatenus *res* aliqua tristitia afficitur,' &c. Modern editions have *re.*

Part 5, Prop. 33, Schol.: '... nisi quod *mens* easdem has perfectiones... aeternas habuerit,' &c. Modern editions (except

Gfrörer) have *metus*. Errors in the original edition of the *Opera Posthuma* have likewise remained uncorrected. See Ed. Böhmer, Spinozana, in Fichte's Zeitschrift für Philosophie und philosophische Kritik, 1860, vol. xxxiii. p. 153. But as to two of the remarks there made, see *ib.* vol. xlii. 1863, p. 97, *n.* where they are retracted by the author.

Gfrörer's edition has a Latin preface of considerable merit, in which the argument for determinism is put with a certain freshness of topics and instances. In this preface there is also a misprint or *lapsus calami* odd enough to deserve special notice. In the part relating to Spinoza's letters we read: 'Penultima a iuvene nobili *Edmundo Burk* [Alberto Burgh] conscripta est.'

Bruder's edition is the handiest and altogether best equipped of the three, and the most convenient for reference.

Dr. Hugo Ginsberg has more lately undertaken a new edition, in which I have seen the Ethics, the Letters, and Tractatus Theologico-politicus. (Leipzig, 1875, &c.) A fourth volume, apparently completing the edition, is announced this year. The introductions contain much useful matter carefully brought together. The text professes to be an improvement on Bruder's; but as regards the Ethics and Letters the editor's intention of collating the original text of the *Opp. Posth.* has not been thoroughly carried out by those entrusted with the work. All the errors above noted are repeated; besides which the number of new misprints can only be called enormous. The additions to the Letters first published in Dr. van Vloten's *Supplementum* are also not fully given. See *Mind,* vol. ii. p. 273.

As to translations: —

Dutch. — A version of the 'Principles of Descartes' Philosophy' (Renatus des Cartes beginzelen der wysbegeerte, &c.) was published at Amsterdam in 1664. The translator, named only as P. B., is stated to have been Peter Balling, one of Spinoza's correspondents *(Bibliogr.* no. 2). The *Tractatus Theologico-politicus* was translated into Dutch as early as 1673, and again in 1694 *(Bibliogr.* nos. 17, 18); and the *Opera Posthuma* appeared in Dutch almost as soon as in Latin *(De nagelate Schriften van B. d. S. &c. Bibliogr.* 23). This last work is well and carefully executed. The purity of the language contrasts remarkably with the Latinisms which infested the current writing of the time, and some errors in the Latin text of the *Opp. Posth.*

are tacitly corrected. There do not seem to be any modern Dutch versions.

English. — There is no complete English translation of Spinoza, nor any trustworthy one of his most important philosophical works. The *Tractatus Theologico-politicus* was translated in 1689, and again (a reprint?) in 1737. The translation of 1689 is, like the original, anonymous; neither is Spinoza's name mentioned by the translator. So far as I have looked at it, the rendering is pretty accurate, but it has no great literary merit. Lastly, in 1862, and in a second edition, 1868, there appeared a version which was on the face of it anonymous, but was known to be the work of the late Dr. R. Willis, and afterwards acknowledged by him. The same writer published some years later a translation of the Ethics and Letters. *(Benedict de Spinoza; his Life, Correspondence, and Ethics.* Trübner & Co., London, 1870.) Of this book Professor Flint has lately said, with perfect judgment and discretion, that it may be recommended to the merely English reader. I should be glad to imitate his reserve, but silence might be misunderstood. The fact is that Dr. Willis, with extensive reading, a fair knowledge of philosophy, and great interest in his subject, had not either scholarship adequate to his task, or that habit of an exact use of language which is almost as needful to the translator as knowledge of the original tongue. The result (though, for many reasons, it is painful to have to say it) is that this version is far too inaccurate to be of any serious use. Not only shades of meaning are missed, and Spinoza's terse Latin spread into loose paraphrase, but there are constant errors in the rendering of perfectly common Latin particles, idioms, and constructions. The same remarks apply to the translation of the *Tractatus Theologico-politicus.* There is a still later anonymous translation of the Ethics (New York and London, 1876). Unfortunately the writer looked upon Dr. Willis as an authority, and copied nearly all his mistakes. In 1854 there appeared a translation of the *Tractatus Politicus* by W. Maccall *(Bibliogr.* no. 32, in Corrigenda), a small book in an apparently obscure series called *The Cabinet of Reason.* It is in the British Museum, but has escaped the libraries of both Oxford and Cambridge Universities. The translator speaks with enthusiasm of Spinoza; why this particular work was chosen for translation does not plainly appear.

It appears from a diary kept by Shelley's friend Williams at Pisa and Lerici in 1821-2, that Shelley not only planned but executed to some extent a new translation of the Tractatus Theologico-politicus: 'to which Lord B. [Byron] has consented to put his name, and to give it greater currency, will write the life of that celebrated Jew to preface the work.' This passage was first published in Mr. R. Garnett's article, 'Shelley's Last Days,' *Fortnightly Review,* June 1878 (vol. xxiii. N.S., p. 858). A fragment of the first chapter, written it would seem in England, and accidentally preserved, and a fac-simile of the MS., may be seen in Mr. C. S. Middleton's 'Shelley and his Writings' (London 1858). See p.403, below. No other trace of Shelley's design remains.

The treatise *De Intellectus Emendatione,* the *Principia Philosophiæ* and *Cogitata Metaphysica,* and the book *De Deo et Homine,* have never to my knowledge been done into English.

French. — The *Tractatus Theologico-politicus* was translated in 1678, and appeared under several false titles at once *(La clef du sanctuaire... Réflexions citrieuses d'un esprit désintéresse... Traié des Cérémonies superstitienses des Juifs,* Bibliogr. nos. 10, 11, 12). More recently the principal works of Spinoza have been translated by E. Saisset (*Œuvres de Spinoza.* Paris, 1842; 2nd ed. 1861, 3 vols.: reprinted without alteration, 1872). The first volume is a critical introduction. The translation is faithful, but the *Principles of Descartes' Philosophy* and a good many of the letters are omitted. The critical and bibliographical information has to some extent become obsolete since Dr. van Vloten's publication of new matter. Another version, intended to be complete, has been begun by M. J. G. Prat, and is still in progress *(Œtivres completes de B. de Spinoza.* Premiere serie: 'Vie de Spinoza, par Lucas;' 'Vie de Spinoza, par Colerus;' 'Principes de la Philosophic de Descartes et Meditations metaphysiques.' Paris, 1863. Deuxieme serie: Traite Theologicopolitique, 1872. Ethique, Premiere Partie, 1880). A version of the *Tractates Politicns,* by the same hand, appeared separately in 1860. In 1878 M. Paul Janet gave for the first time a French version of the *De Deo et Homine,* of which more presently.

German. — There have been several German translations of the *Ethics* and other works of Spinoza. It will suffice to mention here Auerbach's (last edition entitled *B. de Spinoza's sdmmtliche Werke,* Stuttgart, 1871, 2 vols;), and a yet more recent one in J. H. von Kirchmann's *Philosophische Bibliothek,* Berlin, 1868-72, which since its completion is also to be had in a collected form. Auerbach's version contains the whole philosophical works of Spinoza, including in the last edition the essay *De Deo et Homine,* and is wonderfully close to the original. The preface and life of Spinoza prefixed to the first volume contain in a short compass nearly all the extraneous information which the reader is likely to want, and form an excellent introduction to fuller study.[1]

Italian. — The *Tractatus Theologico-politicus* has recently appeared in an Italian version, namely:

Trattato Teologico-politico di Benedetto de Spinoza, &c. (translating full title of original), tradotto dal testo latino per Carlo Sarchi. Milan, 1875. Pp. xlii and 368. Preface by way of dedication to S. Cesare Correnti. At p. xxxiii the translator says: 'Non solamente concorda lo Spinoza colla metafisica del Vico, di cui non fu mai incolpata la cattolica ortodossia, ma sono consentanei i suoi principii con quelli di S. Tommaso, del Dottore angelico, siccome se ne può accertare chiunque voglia meditare le Quest. ii, iii, iv, v, e seguenti della *Somma Teologica.*'

Spanish. — Still more lately there has appeared the first instalment, containing the *Tractatus Theologico-politicus,* of a Spanish version of Spinoza's philosophical works:

Obras filosóficas de Spinoza vertidas al castellano y precedidas de una introduccion por Don Emilio Reus y Bahamonde, &c. Madrid, 1878, 8vo. pp. cxvi and 368.

II. AUTHORITIES FOR SPINOZA'S LIFE

1. *Colerus.* — First and chiefly we have the life of Spinoza by Johannes Colerus (Köhler), German minister of the Lutheran congregation at the Hague. This congregation, existing side by side with the Dutch Reformed Church in freedom and security much beyond any rights officially allowed to it, was to some extent under the protection of German Lutheran princes;

---

[1] I may here mention that Auerbach's novel *Spinoza: ein Denkerleben,* is still practically inaccessible to English readers who do not know German. A French version appeared some time ago in the *Revue Germanique,* but has not been separately published. There are two Dutch translations, the latest dated 1875; and a Spanish one by Gonzales Serrano (*n.d.*).

and, for the convenience of Germans residing at the Hague in the
service of the States or otherwise, there was a German minister
as well as a Dutch one. This office was filled by Colerus from
1693 to 1707. The usage of a bilingual ministry was kept up till
1832, when the last German pastor died. Colerus first published
his life of Spinoza in Dutch, together with a controversial sermon against Spinozism (Amsterdam, 1705. *Bibliogr.* 88). This
original edition is extremely rare. Only two copies are known,
one of which is in the Royal Library at the Hague and the other
at Halle *(Bibliogr.* p. vii). It was almost immediately followed,
and for all practical purposes supplanted, by a French version
(La vérité de la résurrection de Jésus Christ défendue contre B.
de Spinoza et ses spectateurs [sectateurs]. Avec la vie de ce
fameux philosophe, tirée, tant de ses propres Ecrits, que de la
bouche de plusieurs personnes dignes de foi qui l'ont connu. Par
Jean Colerus, Ministre de l'Eglise Luthérienne de la Haye. The
Hague, 1706. *Bibliogr.* 90.) This French version of the life has
been several times reprinted; it is to be found in Paulus' edition
of Spinoza, in Saisset's and Prat's translations, and at the end of
Dr. Ginsberg's edition of the Letters. An English translation of it
appeared in the same year, which is reprinted at the end of this
book (Appendix A), and a German one in 1723, remarkable for a
portrait of Spinoza, in the lettering of which he is described as
'characterem reprobationis in vultu gerens.' There was a later
German translation from the original Dutch, 1734 *(Bibliogr.* 91-
93). Many details have been added or cleared up since, but Colerus remains the principal authority. What gives his witness a singular value is its freedom from all suspicion of designed
panegyric. He detests the philosophy of Spinoza, but is too honest to slander his character as a man, or even to conceal his admiration for it.

    2. *Opera Posthuma* and *Supplementum.* — Some bio-
graphical information is given in the editors' preface to the *Opera Posthuma,* and something may be gathered from various
passages in Spinoza's correspondence, notably in the portions
first made known by Dr. van Vloten, who has also given other
documentary evidence bearing on Spinoza's life both in the *Supplementum* and in his Dutch work on Spinoza (see below).

    3. *Leibnitz.* — A few personal recollections of Spinoza
are preserved in Leibnitz's writings. They will be specially men-

tioned in their place in the biographical part (Paulus, *Collectanea;* Foucher de Careil, *Leibniz, Descartes, et Spinoza).*

The remaining sources of information are of less weight.

4. *Lucas.* — Early in the eighteenth century, we cannot say when first, but it seems before 1712 at all events (see extract from Brit. Mus. MS. below), there became current in MS. a biography of Spinoza, attributed in the preface to one Lucas, a physician of the Hague. It was often associated, under the common title *La vie et l'esprit de Mr. Benoît de Spinosa,* with a certain *Traité des trois imposteurs,* which has nothing to do with Spinoza, and is again distinct from the Latin book *De tribus impostoribus,* though it pretends to be from a Latin original. In this form the life was printed at Amsterdam in 1719, in a publication called *Nouvelles Littéraires,* and also in a separate book. The book was almost immediately called in; the life was reissued alone at Hamburg [?], 1735, and this edition also became very scarce (the British Museum has a copy). Meanwhile the Count de Boulainvilliers, who possessed an early MS. copy, had worked it up with the life by Colerus into a not very coherent whole *(La vie de Spinosa écrite par M, Jean Colerus... augmentée de beaucoup de particularités tirées d'une vie manuscrite de ce philosophe, faite par un de ses amis)* in his book called a refutation of Spinoza, but really a popular exposition, which was published after the author's death (Brussels [?], 1731. *Bibliogr.* 107, where the date is given as 1726 by the misprint of XXVI. for XXXI.).

The additions in Boulainvilliers, and some passages of Lucas omitted by him (these from a MS. copy), are given in Paulus' edition as footnotes to Colerus; and Lucas is reprinted at large from ed. 1735 by M. Prat (he does not mention whence he obtained the use or a transcript of the book) in his *Œuvres completes de B. de Spinoza,* 1re série. The history of this work, and the connexion of the different forms in which it has existed, were first unravelled by Paulus (preface to vol. ii. of his edition). One could wish it were better worth so much trouble. It is the production of an ardent and undiscriminating panegyrist, confused in its narrative, and not always consistent with what is known from other quarters. As Auerbach justly says, Lucas' enthusiasm prevents him from telling his story clearly or soberly. His unsupported evidence is, in my opinion, worth very little, and at best

we can only use him as a witness auxiliary and subordinate to
Colerus. The authorship of this biography has been called in
doubt on the ground that Lucas (of whom, by the way, very little
seems to be known, save that he was the author of a satirical
work called *Les Quintessences)* was not capable of it (Prosper
Marchand, *Dict. Historique,* article 'Impostoribus'). But the
question is not worth discussing.

    5. *Bayle, Kortholt, &c.* — The remaining evidences may
be taken in the lump. A few touches are contributed by the article on Spinoza in Bayle's *Dictionary* (reprinted as appendix to
Dr. Ginsberg's edition of the *Tractatus Theologico-politicus)*,
which however is very loose in its facts, and by a notice prefixed
by Sebastian Kortholt to a second edition of his father's book *De
tribus impostoribus magnis* (Hamburg, 1700. *Bibliogr.* 82: the
passages about Spinoza are given in Paulus' *Collectanea).* The
'three great impostors' of the last-named book are Lord Herbert
of Cherbury, Hobbes, and Spinoza. What is said of Spinoza per-
sonally in the preface is remarkable as the testimony of a very
unwilling witness to the simplicity and blamelessness of his life.
Colerus had Bayle and Kortholt before him when he wrote his
life of Spinoza. Then we have a little book by one Stoupe,[2] a
Swiss officer in the French service, *La religion des hollandois,*
1673 *(Bibliogr.* 63, where the passages in question are given),
containing a rather confused account of Spinoza, who was then
living, and of the *Tractatus Theologico-politicus.* The Dutch
theologians are accused of lukewarmness, or worse, for not
coming forward more strongly to refute Spinoza; this piece of
evangelical zeal is not unlikely, as Paulus suggests, to have had a
politictal motive. Dutch writers presently replied to these
charges. One of them, described as 'Jean Brun, Ministre du Roy
des Armées,' expresses astonishment at Stoupe's zeal against
Spinoza; for Stoupe, he says, himself sought Spinoza's acquaintance, and made much of him on the occasion of his visit to
Conde's head-quarters at Utrecht *(Bibliogr.* 67). In 1847 there
appeared in the Berlin *Allgemeine Zeitschrift für Geschichte*
some notes of travel made in 1703 by Gottlieb Stolle, afterwards
a professor at Jena *(Bibliogr.* 86). At Amsterdam he picked up

---

    [2] The name is variously spelt. Dr. van Vloten, in his recent address on
the unveiling of the Spinoza statue, prints it *Stoppa.*

some gossip about Spinoza from an old man who professed to have known him well. This communication is of no importance, and in part manifestly absurd. But Stolle likewise made the acquaintance of Rieuwerts (or Riewerts, as the name appears on the title-page of the *Principia Philosophiæ)*, the publisher of the *Opp. Posth.,* and got from him some interesting particulars; he also visited Bayle, and spoke with him of Spinoza. See Ginsberg's Introduction to his edition of the *Ethics,* pp. 20-25, where these passages are reprinted.

Some other miscellaneous publications of the eighteenth century contain statements or allusions touching Spinoza's life; but, so far as I know, these are either copied from the authorities already mentioned, or were idle tales contradicted by the known facts (e.g. *Bibliogr.* 98, 110).

I may here say a word of the portraits of Spinoza. Three only that I know of (if so many) may be reasonably considered authentic: —

1. Engraving found in some copies of the *Opp. Posth.* It is not described as rare in *Bibliogr.,* but is difficult to meet with in this country. After searching without result in public libraries, we found an example in the copy of the *Opp. Posth.* belonging to the London Institution, of which the frontispiece to this book is a reproduction.

2. Miniature belonging to the late Queen of the Netherlands, in the Summer Palace at the Hague. A chromolithographic copy is given as frontispiece to Schaarschmidt's edition of *De Deo et Homine.*

3. Painting formerly belonging to Professor Paulus, the editor of Spinoza, since to Dr. van Vloten, and by him presented to the Town Museum at the Hague. Comparison of the three suggests that No. 1 may be to some extent idealised. On the other hand, No. 1 is by far the most artistic and lifelike. *Cf.* Ed. Böhmer, *Spinozana,* i. p. 144, ii. pp. 86, 87 (in *Zeitschr. für Philosophie und philosophische Kritik,* Halle, vol. xxxvi. 1860, vol. xlii. 1863).[3]

---

[3] No. 1 also occurs without the inscription, but in that state is very rare. No. 2 was bought at Leyden in 1866, with some sort of tradition of Spinoza being the person represented. Opinions differ as to the value to be attached to it. No. 3 has been engraved as frontispiece to Paulus' edition of Spinoza. Recent inspection of the original has led me to suspect that it may be

III. EARLY LITERATURE RELATING TO SPINOZA

Andala. — The following book, not without curiosity for the elaborate comparison of Spinoza's philosophy with Stoicism, is not in *Bibliogr.*: —

Apologia | pro | vera & saniore | philosophia | quatuor partibus comprehensa, | auctore | Ruardo Andala, | Phil. et SS. Theol. Doctore & Professore | ordinario. | Franequeræ, | Ex Officina Wibii Bleck, Bibliopolæ | MDCCXIX. 4to. pp. 3 unnumbered (title-page and preface) and 210.

Parts I. and II. relate to Spinoza; the pages of Part I. are headed: 'Philosophia R. Descartes | Spinosismo opposita.' Those of Part II.: 'Spinosus Stoicismus fons Spinosismi | et puritas philosophiæ R. Descartes.' The Stoic philosophy is compared with Spinoza's in parallel columns through a series of numbered heads.

For my acquaintance with this book (as for the references to some of the others hereafter mentioned) I am indebted to the kindness of Mr. I. Bywater, of Exeter College, Oxford, the owner of the copy I have seen. It is not in the British Museum, the Bodleian, or the Cambridge University library.

The full title of the same author's book described in *Bibliogr.* 303 is: —

Cartesius | verus Spinozismi | eversor, | et | physicæ experimentalis | architectus, | auctore | Ruardo Andala, | Phil. et SS.Theol.Doctore et Professore | ordinario. | Franequeræ | Ex officina Wibii Bleck, Bibliopolæ, MDCCIX. 4to.

Pp. 1-282, headed: 'Cartesius verus Spinozismi eversor.' New title: Dissertatio physica | qua repræsentatur | Cartesius | physicæ experimentalis architectus, | ventilata publicè A.D. 21. Jun. MDCCXIX. | Defendente | Georgio Szoboszlai, | Transylvano-Hungaro.

Pp. 1-44, headed: 'Cartesius physicæ experimentalis architectus.'

The same author's *Dissertationum philosophicarum heptas* (Franeq. MDCCXI) contains at least one incidental attack on Spinoza, of whom it is said, among other amenities, in the fifth dissertation, *De voluntatis libertate* (p. 190): 'Hæc et alia

---

only a fancy picture by some painter who had no. 1 before him: if this were so, it would of course be of no authority.

ostendunt Atheum αὐτοκατάκριτον.'

Bontekoe. — Dr. Cornelius Bontekoe's unexecuted intention of refuting Spinoza is noticed in the text further on (ch. xii.).

Boulainvilliers. — Spinoza's name was strangely mixed up, as above mentioned, with a certain *Traité des trois imposteurs* which had a half-occult circulation in MS. in France and the Low Countries; a performance, for the rest, of no particular merit, and itself a clumsy imposture as regards its pretended origin and date. Later in the eighteenth century it was printed, but without the use of Spinoza's name in any way. See for detailed bibliography of this work Ed. Böhmer, *Spinozana,* 1860 *(ubi supra),* pp. 156 sqq. I now add my contribution for what it may be worth. In an eighteenth century MS. in the British Museum (Add. 12064) there occurs, after a copy of this treatise, a note which may be worth transcribing. It is as follows (I modernize the spelling and accents, and correct one or two words):

'J'ai vu une copie MS. de l'ouvrage de Monsieur le comte de Boullainvilliers touchant la doctrine de Spinoza faite sur l'original de l'auteur au mois d'août 1712, in-4to. Ce MS. contient la Métaphysique et l'Ethique de Spinoza, son Esprit [*i.e.* the *Traité des trois imposteurs*] et sa vie, comme il [*sic*] porte le titre. Il commence par la vie de Spinoza, qui est fort abrégée, et dont le plus essentiel et remarquable a été ajouté à la vie de Spinoza écrite par Colerus, et a été imprimé depuis peu dans le livre de la Réfutation des erreurs de Benoît Spinoza, à Bruxelles chez François Foppens en 1731, in-8vo, comme porte le titre, mais véritablement en Hollande. [*Bibliogr.* 107, and see above.]

'Après la vie de Spinoza est placé l'ouvrage de Monsieur Boullainvilliers avec ce titre:

'Essai de Métaphysique dans les Principes de B... *de* Sp... composé par M.L.C.D.C.D.B., c'est-a-dire —

'Il y précède un avertissement qui fait la préface de l'imprimé dans la Réfutation de Spinoza, mais au commencement, où il est dit: J'entreprends de faire parler dans les trois traités suivans — on a retranché le mot trois — parce qu'on n'a pas osé d'imprimer l'Esprit de Spinoza, qui fait le troisième traité... Le troisième traité est intitulé: L'Esprit de Monsieur de Spinoza, c'est-á-dire ce que croit la plus saine partie du monde.'

It would be rash to infer anything from this memorandum as to the authorship of the *Traité des trois imposteurs,* which is indeed quite beneath Boulainvilliers' ability, particularly as shown in the so-called *Réfutation,* with which it was associated in the MS. of 1712 seen by the annotator. But it does appear to connect Boulainvilliers with the affixing of Spinoza's name to the work. It is not surprising that the writer of the MS. now cited did not know (as he obviously did not) that it had been printed in 1719. The 'copie MS.' mentioned by him would seem to be that in the library of the Arsenal at Paris, described *ex relatione* by Böhmer, *Spinozana,* ii. p. 157. The British Museum possesses another MS. copy of the *Traité,* which, however, does not offer any peculiar feature.

In Paris MSS. have apparently been searched for by Böhmer. One would think, however, there must yet be several unexamined copies in French libraries *(cf. Spinozana,* ii. 89,90).

Langenhert. — Arnoldi Geulincx | compendium physicæ | illustratum | à | Casparo Langenhert. | | Franequeræ, | Ex Officinâ Leonardi Strick Bibliopolæ | Anno MDCLXXXVIII.

At p. 116: 'Quomodo autem Philosophi nonnulli atque Theologi, liberrimum hoc arbitrium cum Deo non competere vaferrimo Spinosæ (qui libertatem hanc, ut suo tempore dante Deo demonstrabimus, ne quidem per somnium novit) largiantur, ex ejus sese liberent tricis, id ego me ignorare profiteor.'

Langenhert's intention, like Dr. Bontekoe's, appears to have remained unperformed.

Rijcke. — Theodori Ryckii, etc. ad diversos epistolæ ineditæ. Ed. G. D. J. Schotel. Hagæ Comitum, 1843. At p. 6, in letter to Adrian Biyenburg, Aug. 14, 1675: — 'Inter nos rumor est auctorem *Tractatus Theologico-politici* in promptu habere librum de Deo et Mente multo priore isto periculosiorem.'

Compare Spinoza's Ep. 19, of about the same date. *Ryssel* (J. J. à) gives a short account of Spinoza and his philosophy in his edition of Vossius de philosophorum sectis, Lips. 1690, 4to. p. 203.

Witte (Henning). — Diarium biographicum, in quo scriptores seculi post natum Christum xvii. præcipui... concisè descripti magnô adducuntur numerô. Gedani [Danzig] 1688, 4to. At sig. Nnnn, fo. 4, *verso* (the book is unpaged) *sub ann.* 1677, is the name of Spinoza and a list of his works: the exact date of his death is added in a supplement.

An anti-Spinozist bibliography was attempted as early as 1725 by Joh. Albert Fabricius in his wordily entitled book:

Delectus argumentorum et syllabus scriptorum qui veritatem religionis Christianæ adversus atheos, Epicureos, Deistas seu naturalistas, idololatras, Judæos et Muhammedanos lucubrationibus suis asseruerunt. Hamburg 1725, 4to.

Cap. XIII., p. 355:

Adversus Spinosam et alios mundum æternum confingentes.

At p. 357 is a list of writers against Spinoza: some names of authors and books are given which I do not find in *Bibliogr.* Besides Brampton Gurdon (as to whom see below among English writers) the following are referred to, if reference it can be called.

Gerardus de Vries in exercitationibus rationalibus de Deo.[4]

D. Jo. Jachimi[5] Weidneri Homo Spinosæ religionem exercens: *qu.* whether a separate work from 'Numen Spinozæ in refutationem erroris atheistici,' &c. *(Bibliogr.* 394), the title of which is inaccurately cited by Fabricius.

Petrus van Mastricht in Gangræna. (Novitatum Cartesianarum Gangræna, s. Theologia Cartesiana detecta. Amstelod. 1677. In University Libraries of Cambridge and Leyden, and in the Bodleian: not in Brit. Mus. The author was Professor of Theology at Utrecht, 1677-1706). The full title is: Novitatum Cartesianarum Gangræna, nobiliores plerasque corporis theologici partes arrodens & exedens. Seu theologia Cartesiana detecta auctore Petro van Mastricht, S. literarum in ecclesia & academia Duisburgensi doctore & professore. Prostant Amstelodami: apud Janssonio-Waesbergios. Anno MDCLXXVII.

In cap. 3, De Philosophia non ancilla Theologiæ, occurs criticism of the 'Tractatus Theologico-politicus.' Spinoza is described as 'Atheus quidem, sed Cartesianus tamen' on p. 35, and

---

[4] Gerardi de Vries exercitationes rationales de Deo, divinisque perfectionibus, necnon philosophemata miscellanea, &c. Trajecti ad Rhenum, MDCXCV, 4to At p. 34 is a pious wish for unhappy persons who may be 'istis *Spinis* suffocati': at p. 43 the *Ethics* are named: 'consonant hæc per omnia eis, quæ occurrunt in ipso limine profanæ Ethicæ ordine geometrico demonstratæ.' The book is mainly anti-Cartesian. The author was a Professor at Utrecht.

[5] Read Jo. Joachimi. The D. apparently stands for 'Domini.'

on p. 44 we find an early instance, perhaps the earliest, of a pun
which afterwards became current (see citations from Andala and
De Vries above): 'Spinosam Spinosæ argutiam prolixius obtun-
dere visum.'[6] Van Mastricht shared the mistake, not uncommon
at the time, of attributing to Spinoza the anonymous book 'Philosophia Scripturæ interpres,' really by Dr. Meyer. 'Idem (et
forte etiam ipse idem) aliis licet verbis, habet *Exercitator para-
doxus de Philos. Interp. Script.*' &c. (p. 35).

　　　Jo. van de Weyen (read van der Waeyen) in Summa
Theologiæ (Pars Prior, Franeq. 1689).

　　　The following English works of the late seventeenth and
eighteenth century, more or less concerned with Spinoza, are not
in *Bibliogr.*

　　　Cudworth (Ralph, D.D.). — True Intellectual System of
the Universe, book i. c. 5, p. 707 (the pagination is the same in
ed. pr. 1678, fo., and ed. 1743, 2 vols. 4to.):

　　　'As for that late theological politician, who, writing
against miracles, denies as well those of the former [by natural
power of angels, &c.] as of this latter [supernatural] kind... we
find his discourse every way so weak, groundless, and inconsiderable, that we could not think it here to deserve a confutation.'

　　　Blackmore. — Creation. A philosophical poem. In seven
books. By Sir Richard Blackmore, Knt. M.D., and Fellow of the
College of Physicians in London. London: MDCCXII. 8vo. Also
to be found in the collection of English Poets edited by Johnson.
It is a didactic poem on natural theology; in the course of which,
as the author announces (Preface, p. xviii.) 'the modern atheists,
Vaninus, Hobbs, and Spinosa' are spoken of in their turn. Again
he says in the Preface (p. xlv): —

　　　'Will they [the irreligious gentlemen of the age] derive
their certainty from Spinosa? Can such an obscure, perplext,
unintelligible Author create such Certainty, as leaves no Doubt
or Distrust? If he is indeed to be understood, what does he al-
ledge more than the ancient Fatalists have done, that should
amount to Demonstration?'

　　　The confutation of Spinoza in the body of the work is in

---

[6] Such ornaments of argument were then in fashion, and Spinoza is
here in no less orthodox company than Hildebrand's, of whom our author
speaks thus (p. 3). 'Gregorius septimus, Hildebrandus (Hellebrandum suo
nomine dixeris)'.

Book 3, v. 742. It is not without curiosity as a specimen of what then passed muster in England as philosophy and poetry: —

> *Spinosa* next, to hide his black design,
> And to his Side th' unwary to incline,
> For Heav'n his Ensigns treacherous displays,
> Declares for God, while he that God betrays:
> For whom he's pleas'd such Evidence to bring,
> As saves the Name, while it subverts the Thing.
>
> Now hear his labour'd Scheme of impious Use;
> No Substance can another e'er produce.
> Substance no Limit, no Confinement knows,
> And its Existence from its Nature flows.
> The Substance of the Universe is one,
> Which is the Self-existent God alone.
>
> The Spheres of *Ether,* which the World enclose,
> And all th' Apartments, which the Whole compose;
> The lucid Orbs, the Earth, the Air, the Main,
> With every diff'rent Being they contain,
> Are one prodigious Aggregated God,
> Of whom each Sand is part, each Stone and Clod.
> Supream Perfections in each Insect shine,
> Each Shrub is Sacred, and each Weed Divine.
>
> Sages, no longer *Egypt's* Sons despise,
> For their cheap Gods, and Savoury Deities!
> No more their course[7] Divinities revile!
> To Leeks, to Onions, to the Crocodile,
> You might your humble Adorations pay,
> Were you not Gods your selves, as well as they.
>
> As much you pull Religion's altars down,
> By owning all Things God, as owning none.
> For should all Beings be alike Divine,
> Of Worship if an Object you assign,
> God to himself must Veneration shew,
> Must be the Idol and the Vot'ry too;
> And their assertions are alike absurd,
> Who own no God, or none to be ador'd.

Colliber. An Impartial Enquiry into the Existence and Nature of God &c. The third edition. By Samuel Colliber. London, 1735. 8vo, pp. 276. Spinoza is several times cited in order

---

[7] Sic.

to be contradicted; in some places the words of the original are given.

Brampton Gurdon. A Defence of Natural and Revealed Religion: Being a collection of the sermons preached at the lecture founded by the Honourable Robert Boyle, Esq.; (from the year 1691 to the year 1732). 3 vols. Lond. 1739, fo.

At p. 277. The Pretended Difficulties in Natural or Reveal'd Religion no Excuse for Infidelity. Sixteen Sermons preached in the church of Saint Mary le Bow, London; in the years 1721 and 1722. At the lecture founded by the Honourable Robert Boyle, Esq. By Brampton Gurdon, A.M. Chaplain to the Right Honourable Thomas Earl of Macclesfield, Lord High Chancellour of Great Britain.

Criticism of Spinoza occurs at pp. 297, 299-308, 329-30, 345, 358, 363-5.

Ramsay. The | philosophical | principles | of | natural and revealed | religion. | Unfolded | in | a geometrical order | by the Chevalier Ramsay | author of the travels of Cyrus. | Glasgow: | printed and sold by Robert Foulis. | MDCCXLVIII. 2 vols. 4to. Vol. I. (pp. viii and 541) contains frequent criticism on Spinoza. At p. 497:

Appendix | to the | foregoing work: | containing | a | refutation | of the first book of | Spinosa's Ethics; | by which | the whole structure | is undermined. At pp. 539-541:

'From all this it appears that Spinosa's monstrous system is composed of Cabbalism, Cartesianism, and Predestinarianism differently conjoined and interwoven... With regard to moral actions, the Spinosian errors are not so much abuses, as natural and necessary consequences of the Predestinarian scheme. If this be so, then it is possible that Spinosa did not think himself an Atheist...

'Those who have undertaken the confutation of this philosopher have not as yet succeeded. All that Bayle says against Spinosa is unworthy of our notice. That ingenious author scarce ever dipt beyond the surface of things...

'We have endeavoured to disclose the mysterious jargon of this dark system, represent it in its true light, and confute it in two different manners, by demonstrating truths diametrically opposite to its principles, and by proving that all its demonstrations are sophistical. We conclude with this sole remark, that till

Predestinarian and Cartesian principles be banished from the Christian schools, Spinosism can never be solidly confuted.'

Vol. ii. (pp. 462) is on ancient religions and mythology, and appears to contain no further mention of Spinoza.

Dugald Stewart. In the First Preliminary Dissertation of the *Encyclopædia Britannica* (vol. 1, p. 144 in 7th ed.) a few pages are given to Spinoza. They are of no value at the present day.

Gibbon. In the *Critical Observations on the Sixth Book of the Æneid (Misc. Works,* ii, 510), Gibbon speaks of 'the principles which the impious Spinoza revived rather than invented.' The context sufficiently shows that 'the impious Spinoza' was for Gibbon merely a stick to beat Warburton with.

One other book may be noticed under this head, merely to save trouble to other students of Spinoza literature who may come across it. It is: 'ΑΡΕΤΗ-ΛΟΓΙΑ, or An Enquiry into the Original of moral Virtue; wherein the false Notions of Machiavel, Hobbes, Spinoza, and Mr. Bayle, as they are collected and digested by the Author of the Fable of the Bees, are examined and confuted, and the eternal and unalterable Nature and Obligation of moral Virtue is stated and vindicated. To which is prefixed a prefatory Introduction, in a Letter to that Author.' By Alexander Innes, D.D., &c. Westminster, MDCCXXVIII, 8vo., pp. xlii and 333.

There is not a word in the body of the book about Spinoza, nor yet about Hobbes and Bayle. Machiavelli is once cited as an authority. The argument against Mandeville, who is the sole object of attack, proceeds on hedonistic principles, and there is even an attempt at what late writers have called a hedonic calculus (p. 199), so that I fancy the work may be of some interest for the history of utilitarianism.

IV. Not as a matter of bibliography, but for the reader's general convenience, I shall here mention some of the modern accounts of Spinoza.

It will be generally admitted, I believe, by competent persons that Kuno Fischer's *(Geschichte der neueren Philosophie,* vol. i. part 2) is on the whole the fullest and best. The author has the merit, too rare in philosophical literature, of combining thorough analysis with clear exposition and an admirable style.

In English the best general view is still given by Mr. Froude's essay reprinted from the 'Westminster Review' in *Short Studies on Great Subjects*. The chapter on Spinoza in Lewes' *History of Philosophy* is good for the biographical part; as to the philosophy, it excites an interest which it hardly does enough to satisfy. There is a good article in Blunt's *Dictionary of Sects, Heresies, &c.* (London, 1874),s. v. 'Spinoza,' showing careful study and great familiarity with the Ethics; but it is of necessity much condensed. Compare 'Spinozism' in the same editor's *Dict. of Doctrinal and Historical Theology*. London, 1871.

Hallam's account must be mentioned as occurring in a work classical in its own line ('Literature of Europe,' part iv. ch. iii., ss. 71-96, ch. iv. ss. 9-12). It is painstaking and perhaps as free from material inaccuracy as a mere abstract can be. A more popular one, candid and careful as far as it goes, is in Milman's 'History of the Jews,' vol. iii. p. 374, sqq. (3rd ed. 1863).

Dr. van Vloten's *Benedictus de Spinoza naar Leven en Werken* (2nd ed., Schiedam, 1871) is a work more addressed to non-philosophical readers than Kuno Fischer's, but his account is thus far, unfortunately, accessible only to those who can read Dutch. Spinoza's doctrines are stated, as far as possible, in his own language, so that the book has a value independent of Dr. van Vloten's interpretation, which on many points is open to discussion. I am bound to say, however (the more so as divers philosophers by profession, both in the Netherlands and in Germany, have unduly slighted his work), that in the main I agree with his results.[8]

The most determined adversary of Dr. van Vloten is Dr. Spruyt, now a professor of philosophy at Amsterdam (Van Vloten's Benedictus de Spinoza beoordeeld door C. B. Spruyt. Utrecht, 1876. 8vo., pp. xi. and 100). His work, though short, has three distinct aims: vindication of Descartes, especially as to his services to physical science; criticism of Dr. van Vloten's treatment of Spinoza; and criticism of Spinoza himself. As to the first

---

[8] On the unveiling of the statue of Spinoza at the Hague on September 14, 1880, Dr. van Vloten delivered an address, which is printed in the form of a pamphlet (Spinoza de blijde boodschapper der mondige menschheid. 's Gravenhage, 1880).

topic, I do not know that Dr. van Vloten would really have much to say to the contrary, and I certainly have nothing. As to the second, Dr. van Vloten is well able to take care of himself, and moreover Mr. Lotsy has come to support him. But it is curious that, notwithstanding Dr. Spruyt's vehement and supercilious criticism of most parts of Dr. van Vloten's work, his own remarks on Spinozism amount to a virtual admission that Dr. van Vloten's view of the general effect and tendency of Spinoza's philosophy is correct. The real difference is on the question how far Spinoza was himself aware of its tendency, and a question of this kind is seldom so free from doubt as to justify one in treating with absolute contempt an opinion different from one's own. As to Spinoza himself, there is only one thing to be said of Dr. Spruyt's criticism. *Haeret in cortice.* It is the kind of criticism that naturally occurs to a reader instructed in modern philosophy who looks into Spinoza without any serious endeavour to discover what was really in his mind. It makes verbal points effectively, but adds no more to our understanding of Spinoza than the abundant criticism of the same kind that has gone before it. One point of substance is well seen, namely, that Spinoza's philosophy is not the flawless miracle of consistency imagined by many writers. But Dr. Spruyt runs into the other extreme, and seems to think no inconsistency too gross to ascribe to him. Dr. Spruyt is especially scandalised at Spinoza's theory of politics (which, according to him, is quite irreconcilable with the Ethics), and has devised for it the neat phrase 'brutale machtsvergoding;' which has, I believe, been a source of great comfort to anti-Spinozistic clergymen and journalists.

In the last year or two there have appeared Herr Theodor Camerer's *Die Lehre Spinoza's* (Stuttgart, 1877), and Mr. Lotsy's *Spinoza's Wijsbegeerte* (Amsterdam, 1878). Herr Camerer's book is a minute analysis of the philosophy of the Ethics, which has the merit of never shirking a difficulty, though the difficulties are sometimes exaggerated. Those who know Spinoza already may find it suggestive; and for such only it appears to be written. The total absence of historical criticism is a rather serious defect. Some things in Spinoza are naturally obscure if one does not look back at least as far as Descartes. Mr. Lotsy takes much the same line as Dr. van Vloten, but even more emphatically. The book is vigorous, clear-headed, and often original in treatment. It is noticed more at length in a review contributed by myself to *Mind* (July 1879, p. 431).

Then there is a class of writings which may be described as mixed exposition and criticism, with criticism predominating. Among these, which are very numerous, a chief place is held by Trendelenburg's essays, *Ueber Spinoza's Grundgedanken und dessen Erfolg* and *Ueber die aufgefundenen Ergänzungen zu Spinoza's Werken und deren Ertrag für Spinoza's Leben und Lehre (Historische Beiträge zur Philosophie,* vol. ii. p. 31, and vol. iii. p. 277). The later of the two essays is occasioned by the publication of *De Deo et Homine,* but is by no means confined to points immediately raised thereby.

H. C. W. Sigwart's *Der Spinozismus historisch und philosophisch erläutert, &c.,* Tübingen, 1839 *(Bibliogr.* 310), has suffered the fate of many good books in being assimilated by later ones, till there is little actual need to consult it in its original form. But a good and valuable book it remains.

An elaborate criticism is given in the introductory volume to Saisset's translation. It is avowedly polemical, and belongs to a school of philosophy which may now happily be considered pretty well extinct even in its own country, where till quite lately it sat in high places. But Saisset is an able and fair combatant, and stands, I think, at or near the head of the distinctly adverse writers on Spinoza. In English it has not been my fortune to meet with anything of the kind (save Prof. Flint's work mentioned below) showing competent acquaintance with the subject.

One or two recent works are on the line between general and special monographs. I will name here: —

Busolt (Dr. Georg): Die Grundzüge der Erkenntnisz-Theorie und Metaphysik Spinoza's dargestellt, erläutert und gewürdigt. Von der Universität zu Königsberg gekrönte Preisschrift. Berlin, 1875.

Turbiglio (Sebastiano): Benedetto Spinoza e le trasformazioni del suo pensiero. Libri tre. Rome, 1874.

Signer Turbiglio seems to hold that Spinoza never fully developed his own thought; he distinguishes between 'lo Spinoza reale,' and 'lo Spinoza fenomenico.' Of Spinoza's influence he says, *ad fin.:* 'In qualunque punto dell' età moderna voi interroghiate il pensiero filosofico, vi si revela la presenza dello Spinoza.'

Last, not least, come M. Renan's commemorative address (Spinoza, Discours prononcé à la Haye le 21 février 1877, à l'occasion du 200ᵉ anniversaire de sa mort. The Hague, 1877), a masterpiece in its kind; and Professor Land's lecture *Ter Gedachtenis van Spinoza* (Leyden, 1877), which, with its illustrative notes, gives in a small compass an accurate historical and critical survey of Spinoza's philosophy, and extracts from many authorities in the originals. I may here note that any one who wishes to make a special study of Spinoza will find it amply worth his while to be able to read Dutch.

The only formal commentary on Spinoza's works which I know of is J. H. von Kirchmann's. It has appeared in parts in the *Philosophische Bibliothek,* and is now to be had as a book complete in itself, or together with the translation *(subtit.* Benedict von Spinoza's sämmtliche philosophische Werke übersetzt und erläutert von J. H. v. Kirchmann und C. Schaarschmidt).

It is hardly needful to add that the general histories of philosophy, such as Erdmann's and Ueberweg's, may also be usefully consulted.

V. Among special monographs and discussions those on the treatise *De Deo et Homine* form a class apart.

Avenarius (Dr. Richard): Ueber die beiden ersten Phasen des Spinozischen Pantheismus, &c. Leipzig, 1868 *(Bibliogr.* 146).

Schaarschmidt (Prof. C.): Benedicti de Spinoza korte Verhandeling van God, de Mensch en deszelfs Welstand, tractatuli deperditi de Deo et homine ejusque felicitate versio Belgica. Ad antiquissimi codicis fidem edidit et praefatus est de Spinozae philosophiae fontibus Car. Schaarschmidt. Amstelodami 1869 *(Bibliogr.* 51).

Sigwart (Dr. Christoph): Benedict de Spinoza's kurzer Tractat von Gott, dem Menschen und dessen Glückseligkeit, &c. Tübingen, 1870 *(Bibliogr.* 53). A translation with commentary: *cf.* the same author's earlier monograph *Spinoza's neuentdeckter Tractat, &c.* Gotha, 1866 *(Bibliogr.* 144).

All these are important, and also Trendelenburg's essay already mentioned. I must be allowed to express the pleasure I have found in Professor Schaarschmidt's preface, apart from its considerable philosophical merits, as an example of elegant and unaffected modern Latinity. Quite lately M. Paul Janet has given us the first French version of the treatise, with an excellent introduction:

Supplément aux Œuvres de Spinoza: Dieu, l'homme et la béatitude: traduit pour la première fois en français et précédé d'une introduction. Paris, 1878.

Monographs on special aspects and relations of Spinoza's philosophy are too numerous to be effectively dealt with here. Dr. Joël's researches on the Jewish predecessors of Spinoza *(Beiträge zur Geschichte der Philosophie,* Breslau, 1876, a reissue of several earlier published essays of various dates) are mentioned in the body of the work (ch. iv.). Dr. Joël's inferences are criticised by Mr. W. R. Sorley in *Mind,* No. 19, July 1880, 'Jewish Mediæval Philosophy and Spinoza,' who holds that Spinoza's relation to these thinkers 'was as much one of antagonism as Descartes' relation to Christian Scholasticism, and indeed much more so.'

Spinoza's Relation to Descartes. — Bouillier, Histoire de la Philosophie Cartésienne, 3rd ed., Paris, 1868, 2 vols., chaps. xv-xix in vol. i. being on Spinoza (not in *Bibliogr.).*

Dr. F. G. Hann: Die Ethik Spinoza's und die Philosophie Descartes, Innsbruck, 1875.

Encyclopædia Britannica, 9th ed., art. *Cartesianism,* by Professor Caird.

All these writers adhere to the view that Spinoza's philosophy is a direct development from Descartes, and little or nothing else.

Bearings of Spinoza on Modern Theology. — Heine: Zur Geschichte der Religion und Philosophie in Deutschland, 2tes Buch. *Sämmtl. Werke,* vol. v. p. 123 *sqq.*

Matthew Arnold: Spinoza and the Bible. In *Essays in Criticism,* 3rd ed. London, 1875, at p. 357.

Prof. Robert Flint: Anti-theistic theories. Being the Baird lecture for 1877. Edinburgh and London, 1879.

Pp. 358-375 are on Spinoza; also note xxxviii. pp. 547-552.

Prof. Flint's opinions as to the value, speculative and practical, of Spinoza's philosophy belong to a school from which

I widely differ: he speaks, for example, of the ethical and political applications of Spinoza's doctrine as 'immoral and slavish.' But his work deserves respect as that of a thoroughly competent scholar. The note will be found useful by students.

Dr. M. M. Kalisch: Path and Goal. London, 1880: see pp. 377-405, in title 'Pantheism.'

Relations of Spinoza to Modern Philosophy and Literature. — Conrad von Orelli: Spinoza's Leben and Lehre, &c., 2nd ed. Aarau, 1850 *(Bibliogr.* 130).

The specific object of this work is to defend Spinoza against the criticisms of Schelling, Hegel, and their followers. It contains a careful discussion of Spinoza's philosophy, and collects many opinions and sayings of modern writers on him.

Nourrisson: Spinoza et le naturalisme contemporain. Paris, 1866 *(Bibliogr.* 141).

In this little book literary and bibliographical notices of real interest are strangely associated with superficial and declamatory criticism. Cf. M. Paul Janet's article in *Revue des Deux Mondes,* July 15, 1867.

Dr. S. E. Löwenhardt: Benedictus von Spinoza in seinem Verhältnisz zur Philosophie und Naturforschung der neueren Zeit. Berlin, 1872.

An able vindication of the harmony of Spinoza's doctrine with modern physiology and psychology. Several modern criticisms of Spinoza are considered in detail.

Paul Janet: French Thought and Spinozism. In *Contemporary Review,* May 1877.

Dr. Karl Rehorn: G. E. Lessing's Stellung zur Philosophie des Spinoza. Frankfurt am Main, 1877.

Guyau: La morale d'Épicure et ses rapports avec les doctrines contemporaines. Paris, 1878.

Pp. 227-237 are on Spinoza. 'Le vaste système de Spinoza, où ceux d'Épicure et de Hobbes sont absorbés, contient d'avance les théories fondamentales de l'école utilitaire française et anglaise.'

Jellinek (Dr. Georg): Die Beziehungen Göthes zu Spinoza. Vortrag gehalten im Vereine der Literaturfreunde zu Wien. Wien, 1878.

Frohschammer (Prof. J.): Ueber die Bedeutung der Einbildungskraft in der Philosophie Kant's und Spinoza's.

München, 1879. The part concerned with Spinoza (pp. 118-172) is an ingenious attempt to read into Spinoza, or exhibit as necessary for the completeness of Spinoza's system, an approximation to the author's own point of view.

In conclusion, it may be proper to say a word of the method I have myself followed. While I have endeavoured to make myself acquainted as far as practicable with the modern literature of the subject, my opinions of the meaning and value of Spinoza's philosophy have been formed by the study of Spinoza at first hand; and if this book induces even a few readers to do the same thing for themselves, and to forget as far as possible, in so doing, what they may have read about Spinoza here or elsewhere, I shall desire no other success. The only way to understand a great philosopher is to meet him face to face, whatever the apparent difficulties. A certain amount of historical preparation is indeed at least advisable; for to apprehend rightly the speech of a past time one must know something of its conditions. Apart from this, the author is his own best interpreter, and it has been my aim rather to make Spinoza explain himself than to discover explanations from the outside. As Herder says, 'Einen Schriftsteller aus sich selbst zu erklären ist die *honestas* jedem *honesto* schuldig.'

CHAPTER I

THE LIFE OF SPINOZA

Quae cum magna modis multis miranda videtur
gentibus humanis regio visendaque fertur,
rebus opima bonis, multa munita virum vi,
nil tamen hoc habuisse viro praeclarius in se,
nec sanctum magis et mirum carumque videtur.

LUCRETIUS, i. 726.

BARUCH DE SPINOZA was born at Amsterdam on November 24, 1632.[9] His parents, of whose circumstances and position in life nothing certain is known, were members of the community of Jewish emigrants from Portugal and Spain which had then been established in the Netherlands for something more than a generation. Before we enter on Spinoza's life, it may be not amiss to let our attention rest for a while on the society in which he was brought up, the vicissitudes of its foundation and growth, and the tone of thought and instruction which prevailed in it.[10] Something we may there find to throw light on the manner in which the early signs of Spinoza's philosophical genius were received by his own people, though we shall assuredly be disappointed if we look in external circumstances of education or study, in the influence of masters or companions either Jewish or Gentile, for an explanation of that genius itself. It was well said of an Indian poet: 'Of mighty men and of great rivers the springs are obscure.' The enlarged and purified vision of modern science may perceive much, and guess more, of the conditions that make the appearance of genius possible. But the conditions which fix it at the very time and place, the secret workings of nature which bring it to pass that an Æschylus, a Lionardo, a Faraday, a Kant,

---

[9] The house has been identified with great probability within the last few years. Certainty is to be attained, however, only by the inspection of documents which the owner of the house refuses to produce.

[10] My chief authority on this subject is Grätz, *Geschichte der Juden,* vols. ix. and x. I have also consulted Koenen, *Geschiedenis der Joden in Nederland* (Utrecht, 1843).

or a Spinoza is born upon the earth, are as obscure now as they were a thousand years ago. The power of these men still bears with it the reverence and awe that belong to great things unaccountable.

The result of the persecutions, banishments, and forcible conversions which had earned for the sovereigns of Spain the title of Catholic, and laid the foundation of their country's ruin at the very height of its prosperity, had been to leave in Spain and Portugal a large class of 'new Christians,' nominally converted and openly conforming Jews who in many cases kept up in secret, from generation to generation, some remnant of Jewish usages. Their tendencies to covert persistence in the faith and customs of their fathers were watched by the Inquisition with an evil and sleepless eye. Persecutions, *autos da fé,* and, notwithstanding all the vigilance of the Spanish government, flights from the land of the oppressor were constant. Towards the close of the sixteenth century it seemed as if the precarious state of the Marranos — so these unacknowledged Jews were called — was about to become hopeless. The power of Spain still waxed in Europe; where Spain went, there the Inquisition followed; and where the Inquisition came, there justice and mercy ceased to be.

The Italian States, which had formerly offered a refuge to the exiles, were no longer safe for them. England, now the chief Protestant country, had driven out the Jews three centuries before, and they did not again find admission till the last days of the Commonwealth. It was out of the dominion of Spain herself that the light of deliverance first shone. The fury of the Inquisition defeated its own purpose. The Netherlands revolted from the intolerable combination of secular with spiritual tyranny; and from the desperate rising, as it at first seemed, of a handful of subjects in a corner of the Spanish Empire there sprang a commonwealth which for the greater part of a century was the most free, the most prosperous, and the most tolerant in Europe.

No sooner was the independence of the Netherlands practically secure than the new Christians of Spain and Portugal began to look thither for a refuge. In or about 1591 overtures were made to the magistrates of Middelburg for a settlement of Marranos, which would have secured to the province of Zealand the first advantages of Jewish industry and commerce. The civil authorities were disposed to enter into the plan, but theological prejudice stood in the way. The Reformed clergy set themselves against the proposal, and nothing came of it. But in the spring of 1593 a vessel sailed in secret from Portugal with a small company of Marranos,[11] determined to adventure themselves on the Dutch coasts, and trust their fortunes to the principles of toleration that had been proclaimed by William of Orange. After a not uneventful voyage they landed at Emden, and found assistance at the hands of German Jews already settled some time past in East Friesland. By their advice the fugitives made their way to Amsterdam, where they arrived on April 23. This little nucleus of a colony soon received accession. In 1596 the English fleet under Essex, returning from the sack of Cadiz, brought a number of new Christians, presumably not unwilling prisoners, who openly returned to Judaism as soon as they were safe in Holland. It was some time before any official notice was taken of the new community, and its recognition was hastened by a curious accident. The celebration of the Day of Atonement attracted the suspicion of the citizens, who knew that the immigrants came from Popish lands, and guessed that their mysterious meeting could be nothing else than a Popish plot. The congregation was surprised by armed force, and the leaders arrested. These, once in the presence of the magistrates, speedily convinced them that the Pope and the Inquisition were as odious to themselves as to the Protestants of the United Provinces. Being thus made known to the civil powers, the Jews were emboldened to ask leave to build a synagogue. After some discussion this was granted, and the first synagogue of Amsterdam was opened in 1598. Ten years later the numbers of the colony had so much increased that a new synagogue was needed. This was itself only temporary. In 1675, when the Jewish community of Amsterdam had reached the height of its prosperity, the present Portuguese synagogue was completed, amidst the felicitations not only of Jewish but of Christian theologians and poets.

Meanwhile some years more seem to have passed before the Jews acquired a distinct legal status. They were exposed to inconvenience from an unexpected quarter; for in the battle of Remonstrants and Contra-Remonstrants the worsted Remonstrants took the line of complaining that various strange sects,

---

[11] Grätz, ix. 492, and, as to the exact date, *ib.* note 10.

including Jews,[12] enjoyed a freedom of worship which was denied to themselves. These complaints did the Remonstrants no
good, but they did the Jews some little harm. Mixed marriages
were forbidden; the Jews were once threatened, if not more, with
the closing of the synagogue; and it seems that in other parts of
the Netherlands they were not always sure even of personal liberty. In 1619 an ordinance was made by the States of Holland, on
the report of a commission appointed some time before, by
which provision was made for the regular admission and government of the Jews.[13] After this the Hebrew colony waxed and
throve apace. We have still a living record of their prosperity in
Rembrandt's grave and majestic portraits of Jewish merchants
and rabbis. And they increased and multiplied with every fresh
act of persecuting folly in the Spanish peninsula. Had the Catholic rulers intended to impoverish their own countries and enrich
the heretical provinces, they could not have done it better. The
exiles, though they preserved among themselves (as their de-
scendants still preserve for official purposes) the use of the Portuguese and Spanish languages, and even in their ceremonies and
manners had some remnants of their old outward conformity to
the Church of Rome, soon repaid the hospitality of their adopted
country with faithful attachment, as well as with the material
advantages that accompanied their settlement. Spinoza was a
good citizen if not an active one; and several passages of his
writings show that the free institutions of the Dutch Republic
were to him the object not merely of esteem but of patriotic affection. Yet he has been accused even in our own time of
preaching maxims of despotism. But for the present let us return
from his critics to his immediate ancestors and contemporaries.

The occasion was a great one for the rising Jewish community, the New Jerusalem, as it was already called in Spinoza's
generation. The leaders of the Amsterdam synagogue might, in
the opinion of the latest and most exact historian of the Jewish

---

[12] 'Ja de Joden zelfs, die Christus verzaken, welke zij supplianten (i.e.
your petitioners) houden voor hun eenigen Heiland.' — Remonstrant Petition,
1617, ap. Koenen, p. 145.

[13] Koenen, 147. Each Province was to make its own rules, subject to
the condition that no distinctive dress or badge (such as was usual in Catholic
countries) should be imposed. Koenen gives no particulars of what was done at
Amsterdam.

nation, have done wonders if they had been capable of making the most of their fortune. But they were not men of that stamp. Ability, industry, and fortitude they possessed: the renovating power of genius was wanting. Their learning was rather of that formalist kind which is disconcerted by genius, and forces a quarrel on it. And so it was when genius appeared among them in the person of Spinoza. The conjecture which deals with lost possibilities might amuse itself worse than with the contemplation of what the author of the 'Tractatus Theologico-Politicus' and friend of De Witt might have done for his people in civil and political matters if he had remained in their community.

Saul Levi Morteira, said to have been Spinoza's instructor, was a man who had no claim to original powers. He was not specially remarkable for eloquence, nor did he stand in the first rank of Jewish learning; altogether he was of those who care not to commit themselves out of beaten paths. His colleague, Isaac Aboab de Fonseca, presided over the synagogue of Amsterdam for nearly seventy years. Eloquence was his chief, it would seem his only gift. His discourses commanded admiration, but he was neither eminent in learning nor fitted to deal with questions of practical moment. His character was lacking in force, his perceptions in width and comprehension; he was not capable of firm and clear-sighted action.

A better known personage than either of these two was Manasseh ben Israel. His father, like others of the first founders of the colony, had escaped from the pious cares of the Holy Office, shattered in body and ruined in estate, to find his last resting-place among his own people. The son has a place in the social history of England by his unsparing efforts to procure from Cromwell the readmission of the Jews. He had to encounter much opposition, including an extraordinary polemic from Prynne, in which a great deal of curious learning was mixed up with repetition of all the mediæval stories of Jewish child-murder, cannibalism, and sacrilege. Nor did he live to see his purpose effected: he died in 1657, and the Jews found their way back into England on a footing of informal but unquestioned liberty only after the Restoration. But the way had none the less been made for them by Manasseh ben Israel's endeavours. It may be (as Dr. Grätz suggests) that the very foibles of his character, his turn for mystical interpretations of theology, and his credulity as to prophetic signs and seasons, were additions to his strength for that particular work, and that a stronger man would not have done it so well. His credulity was indeed nothing singular: about the same time a deputation of Asiatic Jews came to England to inquire if Cromwell were not the Messiah. For his learning, it was ample and various, and extended to European as well as Hebrew literature. But it did not save him from giving himself over to superstition and letter-worship which often ran into puerilities. He was a voluminous writer, but wrote with an undiscerning hand, mixing up in his compilation things wise and foolish. Yet he had one power which may at times almost fill the place of genius — the power of winning men's friendship. He was of an open and generous nature, which showed itself in that frank urbanity and polished conversation which is wont everywhere to draw confidence to it.

At the time when the congregation of Amsterdam condemned Spinoza, Manasseh ben Israel was absent on his mission to England. It may be doubted whether his presence would have ensured any more rational course of action. A believer in the verbal inspiration of the Talmud could have had nothing to urge for moderation, unless on grounds of secular policy; and in this case it is by no means clear that policy was not for once on the side of the fanatics.

In the generation before Spinoza the Jewish commonwealth of Amsterdam did not enjoy unbroken peace within itself. For many years there was a schism in the synagogue, arising out of the scandal caused to the stricter members by the survival of Spanish-Catholic practices and manners; and in Spinoza's first years the congregation was troubled by the strange career of Uriel da Costa. He too, deserves brief mention here; not that he was a person of any weight or influence, much less a precursor of Spinoza; but his fate illustrates the temper of the times, and his excommunication may have served as a precedent in Spinoza's case. He was born of a New Christian family in Oporto; his parents were, however, orthodox in conviction as well as in name, and he received a learned education under Jesuit instructors. Dissatisfied with their formal dogmatism, he betook himself to the study of the prophets of the Old Testament; and the result was that he fled to Amsterdam, together with his mother and brothers, joined the synagogue, and changed his former Christian

name Gabriel for the purely Jewish one of Uriel. But here also
disappointment awaited him. He was perplexed and shocked by
the discrepance between Judaism such as he found it, or thought
to find it, in the Scriptures, and such as it had been made by
Rabbinical gloss and tradition. He denounced the modern teachers and rulers as Pharisees, and set their ceremonies at naught;
they replied to his criticism by excommunicating him. He went
on to publish a controversial tract against the immortality of the
soul; upon this the chiefs of the synagogue denounced him to the
civil authorities, and he was fined and imprisoned, and his book
publicly burnt. For fifteen years he endured the social penalties
of excommunication, but at length his patience gave way, and he
was formally reconciled. But he seems to have made no secret of
the purely outward character of his conformity.[14] At this very
time his course of unregulated speculation was leading him on
from an anti-Rabbinical and as it were Puritan Judaism to a doctrine of bare natural Deism. Nor did he observe ordinary caution
in his conversation. There followed a new and more stringent
excommunication, to be taken off only on condition of a solemn
and public act of penance. Da Costa held out this time for seven
years, and then again submitted. He underwent a humiliating
ceremony, modelled on those of the Inquisition, which were
probably known by bitter personal experience to some of those
present.

It is a general fact in human history, and one of the sad-
dest, that no sooner has a persecuted community secured its
freedom than it takes to persecuting in its turn. This was shown
at the very same time by the Reformed Church of the Netherlands: 'Those who but a few years before had complained of the
cruelty of the Church of Rome were no sooner delivered from
that, than they began to call for the same ways of persecuting
those who were of the other side.'[15] And it was not far from this
time that the Puritan colonists of New England set up an ecclesiastical tyranny far more oppressive and searching than that from
which they had fled. Da Costa's penance was completed by his
lying down athwart the threshold of the synagogue, so that the

---

[14] Er wollte, wie er sagte, 'unter Affen auch ein Affe sein.' Grätz, x.
137.

[15] Burnet, History of his own Time, i. 315.

whole congregation stepped over him as they passed out. Humiliation he must have expected, but the reality was too much for his pride. He determined to live only so long as was needful to commit to writing, in the form of an autobiography, a fierce denunciation of his enemies and persecutors. Having completed this writing, he shot himself in his own house.

It does not seem that Da Costa's speculations had any value, and his character cannot be said to call for admiration. Martyrs and confessors in the cause of free thought have not been so few or so weak that one who was twice excommunicated, and twice recanted, can claim a high place among them; and there was at least a large element of personal pique and resentment in Da Costa's later courses. But we cannot refuse our pity to a life cast among such untoward surroundings, nor can we acquit the chiefs of the synagogue of excessive and ill-judged harshness throughout their dealings with this unhappy man. His story prepares us to hear with much less surprise of Spinoza's treatment sixteen years later.

As to the general state of education among the Jews of Amsterdam, they were exceedingly well provided with the appliances of learning and literature then current. So much would sufficiently appear from Spinoza's works and correspondence alone. His writing is that of a man who has been brought up among scholars and has mastered betimes all the knowledge that a scholar is expected to possess. But high literary culture and great literary facility are compatible with great feebleness of intellectual grasp. Scholarship is in itself no warranty of sound thinking. And so it was that the Hebrew scholars who exchanged more or less elegant Latin verses with European scholars of the stamp of Grotius or Barlæus were ready and even eager to give ear to the wildest and most idle fancies in matters of theology and philosophy. The doctrine of the Kabbalah, likened by the historian to whom I am so much indebted to a fungus growth creeping over the body of the Law and the Traditions, was almost universally received. A generation filled with the east wind of mystical ravings hungered after signs and wonders, and signs and wonders came without stint. Demoniacs, exorcisms, miracles, false prophets, even false Messiahs, fed the credulity of the Levantine Jews, and deceived not a few elsewhere. The most singular appearance of this kind, the career of Sabbatai Zevi, belongs however to a somewhat later date. Accounts of the dreams, revelations, and supernatural feats of the new prophets were published and eagerly read; and besides these the epidemic of superstition produced a speculative literature of its own. One of these works, composed by a Polish Jew, Naphtali ben Jakob Elchanan, who had caught the Kabbalistic contagion in Palestine, and published at Amsterdam in 1648, is described by Dr. Grätz[16] as not containing a single rational sentence: 'yet leading rabbis of Germany and Poland accepted this puddle of nauseous blasphemy as a fountain of divine wisdom.' If these were the studies in favour among Spinoza's teachers and companions, we can hardly wonder at the tone of something like contempt in which he generally speaks of current Jewish opinion.

Such, then, was the society into which Spinoza was born. The accustomed course of education was almost if not altogether confined to the Hebrew language and literature. With these, therefore, Spinoza was early made familiar, and at the age of fifteen he had gone so far in the study of the Talmud as to be one of Rabbi Morteira's most promising pupils. In the advanced classes of the Amsterdam school he had the opportunity of mastering the philosophical writings of the golden age of modern Jewish learning, the commentaries of Maimonides and Ibn Ezra. The probable effect of these on the development of his thought will be more fully spoken of in a later place. Enough to say here that he found in the hints and questionings of these men much more than his teachers expected him to find or were themselves capable of finding.

Secular learning and accomplishments had to be sought in other quarters. The elements of Latin were imparted to Spinoza by a German master whose name is not known; he continued the study with Francis van den Ende,[17] a physician as well as a man of letters, whose high reputation as a teacher was qualified by the suspicion that he taught his pupils free-thinking as well as Latin. The charge may have been true, but it may just as well have been a mere popular inference from the known fact that he was a proficient in the natural sciences. So much is certain, and it

---

[16] Grätz, x. 131.

[17] His name is given in the documents relating to the Chevalier de Rohan's plot as Francis Affinius van den Enden. See Clément, *Episodes de l'Histoire de France*, Paris, 1859.

is probable that he communicated this part of his knowledge, no less than that which he specially professed to teach, to those who showed themselves apt for it: for Spinoza's works afford unmistakable evidence of thorough and sound instruction in physical science, and more especially physiology, which cannot well have been acquired at a later time of his life; not that he makes any great display of knowledge, but that with many occasions for mistakes he commits few or none. As to Latin, at all events, Van den Ende's charge was efficiently performed. Spinoza mastered it completely, not indeed according to the fine and exacting standards of later scholarship, but more completely in one sense, for he made it a living instrument of thought. His language is not what we call classical, but it is handled with perfect command and perfectly adapted to its ends. At the same time it appears by quotations and allusions that he was fairly well at home with the Latin classics. His knowledge of Greek was more limited, and by his own account not critical.[18] Of modern languages he knew French, German, and Italian, besides Portuguese and Spanish, one or both of which were native to him. It appears from evidences made public early in the last century, but afterwards lost sight of until quite recently, that he always regarded Dutch as a foreign language, and wrote it only with difficulty. Such little circumstances help us to realize the self-contained isolation in which the Hebrew community must have dwelt even among well-wishers.

It was perhaps through his intercourse with Van den Ende that Spinoza became acquainted with the writings of Giordano Bruno and Descartes. As to Descartes, indeed, explanation may be dispensed with; no young man with a philosophical turn of mind could help reading him. But as to Giordano Bruno, if one assumes (on the grounds to be mentioned hereafter) that Spinoza had read him, one may be fairly called on to assign the occasion for it. Giordano Bruno would not otherwise have come naturally in Spinoza's way; his theories were scarcely less abhorrent to Jews and Protestants than to Catholics. But it is quite possible that Van den Ende may have more or less cherished Bruno in private, and discussed him with a select few of his learners. This would have been just the kind of study to procure for Van

---

[18] *Tract. Theol.-Pol.* cap. x. *ad fin.*

den Ende the alarming reputation handed down to us by Colerus. Besides his graver pursuits Spinoza contrived to acquire considerable skill in drawing: he filled a book with portrait sketches, many of them being of distinguished persons. This book was at one time in the possession of Colerus, but there is no further trace of it.

There is a story that Van den Ende was assisted in his teaching by a daughter, of singular wit, learning, and accomplishments. Spinoza, the story goes, was among her pupils, and from a pupil became a lover. But he had a rival in a fellow-pupil named Kerkering, who finally won the lady's hand by the help of a valuable pearl necklace. Now it is true that Van den Ende had a daughter named Clara Maria, who married Theodore Kerkkrinck (such is the authentic form of the name). The date of the marriage, however, has been ascertained by Van Vloten to be 1671 (the year when Van den Ende left Holland), and it appears by the register that the bride was twenty-seven years old. Now Spinoza was excommunicated and left Amsterdam in 1656. Clara Maria van den Ende was therefore eleven or twelve years old at the latest time when Spinoza could have been her father's pupil, and the tale of the students' rivalry and the pearl necklace must be dismissed. Kerkkrinck was a physician, who published works on medicine, anatomy and chemistry, and earned a considerable scientific reputation, so that the match was in itself a natural one enough for Van den Ende's daughter. The question remains whether the tale of Spinoza's love for her is absolutely without foundation. There is no reason whatever to suppose that Spinoza did not keep up his acquaintance with Van den Ende in the visits which we know that he made from time to time to Amsterdam; and thus we have occasion and room enough for a friendship extending into Klaartje's riper years, which may have passed into a serious inclination. A romantic affection we cannot ascribe to Spinoza at this time: it would be too much out of keeping with all his habits and character; and one may shrewdly suspect that his inclination never in truth got beyond a hypothetical stage. He was likely enough to be rallied by host or friends on his hermit life, and not unlikely to put them off with some such answer as that, if he married a wife, it should be Van den Ende's daughter. A speech or two of this kind would be ample foundation for the story given by Colerus, and a simple confusion of dates would do the rest.

Yet there is one chance left if we are minded to hold fast to the solitary piece of romance that can be suggested in Spinoza's life. Nothing forbids us to suppose that at the earlier time there sprang up some half ideal, half childish affection between Spinoza and Clara van den Ende; there is no violation of possibility in conceiving her as standing to him in a relation like that of Beatrice to Dante. As far as ages go the probability is even greater than in Dante's case; so that, unless we join ourselves to those over-curious persons who would allegorize away the *Vita Nuova,* we have a fair precedent enough. Beatrice was nine years old, Dante himself only ten, when the 'glorious lady of his soul' first showed herself to his eyes, and the word came to him, *Ecce deus fortior me, qui veniens dominabitur mihi.* Spinoza was not a poet, some one will say. No, but he was a mystic at the time in question, which for this purpose will do at least as well. But I throw out this merely for the chance of anyone finding comfort in it. As a hypothesis it seems to me much less probable than the other; and even if the facts had been as suggested, Spinoza was not the man to be very communicative about them. The truth is that we have no positive evidence at all. We have only a story which, as it stands, cannot possibly be true, and which does not rest on any satisfactory authority. The absence of any apparent motive for inventing the whole of it raises a certain presumption that it contains in a more or less distorted form elements of genuine fact, derived from statements made by Spinoza himself. But what those elements may be we have no means of determining.

As to Van den Ende himself, one is sorry to know that he came to a bad end. In his old age he settled in France, and had been there only a few years when he was drawn into the conspiracy of the Chevalier de Rohan and La Tréaumont, partly by working on his patriotism with hopes that the affair would turn to the profit of the Netherlands, partly by flattering his speculative fancy with dreams of a Utopian republic to be established on the ruins of the French monarchy. A general rising in Normandy was to be supported by a descent of the Dutch fleet: the admiral, Cornelius Tromp, was fully prepared to take his part, and long hovered on the French coast awaiting the signal, which never came. But the conspiracy, though carefully planned, was hollow from the first; it was a venture of disappointed and desperate personal ambitions. It was discovered before any part of it could be put in execution, and its leaders paid the usual penalty of unsuccessful conspirators. Van den Ende was hanged at Paris on November 27, 1674.

So much is known of Spinoza for the first twenty-three years of his life. Not long after he had fully attained man's estate the elders of his people began to remark in him an unwonted freedom of discourse, and possibly some laxity in ceremonial observances which would of itself have sufficed as an ostensible ground of censure. One anecdote of this time, plausible enough to be worth repeating, has come down to us.[19] Two fellow-students, it is said, questioned Spinoza closely on theology; he put them off with general reference to the authority of Moses and the Prophets as sufficient for all true Israelites. But as far as their authority goes, answered one of his companions, I cannot find any such thing as that God is incorporeal, the soul immortal, or angels real beings. What say you, then, to these matters? Spinoza replied that he could see no objection in point of orthodoxy to holding that God has a body,[20] or that angels are mere apparitions created for the special occasion of their ministry (for which, indeed, or for something very like it, there is Talmudic authority: a circumstance likely enough to be known to Spinoza and overlooked by his questioners), and that the Scriptures use *soul* as a pure synonym of *life,* without saying anything about immortality. The two friends were only half satisfied; but Spinoza, while he promised to give them fuller explanations another time, contrived not to find any opportunity of renewing the discourse. We have no trustworthy or distinct account of the events that led to Spinoza's rupture with the congregation; but certain it is that in the early part of the year 1656 it was considered by Morteira and his colleague that action of a decided kind must be taken.

It has already been remarked that the persecuted of Spain and Portugal had brought a leaven of persecuting zeal to their new asylum. But in this case reasons of secular policy were po-

---

[19] This is from Lucas; in other words we may give it just so much credit as it appears on the face of it to deserve.

[20] Compare Hobbes's arguments on this point.

tent counsellors to the same effect. The Jewish community was a kind of state within a state, a society foreign in religion, language, and manners to its hosts. To expose themselves to the charge of fostering novelties in speculation might well have been a serious danger to them. As prudent governors of their household, it behoved the chief men to suffer no more scandals within it like that of Da Costa. And Spinoza's particular novelties might be thought eminently fitted to bring them into trouble. He busied himself with Descartes, and the Synod of Dort (not the first and famous, but a second one) had just condemned Cartesianism. The best way would be to make things quiet while it was yet time; the next best, if the erratic member could not be brought to take the fitting measure of heed, at least in his public ways, was to cut him off at once and disclaim all responsibility for him. Accordingly the way of compromise was first tried, and an annuity of 1000 florins was offered to Spinoza as the price of apparent conformity. This however was positively declined. The next step[21] was to summon Spinoza before the congregation and inflict on him the first degree of ecclesiastical censure, the lower excommunication, which excluded the offender for thirty days from the society of the faithful, and was intended to operate as a serious invitation to repentance.

During the period of suspense which followed, Spinoza's life was aimed at by an unknown enemy, presumably some fanatic outrunning the zeal of his masters, or thinking himself a divinely appointed messenger to rebuke their tardiness in defending the faith by a striking example. This man set upon Spinoza with a dagger one evening as he was leaving the Portuguese synagogue.[22] But he avoided the blow in time, and it pierced only his coat, which he afterwards kept in the same condition as a memorial. Being warned by this attack that Amsterdam was no longer a safe place for him, he betook himself to the

---

[21] Our data for these events are still meagre, and their order in time uncertain: but we cannot doubt that a lesser excommunication preceded the final one. See Grätz, x. 175. Lucas gives what purport to be details of the earlier proceedings, but in his usual confused manner and with improbable circumstances.

[22] I follow Colerus's account as the best supported and most probable. Difficulties have been raised about the incident: they are discussed in Van Vloten's *Levensbode,* ix. 419.

hospitality of a friend who dwelt a little way out of the city, on the Ouwerkerk road. His host belonged to the small dissenting community of Remonstrants or Collegiants. Here, under the roof of heretics anathematized by the Synod of Dort, he learnt the final decision of the Jewish congregation on the charge of heresy against himself. The sentence was pronounced on July 27, 1656, in the Portuguese language, and its effect is as follows: —

'The chiefs of the council do you to wit, that having long known the evil opinions and works of Baruch de Espinoza, they have endeavoured by divers ways and promises to withdraw him from his evil ways, and they are unable to find a remedy, but on the contrary have had every day more knowledge of the abominable heresies practised and taught by him, and of other enormities committed by him, and have of this many trustworthy witnesses, who have deposed and borne witness in the presence of the said Espinoza, and by whom he stood convicted; all which having been examined in the presence of the elders, it has been determined with their assent that the said Espinoza should be excommunicated and cut off from the nation of Israel; and now he is hereby excommunicated with the following anathema: —

'With the judgment of the angels and of the saints we excommunicate, cut off, curse, and anathematize Baruch de Espinoza, with the consent of the elders and of all this holy congregation, in the presence of the holy books: by the 613 precepts which are written therein, with the anathema wherewith Joshua cursed Jericho, with the curse which Elisha laid upon the children, and with all the curses which are written in the law. Cursed be he by day and cursed be he by night. Cursed be he in sleeping and cursed be he in waking, cursed in going out and cursed in coming in. The Lord shall not pardon him, the wrath and fury of the Lord shall henceforth be kindled against this man, and shall lay upon him all the curses which are written in the book of the law. The Lord shall destroy his name under the sun, and cut him off for his undoing from all the tribes of Israel, with all the curses of the firmament which are written in the book of the law. But ye that cleave unto the Lord your God, live all of you this day.

'And we warn you, that none may speak with him by word of mouth nor by writing, nor show any favour to him, nor be under one roof with him, nor come within four cubits of him, nor read any paper composed or written by him.'

From the terms of the excommunication something, but not much, may be gathered as to the form which the accusation had assumed. It is not on the face of it a condemnation for mere speculative opinions; indeed such a condemnation would not be warranted by Jewish law. The 'heresies practised and taught' ('horrendas heresias que praticava e ensinava') point at some active attempt to spread his opinions, and the mention of 'other enormities' on Spinoza's part ('ynormes obras que obrava') probably refers to breaches of ceremonial rules, and is not (though to an English reader it looks so at first sight) a meaningless addition like the *alia enormia* of old-fashioned English pleadings.

Thus was Baruch de Spinoza made an outcast from Israel, and cut off from his own people and from his father's house. The ties of kindred, ties which for that people have ever been of exceeding strength and sanctity, were for him severed beyond recall. The bond of fellowship among Israelites is of strength and sanctity only less than that of actual kindred; and this also was at once and irrevocably dissolved. The excommunicated Jew became as it were a masterless man; he had no title by which he could call upon either Jew or Christian to stand by him or answer for him. If it is a good preparation for philosophy to be alone in the world, the needful discipline came upon Spinoza with terrible completeness. It is hardly possible for men at this time, either in Spinoza's country or in our own, to realize the full effect of such a blow. But Spinoza never faltered under it: the passionate weakness of Uriel da Costa was far from his nature. 'This compels me,' he said on receiving the news, 'to nothing which I should not otherwise have done.' Thus it would seem that he held himself to have renounced the synagogue of his own motion rather than to have been driven from it; and the title of a defence which he wrote in Spanish and sent to the elders points the same way. This paper itself has never been found;[23] it is supposed, however, to have contained some foreshadowing of the 'Tractatus Theologico-Politicus.' It is said that

---

[23] Unless it was identical with or developed into the polemic against the Jews mentioned by Rieuwertz, the publisher of the *Opera Posthuma,* to the German traveller Stolle as existing in MS. and having been in his possession. See Ginsberg's edition of the *Ethics,* p. 20.

the chiefs of the synagogue were not content with inflicting their utmost ecclesiastical penalty. They represented to the civil authorities that Spinoza was a dangerous person; their request was backed by the Reformed clergy, and a sentence of banishment for a short time was pronounced against Spinoza, who must have already left the city. But sentences of this kind against men who have forestalled them by absence are common enough in history. The incident does not rest on good authority,[24] but the fact that similar proceedings had been taken in the case of Da Costa renders it not improbable in itself. From this time forth, in any case, we have to think of Spinoza as removed from Amsterdam and the associations of his youth. He marked the severance himself by disusing his Hebrew name Baruch, and substituting for it the Latin equivalent Benedict. Only once more in his lifetime do we hear anything of dealings with his family. Spinoza became entitled upon the death of his father to share the inheritance with his two sisters. The sisters disputed his title, presumably under the belief that an excommunicated heretic would have no part in the estate of a faithful Israelite. Spinoza has left on record his opinion that in a state where just laws are in force it is not only the right of every citizen, but his duty towards the common weal, to resist injustice to himself, lest peradventure evil men should find profit in their evil-doing. In his own case, then, he acted on this principle: the civil law was just, whether on the high ground of indifference to theological strife, or, as is more likely, because Judaism was only a tolerated religion; and Spinoza's claim to share with his sisters was made good. But, having established his rights, he did not choose to take any material advantage by them. When the partition came to be effected he gave up to his sisters everything but one bed: 'qui était en vérité fort bon,' says Colerus in the French version.

Spinoza was now dependent on his own work for a livelihood. In compliance with the Rabbinical precept which commands every man to learn some handicraft, and guided by his philosophical and scientific temper, he had acquired the art of

---

[24] It is in Lucas, with confusion of time and circumstance, as usual. Colerus knows nothing of it, and Spinoza's tone of admiration and deference for the civil powers of his country (in the *Tractatus Theologico-Politicus*) is likewise against it. The precedent of Da Costa turns the scale in favour of giving it a place in the text.

making and polishing lenses for optical instruments. Perhaps a
desire to imitate the example of Descartes, who had likewise
made himself a practical optician, may have entered into Spinoza's motives. At this time his admiration of Descartes was
probably at its height. The art enabled him to earn an income,
slender indeed, but sufficient for his limited wants, and a reputation for skill and knowledge of optics which preceded his fame
as a philosopher. The lenses made by him were sought after, and
those left undisposed of at his death fetched a high price. It was
as an optician, moreover, that he made the acquaintance of
Huygens and Leibnitz. In 1671 Leibnitz wrote to consult him on
certain optical questions, and his letter addresses Spinoza as a
critic of recognized authority. It was believed by Spinoza's
friends that but for his early death he would have made some
considerable contribution to the science; as it was, the only work
of that kind which he completed was a small treatise on the
Rainbow, long supposed to have been lost. It was in truth published at the Hague in 1687, and has been found and reprinted in
our own time by Dr. Van Vloten.[25] We are also told that Spinoza
had formed the plan of writing a concise treatise on Algebra
('breviori et magis intelligibili methodo'), and other unspecified
works.

It appears that Spinoza stayed with his Remonstrant
friend till the end of 1660 or beginning of 1661, when they removed together to the village of Rijnsburg, near Leyden, then the
headquarters of the sect. The house where they lived is still
standing, and the road bears to this day the name of 'Spinoza
Lane.' The Remonstrants were by this time practically tolerated,
but had no regular clergy or public ministrations. There could
therefore be no outward evidence that a person living among
them, and not being a member of any other religious community,
was not one of themselves. Hence the report that Spinoza had
become a Christian would very naturally arise. It gained currency enough to be thought by Colerus worth an express contradiction.

The meagre information given by Colerus and others of
the philosopher's movements and occupations in after years is

---

[25] The original copy, believed to be unique, is in the Royal Library at
the Hague.

partly filled in by his letters, of which we possess only the selection made, unhappily with a far too sparing hand, by the editors of his posthumous works, and a few more which have been discovered in the orphan asylum at Amsterdam formerly belonging to the Collegiants. Spinoza paid frequent visits to the Hague, where he became well known in the society of men of letters; and it is clear that as time went on he found more and more content in his entertainment there, for in 1664 he moved again to Voorburg, which is a suburb of the Hague, and in 1670 to the Hague itself, where he spent the rest of his life.

In 1663 we find that Spinoza had already sketched out some of the leading ideas of his metaphysical system, substantially in the same form in which they eventually appeared in the 'Opera Posthuma,' and had entrusted his papers to a number of his younger friends at Amsterdam. They had formed a sort of philosophical club,[26] at whose meetings the members took it in turns to read out and comment on Spinoza's manuscript. If after discussion any point remained obscure, a note was made of the difficulty, and one of the company would write to Spinoza for explanation. Such a letter is extant, written by Simon de Vries, a young student of medicine, and of much promise, who had conceived for Spinoza an intellectual attachment which grew into a warm friendship. He would willingly have shown his gratitude to his master by substantial benefactions; we are told of a gift of 2000 florins offered by him to Spinoza and declined.

Spinoza's life, as we shall see, was not a robust one; but that of his young disciple seems to have been yet frailer, for he died in Spinoza's lifetime, and not so unexpectedly but that he had time to form the design of making Spinoza his heir, and to be dissuaded from it by his friend's own entreaties. De Vries had a brother living, and Spinoza pressed upon him the duty of thinking first of his own kindred. The master prevailed with the disciple against his own interest, and the bulk of the estate was left by De Vries to his brother, charged however with a sufficient annuity for Spinoza's maintenance. Even this was accepted only in part. The heir offered to fix the amount at 500 florins; but Spi-

---

[26] Perhaps a section or offshoot of the society *Nil volentibus arduum* (it was and is the practice in Holland for the motto of a society to be used as the name of the society itself), of which Dr. L. Meyer is known to have been an active member. (Van Vloten, *Bened. de Spinoza*, p. 29.)

noza pretended that it was too much, and refused to take more than 300. De Vries's letter to Spinoza shows all the generous enthusiasm of a learner in presence of a beloved teacher.

'I have long desired,' he says, 'an occasion to be with you, but weather and the hard winter have not allowed me. Sometimes I complain of my fate in being removed from you by a distance that keeps us so much apart. Happy, most happy, is that companion who dwells with you under the same roof, and who can at all times, dining, supping, or walking, hold discourse with you of the most excellent matters. But though we are so widely separated in the body, yet you have constantly been present to my mind, especially when I apply myself to your writings.'

Spinoza's answer approves the plan of the society, and gives the desired explanations. To De Vries's complaint of their long separation he replies as follows: —

'Your long continued absence has been no less disagreeable to me than to you; but meanwhile I am glad that my exercises *(lucubratiunculae)* are of use to you and our friends. For thus I speak with you while we are away from one another. As to my fellow-lodger, you need not envy him. There is no one I like less, or with whom I have been more cautious; so that I must warn you and all our friends not to communicate my opinions to him till he has come to riper years. He is still too childish and inconstant, and cares for novelty more than truth. Yet I hope he will amend these youthful failings some years hence; indeed I am nearly sure of it, so far as I can judge from his disposition; and so his general character moves me to be friendly with him.'

It appears that Spinoza's expectations of this young man were too sanguine. He is identified by plausible conjecture with one Albert Burgh, who many years afterwards was received into the Church of Rome, and on that occasion favoured Spinoza with an extraordinary letter, of which a specimen will come before us hereafter.

A solitary letter of 1665 containing some personal details has been lately discovered.[27] An allusion to the fleet then fitting out against England, and the mention of a journey of Spinoza's to Amsterdam, of which we have other indications, fix the date towards the end of May, or in the first days of June. The person addressed is supposed to be the 'J. B.,' to whom a letter

---

[27] Ep 42a. Van Vloten, Suppl. p. 303.

of the following year (Ep. 42) was written, and who is identified with the Dr. J. Bresser mentioned elsewhere in Spinoza's correspondence. Spinoza complains of having missed him both when he went to Amsterdam and when he came back to Voorburg. He then begs his friend to be diligent in philosophy while he is young and has time, and not to be afraid of writing to him freely.

'I have before now suspected, and I am pretty sure, that you have some unreasonable distrust of your own parts, and fear to ask or propound something unworthy of a scholar. It is not fit for me to praise your talents to your face; but if you fear my showing your letters to others who may ridicule you, I give you my promise on this point that I will scrupulously keep them, and will communicate them to no mortal, unless with your leave. On these terms you may begin your correspondence with me, unless indeed you doubt my good faith, which I do not suppose possible. I trust to hear your opinion of the matter by your first letter, and to have with it some of the conserve of red roses, as you promised, though I am now much better. After I left this [for Amsterdam] I once let myself blood, yet the fever did not cease (though I was somewhat brisker even before the blood-letting, I think by the change of air), but I was twice or thrice troubled with a tertian; but by dint of good diet at last I drove it out and sent it packing; where it has gone I know not, but I am taking care that it shall not come back.'

He then promises to send 'the third part of my philosophy,' or a considerable part of it, as far as the 80th proposition or thereabouts. As the third part of the 'Ethics,' as it now stands, contains nothing like that number, the third and fourth parts must in the first draft have formed but one. He ends by asking for news of the fleet.

This is the only letter preserved to us in which Spinoza says anything about himself as distinct from his works, and it is preserved only by chance: the editors of the 'Opera Posthuma,' adhering rigidly to the principle of selecting only what illustrated the philosophy, had put it aside as 'of no value.'[28] Ten years later we hear of Dr. Bresser as returned to Amsterdam from a journey to Cleves, and having brought a cask of beer as a present for Spinoza.[29]

Another constant friend of Spinoza's was Henry Oldenburg, well known in the scientific history of England as the first

---

[28] Adscripserunt enim: 'is van geender waarde.' (Van Vloten, *l. c.*)
[29] Ep. 65a, Supp. p. 316.

secretary of the Royal Society and the intimate friend of Robert
Boyle. He had settled in this country, where he spent the best
part of his life, in 1653; and in the course of a journey on the
Continent he visited Spinoza at Rijnsburg and formed an acquaintance with him, which, though opportunities of meeting
were few, was assiduously kept up by correspondence. Oldenburg had, within discreet limits, a lively interest in philosophy,
and in the earlier years of his intercourse with Spinoza was always pressing him not to keep back his knowledge from the
world. In the same letter in which he informs Spinoza of the in-
corporation of the Royal Society, Oldenburg thus exhorts him to
boldness: —

'I would by all means advise you not to begrudge to men of
letters the ripe fruits of your learning in philosophy and theology, but
let them go forth into the world, whatever grumblings may proceed
from petty theologians. Your commonwealth is most free, and therein
the philosopher should work most freely. Your own prudence will
counsel you to publish your thoughts and opinions with as little ostentation as may be; I would have you, for the rest, commit the issue to
fortune. Come, then, my friend, cast out all fear of stirring up against
you the pigmies of our time; too long have we made sacrifices to their
ignorance and trifling scruples; let us spread our sails to the wind of
true knowledge, and search out the secrets of nature more thoroughly
than has yet been done. In your country it will be safe, I should think,
to print your reflections; nor is any offence from them to be feared
among men of learning. If such are your patrons and promoters — and
such, I answer for it, you will find — why should you fear the detrac-
tion of the ignorant?'[30]

Writing some little time afterwards, in the spring of
1663, Oldenburg presses Spinoza yet more urgently to complete
his work then in hand.

'Permit me to ask you,' he says, 'whether you have finished
that important essay in which you treat of the origin of things and their
dependence from their first cause, as well as of the amendment of our
understanding? Surely, my excellent friend, I believe that nothing can
be published more pleasant or acceptable to men of learning and discernment than such a treatise as yours. This is what a man of your wit
and temper should regard, more than what pleases theologians of the
present age and fashion, for by them truth is less regarded than their

---

[30] Ep. 7.

own advantage. I adjure you, therefore, by the bond of our friendship, by every duty of multiplying and spreading abroad the truth, not to withhold from us your writings on those subjects. But if there is any reason more grave than I perceive which hinders you from setting forth the work, I heartily beseech you to be at the pains to give me a summary of it by letter; and by this service you shall know that you have earned a friend's gratitude.'[31]

In the following letters these requests and exhortations are repeated in even stronger terms. We collect that Oldenburg had some knowledge, though it was by no means exact, of the 'Tractatus Theologico-Politicus,' of the treatise 'De Intellectus Emendatione,' which was never finished, and has come down to us as a fragment, and perhaps of an early draft of the 'Ethics.' Oldenburg's language seems to mix up the different works, and his later conduct still more plainly shows that he did not at this time know much of their contents.

He was abundantly valiant in counsel before he had measured the risk; but after the publication of the 'Tractatus Theologico-Politicus' we find that his valour has all evaporated. In 1675, when Spinoza thought of publishing the 'Ethics,' Oldenburg's talk was no longer of spreading all sail and defying the malice of theologians. Now he is all for caution and conformity; he again invokes friendship, but this time to warn Spinoza against giving any sort of ground for attacks upon religion and virtue. Not that he refuses to take some copies of the book; they may be consigned to a Dutch friend in London for him, and he can doubtless find purchasers for them; but he would rather not have it talked about. And when he learnt from Spinoza that the publication was indefinitely put off, his expression of regret was, to say the least, but lukewarm.[32]

In the earlier days of which we are now speaking Oldenburg was not unaided in his encouragement to Spinoza's philosophical work. Boyle's name is joined once and again in his messages of greeting and exhortation, and considerable parts of these letters are taken up with communications on questions of chemistry and pneumatics, conveyed through Oldenburg, which amount in effect to a scientific correspondence between Spinoza

---

[31] Ep. 8.
[32] Epp. 18-20.

and Boyle. They obviously knew and esteemed one another's work; but there is no trace of any more direct intercourse.

The miseries of the great plague and of the war between England and Holland are brought before us by a letter of Oldenburg's in the autumn of 1665. He has no news yet of a book about which Spinoza had asked him, 'because the plague forbids almost all traffic; besides which, this cruel war brings in its train a very Iliad of mischiefs, and is like to leave but little civility in the world.' The public meetings of the Royal Society, he adds, are suspended by the danger of the times; but the individual fellows are not unmindful of their quality, and pursue their experiments in private. Indeed meetings were shortly afterwards held at Oxford, whither several of the members had followed the Court.[33] But the war did not, for some time at least, interrupt the correspondence, nor abate Oldenburg's curiosity for information.

In December 1665 he writes of a wide-spread report that the dispersed nation of Israel was about to return to its own country. The news not having been confirmed from Constantinople, Oldenburg refuses credit to it, but would like to know how it has been received in the Jewish society of Amsterdam. The allusion is to the stir produced throughout the Jewish world by the impostor Sabbatai Zevi, of Smyrna, who proclaimed himself as the Messiah or something more, and obtained a large following not only in the Levant but in all the synagogues of Europe. In London the believers in his mission were testifying to their faith by laying heavy odds that Sabbatai Zevi would be the crowned and anointed king of Jerusalem within two years.[34] But within an even shorter time, so far from being crowned at Jerusalem, he was a prisoner at Constantinople, and completed the discomfiture of those who had committed themselves to him by turning Mahometan: a step which, decisive as it seemed against his pretensions, was ineffectual to sober a certain number of enthusiasts. The delusion survived in various forms for at least two or three years longer.[35] One would give something to know what

---

[33] Epp. 13a, 14.

[34] Grätz, x. 226, 229.

[35] 'And yet most of them affirm that Sabatai is not turn'd Turk, but his Shadow only remains on Earth, and walks with a white Head, and in the habit of a Mahometan: But that his natural Body and Soul are taken into Heaven, there to reside until the time appointed for the accomplishment of

were Spinoza's reflections on seeing the orthodox elders who had excommunicated him (for Isaac Aboab was carried away with the rest) fall an easy prey to a new heresy of the most gross and vulgar kind. But his answer to Oldenburg's inquiry is unluckily not preserved: we know not, indeed, if any answer were sent, for at this point there ensues a break of ten years in the correspondence of the two friends.

In 1663 Spinoza published the only work to which he ever set his name; the origin of it is described by himself in one of his letters to Oldenburg. He had prepared a summary of the second part of Descartes' ' Principles of Philosophy' for the use of a pupil whom he did not choose to make fully acquainted with his own opinions, probably the young man of whom we have already heard. Certain of Spinoza's friends became curious about this manual, and desired him to treat the first part of Descartes' work also in the same manner. This was done within a fortnight, and Spinoza was then urged to publish the book, which he readily agreed to do upon condition that one of his friends would revise the language, and write a preface explaining that the author did not agree with all the Cartesian doctrine set forth by him in the text.

This task was undertaken by Dr. Meyer, and the book appeared at Amsterdam in the same year; in the following one a Dutch translation was issued by the same publisher. The contents were the exposition of two parts of Descartes' Principles, a fragment of a third part, and an appendix of 'Metaphysical Reflections,' professedly written from a Cartesian point of view, but often giving significant hints of the author's real divergence from Descartes. Spinoza took little trouble in the matter himself, and attached no value to the publication except as a means of preparing the way for more important things. 'On this opportunity,' he writes to Oldenburg, 'we may find some persons, holding the highest places in my country' — meaning the De Witts, who certainly were among Spinoza's visitors at Rijnsburg and the Hague — 'who will be anxious to see those other writings which I acknowledge for my own, and will therefore take such order that I can give them to the world without danger of any

these Wonders.' — 'The Counterfeit Messiah of the Jews at Smyrna, 1666' (in *Two Journeys to Jerusalem, &c.,* collected by R. Burton, London, 1738).

inconvenience. If it so happens, I doubt not that I shall soon publish something; if not, I will rather hold my peace than thrust my opinions upon men against the will of my country and make enemies of them.' The design of Spinoza and his friends was but partly effected. The book on Descartes excited considerable attention and interest, but the untoward course of public events in succeeding years was unfavourable to a liberal policy, and deprived Spinoza of the support for which he had looked.

We may here make a note in passing of two facts which are established by this exposition of Descartes, and which have been often overlooked. One is that if Spinoza had ever been a disciple of Descartes, he had completely ceased to be so by the time when he was giving lessons in philosophy to Albert Burgh. The other is that he did not suppose the geometrical form of statement and argument to be an infallible method of arriving at philosophical truth; for in this work he made use of it to set forth opinions with which he himself did not agree, and proofs with which he was not satisfied. We do not know to what extent Spinoza's manual was accepted or taken into use by Cartesians, but its accuracy as an exposition of Descartes is beyond question. One of the many perverse criticisms made on Spinoza by modern writers is that he did not understand the fundamental proposition *cogito ergo sum.*[36] In fact he gives precisely the same explanation of it that is given by Descartes himself in the Meditations.

The next notable event in Spinoza's life is the publication of the 'Tractatus Theologico-Politicus:' the full title, as Englished by an early translator (1689), runs thus: —

'A treatise partly theological and partly political, containing some few discourses to prove that the liberty of philosophizing (that is, making use of natural reason) may be allowed without any prejudice to piety, or to the peace of any commonwealth; and that the loss of public peace and religion itself must necessarily follow, where such a liberty of reasoning is taken away.'

The scope of the book is political and practical, not speculative. The final thesis to which all its apparatus of criticism leads up is that 'in a free commonwealth it should be lawful

---

[36] Foucher de Careil, *Leibniz, Descartes, el Spinoza,* Paris, 1862, p. 75: 'il n'a jamais compris le *cogito ergo sum.*'

for every man to think what he will and speak what he thinks:' a proposition which, with due reservations in behalf of decency and civil order — and the reservations were in no wise neglected by Spinoza — has now become common learning for the greater part of the civilized world. It looks to our modern eyes infinitely less bold than the arguments by which Spinoza maintained it. In order to gain his desired foundation for the freedom of speculative opinion, he plunges into an investigation of the nature of prophecy, the principles of Scriptural interpretation, and the true provinces of theology and philosophy, anticipating with wonderful grasp and insight almost every principle, and not a few of the results, of the school of historical criticism which has arisen within the last two or three generations; a school which, through Lessing and his circle, is connected by direct descent with Spinoza. Taking the whole contents of the treatise together, we cannot be surprised that even in the United Provinces, then the freest country in the world, it was thought needful to issue it without the name of the author and with that of a fictitious printer at Hamburg. The tone and form are conciliatory, but with the kind of high-handed conciliation that exasperates. Much hard hitting will be taken without complaint in downright argument; but few men can endure to be confuted from their own premises by an adversary who never fully shows his hand. It is more tolerable for a dogmatist to be confronted with novelties in speculative opinion than to be told that speculative opinions are in themselves indifferent; and the truth that conduct does not depend on speculation, though exemplified abundantly by all generations of men, is still unfamiliar and unwelcome to most of us. It is just to this unwelcome truth that Spinoza bears a testimony of unsurpassed power in the 'Tractatus Theologico-Politicus;' but if anything more were needed to explain the storm of polemic that burst upon him, there is yet more to come. We have said that Spinoza does not omit the necessary reservations in favour of the civil power; we must add that he makes them not only freely but amply, so amply that he has been charged by some of his modern censors with going about to deify mere brute force. He appeals, moreover, from the Churches to the State, as representing the worldly common sense of the lay mind. He looks to an enlightened civil magistrate to deliver men from the barren clamour of anathemas, almost as an Indian heretic vexed by the Brahmans may look to the impartial secular arm of the British Government. 'This is the conclusion of the whole matter for him; a fervent appeal to the State to save us from the untoward generation of metaphysical Article-makers;' so Mr. Arnold sums it up in his admirable essay.[37] If the English translator had been minded to give the book a second title, after the manner of English controversialists of that day, he might fairly have called it 'Erastianism not Unscriptural.' Now it is a great error to suppose that the metaphysical Article-makers are stupid or undiscerning people. Whatever qualities may be desirable in those who are to believe articles after they are made, a great deal of energy and acuteness have gone to the making of them; and the faculties thus employed are, as a rule, very sufficient to perceive the drift of any new ideas that may imperil their finished handiwork. In 1670 the generation of Article-makers was mighty in the Netherlands, and still pretty fresh from its great exercise at the Synod of Dort. It was fully on the alert, and lost no time in showing itself equal to the occasion. And the occasion was no common one, for the attack was not only powerful, but vital. If there is anything that ecclesiastical dogmatists of all parties are united in hating with a perfect hatred, it is the Erastian view of the relation of the State to religious differences.

Spinoza probably never disguised from himself the opposition he would have to encounter. In 1671 he wrote thus to his friend Jarig Jellis: —

'When Professor N. N. [Wittichius?][38] lately saw me, he told me, among other things, how he had heard of my Theologico-political treatise being translated into Dutch, and that a person whose name he did not know was on the point of printing the translation. I therefore earnestly entreat you to inquire diligently into the matter, and stop the printing if it can be done. This request is not from me alone, but also from many of my friends and acquaintance who would be sorry to see the book prohibited, as it certainly will be if it appears in Dutch.'

It seems that Spinoza's wishes were attended to, for no Dutch version appeared until 1693,[39] some years after an English one had been published in London. But the Synods were already

---

[37] 'Spinoza and the Bible,' in *Essays in Criticism.*

[38] Van Vloten, *Bened. de Spinoza,* p. 81, note.

[39] *Bibliografie,* No. 17.

up in arms, and in the spring of 1671 addressed a solemn complaint to the States-General concerning the printing and publishing of divers 'Socinian and blasphemous books, to wit, the books called "Bibliotheca Patrum Polonorum quos unitarios vocant," the famous book of Hobbes called "Leviathan," and moreover the book entitled "Philosophia Sacrae Scripturae interpres,"[40] as well as that called "Tractatus Theologico-Politicus."' In 1674 effect was given to this by a formal prohibition of the book, which, either in anticipation of such a measure, or in order to obtain a sale in Catholic countries, had already been issued in a second edition with various false title-pages, as of works on medicine or history.[41] Rome was not far behind the Reformed churches in diligence. The 'Tractatus Theologico-Politicus' was ere long put on the Index, and it still holds its place in the strangely mixed company of that catalogue with many of the best and some of the worst books of the world. But the celebrity which came to Spinoza by reason of this publication was not altogether of a disagreeable kind even in official quarters. When his treatise had been some three years before the world he received an invitation to the Chair of Philosophy at Heidelberg, written by Professor Fabritius at the command of the Elector Palatine Charles Lewis, and couched in the most honourable terms. The only hint of a restriction was in the following sentence: 'You will have the largest freedom of speech in philosophy, which the prince is confident that you will not misuse to disturb the established religion.' Now it is hardly possible to suppose that the Elector and his advisers were unacquainted with the 'Tractatus Theologico-Politicus;' and if they were acquainted with its general purport, one is tempted to suspect that a phrase of such very mild caution may have been inserted only as a matter of form; especially when we remember that established religion, as such, is treated by Spinoza with great respect in the treatise itself. The test seems almost framed to invite evasion.

But even the semblance of evasion was repugnant to Spinoza's ideal of intellectual truthfulness. He answered the invitation thus: —

---

[40] This was for a time erroneously attributed to Spinoza.

[41] *Bibliografie,* Nos. 4-7. See Appendix B for the text of the ordinance.

'Had it ever been my desire to occupy a chair in any faculty, I could have wished for no other than that which the Most Serene Elector Palatine offers me by your hands; and especially on account of that freedom in philosophy which the prince is pleased to grant, to say nothing of the desire I have long entertained to live under the rule of a prince whose wisdom is the admiration of all men. But since I have never been minded to give public lectures, I cannot persuade myself to accept even this splendid opportunity, though I have given long consideration to it. For I reflect, in the first place, that I must give up philosophical research if I am to find time for teaching a class. I reflect, moreover, that I cannot tell within what bounds I ought to confine that philosophical freedom you mention in order to escape any charge of attempting to disturb the established religion. Religious dissensions arise not so much from the ardour of men's zeal for religion itself as from their various dispositions and love of contradiction, which leads them into a habit of decrying and condemning everything, however justly it be said. Of this I have already had experience in my private and solitary life; much more, then, should I have to fear it after mounting to this honourable condition. You see, therefore, that I am not holding back in the hope of some better post, but for mere love of quietness, which I think I can in some measure secure if I abstain from lecturing in public. Wherefore I heartily beseech you to desire the Most Serene Elector that I may be allowed to consider further of this matter.'[42]

The call to Heidelberg was in 1673. We have anticipated the order of events to keep the philosophic side of Spinoza's life distinct from the one point at which it was visibly touched by the turmoil of public affairs. The misfortunes of the Netherlands in 1672 are the property of general history. Then took place the sudden and overwhelming invasion in which 'the king of France came down to Utrecht like a land flood;'[43] and this war of insolent aggression, so far from uniting all parties in resistance to the enemy, bred in the Commonwealth a passion of panic that let loose the worst excesses of domestic faction. The brothers De Witt, after lives spent in the service of their country, were massacred by a frantic mob at the Hague. Spinoza had been the friend of John de Witt; he had accepted a small pension from him, and is said to have been consulted by him in affairs of State. It was not common with Spinoza to be visibly disturbed or angry, but by this event he was moved as by no other in his life. So

---

[42] Ep. 54.
[43] Burnet, i. 321.

much was his wonted self-control shaken that he was hardly re-strained from expressing his indignation in public at the risk of his life.[44] He was shortly afterwards, as it fell out, to be exposed to a similar risk, and for a not dissimilar cause. While the head-quarters of the French army were at Utrecht the Prince of Condé, then in command of it, invited Spinoza to visit him. There is no reason to suppose any other motive than a genuine desire to make the philosopher's acquaintance, still less to imagine (as one or two writers have done) a secret political errand. Spinoza pro-ceeded to Utrecht with a safe-conduct, but found that Condé had been in the meantime called away. He waited some days, but Condé's absence was prolonged, and he finally returned to the Hague without having seen him. The French officers who enter-tained Spinoza suggested that if he would dedicate some work to Louis XIV. he might probably count upon a pension; but the proposal fell upon deaf ears. A man who could scarcely be pre-vailed on to accept favours from his friends at home was not likely to sell the reputation of patronizing him to the ruler of a hostile country. But at the Hague, men's minds being still in a ferment, sinister rumours about Spinoza's journey had got abroad; and he found himself on his return the object of the most alarming and most insidious charge that can fall upon a citizen in time of war. The landlord feared an assault, if not the sack of the house, from the populace among whom these reports were pass-ing, and who might at any moment resolve to lay violent hands upon Spinoza as a French spy.

Spinoza, however, comforted his host with these words:
—

'Fear nothing on my account; I can easily justify myself; there are people enough, and of chief men in the country too, who well know the motives of my journey. But, whatever comes of it, so soon as the crowd make the least noise at your door, I will go out and make straight for them, though they should serve

---

[44] This was communicated by Spinoza himself to Leibnitz. 'J'ay passé quelques heures après dîner avec Spinoza; il me dit qu'il avait esté porté, le jour des massacres de MM. de Witt, de sortir la nuit et d'afficher quelque part, proche du lieu, un papier où il y aurait *ultimi barbarorum.* Mais son hôte luy avait fermé la maison pour l'empêcher de sortir, car il se serait exposé à être déchiré.' MS. note of Leibnitz, ap. Foucher de Careil, *Leibniz, Descartes, et Spinoza,* p. 74.

me as they have done the unhappy De Witts. I am a good republican, and have never had any aim but the honour and welfare of the State.'

The danger passed off; but Spinoza's conduct under it is none the less worthy of admiration, for it was unquestionably a very serious one. Even in our own times, notably in France during the war of 1870, many innocent persons have been in imminent peril, or have actually lost their lives, on far slighter circumstances of supposed evidence than appeared in this case. The incident also has its value in the light it throws on the general esteem in which Spinoza then stood. For the consciousness, not merely of an innocent purpose, but of a character above the possibility of rational suspicion, was necessary to make his visit to the French headquarters prudent or justifiable; and the authorities of his own country would assuredly never have consented to it had they not felt absolute confidence that the public good would in no way suffer by it. It is indeed almost surprising that Spinoza, a known friend of John de Witt, was in the existing state of affairs allowed to go to the French camp at all.

Meanwhile Spinoza had been working at the Ethics, and before the end of 1674 manuscript copies of the finished work were in the hands of some of his friends.[45] About the end of July 1675 he made an excursion to Amsterdam in order to arrange for the publication of the book. What befell him there is best told in the words of his own letter to Oldenburg.

'While I was busy with this, the report was spread everywhere that a certain book of mine was in the press, wherein I endeavoured to show that there was no God; and this report found credence with many. Whereupon certain theologians (themselves perhaps the authors of it) took occasion to complain of me to the prince and the magistrates; moreover the stupid Cartesians, being supposed to side with me and desiring to free themselves from that suspicion, were diligent without ceasing in their execration of my doctrines and writings, and are as diligent still. Having knowledge of these matters from trustworthy persons, who likewise told me that the theologians were laying plots against me on all sides, I determined to put off the publication until I could see the issue of the affair, and then to signify my designs to you. But the business inclines, as it seems, to the worse from day to day, and I know not yet what I shall do.'

---

[45] Epp. 63, 66.

The result was that nothing more was done in Spinoza's lifetime. He had shown that he could endure much in silence rather than barter a jot of his freedom, but he did not choose to be vexed with the petty warfare of clerical controversy; he must have felt the assurance that his work would live, and that a few years sooner or later in the date of its appearance would be indifferent. Can he have surmised that the few years by which the publication was postponed would be a mere fraction in comparison with the time during which his thoughts were in the world but not perceived by it, misunderstood by those who took notice of them, and unheeded by those who might have understood? Can he have even dreamt of the splendour with which his work was to shine forth to a newer world after the period of eclipse, giving up its hidden treasures of light and vital fire to inform the philosophy and poetry of a mighty nation? Such fame as Spinoza's is the reward only of those who are above fame in their lives.

Spinoza had now but little more of life before him. For many years he had suffered from consumption, aggravated perhaps by his work of glass-polishing. On Sunday, February 21, 1677, the end came unexpectedly, and almost suddenly. Spinoza had indeed sent to Amsterdam for his friend and physician Lewis Meyer; but on the Saturday he had spent the afternoon in talk with his hosts as usual; and on the Sunday he came down again in the morning, and spoke with them before they went to hear Dr. Cordes, Colerus's predecessor in the Lutheran church at the Hague. They were so far from any immediate apprehensions that they went out again in the afternoon, leaving him alone with Meyer. When they came home they found, to their surprise, that Spinoza was no longer alive. Dr. Meyer, the only person who was with him at the last, returned forthwith to Amsterdam. He is charged by Colerus with neglect of duty and rapacity; or rather, in plain terms, with making booty of a silver-handled knife and the loose money in the room. But this is so grossly improbable that we can only disregard it. Colerus may have not been sorry to compensate himself for the admiration his native honesty compelled him to yield to Spinoza's character by giving currency to a piece of malignant gossip about a friend of Spinoza's, known or suspected to share Spinoza's opinions, and who, as a person only coming incidentally into the story, had no particular claim to be treated with justice. But credit must be given to Colerus, on the other hand, for his downright contradiction of the tales concerning Spinoza's death-bed which were circulated, it would seem, by persons who thought it would tend to edification to represent Spinoza as the blustering infidel of popular orthodox polemics, who is invariably assailed by doubt and disquietude in his last moments, and as invariably strives to disguise them with feeble bravado.[46] Colerus very honestly says that the people of the house, whom he more than once questioned, knew nothing of any such matters, and did not believe a word of them.

Spinoza left behind him but a scanty estate: some thirty or forty volumes, a few engravings, the tools of his trade, and a certain number of finished lenses; which last, we are told, fetched a good price; besides these a modest list of personal effects, carefully enumerated by Colerus, and in all so little more than would cover debts and expenses that the surviving sister Rebekah, who at first was disposed to assert her rights, concluded that the inheritance was not worth having. Yet Spinoza had one precious legacy to dispose of — the desk containing his letters and unpublished work. Van der Spijck had been charged to convey this after Spinoza's death to Jan Rieuwertz, a publisher at Amsterdam. The trust was faithfully executed, and the 'Opera Posthuma' appeared in the course of the same year, but without the author's full name. The editors' preface explains that this was by his own request.

'The writer's name,' they say, 'is expressed on the title-page and elsewhere only by his initials; which is done for no other reason than that, shortly before his death, he specially desired that his name should not be prefixed to his Ethics, while he directed the printing of them. The only reason for this prohibition was, as we think, that he chose not that his doctrine should be called after his name. For he says in the Appendix to the fourth part of the Ethics, cap. 25, that they who desire to aid others by counsel or deed to the common enjoyment of the chief good shall in no wise endeavour themselves that a doctrine be called after their name. Moreover in the third part of the Ethics, in the 11th definition of the Passions, where he explains the nature of ambition, he plainly charges with vain-glory those who do after this sort.'

---

[46] One of these stories is circumstantially repeated by Bayle, *Pensées Diverses,* § 181, 'Vanité de Spinoza à l'heure de mort.'

In the following year the States of Holland and West Friesland, being satisfied that the book entitled 'B. D. S. Opera Posthuma' 'labefactated' various essential articles of the faith and 'vilipended the authority of miracles,' expressed 'the highest indignation' at the disseminating thereof, declared it profane, atheistic, and blasphemous, and forbad printing, selling, and dealing in it, on pain of their high displeasure.[47]

The framers of this well-meant enactment earned a permanent remembrance for their work, but not quite as they desired. Instead of their ordinance extinguishing Spinoza's 'Ethics,' the 'Ethics' have preserved the memory of the ordinance.

It remains to say something of Spinoza's manner of daily life and outward habit; which however, as we know them almost entirely through Colerus's account, so they are presented by Colerus with a kind of simple quaintness more impressive than any studied description can be. The effect of those particulars which we possess is to show us a man who was led to a retired life by choice and circumstance, not by ostentation; to an almost incredible frugality by reasons of health and economy, not by ascetic pride; who could be freespoken and of good will towards all sorts of men, but would be dependent on none. His living and diet were of the simplest, his expenses amounting sometimes only to a few pence for the whole day. But he kept down his expenses in this manner chiefly, if not wholly, in order to keep them within his means; just making both ends meet, as he would say of himself, like a snake with its tail in its mouth. And his means remained slender to the last because he did not choose to live on patronage, and the studies to which he devoted the best of his mind had even less bread-winning virtue then than they have now. It is reported that Spinoza, on hearing that a man who owed him 200 florins had become bankrupt, said with a smile, 'I must retrench my allowance to make up for this little matter; at this price one buys equanimity.'[48] But the story seems

---

[47] June 25, 1678. *Groot Placael Boek,* 3de deel, p. 525: *Bibliografie,* No. 24.

[48] This anecdote is only in Lucas, and as given by him has a slightly theatrical air. He adds a sort of apologetic explanation: 'Je ne rapporte pas cette action comme quelque chose d'éclatant, mais comme il n'y a rien en quoi le génie paraisse davantage qu'en ces sortes de petites choses, je n'ai pu l'omettre sans scrupule.' I cannot but suspect that the turn of the saying at least is borrowed from Epictetus *(Man.* c. 12, 2), ἐπίλεγε ὅτι τοσούτου πωλεῖται ἀπάθεια, τοσούτου ἀταραξία.

doubtful.

Again, Spinoza lived in a retirement which at times might be called solitude; when absorbed in work he would hardly leave his chamber for many days together; once he did not leave the house for three months.[49] But if on these occasions he chose to be alone, it was not that he loved solitude for its own sake. He had none of the shallow pride and arrogance which fancies that the way to show superior knowledge is to disdain the common intercourse of mankind. There was no touch of misanthropy in the retirement from the world which he imposed upon himself. Besides keeping up a not inconsiderable correspondence, Spinoza visited and was visited by not a few men of letters and learning; there was a time, as we gather from his own statements, when their civilities left him few hours to call his own.

Nor did he limit his converse to scholars: he knew how to win the esteem and affection of the simple folk of the household where he dwelt, an esteem which, as M. Renan has well said, is in truth the most precious of all. He talked freely and familiarly with his hosts the Van der Spijcks, and would counsel their children to good behaviour and obedience. He discussed with them the sermons of Dr. Cordes, the Lutheran pastor who preceded Spinoza's biographer Colerus in the charge of the Lutheran congregation at the Hague, and recommended them to give all attention to the discourses of so excellent a teacher. Bold as he was in speculative thought, and detached in his own person from all sects and doctrines, Spinoza was no furious iconoclast in private life. He did not seek to make nominal proselytes who would have been neither the wiser nor the happier for their conversion, and when the good woman of the house attacked him with a point-blank question as to the sufficiency of her religion for salvation, he answered that her religion was good if it led her to a good life, and she had no need to seek further.

But the strength of Spinoza's social feelings, and the importance he attached to fellowship among men as the only means by which man can live a life worthy of his nature, are most evidently shown in his 'Ethics;' and the ideal of human life which he there sets forth, and to which he himself was faithful in action, will come under our notice when we endeavour to obtain a view of his philosophy.

---

[49] Pref. to *Opera Posthuma*.

CHAPTER II

SPINOZA'S CORRESPONDENCE.

Treu dem Gesetz und treu
Dir selbst — so bleibst du frei. — PROVERB.

He that feeds men serveth few;
He serves all who dares be true. — EMERSON.

WE have already made use of some of Spinoza's letters in order to supplement the rather meagre outlines of his biography which we possess from other sources. Hereafter we shall have to refer to others as containing important passages of authentic commentary on his philosophy. But we have a certain number of an intermediate character, which, while their interest is literary and speculative rather than personal, yet lie outside the main lines of Spinoza's systematic thought. They contain much that is curious in itself, and much that is useful as an introduction to Spinoza's general manner of thinking and discussion; and we may find it worth while to dwell a little upon them before we finally quit the ground of biography and enter upon that of criticism. It is pleasant to linger in a borderland where speculation is still relieved by personal incidents. Of Spinoza's correspondence with Oldenburg and De Vries we have already seen something: what remains in those quarters is of strictly philosophical interest. Another friend of Spinoza who must have been in constant intercourse with him was Dr. Lewis Meyer, who undertook the publication of the 'Principles of Cartesian Philosophy,' and was afterwards joint editor of the 'Opera Posthuma.' What has become of the letters which passed between these two? At present, unfortunately, the answer is that we have one, and only one, preserved in the 'Opera Posthuma,' this being an answer to a letter of Meyer's, probably written on behalf of the philosophical club at Amsterdam, and asking Spinoza for the result of his speculations on the Infinite. Here, again, we must leave the contents for the present untouched, only remarking the comparatively early date (1663) of the letter. It belongs to the Rijnsburg time, and shows, together with the letters to De Vries, that the groundwork at least of Spinoza's system as we now have it was by that time fully formed.

Oldenburg, Meyer, and De Vries naturally wrote, as scholars, in Latin (De Vries not without a touch of Batavism), and Spinoza replied to them in the same language, writing carefully, and even indulging in purisms: he will not put the scholastic form 'essendi' before Meyer without an apology.[50] But there were other less learned correspondents who preferred the vernacular.

The originals of their letters are apparently preserved in the Dutch version of the 'Opera Posthuma,' which was published almost simultaneously with the Latin text. But with Spinoza's own replies to them it is not so. Two of Spinoza's Dutch letters are preserved as he wrote them, and the editors of the 'Nagelate Schriften' found it necessary to make considerable amendments in their composition. In one of them Spinoza expressly apologizes for not being perfect in the language. There is some reason to think the Latin versions of the letters originally sent in Dutch were prepared for publication by Spinoza himself.[51]

The lion's share of the miscellaneous correspondence, in point of bulk at least, belongs to William van Blyenbergh, a worthy merchant and municipal officer of Dort, and a citizen of good family, who was mightily taken, by his own account, with Spinoza's 'Principles of Cartesian Philosophy.' In December 1664 he wrote to Spinoza in these terms: —

'Dear Sir and unknown Friend, — I have already had the pleasure of several times carefully reading over your treatise lately published, together with its Appendix. It will be more proper for me to speak to others than to yourself of the exceeding solidity I found in it and of the pleasure I derived from it. This much I cannot forbear saying, that the oftener I go over it with attention, the more I am pleased with it; and that I constantly find something which I had not marked before.'

He proceeds to enlarge (in a style much improved by the Latin translation) on his sincere love of philosophic truth as the

---

[50] 'Infinitam essendi sive (invita Latinitate) essendi fruitionem.' — Ep. 29.

[51] See Prof. Land's paper, *Over de eerste uitgaven der brieven van Spinoza,* Amsterdam, 1879; and Appendix C below.

only thing deserving of affection in this transitory life, on his admiration for the knowledge and philosophic felicity shown in Spinoza's work, and his desire to make the personal acquaintance of a man so favoured, and on his disappointment in having been prevented, by various causes, from introducing himself to Spinoza face to face instead of by letter. He had meant only to ask, in a preliminary way, whether he might trouble Spinoza with some of his difficulties; but, 'not to leave the letter quite empty,' he states one of them forthwith, which concerns the question of creation, especially as bearing on the origin of evil. If, according to what is said in various places by Spinoza, both in his exposition of Descartes and in his own commentary, God is the immediate cause, not only of the existence of the human soul but of its particular operations, is not God the immediate cause of evil volitions, for example, the determination of Adam to eat the forbidden fruit? Blyenbergh professes himself puzzled, but confidently awaits a satisfactory answer, and adds a sentence ominous of future garrulity: 'Be assured, dear sir, that I ask this for no other cause than desire for the truth, and have no particular interests; I am unattached, dependent on no profession; I live by honest merchandise, and spend my leisure on these subjects. I humbly pray you not to find my difficulties troublesome.'

Spinoza seems to have thought from this first letter that Blyenbergh was a man of some real capacity, and that he had gained a valuable acquaintance. At any rate, he received his unknown correspondent with a warm welcome.

'Unknown Friend, — From your letter I understand your exceeding love of truth, and how that only is the aim of all your desires; and since I direct my mind upon naught else, this constrains me to determine, not only fully to grant your request, which is to answer to the best of my skill the questions which you now send or shall send hereafter, but to perform all else on my part which may avail for our better acquaintance and sincere friendship. For myself, there is among things out of my own control none I prize more than entering into the bond of friendship with men who are sincere lovers of truth. For I believe that nothing in the world, not being under our own control, can be so securely taken for the object of our love as men of this temper; since 'tis no more possible to dissolve that love they have for one another (seeing it is founded on the love each of them hath for the knowledge of truth) than not to embrace the truth itself when once perceived. This love is moreover the most perfect and delightful which can exist towards objects not in our control, since no other thing has such virtue as truth to unite men's minds and affections. I say nothing of the exceeding conveniences that spring from it, that I may no longer detain you with matters which you doubtless well know; I have however done so thus far, the better to show how pleasant it is to me now, and will be in future, to find any occasion of doing you service.'

He then takes up the question proposed by Blyenbergh. After observing that Blyenbergh has not defined his notion of *evil,* Spinoza declares that for his part he cannot allow that sin and evil have any positive reality, much less that anything happens contrary to God's will: nay, it is only an inexact and human fashion of speech to say that man can sin against or offend God. For every really existing thing, if we consider it apart from its relation to other things, is perfect as far as its existence goes (this equivalence of *reality* and *perfection* is one of the key-notes of Spinoza's metaphysic). Thus, taking Blyenbergh's example of Adam's determination to eat the forbidden fruit, there is no imperfection in the act as such. Approval or disapproval implies a standard of comparison; we are simply amused by actions in animals which are the object of moral condemnation in men. Sin is a note of imperfection, and therefore something apart from the action itself, in so far as it partakes of or 'expresses reality.'

Again, we cannot say that Adam's will was evil inasmuch as it displeased God. For we cannot assume anything to happen against God's will without assuming imperfection in God, whose will, indeed, being coextensive with his understanding, an event against God's will could only be an event repugnant to the laws of understanding. Adam's determination, then, was not evil considered in itself, nor yet, strictly speaking, contrary to God's will; and there is no difficulty in admitting God to have been the cause of it, so far as it was a real action. Its evil consisted in Adam's losing in consequence of it the state of perfection he enjoyed before. But loss is merely negative, and the conception of it a relative one which has no place in absolute intellect. Our notion of imperfection arises from an individual not conforming to the type of the class which we have obtained by a process of abstraction. But infinite intellect has no need of abstraction or definition, and therefore does not and cannot regard anything as imperfect. Everything is as real and as perfect as the divine power has made it: in other words, as perfect as it can be. We call things good or bad in their kinds; but the divine intellect sees everything as perfect in itself.[52] This Spinoza thinks a sufficient answer on speculative grounds; but he goes on to the practical bearings of the matter. As to the language of the Scriptures, they speak in a popular, not a philosophic manner, ascribing to God anger, jealousy, and even liability to error. 'Thus the precept given to Adam consisted only in this, that God revealed to Adam that eating of that tree caused death; just as God reveals to us through natural understanding that poison is deadly to us. If you ask for what purpose God revealed this to Adam, I answer, in order to make him to that extent more perfect in knowledge.'[53] If you ask, again, why he did not give Adam a more perfect will, it is like asking why God has not endowed the circle with the properties of the sphere.

Then as to the objection that if all men do the will of God, the wicked do it no less than the good: they do it indeed in their fashion, but their lot is nevertheless very different. Knowing not God, they serve him as a blind instrument in the workman's hand, which perishes in the using; the righteous do their service with knowledge, and are made more perfect therein.

The letter discloses only parts of Spinoza's ethical theory, and in language adapted to the assumptions of his questioner; but these parts are characteristic. Even in this form they may still seem daring to many readers, and Blyenbergh was entirely taken aback by them. Yet the leading idea of the letter — namely, that the notions of good and evil are relative, and have place only in finite intellects — had been enunciated centuries before by Maimonides. Observe also Spinoza's complete Nominalism, and the important practical use he makes of it against the anthropomorphic view of the government of the world.

Ten days later Blyenbergh replied in a very long epistle, the contents of which it is needless to state further than that he

---

[52] Cf. *Cogit. Met.* pt. ii. c. 7, § 4: 'Quum ergo mala et peccata in rebus nihil sint, sed tantum in mente humana res inter se comparante, sequitur Deum ipsa extra mentes humanas non cognoscere.' And § 5: '... Deo singularium cognitionem tribuimus, universalium denegamus, nisi quatenus mentes humanas intelligit.'

[53] Cf. *Tract. Theol.-Polit.* c. 4, §§ 26, 27, where it is said that the revelation was a command or precept only in respect of Adam's imperfect knowledge.

repeats and enlarges on his objections. He protests that Spinoza's doctrine destroys all practical difference between right and wrong, and leaves no ground for preferring virtue to vice. As for desiring virtue for its own sake, human nature is far too weak for that. 'See what ground we give to all godless men and their impiety! We make ourselves like stocks, and our actions no better than the works of a watch.' Blyenbergh also explains to Spinoza at the beginning of the letter that he has two rules wherewith to guide himself in philosophy, Reason and Scripture; and that if the apparently clear conclusions of his reason differ from the revealed word, he can only suppose that his reason is wrong.[54]

This disclosure was a surprise to Spinoza, who answered that on such conditions discussion would not be very profitable.

'When I read your first letter, I thought that our opinions pretty well agreed; but from the second I understand it is quite otherwise, and perceive that we differ not only in the consequences that may be drawn from first principles, but also in the principles themselves; insomuch that I can scarce believe that we shall be able to instruct one another further by letters. For I see that no demonstration, however firm it may be according to the laws of demonstration, may prevail with you unless it agree with the interpretation that you, or other theologians familiar to you, put upon Holy Writ. If you find the light of Scripture clearer than the light of reason (which also is given us by divine wisdom), you are doubtless right in your own conscience in making your reason yield. For my part, since I plainly confess that I do not understand the Scriptures, though I have spent many years upon them, and since I know that when once I have a firm proof I cannot by any course of thought come to doubt of it, I rest wholly upon that which my understanding commends to me, without any suspicion that I am deceived therein, or that the Scriptures, even though I do not search them, can speak against it. For one truth cannot conflict with another, as I have already clearly shown in my Appendix to the "Principles of Descartes" (I cannot give the chapter, as here in the country I have not the book by me).[55] But if in any case I did find error in that which I have collected from my natural understanding, I should count it good fortune, since I enjoy life, and endeavour to pass it not in weeping and sighing, but in peace, joy, and cheerfulness, and from time to time climb thereby a step

---

[54] Ep. 33.

[55] *Cogit. Met.* pt. ii. c. 8, § 5. 'Veritas veritati non repugnat, nec scriptura nugas, quales vulgo fingunt, docere potest. Si enim in ipsa inveniremus aliquid, quod lumini naturali esset contrarium, eadem libertate, qua Alcoranum et Thalmud refellimus, illam refellere possemus.'

higher. I know, meanwhile (which is the highest pleasure of all), that all things happen by the power and unchangeable decree of the most perfect Being.'

He then turns to the matter of Blyenbergh's objections, which depend on his way of regarding God in his relations to man as a magnified human judge; whereas in Spinoza's view the reward of serving God is not as it were a prize, but the necessary consequence of the work itself. The love of God, which is man's highest happiness, follows from the knowledge of God as necessarily as it follows from the nature of a triangle that the sum of its angles is two right angles. 'One may easily give a general proof of this, if one will only consider the nature of God's decrees, as I have explained in my Appendix.[56] But I confess that all those who confound the divine nature with that of man are very inapt to comprehend this.' Spinoza further shows how Blyenbergh had misunderstood both himself and Descartes, and then replies with some warmth to the charge that his doctrine is likely to have mischievous consequences. 'When you say that by making men so dependent on God I make them like the natural elements, herbs, or stones, that is full proof that you take my meaning much amiss, and confuse things which are of the understanding with things of the imagination. For if you had clearly conceived in your understanding what dependence on God is, you would never think that things, forasmuch as they depend on God, are dead, corporeal, and imperfect (as who has ever dared speak so meanly of the most perfect being?); you would understand, on the contrary, that thereby, and forasmuch as they depend on God, they are perfect; so that we best understand this dependence, and the necessary operation of things by God's decrees, when we look, not upon stocks and herbs, but upon the most reasonable and perfect creatures... I cannot forbear saying that I am greatly amazed when you say, If God were not to punish evil (to wit, as a judge doth, with a punishment that the evil itself brings not with it, for that is our only difference), what reason is there that I should not run into all manner of wickedness?

---

[56] *Cogit. Met.* pt. ii. c. 9; cf. c. 7, § 7: Dei volitiones et decreta = eius cognitio circa res creatas: 'Dei idea sive decretum.' Cf. too *Tract. Theol.-Pol.* c. 4, §§ 24, 25: 'respectu Dei unum et idem affirmamus, quum dicimus Deum ab aeterno decrevisse et voluisse tres angulos trianguli aequales esse duobus rectis, vel Deum hoc ipsum intellexisse.'

Surely he who abstains from such things only for fear of punishment (which I will not think of you) is in no way moved by
love towards God, and has mighty little affection for virtue. For
my part, I let such things alone, or endeavour so to do, because
they would be clearly at strife with my proper nature, and lead
me astray from the knowledge and the love of God.'

As to the rule of submission to the Scriptures, Spinoza
says that in his opinion it is a more respectful way of treating the
Scriptures to recognize that they speak in human language and in
parables than to put hasty and absurd interpretations upon them
for the purpose of contradicting natural reason. 'Matters of high
speculation have, I think, nothing to do with the Scriptures. For
my part, I have learnt none of God's eternal attributes from
Scripture, nor have been able to learn any.'

One would think this answer not very encouraging, but
Blyenbergh, nothing daunted, returned to the charge with another
letter[57] nearly as long as the former one. He mildly complains of
Spinoza's censures, but makes a kind of apology for persisting in
his objections. He asks many new questions, most of them unanswerable and some irrational, and winds up with this sage post-
script: 'Through haste I have forgot to add this question, whether
we cannot by our foresight prevent that which otherwise would
befall us?' Spinoza replied[58] in courteous terms, but obviously
beginning to lose patience, that his purpose had been not merely
to criticize, but to point out to Blyenbergh the fundamental nature of their difference. 'I had thought,' he says in substance,
'that you wished to discuss these matters in a purely philosophical manner, but you showed me that it was otherwise, and that
the foundation on which I thought to build our friendship was
not laid as I had supposed.' He consents once more, however, to
address himself to Blyenbergh's objections. The leading passage
is so characteristic that it seems profitable to give it nearly in
full.

'In the first place I say that God is perfectly and truly the
cause of everything whatsoever that hath any being. Now if you can
show that evil, error, crimes, and the like are anything which expresses
real being, I shall fully grant to you that God is the cause of these

---

[57] Ep. 35.
[58] Ep. 36.

things. I have sufficiently shown, to my mind, that that which constitutes the nature of evil, error, crimes, and so forth consists not in anything that expresses real being; and therefore we cannot say that God is their cause. For example, Nero's matricide, in so far as it comprehended anything positive, was not a crime. For the outward act, and likewise the intention to slay his mother, were the same in Orestes' case, and yet he is not blamed, at least not in the same degree as Nero. What, then, was Nero's crime? Nothing else but that by such a deed he showed himself ungrateful, unmerciful, and disobedient. 'Tis certain that none of these things express real being, and therefore God was not the cause thereof, though he was of Nero's act and intent. Further, I would here have you note that while we speak in the manner of philosophy we must not use the language of theology. For since theology constantly represents God as a perfect man (and that not without reason) it suits well enough in theology to say that God has desire, that he is angered at the works of the ungodly, or that he takes pleasure in those of the righteous. But in philosophy, where we clearly understand that it is as little fit to ascribe to God the properties that make a man perfect as if one should ascribe to man such as belong to the perfection of the elephant or the ass, there, I say, the forementioned sort of terms have no place, and we cannot so use them without greatly confounding our conception of the matter. Therefore, philosophically speaking, we may not say that God desires anything of any man, or that anything is displeasing or agreeable to him; for all these are human qualities, which in God have no place.'

He goes on to say, in answer to specific questions of Blyenbergh's, that however indifferent acts may be in themselves, considered from the philosophic or universal point of view, this does not affect our moral judgment of the agents. Blyenbergh asks whether homicide is equally acceptable to God with almsgiving? 'Philosophically speaking,' says Spinoza, 'I do not know what you mean by *acceptable to God.* If the question is whether God hates the one and loves the other, and whether the one has given offence to God and the other done him a favour, then I answer No. If the question is whether murderers are equally good and perfect with those who give alms, I again say No.' The similar question, whether stealing be in the sight of God as good as honesty, is similarly disposed of. The acts of the thief and the honest man, so far as they are real actions, are equally perfect. Spinoza's meaning may want illustration for modern readers; suppose, for example, a thief putting forth his hand to steal, and an honest man laying hands on him to stop him. The motion of the hand, considered as a natural event exhibiting the structure and functions of human limbs, is in itself no better or worse in the honest man's anatomy than in the thief's. Or, again, a thief may steal goods with violence, and an officer of justice may afterwards recover them from the thief, by actions in themselves precisely similar. But the honest man and the thief are not therefore alike in perfection or happiness of estate. 'For by an honest man' (Spinoza continues) 'I understand one who desires that every one should have his own; and I show in my Ethics (as yet unpublished) that this desire necessarily arises in righteous men from the clear knowledge they have of themselves and of God.' Evil-doers, not having this desire, must be without the knowledge of God, and so miss the great foundation of human happiness.

There was yet a third question: if there existed a mind so framed that vice and crime were not repugnant to its proper nature but agreed with it, could any rational motive be assigned why such an agent should do good or avoid evil? Spinoza says that this is to assume a contradiction.

'It seems to me no otherwise than if one asked, supposing it agreed better with his nature to hang himself, whether there would be any reason for not hanging himself.' Assuming that a man could really find hanging to agree better with him than eating and drinking, his only rational course would be to hang himself; assuming that such a perverse human being as suggested by Blyenbergh could exist, vice would with respect to such a being become virtue.

'As to the last question, which you have added at the end of your letter, since one could put a hundred such in an hour without coming to a conclusion in any case, and you do not much press for an answer yourself, I shall not answer it.' The question was indeed a formidably vague one. Probably Blyenbergh wanted to extract from Spinoza something capable of being used as an admission of free-will.

Blyenbergh, still unabashed, paid Spinoza a visit in person, and finding that he could not remember to his own satisfaction what Spinoza had said to him, sent yet another epistle, asking a new string of questions, which rambled pretty well over the whole ground of the 'Principia Philosophiæ' and 'Cogitata Metaphysica.' He concluded by asking, as a favour necessary to his complete understanding of Spinoza's answers, that Spinoza would furnish him with the principal heads of the 'Ethics.'

Philosophers are men (though the contrary seems to be not uncommonly believed), and human long-suffering has limits. After some delay Spinoza now replied very shortly,[59] to the effect that he really could not undertake to answer questions of such a scope, but hoped to find an opportunity of explaining by word of mouth that it was impracticable; the chief reason being that, even if he could do it, the fundamental differences between his views and Blyenbergh's would remain where they were before. He hopes that, on further consideration of the matter, Blyenbergh will waive this last request, and remain his good friend. With this Blyenbergh disappears from Spinoza's correspondence, but we hear more of him from Colerus, who speaks with much admiration of a controversial treatise against the 'Tractatus Theologico-Politicus' published by Blyenbergh in 1674. Notwithstanding his former friendly intercourse with Spinoza, the worthy merchant of Dordrecht pronounced the book to be 'full of curious but abominable discoveries, the learning and inquiries whereof must needs have been fetched from hell.' He undertook to prove Spinoza's opinions ruinous to the welfare of souls and of States, 'Ziel- en Landsverderffelyck.' But such were the usual amenities of controversy at the time. In most cases they probably implied no personal ill-will. Eight years later Blyenbergh also published a refutation of the 'Ethics,'[60] with the motto *Ardua quae pulchra,* probably meant as a counterblast to Spinoza's own concluding words, 'omnia praeclara tam difficilia quam rara sunt.'

The curiosity of Spinoza's questioners was not limited to the proper field of philosophy; they made no scruple of consulting him on omens and ghosts. A friend named Peter Balling, of whom we know very little,[61] but for whom, judging from the tone of the answer, Spinoza must have had a sincere regard, announced the death of a child, and at the same time (seeking perhaps distraction in a speculative question) desired Spinoza's opinion of a supposed forewarning that had come to him. In

---

[59] Ep. 38.

[60] *Bibliografie,* 380.

[61] It appears that he was the translator of Spinoza's *Principles of Descartes' Philosophy,* of which a Dutch version came out not long after the Latin.

other circumstances it is possible that Spinoza might have dealt with such a query rather summarily. We cannot suppose for instance that Blyenbergh would have taken much by throwing it in among his other difficulties. But now Spinoza was full of consideration for his friend's distress, and whatever he may have thought of the wisdom of the question in itself, he answered it,[62] gently and patiently, though with his usual decision. After expressing his sympathy and entreating Balling to write to him again at length, he proceeds to the matter of the warning.

'As to the omen you mention, namely, that while your child was still in good health you heard it groan in the same manner that it did when it had fallen into the sickness whereof it soon after died: I should think these were no real groans, but mere imagination, since you say that when you rose up and set yourself to listen for them, you heard them not so clearly as either before, or afterwards when you had fallen asleep again. Surely this proves that these groans were nothing else than imagination, which, being detached and free, could frame to itself a sound of groans in a more forcible and lively manner than in the time when you rose up to listen in a certain direction. I can both confirm and explain what I now say by another chance which befell me last winter at Rijnsburg. One morning as I woke out of a very heavy dream (it being already day), the images which had come before me in my dream remained before my eyes as lively as if they had been the very things, and specially that of a scurvy[63] black Brazilian, whom I had never before seen. This image vanished for the most part, when, in order to divert myself with somewhat else, I cast my eyes on a book or any other thing; but so soon as I removed my eyes from their object, without looking with attention anywhere, the image of this same negro appeared as lively as before, and that again and again, until it vanished even to the head. Now I say that the same thing which happened to me in the inward sense of sight happened in your sense of hearing. But since the causes were very different, there was in your case an omen, and in mine none. [The effects of the imagination are various, according to the exciting cause, which may be either mental or bodily.[64] Where it is bodily, as in the delirium of fever, there can be no question of any relation to future events.] But the effects of imagination, or images, which have their origin from the condition of the mind, may be

---

[62] Ep. 30.

[63] Or, 'leprous.'

[64] Spinoza is here speaking in a popular manner. We shall see hereafter that he does not admit any causal connexion between mental and material phenomena, but only a parallel correspondence excluding such a relation.

omens of something future, because the mind can have a confused presentiment of such a thing. It can therefore frame to itself as firm and lively an image of such a thing as if the thing were present. Thus, to take an example like yours, a father so loves his son that he and his beloved son are as it were one and the same being.'

Spinoza goes on to say, referring for details to some fuller exposition of the subject which cannot be identified with anything in his extant works, that in so far as the father is united by sympathy with the son, he shares not only in his actual existence, but in the consequences determined by his present state and potentially included in it. Under favourable conditions, then, he may have an extremely vivid imagination of something depending on the son's own constitution and likely to happen to him, and which does in fact happen to him shortly afterwards.

Spinoza's language is not altogether clear. It seems to assume a physiological theory of presentiments and other similar occurrences, designed to afford a natural explanation not only of the subjective facts, but of the supposed warnings being verified in a certain proportion of cases. Some such theory may have been struck out by Spinoza in the days when he still believed in animal spirits; as indeed various physical conjectures of a similar kind have been started in our own time with much less excuse. Even very ingenious persons will try the most improbable suppositions rather than resign themselves to the incredulity of healthy common sense.

It is fairly certain that the 'confused presentiment' spoken of in the letter does not mean a revelation or literal foreseeing of a future event as such, but a sort of unconscious judgment of the possibilities involved in existing conditions. But the exact nature of this operation is not defined, still less the nature and extent of the sympathy which enables us to form a presentiment as to persons closely connected with us. The conception of love as an impulse to union with the beloved object, which is here pressed to an almost fantastic consequence, is taken from Descartes, who himself probably had it from some older source. It plays an important part in Spinoza's essay 'On God and Man,' — confided in manuscript to a limited number of friends, of whom perhaps Balling was one — but has disappeared in the Ethics. On the whole the remarks now in question seem to belong to an early stage of Spinoza's psychology. Compared with

other letters of about the same date (1664) they present something like an anachronism. But such anachronisms must exist in
the mind of every man whose thoughts are still maturing; and,
under the special circumstances, Spinoza was probably willing to
strain a point in favour of treating Balling's question seriously.

Ten years later another correspondent, whose name has
been charitably suppressed by the editors of the 'Opera Posthuma,' wrote to Spinoza, without any particular occasion that
appears, to ask what he thought about ghosts. He comes to the
point without preface or preparation. 'The reason of my writing
to you,' he says, 'is that I desire to know your opinion concerning apparitions, and ghosts or goblins; and if they exist, what you
think of them, and how long they live? for some consider them
mortal and some immortal.' He is quite aware, however, that
Spinoza may entertain the preliminary doubt whether there be
ghosts at all: 'but 'tis certain the ancients believed in them...
Some say they are made of a very thin fine matter, others that
they are incorporeal.' Spinoza's answer[65] begins with a neatly
turned compliment: —

'Your letter, received yesterday, was most acceptable to me,
as well because I desired some tidings of you, as because I see that you
have not quite forgotten me. And though others might perhaps take it
for a bad omen that ghosts or goblins should be the cause of your writing to me, I find on the contrary something much more to the purpose;
for I perceive that not only real things but trifles of the imagination may
thus turn to my profit.'

He deals with the question in a tone of perfect courtesy,
but with a touch of banter. 'I esteem you too much,' he says, 'to
contradict you; much less can I flatter you with a feigned assent.
As a middle course I will beseech you to produce one or two
thoroughly authenticated ghost stories of your own choice. To be
plain with you, I am so far from having met with a satisfactory
account of any ghost, that I cannot even make out what a ghost
is. If the philosophers choose to name those things ghosts which
we do not know, I will not contradict them, for there are an infinity of things whereof I have no knowledge.' He lastly observes that all the ghosts he ever heard of were at best very
foolish creatures, and seemed to have nothing better to do than to

---

[65] Ep. 56.

make dull practical jokes.

The questioner replies[66] that he expected some such answer, as from a friend not sharing his opinion (so it would seem his original purpose was to start a discussion); but friends, he adds, may well differ in things indifferent and yet preserve their friendship.

Before proceeding to give reasons for his belief he notes, with a judicial gravity which need not surprise us, seeing that it is maintained at the present day by believers in table-moving, slate-writing, funipotent and other goblins, that preconceived opinions hinder the investigation of truth. He does not meet Spinoza's challenge, but gives *a priori* reasons why there must be disembodied or semi-material spirits — such creatures being, in his opinion, indispensable for the completeness of the universe. On their natural history he is a little uncertain. 'I think there are spirits of all sorts, though, perhaps, none of the female sex.' Being aware, however, that these reasons will not be convincing to people who think the world was made by chance, he passes to evidence. He does not accept the stories of demons and magicians; but for ghosts in general he cites Plutarch, Pliny the Younger, Suetonius, Lavater, and others; the experience of a burgomaster of his own acquaintance, 'a learned and wise man, yet living, who told me that a noise of working was heard all night in his mother's brewhouse, just like that which brewing made in the day time,' and some similar and never-to-be-forgotten experience of his own — of which no particulars are disclosed.

After a while Spinoza replied,[67] still in the tone of his first answer. He had been able to consult only Pliny and Suetonius among the list of authorities given by his friend; but he found these quite enough, for they convinced him that the historians who report ghost stories do so merely for the sake of astonishing their readers. 'I confess that I am not a little amazed, not at the stories that are told, but at those who set them down.' The suggestion that there are male but not female ghosts is presumably not serious, 'otherwise I could only compare it to the imagination of the common sort, who take God to be masculine

---

[66] Ep. 57.
[67] Ep. 58.

and not feminine.' He explains that he entirely repudiates the notion of the world having been made by chance, but he nevertheless cannot admit his friend's assertion that ghosts are necessary to its perfection. For perfection and beauty are terms relative to the observer. 'He who says that God has made the world beautiful must needs assert one of two propositions: either that God has framed the world according to the desire and the eyes of men, or the desire and eyes of men according to the world. Now, whether you assert the former or the latter, I see not why God must have made goblins and ghosts to attain either of these two ends. For perfection and imperfection, they are terms not much different from beauty and ugliness. So, not to be tedious, I only ask, is the existence of ghosts more necessary to the adornment and perfection of the world than that of various other monsters like Centaurs, Hydras, Harpies, Satyrs, Griffins, Argus, and other like vanities? A pretty world it should have been, indeed, had God adorned and beautified it after the good pleasure of our fancies with such things as any man may easily imagine and dream, but none have yet been able to understand.' Having disposed of the other reasons, Spinoza regrets that his friend has not been able to furnish him with any better example than the burgomaster's ghost in the brewhouse, which he considers laughable. 'To cut the matter short, I take for my authority Julius Caesar, who, as Suetonius reports, made sport of such things and yet prospered. And so must all do who consider the effects of human imagination and passions, whatever Lavater, and others who in this matter dream in company with him, may say to the contrary.'

The rejoinder[68] was delayed by a passing indisposition of the writer. It was mostly taken up with a theological digression. Spinoza's friend asks, among other things, as a retort to his demand for a clearer definition of ghost or spirit, whether he has so clear an idea of God as of a triangle. As to the main point, he takes refuge in the general consent of ancient and modern philosophers. 'Plutarch bears witness of this in his treatises of the Opinions of the Philosophers, and of the Daemon of Socrates; as do all the Stoics, Pythagoreans, Platonists, Peripatetics, Empedocles, Maximus Tyrius, Apuleius, and others.'

---

[68] Ep. 59.

Spinoza must have had reasons of private friendship for being indulgent to this correspondent; for he not only answered him again, but took up his remarks on points quite collateral to the existence of ghosts. Part of this letter[69] is of some importance. Spinoza points out that he conceives freedom as opposed, not to necessity, but to external compulsion. Every one admits, for example, that God's knowledge of himself is both free and necessary. So, again, man's love of life is necessary, but not compelled. The correspondent had expressed surprise at Spinoza's refusal to ascribe human qualities to God. To this Spinoza replies: 'When you say that, if I allow not in God the operations of seeing, hearing, observing, willing, and the like, nor that they exist eminently in him, you know not what sort of God mine is: I thence conjecture that you believe there is no greater perfection than such as can be explained by the attributes aforesaid. I do not wonder at it; for I believe that a triangle, if it could speak, would in like manner say that God is eminently triangular, and a circle that the divine nature is in an eminent manner circular; and thus should every one ascribe his own attributes to God, and make himself like God, counting everything else as misshapen.[70]... When you ask me whether I have so clear an idea of God as of a triangle, I answer Yes. But if you ask me whether I have such a clear image of God as of a triangle, I shall answer No: for we cannot imagine God, but we can understand him.' This distinction between imagination and understanding runs through the whole of Spinoza's philosophy. He repeats that nothing has been advanced to make the existence of ghosts even probable, and altogether declines to submit to the authority of the ancients.

'The authority of Plato, Aristotle, and Socrates does not count for much with me. I should have been surprised if you had cited Epicurus, Democritus, Lucretius, or any of the Atomic school. For it is nothing strange that the inventors of occult qualities, intentional species, substantial forms, and a thousand other vanities, should have also devised goblins and ghosts, and given credence to old wives, in order to destroy Democritus' reputation, whose good name they so envied that

---

[69] Ep. 60.

[70] Cf. the fragment of Xenophanes: —

'If oxen and horses had hands like ours, and fingers,
Then would horses like unto horses, and oxen to oxen,
Paint and fashion their gods.' — (G. H. Lewes's trans.).

they burnt all the books he had published with so much renown. If you choose to believe them, what reason have you for denying the miracles of Our Lady and all the saints? which are described by so many philosophers, theologians, and historians of renown that I can produce a hundred of them for one of the others.'

This last passage is material, as disclosing how very imperfectly Spinoza was acquainted with Greek philosophy. It would seem that he thought Aristotle responsible for all the developments of the schoolmen and knew Plato only by name. His sympathy with the Epicureans is no doubt founded on the fact that their system was a genuine attempt at a scientific explanation of the world, and was in its day the solitary protest against the contempt of physics which prevailed in the other post-Aristotelian schools. But he obviously did not know Lucretius except by hearsay; for Lucretius and his masters, so far from venturing to deny the objective reality of apparitions, provided an elaborate physical hypothesis to account for them.

Alchemy was a kindred topic which still exercised men's minds in Spinoza's time, and we have some evidence of the manner in which he regarded it. In 1667 he wrote to Jarig Jellis on an alleged conversion of silver into gold effected by an unknown stranger in the presence of the naturalized German chemist Helvetius (Schweizer), who had by this time taken up alchemy with full belief.

He made inquiries of both the goldsmith who had assayed the gold and Helvetius himself; and though he expresses no opinion, he was obviously disposed to think seriously of the matter at that time.[71] But in 1675, when Dr. Schaller had sent him an account of some similar experiment, he simply replied that he did not care to repeat it, and that the more he considered it the more sure he felt that no gold was produced which was not there already.[72]

We have also letters more nearly connected with Spinoza's philosophical work, and attached to particular landmarks

---

[71] Ep. 45. See Lewes, *Hist. Phil.* 2. 180. Helvetius published his *Vitulus Aureus* in this same year, 1667. His family is a remarkable example of hereditary talent; his son and grandson were both eminent as physicians in France, where the son settled early in life; his great grandson (1715-1771) was the philosopher by whom the name is best known.

[72] Ep. 75 b. Van Vloten, Suppl. p. 318.

of it. In 1673 the Jewish physician Isaac Orobio de Castro[73] forwarded to Spinoza a long letter, written nominally to him, but for Spinoza's perusal, by a certain Dr. Lambert van Velthuysen of Utrecht. This critic went through all the common topics of censure against the 'Tractatus Theologico-Politicus,' and concluded that the principles of that treatise destroy the foundations of religion, 'introduce atheism, or set up a God himself subject to destiny, whom men can have no reason for worshipping; leave no room for divine government or providence, and abolish all dispensations of reward and punishment.' In short, the author of such a work has no injury to complain of if he is denounced as teaching mere atheism in a disguised form.[74]

Spinoza thought the criticism not only wrong but perverse; so perverse, indeed, as to be hardly consistent with good faith: and he replied with a sharpness beyond his wont. The original draft of the letter has been found, and contains even stronger expressions, which on consideration he struck out. The tone of this letter shows us an aspect of Spinoza's character which we could ill afford to miss. His indignation is not the mere intellectual disgust of a philosopher at the stupidity of an unreasonable critic, it is the moral resentment of a man loving truth and righteousness at the imputation of teaching what he abhors. It seems well to give here a considerable part of the letter.

'He begins with saying it concerns him little to know what is my nation or way of life. If he had known it, he would not have so easily convinced himself that I teach atheism. It is the character of atheists to seek rank and wealth beyond measure, things which I have ever despised, as all know who are acquainted with me.... Then he proceeds: *In order to avoid the reproach of superstition, he seems to me to have cast off religion altogether.* What this writer means by religion and what by superstition, I know not. Does he, I would ask, cast off all religion

---

[73] Balthasar, afterwards Isaac Orobio de Castro *(circ.* 1620-1687) was of a New Christian family, and had lived many years in Spain, where he was a distinguished physician. He fell into suspicion of Judaism, and was imprisoned and tortured by the Inquisition, and finally banished from Spain. After spending some time in France, he settled in Amsterdam and professed himself a Jew. He became well known as a controversial writer, and was the author of a critique on one of Spinoza's critics, whom he charged with being himself a Spinozist. *(Certamen Philosophicum,* etc. *Bibliogr.* 108, 209). Grätz, x. 202.

[74] Ep. 48.

who affirms that God is to be accepted for the chief good, and that as such he is to be loved with a free affection? that in this only consists our perfect happiness and perfect liberty? more, that the reward of virtue is virtue itself, and the punishment of folly and vice is folly itself? and, lastly, that every man's duty is to love his neighbour and to obey the commands of the supreme power? These things I have not only said, but proved by most solid reasons. But methinks I see in what mud this fellow sticks.[75] He finds, it should seem, nothing to please him in virtue and knowledge by themselves, and he would choose to live by the mere impulse of his passions but for this one difficulty, that he fears the penalty. So he abstains from ill deeds and follows God's commandments like a slave, unwilling and with a hesitating mind, and for this service looks to be rewarded by God with gifts far more grateful to him than the love of God itself; so much the more, I say, as he finds the more distaste and repugnance in well-doing. And thus it comes about that in his conceit all men who are not restrained by this fear must live without discipline and cast off all religion. But I leave this, and pass to his conclusions where he would fain show that I *teach atheism by covert and glozing arguments.*

'The foundation of his reasoning is this, that he thinks I take away God's freedom, and make him subject to fate: which is manifestly false. For I have affirmed that all things follow of inevitable necessity from God's nature no otherwise than all affirm that it follows from God's nature that he understands himself. This surely no one denies to follow necessarily from God's nature, and yet no one conceives that God understands himself under any compulsion of fate, but rather that he does so with entire freedom, though necessarily....

'This inevitable necessity of things destroys neither divine nor human law. For moral precepts, whether they have the form of law from God himself [i.e. by direct revelation] or not, are yet divine and wholesome; and the good which ensues from virtue and the love of God, whether we take it from God as a judge [a political superior issuing distinct commands] or as

---

[75] 'Quo in luto hic homo haereat.' Spinoza was scholar enough to know the classical force of *homo* in controversial usage, and I think he intended it.

flowing from the necessity of God's nature, will be neither more nor less desirable; as on the other hand the evil which ensues from evil deeds is not therefore less to be feared because it so comes of necessity: in short, whether our actions be necessary or free, our motives are still hope and fear. Therefore his assertion is false, that *I would leave no room for precepts and commands,* or, as he says later, *that there is no expectation of reward or punishment when everything is ascribed to fate, and it is settled that all things proceed from God by inevitable necessity....*

'It were too long to review all the passages which show that he was in no sober mood when he formed his judgment of me. Wherefore I pass to his conclusion, where he says that *I have left myself no argument to prove that Mahomet was not a true brobhet.* And this he endeavours to show from my principles, whereas it plainly follows from them that Mahomet was an impostor. For that liberty which is granted by the catholic religion, as revealed by the light of both nature and prophecy, and which I have shown is most fit to be granted, is by him wholly done away. But if this were not so, am I concerned, I pray you, to show that such and such a prophet is a false one? On the contrary, the burden lay on the prophets to show that they were truly such. If he should reply that Mahomet also taught God's law, and gave sure tokens of his mission, as the other prophets did, then I grant there will be no cause for *him* to deny that Mahomet was a true prophet.

'For the Turks themselves and heathens in general, if they worship God by justice and charity to their neighbours, I believe that they have the spirit of Christ and are saved, whatever persuasion they may entertain through ignorance concerning Mahomet and their oracles.

'You see, my friend, how far from the truth your correspondent has wandered. Nevertheless I admit that he has done no injury to me, but much to himself, when he scruples not to affirm that *I teach atheism with covert and glozing arguments.*

'I do not think you will find anything in this that you can judge too harsh in its terms towards this writer. But if you light on any such thing I beg you to strike it out, or else amend it as you shall think fit. I have no mind to anger him, whoever he may be, or make myself enemies by my work; and because this commonly happens in disputations of this sort, I could scarce bring myself to answer him, nor could I have done so unless I had promised you.'[76]

This protest is strong and even vehement in its terms, and there is not the least reason to doubt its sincerity. It has an important bearing on that part of Spinoza's sentiments of which it is peculiarly difficult to form an exact estimate, I mean his relation to religious belief in general. We shall have to consider in another place the effect of his philosophical system, taken in itself, on religion as usually understood. His own interpretation of his philosophy is on that question material but not conclusive: here it comes before us as a point in his personal character. It is evident that he considered religion as something very real in man's life, and the charge of irreligion or atheism as the grossest and most wicked of calumnies. But this religion, as he understands it, is not the religion of churches and sects. It is independent of dogmatic theology, independent of any particular knowledge or belief as to revelation, independent even of the so-called natural theology which holds to the conception of God as a Person after all other definitions of his nature have been renounced, and to the expectation of another life which shall redress the balance of the present one in some manner of which all specific knowledge is disclaimed. The essence of religion is in Spinoza's mind a cheerful and willing co-operation with the order of the world as manifested in the nature of man and of society. Irreligion is the self-seeking spirit to which the love that is its own reward is unknown. The atheist is the man who has nothing better to pursue than the satisfaction of his own vulgar appetites, whose only plan of life is 'honores et divitias supra modum quaerere.' The true and saving worship is to do justice and love one's neighbour. And observe that Spinoza does not put this as something beside or opposed to religion; he speaks of it as religion itself, and regards definite religious beliefs (in the popular sense) as things in themselves comparatively indifferent, but good in so far as they serve as a vehicle, so to speak, for the essential virtues of love and well-doing.

His attitude towards Christianity — not the dogmas of Catholic or Reformed divines, but the 'spirit of Christ' which men may have in intellectual and historical ignorance — is one

---

[76] Ep. 49.

of respect and even reverence. In the 'Tractatus Theologico-Politicus' one is not absolutely safe in relying on expressions of this kind, as the treatise is framed throughout on an accommodating and hypothetical plan, which gives occasion for a certain vein of irony. But in this letter he is writing to the Jew Orobio, an escaped and living witness of the tender mercies of the Inquisition, who, even if he shared the liberal tendencies of many members of the Amsterdam synagogue, would not be specially pleased by compliments to Christianity. And it is very certain that Spinoza did not go out of his way to please Van Velthuysen, for whose reading the reply was ultimately intended.

The tone of the *Tractatus* and of Spinoza's remarks in divers passages of other writings is indeed strongly anticlerical. Spinoza regards clerical influence as a bad thing, not so much on the ground that it is wrong to teach with authority and as absolutely certain that which is false or doubtful, as because such influence tends to disturb the order of society and diminish respect for the civil law. Hence the peculiar hostility with which Spinoza has been pursued by professional theologians. But as regards individual belief there is nothing irreligious or antireligious to be found in him. He would never have consented to his name being inscribed on the banner of a materialist crusade.

Notwithstanding the sharpness of this first passage of arms, Van Velthuysen and Spinoza came into direct communication afterwards, and on terms of mutual respect, if not friendship. There is a letter[77] from Spinoza to Velthuysen concerning his intention of publishing, together with some explanatory notes to the 'Tractatus Theologico-Politicus,' certain papers which appear to be no other than the correspondence we have just had before us. The letter seems to be one of a series of at least two or three, and to have been preserved only by accident. I give it here, however, for the fine sense of literary courtesy which it shows.

'I am surprised at our friend Neustadt having told you that I thought of replying to the writings against my treatise which have been published for some time past, and intended to include your MS. in the number. I am sure I never intended to refute any of my opponents, so little did any of them seem to me worth an answer. All I remember to have said to Mr. Neustadt is

---

[77] Ep. 75.

that I purposed to publish some notes explaining the more difficult passages of the treatise, and to add to these your MS. and
my answer, if I had your leave for so doing. This I desired him to
ask of you, and added that in case you should be unwilling to
grant it on the score of certain expressions in the answer being
rather severe, you should be at full liberty either to amend or to
cancel them. Meanwhile I have no cause of offence against Mr.
N.; but I thought it well to show you the real state of the case, so
that, if I cannot obtain your leave, I might at least make it clear
that I had no manner of design to publish your MS. against your
will. I believe, indeed, it may be done without any risk to your
reputation, provided your name is not affixed to it; but I will do
nothing unless you grant me leave and licence to publish it. But I
am free to confess you would do me a far greater favour if you
would set down the arguments with which you think you can
attack my treatise, and add them to your MS.; and this I most
heartily beseech you to do. There is no one whose arguments I
should be more willing to consider, for I am aware that your only
motive is affection for the truth, and I know the candour of your
mind; in the name of which I again entreat you not to decline
giving yourself this trouble.'

The scheme here mentioned was not carried out, and a
year or two afterwards Van Velthuysen published his arguments
as an independent work. It is one of the polemics against Spinoza
mentioned with approbation by Colerus.

Leibnitz, who after Spinoza's death joined the popular
cry against him, appears in his lifetime among the list of his correspondents. In 1671 he wrote to him, enclosing for his opinion a
note on the improvement of lenses. He addresses him as an ex-
pert of well-known standing and authority: 'Among your other
merits known to fame, I understand that you have excellent skill
in optics, which persuades me to address to you my essay, such
as it is, as I shall not easily find a better critic than yourself in
this kind of inquiry.' Spinoza replied courteously, and offered to
send Leibnitz a copy of the 'Tractatus Theologico-Politicus,' if
he had not one already.[78]

In 1675 we hear that Tschirnhausen (of whom presently)
had met in Paris 'a man of excellent learning, accomplished in

---

[78] Epp. 51, 52.

many sciences, and likewise free from vulgar theological prejudice, by name Leibnitz,' who thought very highly of the 'Tractatus Theologico-Politicus,' and had (if he remembered right)
written about it to Spinoza.[79] Tschirnhausen thought he might
safely be trusted with Spinoza's writings (*i.e.*, the Ethics in MS.),
and that, for reasons he could explain on occasion, it would be
well worth Spinoza's while. The answer to this overture was
however more cautious than might have been expected. Spinoza
wrote to the friend through whom it had been communicated that
he thought he already knew this Leibnitz by correspondence, but
could not tell what he was doing in France. From his letters he
judged him to be an accomplished and liberal-minded man, but
he thought it imprudent to trust him with the unpublished work
without knowing more of him. On the whole he would await a
further report from Tschirnhausen.[80]

Leibnitz afterwards, on his way home from Paris, paid a
visit to Spinoza. Whether they talked philosophy does not appear. Leibnitz himself represented the conversation as having
been an ordinary if not trifling one, in which Spinoza told him
some amusing stories about the politics of the time.[81] He doubtless thought it necessary to avoid the suspicion of having had too
much to do with the heretic Spinoza, and prudent to make a sort
of apology for having visited him at all. Leibnitz's depreciation
of Spinoza's merits in philosophy was such as to speak ill either
for his penetration or for his candour.

In the last two years of Spinoza's life we have a series of
important philosophical letters which bring him, as we now
know, into relation with one of the men who in the following
generation were diligent in extending the domain of science.
Ehrenfried Walter von Tschirnhausen (1651-1708) was of a noble Bohemian family, and later in life attained high distinction in
mathematics and physics, and was at a comparatively early age
admitted to the French Academy of Sciences. He became especially known by his improvements in the construction of lenses
and burning glasses, with which he produced extraordinary effects, and his name has left a permanent place in mathematics by

---

[79] There is no such matter in Leibnitz's one extant letter to Spinoza.

[80] Ep. 65b (to Dr. Schaller of Amsterdam), Suppl. p. 317.

[81] 'Anecdota non contemnenda de rebus illius temporis.' See Spin.
Op. ed. Paulus, 2. 672 *sqq.;* and cf. Van Vloten, Supp. p. 307.

his investigation of the class of curves known as caustics. The foundation of his scientific taste was laid during his studies at the university of Leyden, and we may well suppose that it was on the special ground of optics that he first sought Spinoza's acquaintance. When we meet with him in the letters he is already on the footing of an old friend. His name was suppressed by the editors of the 'Opera Posthuma,' like those of several other of Spinoza's correspondents, and his part, formerly attributed by conjecture to Dr. Meyer, has only been restored to him since the full text of these letters was published by Van Vloten. He did not, like Leibnitz, turn against Spinoza's memory; but neither did he make any open attempt to vindicate it. The work by which he is best known, 'Medicina Mentis' (Amsterdam, 1687), draws largely and tacitly on Spinoza's treatise on the 'Amendment of the Understanding.' The borrowing is of an extent which in our more scrupulous age would amply warrant a charge of plagiary; but when we consider the lax habits of the time in this respect, and the prejudice which any open reference to Spinoza would certainly have excited against Tschirnhausen's work, we should be at least cautious in blaming him. If his object was to gain a hearing for Spinoza's ideas among the respectable public, there can be no doubt that the course he adopted was the most plausible if not the only practicable one. At the same time it is certain that Tschirnhausen, without any such excuse, gave some offence to both Huygens and Leibnitz by his use of unpublished matter which they had communicated to him.[82]

Tschirnhausen was an eager student of Descartes, and also of Spinoza's yet unpublished writings. In 1675-6 he made a journey to London, where he exerted himself with success to remove an ill opinion which Boyle and Oldenburg had formed of the 'Tractatus Theologico-Politicus' and of Spinoza himself; and on his way back he stayed in Paris, and, as we have seen, made the acquaintance of Leibnitz. During this time he exchanged letters with Spinoza on several metaphysical points. His questions and objections were the most deserving of attention of any that Spinoza had received. They are always intelligent, and one or two are so acute and forcibly put that it would be difficult for a modern critic to improve upon them. Even an uncritical reader

---

[82] Van Vloten, *Benedictus de Spinoza*, App. III.

may perceive strong evidence of their aptness in the fact that Spinoza himself found considerable difficulty in meeting them. Tschirnhausen's power of appreciation and criticism does not seem however to have been accompanied by much capacity for original work in philosophy. He entertained an exaggerated notion of the advances in physical discovery which might be secured by an *a priori* doctrine of method. We already see traces of this in his correspondence with Spinoza, and at a later time his too sanguine expectations were gently rebuked by Huygens.[83] But with all allowances for errors of judgment and other human infirmities, his career was a useful and honourable one, and to have been Tschirnhausen's master is no contemptible addition to Spinoza's memory.

There is yet one correspondent to be recorded who stands alone. In the autumn of 1675 Spinoza received a strange epistle[84] dated from Florence, and written by one Albert Burgh, now believed to be the same pupil and companion whose facilities of intercourse with Spinoza were so much envied by Simon de Vries, and of whose temper and capacities Spinoza, in writing to De Vries, expressed a very doubtful opinion. He now announced that he had been received into the fold of the Catholic Church; the particular circumstances of his conversion might be seen in a letter he had written to Professor Craane of Leyden; his present purpose was to offer a few remarks important for Spinoza's own welfare. And with that he launched forth at no small length into denunciation of Spinoza's profane and chimerical philosophy, mixed with compassion (of the right ecclesiastical sort) for the wretched estate of his soul if he should persist in his damnable errors. He marvels how a man of Spinoza's abilities, eager in the pursuit of truth, could let himself be so deceived by the devil. 'You assume,' he asks with delightful simplicity, 'that you have at last found the true philosophy. How do you know that your philosophy is the best of all those which have ever been

---

[83] See their correspondence in Van Vloten's Supplement, which is in many respects curious. Tschirnhausen's statements as to an expected pension from the Academy of Sciences, and the amount of assistance he required 'ad studia bona excolenda,' show that the endowment of research is no new invention. Huygens' just estimate of the amount of inevitable labour still lying before science is also worth noting.

[84] Ep. 73.

taught in the world, are now taught, or shall ever be taught hereafter? To say nothing of what may be devised in the future, have
you examined all those philosophies both ancient and modern
which are taught here, in India, and all the world over? And even
supposing you have duly examined them, how do you know that
you have chosen the best?...

'Do not flatter yourself,' cries the triumphant proselyte,
'with the reflection that the Calvinists or so-called Reformed
divines, the Lutherans, the Mennonites, the Socinians, or others
cannot refute your doctrines. All those poor creatures are as
wretched as yourself, and sitting along with you in the shadow of
death. How dare you set yourself up above all the patriarchs,
prophets, apostles, martyrs, doctors, and confessors of the
Church? Miserable man and worm upon the earth that you are,
yea, ashes and food for worms, how can you confront the eternal
wisdom with your unspeakable blasphemy? What foundation
have you for this rash, insane, deplorable, accursed presumption?
What devilish pride puffs you up to pass judgment on mysteries
which Catholics themselves declare to be incomprehensible?'
This and much more of the same fashion is enforced with arguments which it would be intolerably tedious to repeat. One of
them however may deserve to be singled out: it is that, because
Julius Caesar would probably have laughed at a prophecy of
gunpowder, it is unreasonable to disbelieve in the divining rod,
alchemy, magic, and demonology. Burgh protests that he has
written to Spinoza 'with a truly Christian intention; first that you
may understand the love I bear to you, though a heathen; and
next, to beseech you not to persist in perverting others.' Finally
he threatens Spinoza with eternal damnation if he does not repent
of his wicked and abominable errors. It will be remembered that
the immortal discourse of Brother Peter in the 'Tale of a Tub'
ends with invoking similar consequences on the hearers if they
offer to believe otherwise; but the genuine crudity of Albert
Burgh's effusion hardly leaves room for even a Swift to add any
touch of caricature.

Spinoza was at first unwilling to make any answer to
such an attack. But some common friends, who had known
Burgh and, with Spinoza, hoped better things of him, represented
that it was but due to their old friendship to try the effect of re-
monstrance. Being once prevailed upon to write, Spinoza could

not but show his sense of the extreme folly and insolence displayed in Burgh's letter. The arrogance of it would have been sufficiently gross if addressed to a Protestant; to one who had never professed himself a Christian at all it was extravagant. The answer is far the sharpest ever written by Spinoza.[85] For serious argument he had little occasion; the convert's attack on what he called chimerical philosophy was easily answered out of his own mouth.

'You who assume that you have at last found the best religion, or rather the best teachers, and fixed your credulity on them, *how do you know that they are the best among those who have taught other religions, or now teach or shall hereafter teach them? Have you examined all those religions both ancient and modern which are taught here and in India and all the world over? And even supposing you have duly examined them, how do you know that you have chosen the best?*'

Spinoza recalls to the hot-headed proselyte, who fancies that Rome has a monopoly of all the virtues, that in Alva's persecution his own ancestors had suffered valiantly for the Protestant religion. The historical claims of the Church of Rome are met not with direct criticism but with an unexpected counter-attack.

'As for what you add touching the common consent of multitudes of men, the uninterrupted continuance of the Church, and the like, that is the very same old tale as the Pharisees'. They bring forward their myriad witnesses with no less confidence than the devotees of Rome, and those witnesses repeat their traditions, as if they were facts within their own knowledge, no less stoutly than the Roman ones. Their lineage they carry back to Adam. They boast as proudly as any that their Church has been continued to this day, and stands unshaken in spite of the enmity of heathens and Christians. They have more antiquity for them than any other sect. They proclaim with one voice that their tradition comes direct from God, and that they alone possess the

---

[85] Some remarks of Leibnitz's on this letter, of no great importance, may be found at the end of M. Foucher de Careil's *Leibniz, Descartes, et Spinoza;* and some sufficiently absurd reflections by the admiring editor at the end of the 'Premier Mémoire' in the same volume.

word of God both written and unwritten. It cannot be denied that all heresies have branched off from them, while they have remained firm during several thousand years with no political power to compel them, but in the mere strength of fanaticism. The miracles they report would weary a thousand nimble tongues. But their most notable claim is that they count far more martyrs than any other nation, and they daily increase the number of those who have with singular constancy suffered for the faith they profess; and this is no fable. I know myself, among others, of one Judah, called the Believer, who in the midst of the fire, when he was supposed already dead, began to sing the psalm. *To thee, O God, I commit my soul,* and so expired singing it.[86]

'The discipline of the Roman Church, which you so much praise, is, I confess, politic and brings gain to many. I should think, indeed, that there was none more convenient for deceiving the vulgar and subduing men's minds, were it not for the discipline of the Mahometan Church, which far excels it. For since that superstition had its rise, no schism has taken place in their Church.'

Spinoza means, I suppose, that in the history of Islam there is no great doctrinal rupture comparable to the Reformation in Europe. He must have known from his study of the Jewish philosophers, who abound in allusions to the Arabic schools, that Mahometanism has no lack of sects to show. It shares with Judaism, however, the advantage of never having complicated its fundamental formula. But under the circumstances Spinoza

---

[86] This was Don Lope de Vera y Alarcon de San Clemente, a Spanish nobleman who was converted to Judaism through the study of Hebrew, and was burnt at Valladolid on the 25th of July, 1644. Grätz, *Gesch. der Juden,* x. 101. Dr. Grätz supposes that Spinoza here speaks as an eye-witness, and must consequently have been born and passed his youth in Spain. But the sense of Spinoza's words is amply satisfied by referring them to the notoriety which the event doubtless had among the Jewish congregation of Amsterdam. It cannot be suggested that in § 3 Spinoza means to say that Burgh had witnessed the sufferings of his own ancestors under the Duke of Alva. But the phrase (parentes tuos nosti, qui ... ipse quendam Judam ... novi, qui ...) is exactly the same in both cases.

could not be expected to write with minute exactness, even if he were capable of it. A broad and rapid presentation of things was the only instrument that could possibly have any effect on Albert Burgh's sublime ignorance.

CHAPTER III

IDEAS AND SOURCES OF SPINOZA'S PHILOSOPHY

Laudemus viros gloriosos, et parentes nostros in generatione sua. — ECCLUS. xliv. 1.

Lo, thou hast learned that whosoever tells a thing in the name of him that said it brings redemption to the world. — Pereq R. MEIR (in C. Taylor's 'Sayings of the Jewish Fathers').

PART I. — JUDAISM AND NEO-PLATONISM

THE time has passed when systems of philosophy could be regarded as final and absolute. It is not so very long since it was assumed as a matter of course that the key to all the secrets of the universe was in man's hands, and that only culpable perversity could fail to find it. In our own day the nearest approach to a dogmatic philosophy of the old pattern has been a doctrine which proceeds on the systematic assumption that the problems of philosophy are insoluble. There are some who find in this state of things the death-warrant of philosophy itself, and thereupon exult or revolt, according to their temper, as at a matter irrevocably judged. But such are over-hasty, forgetting that the change which has come over men's view of the great problems of the world is not single or casual, but is the last step in a vast movement of human thought which has profoundly modified our whole conception of the nature and limits of knowledge. Science has for good and all abandoned the dream of finality. The discoverer well knows that his discovery, while it brings new certainty and new power over things, will also throw open a new series of questions. In the first flush of conquering advance, armed with instruments whose power seemed unbounded, and mighty in their new-born freedom of mind, the leaders of the great revival saw visions of a goal near at hand. Let the right method be once obtained, and a few simple principles might suffice to explain the whole course of nature. So thought Descartes and his ardent followers, among whom we have already seen

Spinoza's friend Tschirnhausen. So thought Leibnitz even after the warning of their failures. A few more cautious workers, with the prescience which only practical experience gives, refused to be dazzled by these magnificent and facile promises. Thus Huygens perceived that the course which lay before scientific explorers was at best a long and arduous one. Thus Newton taught the world the lesson of patient exactness by his great example of self-denial. But the world is slow to learn, and as the work of science grew and multiplied it admired with imperfect knowledge, accepting provisional or even erroneous results as absolute truth. At last the various paths of science were seen to converge into a broad road. The atomic theory brought chemistry into relation with general physics, and the ideas of correlation and continuity drew together the several branches of physical knowledge, while the undulatory theory of light opened to the scientific imagination a new world coextensive with the sensible universe. But it was also seen that this was not the end of questionings, but the beginning of new and higher questionings. A fresh problem arose in the place of every one that had been solved or set aside: and, so far from resting on her conquests, science only girded herself for a more strenuous continuance of the campaign. We stand face to face with infinite mysteries in the things we see and handle; we have to do no longer with inert masses pushed and pulled through space by a convenient something called Force, but myriadfold complexities of rushing, vibrating, pulsating units, each of them endowed with a definite character and persisting in it against the assaults of the whole universe; endless motion, shock and counter-shock, taken up and reverberated by the all-pervading ether; everywhere restless activity, and changes rapid beyond our conception, though numbered and measured in our calculations; a new and immense variety in the manifestations of nature, a boundless and unexplored wealth in her powers. The very elements of our physical knowledge are transformed. Only a few years ago we talked of Matter and Force as if they were things obvious and within our grasp. The doctrine of Energy has come to tell us that even in the elements we must always be learning afresh. Descartes, and Spinoza after him, spoke of Motion as if it were a real thing. Down to the present time we have been brought up to speak of Force as if it were a real thing. Now Force has become either a mere compendious symbol in the description of motion, or a worse than idle name to hide our ignorance; and matter is almost reduced to a vehicle for Energy. Yet the certainty of the natural sciences is not shaken, nor is the ardour of research abated. We still seek knowledge, knowing that when we have found it we shall have to seek still farther.

Was it any wonder, then, that philosophy, having not only the difficulties of scientific inquiry to contend with, but other peculiar ones differing in kind from those encountered in the natural sciences, should be slower to enter into the critical period in which knowledge becomes conscious of its provisional character? Is it surprising, on the other hand, that philosophy also should at last conform to the conditions that science has already recognized? And if it does submit to those conditions, why should its work become fruitless or worthless any more than the work of science? We can see, indeed, that it is not so. There are no longer Platonist and Aristotelian schools, but Plato and Aristotle are more exactly studied, more truly honoured and revered, than they ever were in the days when men blindly worshipped them. The same is true, though less conspicuously true, of the great names of more modern times. Kant certainly has disciple who may be called after his name; but that would be a very shallow estimate which should reckon the power of Kant in philosophy by the number of professed Kantians in the world. For the work done by Kant was not that he established this and that proposition about the mental mechanism of perception and thought, but that he announced the entry of philosophy into her critical age. His own application of the critical method may or may not be correct, it may or may not be complete; but his work stands nevertheless. Ardent and strenuous thinkers began to strive against it when it was barely finished; they have striven ever since to find some form in which dogmatic philosophy could be revived, and they have all striven in vain. The harvest of the 'Critique of Pure Reason' is reaped by hundreds and thousands who know nothing of the Categories and Antinomies. It is not systems that make the life of philosophy, but the ideas of which systems are the perishable framework; and the philosopher's place among his fellows is determined not by counting the heads of those who accept his system as a whole, but by the strength and fruitfulness of the ideas which he sets astir in men's minds.

In every scheme of philosophy, then, which is worth serious consideration, there is a vital core of ideas embodied in a
frame of more or less artificial construction. It is the task of the
history of philosophy to trace from generation to generation the
life and growth of these underlying ideas; to disengage them
from their local and temporary incidents; and thereby to keep a
clear pathway for the work of philosophy itself. This is the spirit
in which we would fain approach that splendid effort of constructive genius which Spinoza has left us in his 'Ethics;' not
with a minute curiosity seeking for mere curiosity's sake to re-
trace each individual stone of his building to the quarry whence
he may have hewn it, nor yet with the incurious and barren admiration which forgets that even the loftiest genius is conditioned
by the materials given to the workman's hand. It has been said of
Spinoza that his theory was after all but a system, and that like
all other systems it has passed away never to come back. Such a
charge, if a charge it be, we can freely afford to admit. Spinoza
did not seek to found a sect, and he founded none. Nay, we will
go farther; it is at least doubtful whether a single person can be
named who has accepted the system of the 'Ethics' in all points
as it stands. But that is because Spinoza's mind is above the level
of the people who hunger and thirst after systems; and for that
very reason the thought of Spinoza's 'Ethics' has slowly but
surely interpenetrated the thought of the world, and even now
works mightily in it, while other systems welcomed in their own
day as new revelations are now in very truth past and forgotten.
Or are we to go, perchance, in search of systems which have not
passed away? Assuredly such are to be found: they drag on their
barren life, a fixed monotony of centuries, in the schools of
Brahmans and Buddhists and Confucians, who have drained off
the life-giving words of their ancient masters into labyrinthine
canals and stagnant pools. There in the overteemed East is the
limbo of unchangeable systems, preserved from the fertilizing
breath of change by a universal inertia. If Spinoza's philosophy
were identical, as not a few shallow critics have fancied, with
Indian pantheism or indifferentism, then Spinozism would be an
existing, unchanged, and unshaken system; but such an existence
and such security are the death of philosophy.

In order to consider the origin and growth of Spinoza's

philosophical ideas, it will be necessary to anticipate to some extent our account of his finished doctrine. The first and leading idea in Spinoza's philosophy — the only part of it, in fact, which has at all entered into the notion commonly formed of his system — is that of the unity and uniformity of the world. Nature, as conceived by him, includes thought no less than things, and the order of nature knows no interruption. Again, there is not a world of thought opposed to or interfering with a world of things; we have everywhere the same reality under different aspects. Nature is one as well as uniform. Now there is a thing to be well marked about this conception of Spinoza's; it is itself two-sided, having an ideal or speculative, and a physical or scientific aspect. On the one hand we find a line of reasoning derived from the metaphysical treatment of theology; in other words, a philosophy starting from the consideration of the nature and perfection of God. On the other hand, we find a view of the existing universe guarded by the requirements of exact natural science, so that the philosopher who follows this track is bound over to see that his speculation, whatever flights it may take, shall at all events not contradict physics. The combination of these two elements is one of the most characteristic features of Spinoza's philosophy. No one had before him attempted such a combination with anything like the same knowledge of the conditions of the task. Few have even after him been so courageous and straightforward in the endeavour. The pantheist or mystical element, as we may call it (though both terms are ambiguous and liable to abuse), is not merely placed beside the scientific element, but fused into one with it. Here, then, is a twofold root of Spinoza's conception of the universe, and each branch of it calls for an account of the soil that nourished it.

The greater part of Spinoza's 'Ethics' is occupied with the application of his general ideas to investigating the nature of man. The body and the mind are not treated as two separate entities working upon one another, much less is the one allowed to be the product of the other. Mind and body are in truth one and the same. That which is mind to the inner sense is (or if accessible would be) body to the outer sense. There is no mind without body; but also there is no body without mind. Physical and mental events run exactly parallel to one another; the physical sequence cannot interfere with the mental sequence, or the mental with the physical, just because they are two sides of the same thing. Such is the metaphysical theory which determines Spinoza's psychology. It is implied in, and directly deduced from, his general view of the world; but it is convenient to speak of it separately, for reasons which will appear, as the monistic element.

When he comes to human actions, Spinoza regards them as a particular case of the operation of universal causes. Every living thing has *appetite,* an impulse making for certain ends and determined by the tendency or effort *(conatus)* of all things towards self-preservation, which effort is given by the very fact that the individual thing does exist as such. When appetite as thus understood is conscious, it becomes desire. With this fundamental idea Spinoza works out an account of the passions which is by general consent his masterpiece, and which even now may be said to stand unsurpassed. In the ethical field of action also the self-preserving effort is the ultimate fact of life. 'The foundation of virtue is no other than the effort to maintain one's own being, and man's happiness consists in the power of so doing.'[87] That is the first law of our moral nature in the scientific sense of law; it is a universal fact which must be faced and reckoned with. But this does not lead to a system of selfishness. For man is known by experience to be a social animal, and this is no less a law of his being. Thus he can maintain his being only in society. As an individual living in society, and unable to be solitary if he would, he must preserve society in order to preserve himself; or rather the preservation and welfare of society are his only true preservation and welfare. Thus the foundation of morality is essentially social. To this element of Spinoza's doctrine we shall refer as the idea of natural law. The choice of that term will explain itself hereafter.

We need not say anything thus early of Spinoza's following out of this idea in politics. Of the last part of the 'Ethics' we shall only say here that, notwithstanding its place in the finished work, it is in the main to be assigned to what we have called the mystical element in the principles of Spinoza's philosophy, and is to be explained, so far as it may be capable of historical explanation, by reference to the same sources. The in-

---

[87] Eth. 4, 18, Schol.

terpretation is, however, difficult at best: the result I have myself arrived at after much doubt will be submitted to the reader in its due order.

This division enables us to give at once in a summary way some kind of introductory general notion of what is at present known or surmised about the birth and growth of Spinoza's philosophical ideas.

The pantheist or mystical element is traced to the mediæval Jewish philosophers, with whose works we know that Spinoza was familiar. This is to some extent matter of direct evidence. A claim has also been put in, and with likelihood practically amounting to certainty, for Giordano Bruno. Now Bruno himself was subject in certain ways to Oriental influences, while the Jewish and Arabic schools of the Middle Ages were again strongly imbued with Neo-Platonism, and Neo-Platonism in turn has a semi-Oriental character. It seems impossible, even if it were worth while, to disentangle all the details. But it remains sufficiently clear, whatever theory we may adopt, that the East has a considerable share in this portion of Spinoza's materials.

The scientific element may be assigned without hesitation to Descartes, though Spinoza carried out the scientific view of the world farther and more vigorously than Descartes himself. But as regards its union with the mystical element it is material to remark that a nascent scientific impulse runs through the naturalism of the Renaissance philosophy as represented by Bruno and others; and thus the line of contact was in a manner already traced.

The monistic element is given by reaction from the dualism of Cartesian philosophy, and determined chiefly, as I think, by considerations of a scientific order. The pantheist idea may also have its part. But we can strike no exact account between the two, for Spinoza had completed the fusion of the mystical and the scientific principles before he settled his monism in its final form.[88]

The idea of natural law remains, and is the most independent work of Spinoza's genius. Ideas and suggestions of a general kind he had from Descartes, and a good deal of more

---

[88] This appears from the advance of the *Ethics* on the *Tractatutus de Deo et Homine* (see next note) in that respect.

definite material from Hobbes, who is in fact his master in politics; and there is an extraordinary amount of resemblance to Stoic doctrine, suggestive at the first glance of imitation. But closer attention will show that such a supposition presents greater difficulties than that of coincidence.

It would seem, if the foregoing statement can be accepted, that the really practical part of Spinoza's philosophy, that by which it is now operative and keeps hold on men's living interests, is also the part which is most peculiarly his own. I am aware that such a conclusion may not be free from unconscious bias, nor is it to be assumed that historical criticism has said its last word. It is certain that critics have hitherto busied themselves much more with the metaphysical than with the ethical part of Spinoza's system; and it is yet to be seen whether the revival of interest in ethical problems which has lately shown itself may not be fruitful in this region. It may be, though such is not my own judgment, that if little has been found here, it is because there has been little search. In the meantime I can only beg the reader to use his own diligence in verifying whatever is advanced.

First let us take in its purely speculative aspect the idea of the nature of things as one and uniform. Much light has been thrown on the growth of this idea in Spinoza's mind by the discovery of his unpublished 'Essay on God and Man.'[89] The date of its composition is only approximately known, nor is the work itself a uniform whole. On the one hand it must be earlier than any of Spinoza's other writings, and the absence of any mention of it in the letters goes to show that by 1661 at latest it was for Spinoza himself a superseded work. On the other hand it was written originally in Latin, and therefore after he had mastered the language under Van den Ende, and it shows familiarity with Descartes. We shall probably not be far wrong in placing it about the time of Spinoza's excommunication. Possibly the essay or some portions of it, privately circulated among friends, may have

---

[89] See the account of Spinoza's works in the Introduction, and the monographs on this essay there cited. It is preserved only in an indifferently executed Dutch version, which seems to have been made in the early part of the eighteenth century. The original title, rendered by 'Korte Verhandeling van God, den mensch, en deszelfs welstand,' was probably *Tractatutus de Deo et Homine eiusque Felicitate.*

been the 'abominable heresies which he taught.' Compared with the 'Ethics' or even with the earlier treatise on the Amendment of the Understanding, it is a brilliant but immature performance. Inasmuch as we possess the 'Ethics,' the essay has only a historical value, but that value is very great. It shows us the ferment and conflict of elements received from different quarters and not yet subdued to their places and proportions in a new structure. As to the matter now in hand, it gives positive proof that Spinoza really worked out his metaphysic by starting in the first instance from theology, and did not first conceive his metaphysic and then clothe it in theological terms. In psychology and everything that has a scientific bearing he was still dominated by Descartes when he wrote the essay. Not that he even then adopted the Cartesian doctrines.

He was struggling, but as yet without a perfectly fixed aim, to work out for himself the reconciliation of Cartesian analysis with *a priori* speculation. The leaders of mediæval Jewish thought had endeavoured to recast their theology in an Aristotelian mould given them by the ptilosophic culture of their time. Spinoza in turn, beginning where they had left off, set himself to refashion their handiwork with the instruments furnished by Descartes. But he took up the work with the resolve to carry it through at all costs, and the result was that both matter and method became transformed in his hands. It must remain doubtful, I think, whether Spinoza himself was ever fully aware of the amount of the transformation he had effected, especially as regards his theological premises. He could not have been what he was without the Jewish doctors or without Descartes, but his philosophy is neither Cartesian nor Jewish.

The essay likewise gives to my mind strong reasons against holding (though it is commonly assumed as if it were certain) that Spinoza was ever actually a Cartesian. For though as to certain parts it is Cartesian in language and arrangement, in those very parts the essay enunciates anti-Cartesian doctrine even more pointedly than the 'Ethics' afterwards did. Not only is it denied that sorrow and the passions derived from it can ever be useful — whereas Descartes says that sorrow is in a manner even more necessary for men than joy — but all passions whatever, except the divine love,[90] and, in a qualified sense, one or two others of the more active kind, are repudiated as unworthy of the philosophic life. If Spinoza was a Cartesian at any time it must have been before the essay was written; and moreover he could not have become a Cartesian without utterly breaking with the Jewish philosophic traditions, on whose lines, however, or at any rate from out of them, he is working in the essay. We should be driven to suppose, then, that Spinoza broke with Jewish literature to take up Descartes, and becoming dissatisfied with Descartes, turned back again to the Jewish authors.[91] But violent oscillations of this kind are not in Spinoza's character, to say nothing of the time between Spinoza's introduction to Descartes and his composition of this essay being too short to afford room for them. And even so the essay should present to us, not a juxtaposition of non-Cartesian metaphysic and Cartesian psychology, but modified Cartesian doctrine throughout. And this it certainly does not. I conclude, therefore, not only that Spinoza was not solely dependent on Descartes, but that he was never a Cartesian at all.[92]

The argument of the essay starts, in a purely *a priori* manner, from the nature and attributes of God. The absolute uniformity of nature, and the implied rejection of final causes, are deduced from the consideration of his freedom and perfection. The universe is governed by divine laws, which, unlike those of man's making, are immutable, inviolable, and an end to themselves, not instruments for the attainment of particular objects. The love of God is man's only true good. From other passions we can free ourselves, but not from love, 'because for the weakness of our nature we could not subsist without the enjoyment of something that may strengthen us by our union with it.' Only the knowledge of God will enable us to subdue the hurtful passions. This, as the source of all knowledge, is the most perfect of all; and, inasmuch as all knowledge is derived from the knowledge of God, we may know God better than we know ourselves. This

---

[90] In treating this as a passion the Essay differs from the *Ethics*.

[91] This is in fact the theory of Dr. Joël. He puts the supposed return to Jewish philosophy as late as the composition of the *Tractatus Theologico-Politicus,* in which he finds the occasion for it.

[92] The same conclusion has been arrived at by Dr. Avenarius in his very careful discussion of Spinoza's philosophical development.

knowledge in turn leads to the love of God, which is the soul's union with him. The union of the soul with God is its second birth, and therein consist man's immortality and freedom.

The detachment from ordinary cares and interests in which the essay makes man's happiness to consist is carried so far as to approach quietism. A great contrast is presented to Spinoza's later manner in such passages as the following, which occur in the description of Hate. It is said to be produced, in common with other passions, by false opinion.

'Hate is the right contrary to love, and ariseth from the delusion that is begotten of mere opinion. For when a man hath concluded concerning such and such a thing that it is good, and another comes and doth somewhat to the prejudice of the same, then the first conceives hate against him so doing. The which should have no place in him if the true good were known, as we shall show hereafter. For all that is or may be thought of is in comparison with the true good [the love of God] nothing but mere wretchedness, and is not he that so affects wretched things much more worthy of pity than of hate?'[93]

In the 'Ethics' the ordinary pleasures and amenities of life, though not exclusive or sufficient objects of a reasonable man's pursuit, nor to be lamented for when they are not attainable, are treated as something very different from 'mere wretchedness.' And we shall see that the love of God, though still presented as the crown and perfect state of the human mind, acquires a much more intellectual character, if indeed it can be at all distinguished from pure speculative knowledge.

It appears therefore that the theological element, however transformed subsequently, may claim the right of primogeniture among Spinoza's ideas. We shall be pursuing an order not only historical in point of actual chronology, but just and fitting with regard to the probable history of Spinoza's thought, if we first turn our attention to the Jewish doctors of the middle ages who brought a philosophical treatment to bear upon theological problems.

Partly coinciding in time with Catholic scholasticism, but with their rise and culminating period nearly a century earlier, a series of Jewish philosophers in Spain, Provence, and the

---

[93] *Korte Verhandeling*, part ii. cap. 3.

East, did work which has a far more important place in the general history of philosophy than has commonly been allowed to it. The task they set themselves was the same in kind as that of the schoolmen, who, in spite of religious difference, joined hands with them on the common ground of Aristotle, and used their work with open acknowledgment and respect. They strove, in one word, to systematize theology on an Aristotelian footing. For this purpose it was necessary to embark on a critical and philosophical interpretation of Scripture; and in this undertaking the comparatively undefined character of Jewish orthodoxy secured them a certain amount of freedom.[94] Or rather philosophy presented itself to Jewish speculation as an enlightened interpretation of the hidden meaning of the law. Thus Moses ben Maimon and Ibn Ezra were leaders in biblical criticism no less than in philosophy. The ideas they put forward in this field were to be carried out to their full development in the 'Tractatus Theologico-Politicus.' Spinoza's object is indeed opposite to that of Maimonides. So far from finding philosophy in the Scriptures, he maintains that it is idle to seek it there; and the sharpness of his criticism on Maimonides' artificial system of interpretation has probably distracted attention from that which they really have in common. Maimonides' work was continued by Levi ben Gerson, or Gersonides (born at Bagnal in Provence in 1288, living in 1340), who, professing to be a mere interpreter of the Scriptures and to rely on them as the source of every kind of knowledge, was at the same time more thoroughly Aristotelian than his predecessors. His discovery of Aristotelian metaphysics in the Song of Solomon was probably the extreme feat of the Jewish theolpgico-philosophical dialectic.

The influence of these writers is most marked in the 'Tractatus Theologico-Politicus,' with which we are not immediately concerned in this place. In the purely philosophical part of

---

[94] The Mahometan schools enjoyed the same advantage. Strictly speaking, neither Judaism nor Islam have any dogmatic theology at all. At the same time there must have been in practice a good deal of restraint. Maimonides expressly warns his readers that on many points he will be deliberately obscure; and Ibn Ezra could only hint with elaborate mystery that 'the Canaanite was then in the land' could not have been the language of Moses' generation. The intervals of absolute silence in his commentary on Isaiah are even more significant.

Spinoza's work it was comparatively slight: it is perhaps not too much to say that there are only traces of it in the 'Ethics,' apart from the doctrine of the mind's eternity in the fifth part, which I believe comes from the Averroists through Gersonides. Still the points of affinity are notable. The following are specimens of those which may be found in Maimonides' great work, the 'More Nebuchim.'[95]

The will and the wisdom of God are regarded as inseparable. And not only is there no real distinction between the divine attributes, but no attribute whatever can be predicated of God in the ordinary sense. Even eternity and existence, as applied to him, are not *synonymous,* but merely *homonymous* with the same terms in any other application.[96] This, however, is by no means peculiar to Maimonides; it is a common possession of the scholastic writers, and is distinctly enounced in the treatise on mystical theology which bears the name of Dionysius the Areopagite. Probably it might be traced much farther back by any one conversant with Neo-Platonism. The application of the principle to God's knowledge as distinguished from man's was strenuously disputed by Levi ben Gerson.

The existence of God is involved in his essence; otherwise of the existence of any finite creature, which may be considered as an accident in the logical sense.[97]

God coexists with the creation as its cause *in actu,* not as a cause *in potentia,* which precedes the effect in time.[98]

Perfect intellect forms no conception of good and evil, only of true and false. Such was the first state of Adam. Good and evil belong to the region of probable opinion.[99]

Dr. Joël also calls attention to Maimonides' reflections on final causes as being fitted to prepare the way for Spinoza's

---

[95] Edited by Dr. Munk, *sub tit. Le Guide des Egarés,* with literal French translation.

[96] Cap. 56, and elsewhere.

[97] Capp. 57, 58.

[98] Cap. 69. One may be allowed to note (though not here relevant) Maimonides' answer to the standing question why the world, if created in time, was created at one time rather than another. He says it is just like asking why there exists a certain number, neither more nor less, of individuals of any kind — *e.g.* the fixed stars.

[99] Cap.2.

entire rejection of them.[100] Maimonides holds that the conceptions of design and final cause have no intelligible application except as regards things created in time.

Chasdai Creskas of Barcelona, and afterwards of Saragossa, who lived in the latter part of the fourteenth and early part of the fifteenth century, was a more daring and original thinker than his predecessors, though to a certain extent in the interest of orthodoxy. He broke with the Peripatetic tradition to strike out an independent line of his own, and Dr. Joël's research has shown that he stands in a closer relation to Spinoza than any other of the Jewish philosophers. His principal work, the 'Light of the Lord' (Or Adonai), finished in 1410, contains many things which come near to characteristic points of Spinoza's philosophy. Some of these points are already well developed.

He censures as fallacious the notion of infinite extension being made up of measurable parts (cf. Spinoza, Eth. i. 15 schol., Ep. 29): he also holds matter to be eternal, the act of creation consisting only in the ordering of it; and maintains that the material world, being good in its kind (which he takes, I presume, as a truth known by revelation), participates in the Divine nature. The contrast of this with the Cartesian theory of substances distinct *in genere* probably had something to do with Spinoza's conception of extension as an attribute coequal with thought.

Again, the perfection of God consists not in knowledge, as the Aristotelians say, but in love. This love is what determines God to creation, as at the same time a necessity of his nature and an act of will. Love being the chief attribute of God, the perfection of any creature depends on the extent to which it shares therein: thus the love of God (for its own sake, not as a means of salvation) is the chief end of man. We have already had occasion to see what an important part is assigned to this in the essay 'On God and Man' which preceded Spinoza's Ethics.

Most remarkable of all, perhaps, is Chasdai's thorough determinism. He explicitly denies that any event, whether depending on human choice or not, can be called possible or contingent in an absolute sense. It is inconceivable, he says, 'that two men, being themselves of like temper and character, and having before them like objects of choice in like circumstances,

---

[100] *Zur Genesis der Spinoza's* (in *Beiträge zur Gesch. der Philos.*)

should choose differently.' Volitions are determined by motives as much as anything else in nature is determined. An act of free will is *free* in so far as it is not *compelled,* but *necessary* in so far as it is not *uncaused.* The argument on this topic seems to be fully worked out, and to deal with most of the points that have been made in later controversy on the subject. The fallacy of fatalism, for example, is clearly enough exposed. The objector who says, If all things that happen are necessary, why do men take pains to compass their ends? forgets that things are necessary only with reference to their conditions, and that in the case of human undertakings forethought and labour are among the conditions.

Reward and punishment, as the consequences of good and bad actions, are themselves part of the necessary order of things. If it is asked, How is it just that the wicked should be punished, if their wickedness is necessary? Chasdai answers, with Zeno before him and Spinoza after him, that their punishment is necessary too. Reward and punishment, commands and prohibitions, are nevertheless ordained by Providence as means to lead men to salvation. The love of God is man's chief good, even as love is God's own perfection; and therefore the foreordained sanctions are attached to those actions and thoughts which are free in the popular sense, that is, which are determined by a state of mind involving the love of God or its contrary.

Chasdai holds fast, it must be remembered, to the idea of *designed* order in the universe, though final causes in the ordinary sense are as it were swallowed up in the absolute, self-sufficient necessity by which God's love manifests itself. He likewise holds fast to the necessity of revelation, and goes so far as to say that the fundamental doctrine of the unity of God could not be otherwise known. Thus he cannot be regarded as a forerunner of Spinoza's system. Spinoza took the suggestions in detail and worked them into a systematic connexion of his own which would probably have found little favour in Chasdai's eyes.

Chasdai Creskas deserves to be remembered, apart from his probable influence on Spinoza, as one of the first who ventured to attack the prevalent Aristotelian dogmatism. His motives appear to have been purely theological; the artificial constructions forced on Scripture by the school of Ben Maimon and Ben Gerson were repugnant both to his reason and to his faith. When theologians fall out philosophy sometimes comes by her own. For Spinoza's knowledge of Chasdai's work we have the direct evidence of one express quotation[101] (Ep. 29, *ad fin.*).

A word must also be said of the mystical literature which exercised an even greater influence on modern Judaism than the Aristotelian philosophy, and whose later development was due, according to one high authority,[102] to a reaction against the rationalism of the philosophic writers. The possible influence of the Kabbalah on Spinoza has been discussed from time to time ever since Spinoza's writings have been an object of notice to the learned world. One of his earliest critics, J. E. Wachter, endeavoured to trace his principal doctrines to that quarter:[103] and others in later times, without going so far as to ascribe to the Kabbalists the chief share in Spinoza's philosophical genealogy, have claimed for them a more or less considerable one. In order to put this question on a rational footing it is very necessary to distinguish between the Kabbalah properly so called, which dates from the thirteenth century, and the older mystical traditions which the Kabbalists deliberately confounded with their own fantastic speculations in order to give themselves an apparent sanction of antiquity. The later Kabbalah, starting from an idealist theology and cosmology expressed in highly symbolic language, rapidly became overwhelmed by its own anthropomorphic symbolism, and overran all Jewry with demonology, thaumaturgy, and other wild fancies beyond measure; for all which the professors of this so-called philosophy found warrant in Scripture by trifling and wearisome schemes of non-natural interpretation, anagrammatic readings, arbitrary transpositions and substitutions of letters, allegorical and other occult meanings, virtues of numbers, and the like. The greatest play was made with the numerical values of words and letters, a method which has to some extent found its way into Christian theology

---

[101] 'Verum hic obiter adhuc notari velim, quod Peripatetici recentiores, ut quidem puto, male intellexerunt demonstrationem veterum, qua ostendere nitebantur Dei existentiam. Nam ut ipsam apud Judaeum quendam, Rab Ghasdai vocatum, reperio, sic sonat.'... The passage is identified by Dr. Joël *(Don Chasdai Creskas' Religionsphilosophische Lehren,* etc., p. 9).

[102] Dr. Grätz, in *Gesch. der Juden,* vol. vii.

[103] *Der Spinozismus im Jüdenthumb,* 1699. *Elucidarius Cabbalisticus,* 1706. See Van der Linde, *Bibliogr.* No. 274.

also. The metaphysical foundations of the system appear to have been derived by some road not fully known from Neo-Platonism, and it is said by the best authorities that the very terms bear marks of imitation from the Greek. The doctrine of emanations and intermediate powers between God and the world was laid hold of in order to have a philosophic standing-ground against Maimonides and the rationalists, and at the same time to pre-serve tradition and ritualism in their literal significance. In Spi-noza's generation this system had attained its fullest and most extravagant development: and it seems to have become by that time the most unmitigated nonsense ever put together by the per-verted ingenuity of man, except perhaps the English law of real property. In its application to ceremonial observances it was little else than a mass of ludicrous or disgusting puerilities. Its fruits were seen in the outbreaks of delusion and imposture culminat-ing in the exploits of the false Messiah, Sabbatai Zevi, of which mention has already been made in a former chapter. Such a doc-trine, we may be sure, had little attraction for Spinoza; and in an age when historical criticism did not exist he would scarcely have had the patience to search the rubbish-heap for the jewels that might be buried in it. He has indeed left us in no doubt as to his opinion of the Kabbalists of his time. For he says in the ninth chapter of the 'Tractatus Theologico-Politicus:' 'I have read and moreover known some Kabbalistic triflers, at whose follies I was astonished beyond description.'

It is hardly worth while to insist on the differences be-tween Spinoza and the Kabbalah. The doctrines of emanation and the transmigration of souls are both fundamental in the Kab-balistic account of the world, and are both utterly incompatible with Spinoza's metaphysic.

But on the other hand Spinoza twice refers, in passages of marked importance and in a tone of respect, though in vague terms, to ancient Hebrew opinions and traditions; and these ref-erences may with some plausibility be assigned to the earlier mysticism which undoubtedly preceded the modern Kabbalah, and was afterwards confused with it. Only an accomplished Ori-entalist can be entitled to a positive opinion on the sources and antiquity of these speculations. But all mysticism is Eastern in its ultimate origin, and the choice would seem to be substantially between holding that the Jewish mysticism was indirectly de-

rived from the East through Neo-Platonism and the Alexandrian
schools, or that it came, as we know that modern Jewish theology came, earlier and more directly from the old Persian religion, in which case Jewish and Alexandrian mysticism would be
related to one another, not in a direct line of descent, but as parallel and partly intermixed streams from the same fountain-head.
The question is hardly a proper one to be pursued here, even if I
were qualified for the undertaking. But it is easy to see that, apart
from the evidence of actual coincidences, which in a case of this
kind is difficult to fix at its true value, the last mentioned opinion
has a strong antecedent probability in its favour: and even a
stranger to Oriental literature may be permitted to appreciate the
weight of M. Franck's arguments for it.

The allusions in Spinoza are the following.

In the Scholium to the seventh Proposition of the Second
Part of the Ethics he says: 'A mode of extension [*i.e.* a finite
material thing] and the idea of that mode are one and the same
thing, but expressed in two ways; which certain of the Hebrews
seem to have seen as through a cloud, when they say that God,
the understanding of God, and the things understood by him are
one and the same.' Now this is distinctly said in the commentary
of Moses of Cordova on the Kabbalistic book Zohar. 'It is to be
known that the knowledge of the Creator is not as that of his
creatures. For in these knowledge is distinct from the subject of
knowledge, and is directed upon objects which in their turn are
distinguished from the subject. This is denoted by these three
terms: thought, that which thinks, and that which is thought of.
But the Creator, on the contrary, is himself at once knowledge
and that which knows and that which is known. His manner of
knowledge consists not in applying his thought to things outside
him; in the knowledge of himself he knows and perceives all that
exists. Nothing exists which is not united to him or which he
finds not in his own substance.'[104] The coincidence is striking,
and it is quite possible that Spinoza had read Moses of Cordova.
But then it is quite certain that Spinoza had read and digested the
Kabbalist's far greater namesake Moses ben Maimon. And the

---

[104] Franck, *La Kabbale,* pp. 27, 194; Sigwart, *Spinoza's Neuentdeckter Tractat, &c.,* p. 100. The book Zohar itself, the great armoury of the Kabbalists, is finally ascertained by recent criticism to be a forgery of the thirteenth
century. Grätz, *op. cit.* vol. vii. note 12.

same thought is even more fully and distinctly expressed in a chapter of Maimonides' masterpiece, to which Spinoza makes on another point an unmistakable reference elsewhere.[105] The chapter opens thus: 'Thou knowest the famous proposition laid down by philosophers concerning God, to wit that he is intellect, the intelligent, and the intelligible, and that these three things in God make but one and the same thing, wherein is no multiplicity.' And again at the end of the chapter: 'Hence (from God being intellect always *in actu,* never *in potentia* like the knowledge of finite minds) it follows that he is constantly and perpetually intelligent, intellect, and intelligible; it is his very essence that is intelligent, it is the same that is the intelligible, and still the same that is intellect, as must be the case with all intellect in act.' Maimonides himself is here following Ibn-Síná, and the idea is ultimately derived from Aristotle. Thus we have a warning of some significance against jumping at simple coincidences in matters of this kind. It is practically certain that Spinoza had in his mind the passage of Maimonides; he may or may not have also had before him the adaptation of it by Moses of Cordova to a purpose superficially like Spinoza's own.

The other passage to be considered is in a letter to Oldenburg (Ep. 21).

'I hold God for the immanent cause, as they say, of all things, not the transient. That all things have their being and move in God, I affirm with Paul, and perhaps I may say with all the ancient philosophers, though in another form; I might even make bold to say, with all the ancient Hebrews, so far as one may guess from certain traditions, though they be in many ways corrupted.' The traditions here mentioned might well belong to the metaphysical kernel of the Kabbalah, which Spinoza must, in common with all scholars of the time, have believed to be of great antiquity; and the manifold corruptions of which he speaks would also fit very well with the vagaries of the later Kabbalists, and the opinion expressed of them in the 'Tractatus Theologico-Politicus.' But such a reference is too vague to be much relied upon by itself; and we have seen that the passage in Eth. ii. 7 gives it very little support.

---

[105] *More Nebuchim,* part i. c. 68 (vol. i. p. 301 in Munk's translation, and see his note); Spinoza, *Cogitata Metaphysica,* pt. ii. c. 6, § 3.

It is further to be observed that the Kabbalah was taken up with great ardour by Raymond Lull within the century of its birth, and thus obtained a partial currency in Christendom; and that it was eagerly studied by Pico de Mirandola, Reuchlin, and other scholars of the Renaissance, who, entertaining no doubt of the antiquity alleged for it, thought to find in it a venerable and authoritative confirmation of the Platonic or Neo-Platonic philosophy that prevailed among them.

Giordano Bruno, whose relation to Spinoza will immediately be considered, was probably not free from this influence. At all events the work of the Jewish Neo-Platonist Avicebron (Ibn-Gebirol) was known to him and freely used by him; and thus we have yet another road by which the Neo-Platonic ideas may have found their way to Spinoza. Solomon Ibn-Gebirol, born at Cordova or Malaga about 1020, came at an unfortunate time for his philosophical reputation among his own people. His speculative writings, in which he closely followed Plotinus, were overwhelmed in the Peripatetic flood that was already rising before his death, and while he lived and still lives as a religious poet,[106] he was entirely forgotten as a philosophical writer. But his principal work had been translated into Latin under the name of 'Fons Vitae,' and was current among the schoolmen. The author's name was disguised under the Latinized form Avicebron, and he was set down without further inquiry, by a sort of unreasoned mental attraction, as belonging to the Arabic school headed by Averroes and Avicenna. The identity of Avicebron with Ibn-Gebirol was rediscovered only in our own day by the sagacious industry of the late Dr. Munk. The 'Fons Vitae,' well known to the leaders of mediæval philosophy, fell into the hands of Giordano Bruno, who as a Platonist of the Renaissance naturally received it in a much more kindred spirit than the Aristotelians. Bruno repeatedly cites Avicebron with approval, and there is much likeness in the general strain of their speculations, which however may be due to the use of common sources.

We have no direct evidence that Spinoza was acquainted with Giordano Bruno's writings; but the want of such evidence

---

[106] 'Den Gabirol, diesen treuen
Gottgeweihten Minnesänger,
Diese fromme Nachtigall,
Deren Rose Gott gewesen.' — HEINE, *Hebräische Melodien.*

counts for very little. But for his reply in a letter to a friend's passing question, we should be in the same case as to Spinoza's knowledge of Hobbes; yet his political theory is so evidently founded on that of Hobbes that the letter adds nothing to our certainty. At that time it was still the constant practice for writers to make in silence such use of their predecessors' work as in our day would be thought to demand the most ample acknowledgment. And in this particular case there was a special reason for silence, the same reason which probably accounts for Tschirnhausen's later omission of all reference to Spinoza himself. Any avowed following of Bruno would have been sure to excite the most violent prejudice even among Protestant readers. It was by no means at Catholic orthodoxy alone that Giordano Bruno had struck in his daring and unconfined speculations. We are free, then, to take at its full worth the internal evidence for Spinoza's knowledge of Bruno; and it is of such strength as to carry all but irresistible conviction. Whether Spinoza had actually read Bruno's dialogues, or had become acquainted with their substance in some other way (for example, through Van den Ende), it is impossible with our present materials to decide.

One is tempted to linger on the singular career and tragic fate of the man whose fame, crushed for awhile but not consumed, has revived in our own day for the eternal dishonour of his persecutors. They who curse liberty and the advancement of man's estate in our own day are true and worthy successors of those who burnt Giordano Bruno and were ready to torture Galileo. The philosopher and martyr of whom we now speak is at last fitly celebrated in the verse of one of our own poets, himself full of the spirit of the Renaissance, its ideal ardour for freedom, its impatience of authority in all forms, its height of speculative ambition, and its passionate love of beauty. But my task forbids me to enter on digressions, and I must proceed to notice the points of Bruno's philosophy which bear on the matter in hand.

Bruno admits only one first principle, cause, or substance, in the universe. He is never tired of dwelling on the unity of all things, which he regards as a multiform unity embracing the whole and present in every part. He rejects the notion of formless matter, and maintains that matter and form are inseparable. Finite things differ from one another not in their being, but only in their mode of being, so that in them the one substance is not diverse, but only diversely fashioned and figured; all things are in the universe, and the universe in all things. The study of nature seems to disclose two substances of mind and body, but further contemplation reduces them to one; and the ultimate object of all philosophy and science is declared (with an ironical reservation as to supernatural knowledge) to be the perception of this unity. In one dialogue the speaker who represents Bruno's own opinions asserts that the 'first principle' is infinite in all its attributes, and that one of those attributes is extension *(uno amplissimo dimensionale infinito)*. Again, it is animated, inasmuch as it includes all life as part of one and the same being: all particular lives are effects of the divine life present in all things, 'Natura est deus in rebus.' We find in Bruno the terms *attribute* and *mode,* used in a manner which, though it has not anything like Spinoza's precision, may very well have suggested Spinoza's adoption of the words. The constant polemic against Aristotle is likewise worth noting; if Spinoza was a reader of Bruno, his almost contemptuous view of Aristotle (p. 37 above) might be partly accounted for by this.

In some of Bruno's writings much prominence is given to the identification of the highest kind of speculative knowledge with the love of God, or the one perfect object; and the power and surpassing excellence of this ideal and intellectual love are dwelt upon with exuberant poetic fancy. Notwithstanding the wide difference between Bruno's manner and Spinoza's, the thought and even the expressions are often strikingly like those of the 'Essay on God and Man.' At the same time this topic is so much the common property of all mystic and mystically inclined writers that I can hardly think these resemblances add very much to the evidence of a specific connexion between the two thinkers. It would be no great matter for surprise if an equally good parallel could be produced from the Persian Súfis, whom Spinoza certainly had not studied. Still, when the general probability of Spinoza's relation to Bruno is once established, all points of coincidence have a certain cumulative value, though each may in itself be capable of a different explanation.

It has been suggested that Descartes also may have been indebted to Giordano Bruno, and there is nothing unlikely in it. Leaving this question aside as too remote, we must now turn to

Descartes as the master who gave the most powerful and immediate impulse to Spinoza's thought in another direction. By him were nourished the exact method, the close analysis, the spirit of scientific curiosity, which we find in Spinoza's earliest writing side by side with the ardour of universal contemplation, and in the 'Ethics' interpenetrating and transforming it.

PART II. — DESCARTES

The real merit of Descartes is not to be found in the particular novelties which he started in either natural or universal philosophy. His fundamental axiom in psychology, though first brought into full prominence by him, was not altogether new. His physical principles were unsatisfactory not only in themselves, but as compared with the results already arrived at by other workers to whom Descartes failed to do justice. They were indeed absolutely erroneous in many respects, as we shall presently have occasion to see. The amount of direct edification which a modern reader can get out of Descartes' 'Principia Philosophiae' is in truth exceedingly small. It is only in pure mathematics, where, as the undoubted creator of analytical geometry, he can claim his part in all its later achievements and extensions, that his contributions to man's positive knowledge have retained a permanent value. Yet the name of Descartes, notwithstanding all the shortcomings of his actual performance, marks an epoch in the history of science and philosophy. His fame is great and justly won because he made a serious attempt to give an account of the world on a scientific plan, to apply the same method to the problems of outward and inward experience, and to combine the results into a consistent whole. He saw, with clearness and boldness then without parallel, that physiology was a branch of physical knowledge, and to be investigated on just the same principles as every other branch. He saw that philosophy must leave science alone with the things which pertain to science; that the business of philosophy is not with the particulars which fall within the province of scientific inquiry, but with the interpretation of the facts of experience which for science are ultimate. We have no right to be offended or even surprised when his execution falls short of his intentions. He knew that he ought not to be imposed upon by words or dogmatic fictions, but it was only natural that he should in many cases be unconsciously led away by them. There is another disturbing influence, unfortunately, which has to be allowed for in considering Descartes' work as a whole; I mean his attitude of extreme caution towards the Church. It is certain that he was much hampered by the danger of an open conflict with orthodoxy, which he was determined to avoid at almost any cost. As it was, all his astuteness was too little to save himself or his immediate followers from ecclesiastical hostility which was even more bitter in the Protestant Netherlands than in any part of the Catholic world, and which, though it never rose to the importance of a persecution, was able in various ways to inflict considerable inconvenience. It would be neither generous nor wise to ascribe Descartes' hesitation and reticence in the face of these difficulties to mere personal timidity. He had a sincere aversion to controversies of this kind and a sincere dread of violent changes. He would have liked the Church to adopt modern science and philosophy; failing that, he was content that they should be left unmolested, and thought it no harm to secure immunity, if necessary, by silence on some points and transparent dissimulation on others. Certain apologetic passages in Descartes' physical writings are as manifestly ironical as anything in Hume. Open defiance must have appeared to him an impracticable policy, and disastrous, if it had been practicable, both for society and for science itself. These questions, however, do not touch the physical side of Descartes' teaching, as to which there is no suspicion of reserve. And it was on this side, as I conceive, that Spinoza first approached him and felt his power. In Spinoza's earliest essay the psychology shows a reader of Descartes, but a reader very far from being a disciple; the physics, on the other hand, are simply and solely Cartesian.

Yet, while the influence of Descartes' philosophical conceptions on Spinoza has over and over again been discussed, sometimes with exaggeration, sometimes with depreciation, the not less important and certainly more persistent influence of his physical conceptions has passed, so far as I am aware, almost without notice.[107] The very peculiar account of motion given by Descartes was not only repeated by Spinoza, as in duty bound, in

---

[107] Professor Sigwart, however, has indicated the point here discussed and its significance. Spinoza's *Neuentdeckter Tractat,* &c. Gotha, 1866, p. 49.

his 'Principles of Cartesian Philosophy,' but occurs in the 'Essay on God and Man,' and has left its traces in the 'Ethics.' I venture to say that without going back to the Cartesian theory of dynamic Spinoza's account of the material world is not intelligible.

We read in Spinoza of 'certain things immediately produced by God,' which, though individual things, are infinite in their kind, and necessary in an eminent manner, as being coextensive with the attribute or aspect of existence to which they belong. What these things are is not stated in the Ethics; the explanation must be sought partly in one of the later letters, partly in the early essay which has already come before us.[108] In this last the following explanation is given.

'As concerning *Natura naturata* in general, that is, the modes or creatures which immediately depend on God or are created by him, of such we know two and no more; namely, motions in matter, and understanding in the thinking thing. Of these we say that they have been from all eternity, and to all eternity shall remain unchangeable, a work verily as great as beseemed the greatness of the master-worker.'

The subject of motion is not pursued, as more properly belonging to a treatise on natural science. Motion and understanding, the eternal and immutable creatures, are called by a startling Hebraism Sons of God. Indications of this kind have their value as showing that Spinoza was really striving to find a scientific interpretation for mystical conceptions. Not less significant is the disappearance of such language from the Ethics. We find it stated, again, that extended bodies differ from one another only in 'proportion of rest and motion;' and, what is still more extraordinary, we hear of a body being set in motion by the impact of another body *having motion greater than its rest.*[109] In the 'Tractatus Theologico-Politicus' (c. vii. § 27) we read of 'res maxime universales et toti naturae communes, videlicet motum et quietem, eorumque leges et regulas,' which, though it might

---

[108] *Eth.* 1, propp. 21, 23, and 28, schol.; *Ep.* 66, § 8; *Korte Verhandeling,* part i. cap. 9, to which there is an odd note, presumably by a transcriber, stating that the author really thought motion itself to be capable of further explanation.

[109] *Korte Verh.,* part ii. note *ad init.* (I have no doubt that this note is Spinoza's own), and cap. 19 (pp. 49, 99 in Schaarschmidt's ed.). Cf. *Ethics,* 4, 39.

excite little attention by itself, is significant in connexion with other passages. And in a letter as late as 1675 he gives Motion and Rest as examples of the 'things immediately produced by God.' Motion and Rest, then, were for Spinoza not relative terms describing the state of bodies with regard to each other, but in some sense and for some purposes real things. Indeed he all but defined Matter as Extension modified by Rest and Motion.

For the key to these ideas we must look to the second part of Descartes' 'Principia Philosophiae,' closely followed by Spinoza himself in the professed exposition of Cartesian doctrine which was his first published work. Descartes tells us that the nature of matter, or body generally considered, does not consist in hardness, weight, or any other sensible quality, but only in extension in three dimensions; and that all matter is ultimately homogeneous ('in toto universo una et eadem existit'), and all the differences in its sensible properties depend on differences of motion ('omnis materiae variatio, sive omnium eius formarum diversitas, pendet a motu'). The relative nature of motion is clearly enough pointed out ('nullum esse permanentem ullius rei locum, nisi quatenus a cogitatione nostra determinatur'), and the same illustration of it is given which has (no doubt independently) been repeated by Mr. Herbert Spencer ('First Principles,' c. 3, § 17).

Thus far the modern reader may follow Descartes with admiration; but then it is laid down that the *quantity of motion* in the universe is constant, a proposition which is demonstrated *a priori* from the perfection of God. We are to presume that God observes the utmost constancy in all his operations, and we must not suppose any changes in his works which are not actually known by experience or revelation. Hence we are to believe that in the beginning he created a certain quantity of motion and rest, and preserves them unchanged: 'materiam simul cum motu et quiete in principio creavit, iamque per solum suum concursum ordinarium tantundem motus et quietis in ea tota, quantum tunc posuit, conservat.' The addition of rest, as if that also were a real thing, is shown by the context to be merely rhetorical. Spinoza may have been misled by it, or his own language may be nothing but an excessive imitation of Descartes. It would seem, indeed, that Descartes himself was not free from confusion on this point; for some paragraphs later he speaks of motion as contrary to rest, and of speed as contrary to slowness, 'in so far as such slowness partakes of the nature of rest.' Spinoza, again, speaks elsewhere of finite existence as 'de nihilo participans,' partaking of nullity ('Cogit. Met.' pt. ii. c. 3, § 1); but he certainly did not regard Nothing as a real thing. Here, then, we have the conservation of motion laid down by Descartes as a first principle of physics, and taken over by Spinoza without question. The first remark that occurs on it is that, however we take the supposed principle, it is not true; and it is almost impossible to believe that the supposed proof of it was satisfying to the inventor himself. Yet Descartes had a perfectly distinct and right intention, and one may even say that he came near to a definite truth. But unhappily he had not the patience to abstain from premature generalization; he violated all the rules of sound scientific method, including his own maxims, and his haste led him into deep and irreparable error. He was added to the number of those mighty ones who in their search for the truth of things have, as Lucretius says, mightily fallen: 'graviter magno magni cecidere ibi casu.'

By *quantity of motion* Descartes meant what is now called *momentum,* a quantity measured by mass and velocity jointly. The term 'quantity of motion' has indeed been preserved as a synonym for momentum in several modern books. Now velocity, and therefore momentum, is a quantity having direction as well as magnitude. It seems unaccountable that Descartes should have neglected to consider this, but he did neglect it. He took a sum of directed quantities all over the universe, in all directions indiscriminately, and asserted that it was constant: his proposition would symbolically be expressed thus — $\Sigma\ (mv) = C$. This is not only untrue but unintelligible. For, motion and velocity being relative (as Descartes himself, strange to say, well knew), we are not told how the velocity is to be estimated. Descartes took no account whatever of direction, holding the nature of motion in itself to be something apart from its direction, which he calls 'the determination of motion towards this or that part;' and this is further made clear by the application of his principle which immediately follows. He considers various cases of the collision of two bodies on the assumption that the total quantity of motion must remain the same after the collision as before; and he treats the quantity as still being the same when the direction is reversed. The most curious confusion of all is that, after duly warning us that the two bodies in question must be regarded as an independent system ('a reliquis omnibus sic divisa ut eorum motus a nullis aliis circumiacentibus impedirentur nec iuvarentur'), he proceeds to speak of cases in which one of them is absolutely at rest, and other cases in which they are moving with different velocities. The results he obtains are in part wholly wrong, in part such as might be theoretically true in a limiting and physically impossible case. Spinoza was apparently satisfied with all Descartes' rules except one. (Ep. 15, § 10).

Had Descartes attended to the truth that direction is inseparable from momentum, he might have lighted upon the perfectly true proposition that momentum *in a given direction* is conserved. This is a corollary from Newton's Third Law of Motion, that action and reaction are equal and opposite. For, if any change took place in the momentum of a system resolved along any particular direction whatever, such change would be due to an inequality between action and reaction measured in that direction, which is what the third law of motion excludes.[110] But Newton's third law was unknown to Descartes; and in truth its scope and importance have only in late years been redeemed from general neglect. Descartes, however, had a grand object in his speculations on the first principles of physics. He could not be expected to know that it was unattainable with the means at his command, and the importance of the conception may almost excuse his rashness in clutching at it and seizing a phantom. He was in search of a principle which should enable him to deal with the material universe as a machine self-acting and complete in itself. Given a certain disposition of matter and motion, the whole future series of phenomena was to be involved in it, and was to follow without any necessity for a renewal of interference from outside. Theological criticism was met, if not disarmed, by postulating an original creative act to endow the matter of the universe with its fixed 'quantity of motion.' Descartes was in truth feeling about, without sufficient light, for some such general doctrine as that which is now known as the Conservation of Energy; and if it had been in the nature of things that the Conservation of Energy, or anything equivalent to it, should be either

---

[110] The proposition was also correctly enounced by Leibnitz: *Opera Philosophica* (ed. Erdmann, Berlin, 1840), pp. 108, 133.

discovered or proved *a priori*, Descartes would in all probability have done it. His contemporaries were too much dazzled by the brilliance of his system to perceive its scientific weakness. Spinoza, full of the Hebrew conviction of the perfect unity of the divine nature and of its manifestations in the sensible world, and determined to carry that principle to its utmost consequences, found in Descartes a seeming demonstration, on grounds of scientific evidence, of that unity and uniformity in the physical world which speculation had already led him to expect, and it must have come upon him almost as a revelation.

It is curious that Spinoza's language about Motion and Rest, derived as we have seen from the most confused and erroneous part of the Cartesian physics, is nevertheless in a manner capable of a rational interpretation. He is asked to name the particular things which are infinite in their kind, and necessary to the existence of finite things of the same kind. Matter he does not count as such (at least not in the first rank), though in his view the material universe may be considered as an individual whole no less than any part of it. Probably he regarded matter as nothing but figured extension; and the visible universe, 'facies totius universi,' involves change and motion. He names accordingly 'motus et quies,' as being, in the attribute of extension, the examples desired. Now if for *motus* we might read energy of motion, and for *quies* energy of position, we should have a fairly plausible result. Energy is, according to the notions of modern physics, the most fundamental property of the sensible universe, coextensive with it, and necessary to everything that happens in it. Every physical event may be regarded as a transference of energy. Again, though kinetic energy and potential energy, taken separately, are not constant, the sum of them is constant; so that, if anything in the physical world is to be called infinite and immutable, Energy, taken as this sum, appears to have a good enough claim to the title. And thus (if we chose to disregard historical facts and conditions) we might find in Spinoza's dark saying a kind of prophetic vision, and assign to him the glory of having pointed the way to the latest generalization of science. But this fancy would of course be wholly untenable; first, because it was no more possible for Spinoza than for Descartes to arrive at the modern conception of the Conservation of Energy; secondly, because we have fixed Spinoza's phrase to its only admissible meaning by tracing it to its Cartesian origin. Why then, it may be asked, do I go out of the way to suggest the possibility of such a fancy? I reply that the example is not uninstructive as showing what caution must be used in assigning a meaning to obscure language in the philosophy of past generations, and how important it is, where practicable, to ascertain the history of the ideas and terms we have to do with.

At the same time we have indications that towards the end of his life Spinoza had become deeply dissatisfied with the physical conceptions of Descartes. This appears by his last letters to Tschirnhausen (in the year 1676). Tschirnhausen asks (Ep. 69) how Spinoza would prove *a priori* the existence of bodies figured and in motion, extension in the abstract being conceivable without any such thing. Spinoza makes answer thus: 'From extension as conceived by Descartes, that is, an inert mass (molem quiescentem), it is not only, as you say, difficult, but altogether impossible to prove the existence of bodies. For matter at rest will, so far as in it lies, persist in its rest, and will not be impelled to motion unless by a more powerful external cause, and for this reason I long ago did not hesitate to affirm that the Cartesian principles of natural philosophy are useless, not to say absurd.' Tschirnhausen replied that Descartes did not, in his opinion, profess to account for the existing material universe as a product of inert matter, since he supposes matter to have been animated with motion by a creative act. Spinoza was unable, probably by reason of increasing ill health, to keep up the discussion at any length. His rejoinder is in these terms: 'As to your question whether the variety of existing things can be proved *a priori* from the mere conception of extension, I think I have already sufficiently shown that it is impossible; and that therefore matter is ill defined by Descartes as identical with extension (materiam a Cartesio male definiri per extensionem), but must necessarily be explained by an attribute which expresses an eternal and infinite nature. But perhaps I will discourse of this more clearly with you some day, if life suffices me. For hitherto I have not been able to set down anything orderly on the matter.' The opportunity for fuller explanation never came, and the passage as it stands is, like others in the same correspondence, somewhat obscure. One would expect the meaning to be that matter without motion is as inconceivable as matter without extension, so that

Descartes' assumption that matter was there first, as an inert lump, and motion was put into it afterwards, is illegitimate and irrational. But if Spinoza meant this, I cannot see why he should not have said it with his usual distinctness.

At any rate it is pretty clear that the Cartesian conception of material substance as consisting merely in extension — the confusion of matter with space, as Professor Clerk Maxwell has called it[111] — which leaves the fact and the idea of mass inexplicable, and leads to motion being inconsistently regarded, now as an *ens rationis* like the configuration of a system or part of space, now as a kind of thing-in-itself, was not accepted by Spinoza in his later days. This alone would not show that he did not accept it when he wrote the 'Ethics,' but it is enough to make us wary in reading those propositions which involve physical ideas.

Another physical proposition given by Descartes, and included in Newton's first law of motion, appears to have furnished the groundwork of the more general proposition used by Spinoza as the starting point of human psychology and ethics. Descartes says ('Princ. Phil.' 2, c. 37) that 'everything, in so far as it is simple and undivided, remains, as much as in it lies, in the same condition, and suffers no change unless from external causes.' Spinoza, in his manual of Cartesian philosophy, repeats the proposition in almost the same words. 'Unaquaeque res, quatenus simplex et indivisa est, et in se sola consideratur, quantum in se est, semper in eodem statu perseverat.' The demonstration he gives is framed in such general terms as to show that he regarded the proposition as not merely physical; Descartes having already treated it as the most general law of physical action ('Princ. Phil.' 2, c. 43). And in the 'Cogitata Metaphysica,' published as an appendix to this work, we find the general idea of the self-preserving effort of things, 'conatus quo res in statu suo perseverare conantur.' This effort, Spinoza says, is in truth nothing else than the thing itself; or, as we should now say, the fact of the thing being there. And he gives the first law of motion as a simple example. 'Motion has the power of persisting in its actual condition. Now this power is nothing else

---

[111] Clerk Maxwell was living when these lines were written: I cannot let them pass through the press without adding a word of tribute to a man of profound and original genius, too early lost to England and to science.

than the motion itself, that is, the fact that such is the nature of motion'[112] ('Cogit. Met.' pt. i. c. 6, § 9). In the 'Essay on God and Man' is a curious chapter (pt. i. c. 5) in which Providence is explained as identical with the self-preserving effort.

Let us now turn to the sixth and seventh propositions in the third book of the 'Ethics.' 'Unaquaeque res, quantum in se est, in suo esse perseverare conatur:' every particular thing, so much as in it lies, endeavours to persist in its own being. 'Conatus, quo unaquaeque res in suo esse perseverare conatur, nihil est praeter ipsius rei actualem essentiam:' the endeavour wherewith everything strives to persist in its being is nothing else than the fact of the thing being what it is. The physical aspect of the proposition may be stated in modern language by saying that no change of configuration takes place without work being done; this gets rid of the objectionable term *conatus,* and dispenses with the auxiliary proposition which Spinoza required to guard against the illusions it might lead to. Both the conception and the name of the self-preserving endeavour are older, possibly much older, than Descartes;[113] but the connexion between Spinoza's proposition and Descartes' so-called first law of nature appears to be sufficiently made out by comparison of the passages above given.[114]

Here again we are led to remark the importance of historical criticism. It would be easy, notwithstanding Spinoza's own warning, to find in the *conatus* an inkling of the struggle for

---

[112] Or perhaps, 'of the particular motion:' but if that had been the meaning Spinoza would probably have written *istius motus.*

[113] Giordano Bruno speaks of a 'desio di conservarsi' as common to all creatures. In Dante, *De Monarchia,* 1, § 15, we find it assumed as a principle that 'omne quod est appetit suum esse.' A similar maxim was familiar to the Stoics. 'They say that the first impulse of every living thing is directed to self-preservation (ἐπὶ τὸ τηρεῖν ἑαυτό),... and the proposition is thus stated by Chrysippus in his first book on *Ends,* that the first property of every living creature is the conscious maintenance of itself' (τὴν αὑτοῦ σύστασιν καὶ τὴν ταύτης συνείδησιν). Diog. L. vii. 85 (ap. Ritter and Preller, § 420). I have not been able to trace the idea much farther back. So far as I can learn (though I speak with diffidence) it is not in Aristotle; but it is discoverable in the later Peripatetics. See the fragment on the Stoics in Grote's *Aristotle.*

[114] It is briefly noticed by Trendelenburg, *Historische Beiträge zur Philosophie,* ii. 82.

existence, as we now call it, which is so important in the modern scientific account of the world. It has even been suggested that Spinoza here anticipates the doctrine of evolution. But the facts are inexorable. There is no more of evolution in Spinoza than in Descartes; there is in one sense the general idea of evolution in both, namely, that the whole physical universe, animate as well as inanimate, is to be accounted for by physical causes. What the doctrine of evolution has done is to put this idea into forms whereby it becomes capable of definite scientific treatment, and leads to definite results. The point is not to see that there is in nature a constant endeavour, or even competition, of individuals and kinds to preserve their existence, but to see that the competition is itself an orderly process, and that existing forms are worked out by it in ways which may be investigated and reduced to law. This belongs to natural, not to speculative philosophy; the most the speculative philosopher can do is to know his own business and leave the road clear for natural history. And this is the credit I would claim for Spinoza, not the gift of prophecy but the gift of discernment. But we shall return to this hereafter.

Thus much of Descartes' physical doctrines in their relation to Spinoza. As to his philosophy in general, there is no doubt that Spinoza was profoundly influenced by his doctrine of method and by his manner of approaching metaphysical and psychological questions. Indeed it could not have been otherwise. At the time when Spinoza's mind was opening to philosophy, and his powers ripening for independent work, Descartes was still in the first flush of his renown. Every student who meant to think for himself would turn eagerly to Descartes as the liberator who had set reason on a new footing. Spinoza necessarily dwelt in a Cartesian atmosphere and drew his life from it. But, however much Spinoza must have admired the height and range of Descartes' genius, and been fascinated by the brilliance of his invention, he found the actual performance wanting. Reasons have been given, in the foregoing notice of the 'Essay on God and Man,' for believing that Spinoza was never a Cartesian in metaphysics; it is certain that in psychology he came, though more gradually, to a marked divergence from Cartesian opinions; and we have just seen that even in physics, where until the advent of Newton Descartes seemed to reign without a rival, Spinoza did not give him unreserved allegiance. When he wrote his early essay, Spinoza had already made up his mind to reject the metaphysical dualism of Descartes; the conception of spirit and matter as two distinct substances is entirely put aside. On the other hand he still so far adhered to Cartesian psychology as to hold that interaction took place between the mind and the body by means of the 'animal spirits,' the direction of whose motion, though not the motion itself, could be changed by a purely mental act. This was the philosophical use of the fallacious distinction made by Descartes between motion and its direction or 'determination towards this or that part.' It enabled him to assign, as he thought, a point of contact for the material and the immaterial worlds, and not only to leave room for the operation of free will but to give a scientific explanation of it. The will could impress as much change as might be required on the direction of the animal spirits without violating the axiom of the conservation of motion.[115] Spinoza, as his own work advanced, perceived the weakness of the Cartesian theory, and not only ceased to follow it but explicitly controverted it in the 'Ethics.'

Spinoza's doctrine of the unity of Substance was held by him, I believe, without interruption from the first days of his philosophic activity. He was only strengthened in it by examination of the Cartesian dualism; and, so far as we think of his opinion on this point in relation to Descartes, we must think of it as a critical reaction rather than a development. It is true that philosophy could not in any case have rested content with the form of dualism propounded by Descartes; the school of Descartes himself did not so rest. He had drawn a sharp line of separation between the subjective and objective aspects of the world, the mental and the material series of phenomena, without making any distinct attempt to show how they came into relation and correspondence with one another. The gap was filled up by the ingenuity of his immediate followers with the doctrine of Occasional Causes; which however is really equivalent to giving up the problem as hopeless, and taking refuge in a perpetual miracle. Yet no other way is possible so long as the fundamental distinction of substances is retained. Spinoza saw that the apparent explanation was no explanation at all, and took up the question

---

[115] Attempts have been made quite lately to revive this invention in a form adapted to modern physical knowledge.

again from the beginning. If it can be said of him that he only continued the work of Descartes, it can with equal justice be said of Kant that he only continued the work of Hume. Both found new difficulties probed and laid bare, new lines of search indicated by their great precursors; but the problems thus started had in the one case been solved imperfectly or erroneously, in the other they were conspicuously and of set purpose left unsolved. Kant and Spinoza, men of widely different genius and considering the questions of philosophy under widely different forms, both produced results which have struck deep root and brought forth a manifold harvest in the subsequent course of philosophic inquiry.

Every new step in philosophy is a continuation of the last, in so far as its character and direction are determined by that which has been found wanting in the account of things obtained in the last preceding stage. But it can properly be called a continuation only when it pushes on in the same direction, not when it comes back from it as leading nowhere and strikes out a distinct one. This last was the case with Spinoza as regards Descartes; and to speak of his philosophy as a branch of the philosophy of Descartes appears to me nothing short of a paradox.

CHAPTER IV

THE DOCTRINE OF METHOD

> Et j'avais toujours un extrême désir d'apprendre à distinguer le vrai d'avec le faux, pour voir clair en mes actions et marcher avec assurance en cette vie. — DESCARTES, *Discours de la Méthode.*

THE best general introduction to the philosophy of Spinoza is perhaps that which he has himself given us in his unfinished work, 'On the Amendment of the Understanding.' It was begun some considerable time before the 'Ethics,' probably on the suggestion of Descartes' 'Discourse on Method,' but on a much larger scale; it seems to aim at nothing less than a complete analytical account of the objects, nature, and instruments of philosophic inquiry. Thus it was to prepare the way for a constructive exposition which is now represented, so far as Spinoza was able to carry it out, by the 'Ethics.' At the time of writing this treatise his designs were probably more extensive; and changes, though not fundamental ones, had come over his opinions in some points before the 'Ethics' assumed their present form. But on the whole the 'De Intellectus Emendatione' stands so much nearer to the 'Ethics' than to the 'Essay on God and Man' that it may be fairly regarded as the analytical preface to Spinoza's latest work, bearing to it some such relation as Descartes' 'Discourse' to his 'Principles of Philosophy,' or Kant's 'Prolegomena' to the 'Kritik.' Spinoza himself, if we may trust the statement of his editors, had not dropped the work as out of harmony with his later views, but always intended to take it up and finish it. Several of the foot-notes attached to it in its present shape look as if they had been made by Spinoza on a reperusal some time after the text was written, and were meant as memoranda for his own use in the subsequent revision and completion which was never executed.

The treatise begins by considering the futility of the common objects of human desire, which are reduced to the heads of wealth, power, and pleasures of sense. All these are vain and precarious in themselves, and distract the mind from the pursuit of the true good. But is not that pursuit also precarious? and if for its sake we renounce that which men commonly seek after, may we not lose the substance of life for a shadow?

The answer gives in a few sentences the whole aim of Spinoza's philosophy. 'After I had somewhat thought over the matter, I found, in the first place, that by abandoning these objects and undertaking a new course of life I should abandon a good uncertain in its own nature, as we may plainly gather from what I have said, for one uncertain, not in its own nature (for it was a constant good I was in search of) but only as to the attainment of it. Further, I came by persevering reflexion to see that by so doing, it only I could thoroughly weigh the question, I should abandon certain evils for a certain good. For I perceived that I was encompassed by the utmost danger, and drove myself to seek a remedy with all my power, uncertain as it might be; as one sick of a mortal disease, when he foresees certain death unless a remedy be applied, is driven to seek that remedy with all his power, uncertain though it be, and his whole hope is set thereon. Now all those things which the multitude pursue not only provide no remedy for the maintenance of our being, but actually hinder it, and are oftentimes the occasion of ruin to such as possess them, always to such as are possessed by them.'... Happiness or unhappiness depends on the nature of the object whereon we fix our affection. Strife, envy, hatred, and fear are the constant penalty of loving perishable things. 'But love towards a thing eternal and infinite feeds the mind with pure joy, and is wholly free from sorrow; this is to be greatly desired and strenuously sought for.'

Spinoza, like Descartes, tells the story of his own search for truth, taking us along with him in the path which he struck out, and retracing with us the steps by which at last he found himself in the right way. But the difference of their ambitions is remarkable. Descartes is in search, not of blessedness, not of the supreme good, but of certainty for the conduct of man's action. 'I ever had an exceeding desire to learn how to distinguish truth from falsehood, that I might see the way clearly in my actions and walk with confidence in this life.' There was no ardent disquietude in his pursuit of truth. He found literature instructive and agreeable; mathematics admirable and useful; theology a guide to heaven (whither he meant to go no less than any other man), but too lofty for terrestrial uses; philosophy an art of supporting many diverse opinions with equally plausible reasons; and special branches of learning appeared to him in the same case with philosophy, save that they were practical roads to wealth and honourable employments. From the pursuit of these he could stand apart; he knew enough of vulgar imposture and delusion to be proof against them; and having found the school of books a failure, he went forth into the school of men. It was only after some years that in the leisure of a long winter he turned back upon himself to find some better foundations of knowledge and belief. Meanwhile active life was well enough; every man finds at least some truth in attending to his own business, for therein error brings its own speedy punishment As for the common objects of men's desires and undertakings, their vanity is passed over with the briefest mention. What may be the real object of life is not discussed, not even glanced at. Knowledge is enough for our present search, Descartes seems to say. Let us know where we are, and then there will be time enough for the rest.

It is otherwise with Spinoza. Following a more ancient course of thought than that struck out by Descartes, he is impelled by the futility of earthly desires to set forth on the quest of man's true and perfect good. It is not enough for him to satisfy the practical need of 'walking with confidence in this life;' he would fain understand the consummation of the journey, and the purpose to which all particular knowledge and actions are subordinate. The life of courts and camps, the field of varied activity and observation where Descartes could leave his questionings aside for a season, was not open to him. He set himself, without delay or remission, to attack the problem of life, not in and through the world, but apart from it. Descartes assumes tacitly that human life is good to a reasonable man; Spinoza assumes that there is some human good so sure and so permanent that by finding it the reasonable man can make life good for himself, and help others to find it good also. The alternative of pessimism does not occur to them in any form. Descartes certainly had no reason to complain of the world; Spinoza, so far as outward circumstances went, had as little reason to praise it. But for each of them it was equally impossible to devise that sort of stimulant for jaded philosophical appetites. They lived in too fresh and stirring an air.

Spinoza's early mention of 'love towards a thing eternal and infinite' reminds us in a manner of the 'Essay on God and Man.' But the following paragraphs no less foreshadow the 'Ethics.' He does not rush off to take the Chief Good by storm, but prepares to make sure of it by artificially conducted approaches. But for the glimpse he first gave us we should not know what he had in sight. In considering what is the true or the chief good, it is to be observed, he says, that good and evil are only relative terms. 'Nothing regarded in its own nature is to be called either perfect or imperfect; especially when we are satisfied that everything which happens does so according to an eternal order and fixed laws of nature.' But man can form the conception of a human character more constant than his own, and sees that it is possible for his existing character to be improved by approach to this ideal. He casts about therefore for means which may help him towards this perfection; everything that may so help him is a *true good.* 'And the chief good is to bring it to pass that he, together with other persons, if so it may be, may be endowed with such a character. What that character is we shall show in its proper place, namely, that it consists in knowledge of the union which the mind has with the whole of nature. This then is the end for which I make, to acquire such a character, and to labour that many acquire it with me; that is, it belongs to my happiness to endeavour myself that many others may understand the same that I do, that their understandings and desires may wholly agree with mine.' Here is announced the essentially social nature of all human morality and improvement, which we afterwards find developed in the 'Ethics.' To be wise alone is only half the battle, and the lesser half; the triumph of the seeker for wisdom is to find for his fellow-men as well as for himself. An instructed and enlightened society must be formed if its members are to attain wisdom. For this end moral philosophy and the science of education must be cultivated (and how far, two centuries after Spinoza, we still are from a science of education); and health being an important condition of our undertaking, medicine in every branch is to be perfected;[116] nor are the

---

[116] *Cf.* Descartes, *Disc. de la Méthode,* part vi. whose language is stronger... 'S'il est possible de trouver quelque moyen qui rende communément

mechanical arts to be omitted which multiply the convenience of life. 'But before all is to be devised a method of curing the understanding, and purifying it so far as we are able at this stage, that it may succeed in understanding things as well as possible and without error.' Thus the scope of all knowledge is the same, the perfection of man's nature; and by its tendency to promote that end its usefulness is to be judged.

Some provisional rules are laid down for the conduct of life during the period of inevitable ignorance, but they are of no great moment. One of them looks as if Spinoza thought it possible at one time that a guarded and judicious introduction of his opinions would save them from being unpopular. Then we come to the degrees of perception, or as we should now say, knowledge.

Four kinds are enumerated. We may learn things (1) by hearsay or on authority *(ex auditu);* (2) by the mere suggestion of experience *(ab experientia vaga[117]);* (3) by reasoning *(essentia rei ex alia re concluditur);* and (4) by immediate and complete perception *(res percipitur per solam suam essentiam).* Thus a man's birthday, the names and condition of his ancestors, and the like, are known to him by hearsay; such matters as that oil increases fire, and water puts it out, and most things that make up the common knowledge of life, he knows by unreasoned experience; while by reasoning from the known properties of light and optical instruments we correct the illusions of our sight as to the size of heavenly bodies, or from our peculiar experience of our own bodies, we infer that there is a peculiar relation of some kind between the mind and the body. We know immediately, or by the nature of the thing alone, a few of the simplest and most general truths. A single example, however, will serve to illustrate all the kinds of knowledge; and this example alone is retained in the 'Ethics,' where the classification is repeated, but tradition and loose experience are taken together as sources of knowledge of the first kind; reasoning forming the second kind, and intui-

---

les hommes plus sages et plus habiles qu'ils n'ont été jusqu'ici, je crois que c'est dans la médecine qu'on doit le chercher.'

[117] This is a Baconian phrase. *Nov. Org.* Aph. 100. Sigwart, *Spinoza's Neuentdeckter Tractat, &c.* p. 157. Prof. Sigwart's other evidences of Baconian influence in Spinoza's treatise are not so clear; the influence, at all events, was a transitory one.

tion the third and highest. The example chosen is that of a simple arithmetical proportion.

'Let three numbers be given in order to find a fourth, which shall be to the third as the second to the first. Tradesmen have no hesitation in multiplying the second by the third and dividing the product by the first; either because they have not forgotten the rule they once heard from a master without any proof [knowledge *ex auditu*], or because they have often made trial of it with simple numbers [*experientia vaga*], or by virtue of the proof in the nineteenth proposition of the seventh book of Euclid, that is, by the general property of proportionals [*ratio* or *secundi generis cognitio*]. But with very simple numbers there is no need of this. For example, if the given numbers be 1, 2, 3, no one fails to see that the fourth proportional is 6, and this much more clearly, because we at once infer the fourth number from the ratio which we see by a single intuitive act that the first has to the second.'[118]

We have to choose between these modes of acquiring information as the means of arriving at exact knowledge, and thereby at the greatest possible perfection of man's nature. Tradition and loose experience are obviously uncertain and untrustworthy. It was Spinoza's intention, as we learn by his marginal note, to discuss in this place the whole subject of experimental knowledge and research. Reasoning will lead us to certainty, if rightly carried out; 'yet by itself it will not be a means of attaining our perfection.' The fourth mode of perception alone (the third kind of knowledge in the nomenclature of the 'Ethics') is the only one which is both *adequate,* as giving us the whole nature of the thing perceived, and free from risk. Our task is therefore to find the best and shortest way for bringing things at present unknown to us within its grasp.[119]

'Now that we have learnt what knowledge is needful for us, we have to deliver a way and method, whereby the things to be known shall be known with that kind of knowledge. To which end it is first to be considered, that there shall not be here an infinite search: that is, in order that the best method of discovering the truth may be found, we do not need another method to discover that, and to discover the second method we do not want yet a third, and so on without end. For in this manner we should never arrive at knowledge of the truth, nor at any knowledge at all. The matter stands indeed in the same way as that of

---

[118] *Eth.* 2, 40, schol. 2.
[119] *De Int. Emend*, c. 5.

material instruments, where one might argue in like manner. For to work iron one must have a hammer, which hammer must be made; for which yet another hammer and other tools are needful, and to produce these again we shall need other tools, and so on without end:[120] and in this fashion one might vainly endeavour to prove that men have no power of working iron.'

Man has in fact succeeded in making tools and machines by many progressive steps. At first he used his hands to obtain, by rough and toilsome processes, a few of the simplest instruments. By the help of these he made other and better ones with less labour, and from stage to stage arrived at his command of mechanical arts. So too the human mind, using its native strength to procure instruments for its work, proceeds from one undertaking to another till it attains consummate wisdom. What then are the instruments with which the mind is equipped by nature, and which suffice it for the construction of other and more finished ones? They are true ideas, and the sole and sufficient proof of their truth is furnished by themselves. Accordingly the doctrine of method is not concerned to assign a test of truth to be applied to our ideas after we have got them; the problem is to find the due order in which truth, the representations of the nature of things,[121] or true ideas (all which terms are synonymous) are to be sought for. This naturally appears to a modern reader at first sight as the most absolute dogmatism. The author seems to be claiming an arbitrary right to accept anything he pleases as self-evident. But this is not really the case. Spinoza's drift in this passage, when freed from the technical form of his argument, is that by no logical device whatever can we escape the necessity of starting from something or other as self-evident, and throwing on its self-evidence the whole weight of all the subsequent knowledge we may build on our leading assumptions.

Let us take Spinoza's own explanation in the more con-

---

[120] *Cf.* the Rabbinical list of 'things created between the suns,' in which 'some say, tongs also, made with tongs.' — C. Taylor, *Sayings of the Jewish Fathers,* v. 9.

[121] 'Essentiae obiectivae rerum.' In Spinoza's usage *obiectivus* means represented in, or taken as the object of thought, and is often equivalent to the modern *subjective*. The correlative term, where the thing is considered in itself, or as we should now say *objectively,* is *formalis;* so that true knowledge in the mind is said *referre obiective formalitatem naturae.*

cise and finished form which it assumes in the 'Ethics,' In the second part (Prop. 43) he asserts that 'whoever has a true idea, knows at the same time that he has a true idea, and cannot doubt the truth of the thing perceived.'

After the regular demonstration, which is very artificial, these remarks are added by way of Scholium: —

'It is to be noted that the foregoing proposition is pretty manifest of itself. For no man who has a true idea is unaware that a true idea involves the utmost degree of certitude. For to have a true idea signifies nothing else than to know the thing perfectly or as well as possible; nor can any one possibly doubt of this unless he thinks an idea to be a lifeless thing like a picture on a panel, and not a mode of thought, to wit the very act of understanding. Who can know, I ask, that he understands anything, unless he do first understand the thing? in other words, who can know that he is sure of anything unless he is first indeed sure of that thing? Again, what can be found more clear and certain than a true idea, which may be the test of truth? Even as light makes manifest both itself and darkness, so is truth the measure of itself and of falsehood.'

Spinoza does not say, be it observed, that every apparent certainty is true knowledge, but that there is no true knowledge without certainty, and the certainty is given in the knowledge itself. In other words, there is ultimately no external test of truth; we must be content in the last resort with the clear and persistent witness of consciousness. This doctrine is not necessarily transcendental or dogmatic. It is compatible with a purely empirical account of the origin of all our knowledge, and indeed is adopted in that connexion by one of the leading philosophical authors of our own time and country. Mr. Herbert Spencer's view of the final test of truth, though he puts it in the negative form as the inconceivableness of the contrary, is substantially not distinguishable from Spinoza's. Rightly understood, the doctrine is not an assumption of infallibility, but a warning against any such assumption. When a man is once in possession of the truth, he cannot doubt it; but he may well be deceived into supposing himself in possession of it when he is not. To take an illustration used elsewhere by Spinoza himself, a man dreaming often fancies himself sure that he is awake; but a man really awake can never think he is dreaming. The things I see and feel, my phenomena, are ultimate certainties to me so far as they go. The difficulty is to ascertain how far they really do go, to separate the phenomena from my interpretation of them, which experience has shown to be in many ways liable to error. Again, when I have clearly grasped the relations between the parts of a geometrical diagram, I can entertain no doubt concerning them. Yet before I had sufficiently considered them I might be uncertain, or even entertain a wrong conception of the geometrical relations and imagine it to be certainly right. No one knew better than Spinoza how easy it is to hold confused and erroneous beliefs with absolute confidence. Some of the current notions in philosophy and psychology which he makes the objects of his most unsparing attack are precisely those which have been most commonly maintained on the ground that they are principles given by consciousness as clear, ultimate, and self-evident.

At the same time there is no reason to doubt that Spinoza did underrate (as almost all constructive philosophers have underrated) the difficulty of ascertaining what the ultimate data of sense and thought really are; he nowhere undertakes the analysis of these data, nor does he separate it from the business of ascertaining concrete truth in particular cases. Descartes' own testimony is express that he thought the whole body of possible knowledge to lie, generally if not in detail, within a moderate compass, and to be deducible from principles which might be finally settled in a single generation, when once the problem of method was solved. Spinoza is not so explicit, but it seems probable that his expectations were of the same kind. For men in this sanguine frame of mind it was natural also to underrate the difficulty of procuring acceptance among mankind for the conceptions which to them appeared to shine with the light of evident and self-justifying truth. This kind of excessive hope, however, is capable of being dashed by experience in all but incorrigible visionaries; and while it appears, though not extravagantly, in the fragment 'De Intellectus Emendatione,' no sign of it is left in the 'Ethics.'

So far I have put the matter in my own way, to avoid the difficulties of Spinoza's vocabulary: but his use of the term *idea* calls for some consideration in this place, the point being too important for the understanding of Spinoza's psychology to be omitted or evaded. In the passage now before us[122] *idea* is a conscious state of the knowing mind, in which the object known is represented. This again may become the subject of another representation, and so on. 'The man Peter is an existing thing *(quid reale).* The *true idea* of Peter is the nature of Peter represented in thought *(essentia Petri obiectiva),* and is itself an existing object wholly distinct from Peter.'

This *idea of Peter* may then be the object of another idea which will contain by representation *(obiective)* all that the idea of Peter contains actually *(formaliter);* and again the idea thus formed of the idea of Peter has its own nature which may likewise be the object of another idea, and so on. Thus to know the *idea of Peter* is not a previous condition of knowing Peter himself; in other words, knowing that I know is not a condition of knowledge, but on the contrary the reflective knowledge is a consequence of the direct. And the certainty of knowledge is nothing else than the nature of the thing itself represented in thought; whence we see again that there is no ultimate mark of truth outside the truth itself.

So far, then, and as far as the treatise on the 'Amendment of the Understanding' goes, Spinoza's *idea* seems equivalent to what we now call a concept. But we shall find elsewhere that it has a wider significance. It always denotes a mode of thought considered as corresponding to an object, but the nature of the correspondence may be very different from that which is here dealt with. The most important case is that of the human mind, which is spoken of as the *idea* of the body associated with it. Now a man can easily think of his own body, but he is not always doing so, and when he does his thought will not be accurate unless he has learnt something of physiology. And even if every human being were an accomplished physiologist, the constant relation of the mind as a whole to the body as a whole would still be something different from the relation of the knowing to the known. The organic sensations which furnish the groundwork for a large part of our conscious life are not knowledge or concepts. But Spinoza makes use of the one term *idea* to denote the two kinds of relation, and we have to find out by the

---

[122] *De Int.* Em. c. 6, § 33.

context which he means.[123] If I think of Peter, the state of my consciousness is an *idea* of Peter according to Spinoza's first usage of the term. But according to his other usage, it is the *idea,* not of Peter, but of the corresponding state of my own brain and nerves, or such parts of them as are, in modern language, the organs of that particular phase of conscious thought. In the one sense the object of the idea is Peter, in the other it is the bodily organism correlated to the thinking mind. And it is important to observe that in this other sense *idea* has a far wider application than in the first and more familiar sense. The material correlate which is called the object of the idea may be a living organism, but also it may not. The idea may coincide with a concept in a conscious mind, or with a conscious mind forming concepts, but also it may not. Considering, for example, the whole material universe as the object, we have a corresponding *idea* which, whatever it may be, is not part of any human consciousness. In this sense, accordingly, there can be only one *idea* of any given object; in the former sense, in which *idea* was equivalent to concept, we might have a distinct and individual idea of the object in every finite mind capable of thinking about it.

Taking *idea* in the narrower sense of concept, it is obvious, as Spinoza points out, that the process denoted by it may be repeated on the idea itself; and this either in the conceiving mind itself or in another. When this takes place in the same mind, we have a thought thinking upon itself, or reflective knowledge. The mind's operation thus taking account of itself is in Spinoza's language *idea ideae.* Now Spinoza was firmly minded to hold fast the unity and continuity of mental processes. He would have nothing to do with separate faculties, much less with an ascending scale of them. When the mind knows itself, the knowing and the known are one and the same. In order to enforce this he carries over the term *idea ideae,* naturally framed, as we have seen, on his first sense of the word *idea,* to a new employment in the second sense. Reflective knowledge is *idea mentis* or *idea ideae* (where *idea* is the concept). The mind itself, as united with the body, is *idea corporis* (where *idea* = correlate in the world of

---

[123] The corresponding German term *Vorstellung* is capable of the same latitude. Hence we find the ambiguity of Spinoza's own language to some extent reproduced even by the best of his German expounders. Spinoza himself once calls attention to the distinction: *Eth.* 2, 17, schol.

thought). Spinoza tacitly substitutes correlate for concept in the interpretation of *idea ideae,* and concludes that the *idea mentis* is united with the mind as the mind is with the body. But the mind and the 'idea of the mind' are both modes of thought. If therefore they correspond exactly they must be one and the same thing; not the same thing under different aspects, as the mind and body, but the same thing under the same aspect, and identical to all intents.[124] The blending, logically not to be justified, of the two meanings of *idea,* seems to give us the key to some of the difficulties we must hereafter face in the 'Ethics.'

Spinoza goes on to say that the object of method is neither to find a special test of truth (which has been shown to be needless) nor the actual acquisition of knowledge, but the guidance of the search for knowledge. Method is 'nothing else than reflective knowledge or the *idea of an idea.*'[125] Now the reflective knowledge which has for its object the idea of the most perfect being is more excellent than any other. This idea, then, is the ultimate object of the mind's pursuit. Here, again, the two senses of *idea* are not separated. It is by no means evident that the mind's knowledge of its own operations is more or less perfect as knowledge by reason of those operations being concerned with a more or less perfect subject-matter. To make the assumption intelligible we have to suppose a correlation as well as a relation between the mind which knows in the first instance and the object which is known. What is meant by the idea of the most perfect being is not further explained in this place; except that true ideas in the mind should be produced from 'that which represents the origin and source of all nature,' as the reality of things is derived from that origin itself. Once more the two distinct conceptions of representation and correlation are thrown together under the term *idea.*

The road by which the human mind is to attain its goal is practically to be found in the knowledge of its own powers and of the order of nature. Were the true method once found and followed, advance would be certain. But it is in truth seldom found, by reason of men's prejudices, the toil and clearness of

---

[124] *Eth.* 2, 22.
[125] *De Int. Em.* c. 7, *ad fin. Cf.* Descartes, *Disc. de la Méthode,* part ii.; but the resemblance is not close.

thought needed for the work, and other causes. Even if the method, being found, were exhibited in action without any previous warning, it would probably fail to carry conviction: for it might well happen to lead to unexpected results, which men would be prone to reject without examination. It is therefore not reasonable to call for an immediate production of results to test the value of the method by. As for absolute sceptics, if any such there be, they are by their own showing beyond the pale of reasonable discourse. A man who will admit nothing cannot be certain even of his own doubt, although he cannot live without acting on a great number of assumptions as to the reality of himself and the world.

The inquiry, so far as it has gone, is now summed up. We have ascertained, firstly, what is the ultimate object of our search; secondly, through what kind of knowledge we may best attain perfection; thirdly, what course we must follow to think rightly from the beginning, or how we may enlarge our stock of 'true ideas.' To provide for this demand is the special task of method, and its problems are the following: —

1. To distinguish a true idea from all other conceptions, and restrain the mind from others:

2. To deliver rules whereby things unknown may be brought into knowledge according to this distinction:

3. To establish an order of inquiry whereby we may be saved useless labour:

4. And to arrive at the 'idea of the most perfect being,' as the surest way to the perfection of our method.

This may not look very promising at first sight to a student of modern science: especially the fourth canon of method has an air of hopelessly unpractical mysticism. But reflexion will alter this view. The first three rules are open, in our day at least, only to the objection that they savour of commonplace. Clearness of conception and avoidance of confused thought, a procedure step by step from the known to the unknown, and an arrangement of the whole work such that every step has its value, and no labour is spent in vain, are beyond question among the most essential conditions for the successful conduct of all scientific inquiry. Every one seriously concerned with the investigation of truth in philosophy, law, natural science, or the practical affairs of life, does in fact endeavour to fulfil those conditions in his own business, and the success of the body of his enterprise will be in proportion to his success in fulfilling them.

The fourth rule is in appearance a harder saying. But we have already seen that for Spinoza, attached by race and tradition to the Hebrew sentiment of a one and only supreme power, and by an intellectual passion to the pursuit of exact science, the perfection of God, conceived as the most perfect being, 'constant in all his works,' meant above all things unity and uniformity. Thus the 'idea of the most perfect being' includes, if it is not equivalent to, the belief that the whole nature of things is one and uniform. Now this is the very first principle of all science. The uniformity of the course of nature is that to which all lesser uniformities converge, and by which they are all supported. If we do not call it a law of nature, it is because there could be no laws of nature and no science without it. And Spinoza will have no exceptions from it. In knowing the 'most perfect being,' the mind also knows itself as part of the universal order and at one with it: therein finding, as we have to learn elsewhere, the secret of man's happiness and true freedom. What more Spinoza may have meant is doubtful: that he meant this much is certain. Such is not the mind of a dreamer of dogmatic dreams.

Spinoza proceeds to work out the several departments of method; an operation interesting to us not because it is more likely to lead any one to the actual discovery of truth than other expositions of the same kind, but because it throws light on Spinoza's theory of knowledge and helps to make us familiar with the conceptions afterwards more closely handled in the 'Ethics.' The first part of method was to distinguish true ideas from all others: the nature of fiction, error, and doubt, has therefore to be considered. Fiction or fancy in its most common shape deals with things considered as possible but undetermined. We make a supposition which we know or assume to be consistent in itself, but without knowing the facts on which its actual truth depends. An omniscient mind would be incapable of making suppositions of this kind;[126] nor can we make them as to matters of which we are certain. In another sense, however, we can imagine the con-

---

[126] Reading with Sigwart *eum* or *id* for *nos* in § 54, *ad init.* The correction had already been made by the contemporary Dutch translator: 'Hier uit volgt dat, zo' er enig God, of iets alweetend is, hy gantschelijk niets kan verdichten,' — *Nagelate Schriften,* p. 423.

trary of what is well known to us; for instance, that the sun goes round the earth. This is the mental representation of an erroneous idea which we may have ourselves formerly entertained, or which might be entertained by others. Again, we make suppositions contrary to our immediate perceptions; as that a candle burning before us is not burning. This is nothing but an effort of memory or abstraction; the recollection of unlighted candles we have seen, or the image of the candle before us apart from its flame. Spinoza gives in a note the important remark that the mind can really create nothing by way of 'fiction,' but can only recall and combine the elements already given in experience. We remember spoken words and a tree; and if attention is directed 'confusedly and without distinction' to these mental representations, we can form the notion of a tree speaking. As to the fictions which involve the nature of things apart from or in addition to particular facts, they depend simply on ignorance. The less we know of nature, the more absurdities can we accept from the workshop of unregulated fancy; such as talking trees, magic and apparitions, transformations of men into stones, and the like. On the whole, then, the mere fictions of the imagination are always confused, and will never impose on us if we trace out their consequences, which if they are absurd will show the absurdity of the assumption, or analyse them into elements so simple as to exclude that confused representation of several things at once which is the essence of baseless fancies.

Positive error *(idea falsa)*[127] is of the same nature as fiction, differing from it only in the addition of intellectual assent. The remedy is the same as in the last case, namely, the reduction of our ideas to a degree of simplicity that shall ensure their being clear and distinct. A perfectly simple idea cannot be false, provided we understand truth and falsehood in the sense which Spinoza now proceeds to explain. The truth or falsehood of an idea does not, in his view, depend so much on external things as upon the constitution and operation of the mind itself. An architect conceives in his mind a building of a new design, which may peradventure never be executed. If the plan is not repugnant to the laws of construction,[128] he has an *idea vera*. If a man makes a

---

[127] Cap. 9.
[128] 'Si quis faber *ordine* concepit,' &c. § 69.

reckless assertion without means of knowledge, his judgment is with regard to him not true, though it may turn out to be in accordance with fact. 'The affirmation that *Peter exists* is true only with regard to him who has assured knowledge of Peter's existence.' Again, even a fiction may be *idea vera* when it is used consistently and limited to the purpose for which it was made. Thus we may imagine a sphere to be generated by the revolution of a semicircle; and this conception, though we know that it does not correspond to any physical fact, is perfectly legitimate and true for the purpose of defining our conception of a sphere. If we took it as the statement of a physical event it would become false. So the mathematical ideas of imaginary quantities and loci, the circular points at infinity, and the like, are 'true ideas' in Spinoza's meaning, for they are consistently worked out and lead to intelligible results. Probably Spinoza would have said the same of the non-Euclidean systems of geometry which have been the subject of modern speculations. Truth, in short, is not the correspondence of the concept with an external object, but the result of the normal operation of the mind on elements given by clear and distinct conception. 'Error *(falsitas)* consists only in this, that somewhat is affirmed of a thing which is not contained in the concept we have formed of it; as motion or rest [*i.e.* as physical facts] of a semicircle.' When we make such an affirmation, 'it shows a defect in our conception, or that our thought or idea is as it were maimed and cut short.'[129]

Spinoza's definition of truth may seem to verge on paradox. But his estimate of the value of truth coincides with that which we derive both from common sense and from science. Not the bare possession of a fact, but the possession of it in connexion with other facts which enable us to make the right use of it, is the object we seek in every particular inquiry. Disjointed and accidental knowledge is for the most part little better than none, and may be even worse. On the other hand we may and constantly do use fictitious conceptions as the most convenient way of arriving at real results; and there is no harm in this if we confine the fiction to its proper use. Thus the corpuscular theory of

---

[129] *Cf.* Ep. 42, where Spinoza says even more positively that the chain of 'clear and distinct perceptions' is independent of external circumstances. See especially § 3.

light, though known to be false as a physical hypothesis, may still be used as a legitimate fiction in geometrical optics: and the language and conceptions of the Ptolemaic system are still employed in astronomy for many purposes. Even the formal part of Spinoza's exposition is less alien to our ways of thinking than it appears. When he makes truth consist, in the last resort, in the identity of ideas clearly seen to be equivalent, falsehood in the juxtaposition of incongruous ones, he is really on the same line of thought as more than one recent inquirer. The position becomes dogmatic only on the assumption that we have ideas antecedent to experience; but of such ideas Spinoza knows nothing. He does not dwell, it is true, on the practical necessity of testing our work, in all departments where it can be so tested, by fresh appeals to experience. But this belongs to the art of conducting research in the particular subject-matter, whatever it may be; and Spinoza does not profess to give rules extending so far. At the same time it is hardly open to doubt that Spinoza very much underrated the difficulty of making sure of 'clear and distinct ideas' at the outset. With all philosophers of all times down to his own, he supposed that the ultimate elements of things and of knowledge were comparatively few and simple; and that when the fundamental principles were once ascertained, everything could be explained by deduction from them with very little need for external verification. Previous inquirers, he says, have fallen into error by not understanding the first principles of the universe; 'whereby, proceeding without due order, and confounding the nature of things with rules which, though true, are abstract' — in modern language, by applying general rules or definitions without first ascertaining whether they were really applicable to the particular class of facts — 'they confound themselves and distort the order of nature.' He instances the materialism of the Stoics, who identified the soul with the subtlest kind of matter by mixing up a physical conception which was clear as far as it went with a confused notion of mind. 'But we,' he continues, 'if we proceed with as little abstraction as may be, and begin from first principles at the earliest possible point, that is, from the source and origin of nature, shall be free from all fear of such illusion.' The reason why the danger of abstractions disappears is that (as we are to learn hereafter) the idea of the first principle of nature is not and cannot be an abstraction. 'This is in fact a being single and infinite, that is, it is the whole of being, beside which no being is found.'[130]

This 'being single and infinite' is that which has been already proposed as the final object of all knowledge, the knowledge of it being man's only durable good. And we may fitly observe here the reason why the idea of this being is justly denied by Spinoza to be abstract. We may arrive at an abstract idea of being by forming more and more general notions which, as we proceed from one to another, shall comprise a greater number of subordinate kinds and individuals agreeing in fewer attributes; until at length we arrive at a bare notion of being in which no distinct attribute is left. This is the vanishing-point of logical classification, where there is no longer a handle for the dividing mind to lay hold of. But this abstraction is quite different from our conception of the sum of things as a whole, which is the conception not of a class or genus but of existing things, and is no more abstract than the conception of any object or assemblage of objects which cannot be directly presented to sense. To a certain extent this may be illustrated by simpler examples. We have the general name *army,* and a corresponding general or abstract idea. But the name of the British army, and the idea called up by it, stand for no abstraction, but for a certain real aggregate of men, together with their arms, horses, and various munitions of war, all which are definite existing things. In our idea of the British army as it exists at a given moment, as when the Mutiny Act for next year comes into operation, there is no abstraction at all. There is a sort of abstraction when we regard the army as a body which retains an historical and moral continuity notwithstanding the changes of men, material, and organization which are constantly taking place in it: but this, as may easily be seen, has no analogy in the course of nature as a whole. For changes of this kind are from without, or with regard to something outside the subject of change: but there is nothing outside the whole of nature. Now the idea of the whole of being, as Spinoza calls it, is the idea of the whole actual sum of existence and of all its consequences: and it differs from the abstract idea of being in the same way that our thought of the British army differs from our thought of an army in general, but in an even greater degree. It is

---

[130] Cap. 9, §§ 74-76.

not a vanishing conception which eludes the understanding by having no real contents, but it baffles the imagination because its contents are too rich and manifold to be grasped. And it has the singular property that no abstraction can be formed from it. The universe, as including everything, is manifestly *sui generis,* or rather above all genera and species: we cannot speak of this or that universe, for then it would be a universe no longer. But all this may so far seem to be mere trifling with words. For suppose we have an idea of the universe or whole sum of being, which, embracing as it does all particular existence, is necessarily single and all-containing, what then? Where is the mighty profit which, according to Spinoza, we are to derive from the contemplation of it? Nothing is more certain than that no man ever made or will make a discovery of any moment in art or science by dint of thinking on the nature of things at large. But it is no less an assured fact that discoveries are not made without belief in the nature of things, by which I mean the sure trust that under all diversity of appearances there is a certain and sufficient order, that there is no maze which has not somewhere a clue. Belief in the nature of things is the mainspring of all science and the condition of all sound thinking, unless there be some kind of sound thinking which diverges from sound reason. Now Spinoza's philosophy is the enthronement of reason, and it is this belief that he requires. The truth is that his idea of the sum and source of all being, or the most perfect being, in other words, of God, as he afterwards explained that name in the 'Ethics,' includes the idea of uniformity as ruling all events whatever, and this uniformity is regarded as inseparable from the unity of the only and all-embracing whole. 'Deus est summe constans in suis operibus.' The Mosaic conception of the one God of Israel wedded to the Lucretian conception, revived though with bated breath by Descartes, of the one and inflexible nature of things; such is the mood Spinoza would have us bring to the questioning of the world, such the majesty and gravity of nature in his eyes. Here we have no matter of verbal definitions, but a fundamental principle; and whoever would enter into Spinoza's mind must first feel himself at home in this the central point of Spinoza's philosophy.

Let us return for the present to the fragment on Method which is our text in this chapter. Having spoken of true and false ideas, Spinoza goes on to the nature of doubt, which can take place, he says, only in the case of ideas which are confused or imperfect. We know by past experience that error is possible, but have not the means of ascertaining or removing the possible sources of it in the particular case. Ignorant people are confident because they know nothing of their liability to mistake; thus a rustic stares and disbelieves when he is told that the sun is much bigger than a clod of earth. So that doubt may be said always to arise from our inquiries not being pursued in a due order. Here again there is the tacit assumption that it is possible to conform to an ideal type of order in every kind of investigation, so as to ensure demonstrative certainty for every step; in other words, that a general and infallible theory of method can be found.[131] What Spinoza says of memory in the next chapter is more fully repeated in the 'Ethics,' and may be here passed over: but his summary of the results thus far obtained is important. He dwells on the point that error has been shown to be a product not of the understanding but of the imagination.

'As to a true idea,' he proceeds, 'we have shown that it is simple or compounded of simple ideas; that it shows how and why something is or has become what it is; and that the effects of the object as represented in the mind correspond to the reality of the object itself.[132] Which was indeed the meaning of the ancients when they said that true knowledge proceeds from the cause to the effects; save that they never to my knowledge conceived, as we do here, the mind as acting conformably to fixed laws and like an immaterial automaton. Hence we have gained, so far as we might at the outset, the description of our understanding, and such a rule of true ideas as leaves us in no fear of confounding true things with false or feigned; neither shall we wonder why we understand sundry things that are in no wise subject to the imagination, while others are in the imagination which are wholly repugnant to the understanding, and others again agree therewith. For we know that the operations by which the works of imagination are produced have place according to laws of their own wholly diverse from those of the understanding, and that the mind, as regards the imagina-

---

[131] *De Int. Em.*, cap. 10.

[132] 'Quod ipsius effectus obiectivi in anima procedunt ad rationem formalitatis ipsius obiecti.' One might be tempted to read *affectus* for *effectus*. But *effectus obiectivi is* probably equivalent to the *ordo et connexio idearum* of *Eth.* 2, 7. As to 'automaton spirituale,' which occurs immediately below, *cf.* what Descartes says of the body in the Treatise of the Passions, §§ 6, 16.

tion, is in a merely passive condition. Whence it also appears how easily those may fall into great error who have not been careful to distinguish between the acts of imagination and of understanding.'

This distinction is one of the corner-stones of Spinoza's psychology: and the conception of knowledge as an activity of the mind — which, as we may remember, is not found in the early treatise 'Of God and Man' — is of hardly less importance in his mature work. He now applies his doctrine of the imagination to illustrate the fallacies of common language. The passage is remarkable,

'Since words belong to the imagination (that is to say, we form many notions according as the words expressing them are confusedly put together in the memory by reason of particular bodily conditions), we cannot doubt that words, no less than imagination, may be the source of many grievous errors, unless we are very watchful against them. Besides, they are framed after the fancy and capacity of the common sort, so that they are but signs of things as they are in the imagination, not as they are in the understanding. Which is evident from this, that on all such things as lie in understanding only and not in imagination they have fixed names that are oftentimes negative, as are *incorporeal, infinite,* and the like. Many other things which are in truth affirmative they express in negative terms, and conversely,[133] because in each case the contrary is far easier to be imagined: thus the names occurred in that easier form to the men who first framed them, and they used positive terms for negative ideas. There is much that we affirm and deny because the nature of language allows us so to do, and yet the nature of things doth not; so that, not knowing this last, we might well take falsehood for truth.'

Spinoza proceeds[134] to the second part of the doctrine of method, which prescribes as the ends to be sought, first the possession of clear and distinct ideas 'produced by the pure operation of the mind, not by casual bodily motions;' next the reduction of these to unity. For this purpose we must endeavour so to connect and order our ideas 'that our mind, so far as possi-

---

[133] The Latin here repeats instances of terms negative in form, but gives none of terms affirmative in form but negative in meaning. There seems to be some confusion or omission in the text. In the first sentence of the paragraph here translated, it is not clear whether the subject of *componuntur* is *verba* or *canceptus* I have assumed the former.

[134] Cap. 12.

ble, may represent in thought the reality of nature both as a whole and in its parts.' Finite things must be understood through their immediate causes; 'for the knowledge of an effect is in truth nothing else than acquiring a more perfect knowledge of the cause.' Hence it appears, adds Spinoza in a note, that we can understand no part of nature without at the same time increasing our knowledge of the first cause or God; in modern language, every true explanation of a particular fact gives us a particular piece of the single and universal order of nature, and thereby adds to our knowledge of that order. 'Therefore,' the text continues, 'so long as our business is inquiry concerning actual things, we may never form any conclusion from abstract notions; and we shall use exceeding care not to confound that which is only in the understanding with that which is in the thing itself.'

To appreciate the significance of this we must bear in mind that Spinoza was a thorough-going nominalist. And further on he says that our chief aim should be to acquire knowledge of particulars. Such an outspoken abjuration of all figments and preconceived notions might almost be expected to introduce without more ceremony an exhortation to practical observation. But Spinoza proceeds otherwise: he tells us that the best way is to work from the true definition of the thing investigated, and that the next problem is to fix the conditions of such a definition.

What he says on this topic[135] is very characteristic. 'A definition, if it is to be called *perfect,* must explain the very nature of the thing, and beware of using instead thereof only some of its properties.' He gives as an example the definition of a circle, which he chooses merely for convenience; a circle being, like all geometrical figures, an abstraction, so that it really matters not which of the possible definitions we take.[136] If we define a circle as a figure such that the radii from the centre to the circumference are equal, we get only a particular property of the circle, and have not accounted for the circle itself. And if we were dealing with a real thing this would be serious. The true definition of a created (which practically means finite[137]) thing

---

[135] Cap. 13.

[136] 'Figura non aliud quam determinatio, et determinatio negatio est.' Ep. 50, § 4. Modern readers, however, will have no difficulty in admitting that a circle or hyperbola is not a physically existing thing.

[137] Not exactly, for *res creata* here must = *modus* in the 'Ethics,' and

should satisfy two conditions. 1. It must include the immediate cause *(causa proxima)* of the thing. 2. It must be such that all the properties of the thing, so far as it is considered apart from everything else, can be deduced from it. In the case of the circle these conditions would be fulfilled by defining it as the figure described by the free extremity of a straight line whose other end is fixed. As to the definition of an uncreated thing, it must show that the thing is not explained by reference to anything outside itself, which Spinoza calls the exclusion of a cause; it must make the existence of the thing evident; the explanation must involve no abstract notions; and all the properties of the thing must be deducible from the definition, which however is not so material in this case.

All this is at first sight perplexing, and if we take the terms in their common meaning it is hardly intelligible. We have then to consider what Spinoza really meant by a definition, and what was the *causa proxima* which, wherever a cause is admissible, the definition must include. He requires of a definition, as it appears to me, a great deal more than logicians require; so much that it may fairly be suggested that what he calls a definition would now be called a scientific explanation. It is not merely an equation of names, but an equation of ideas corresponding to a constant relation between facts, and expressing the reduction of something unknown to terms of known elements. If this be so, the 'immediate cause' is the known condition or set of conditions in terms of which the unknown thing can be expressed. Definition is the same process, considered with regard to the observer's mind, which is explanation when we consider it with regard to the object. As the object is to our idea of it, so is explanation to definition; explanation resolves the given phenomenon into better known or more familiar elements of fact, definition resolves the idea of it into better known or more familiar elements of thought. On this view it is quite natural that where there is no real physical sequence, as in the case of geometrical figures, the *causa proxima* should be different as we approach the subject from one or another direction, and that, as Spinoza says, it should matter little which direction we take. The *causa proxima* of a circle, if we confine ourselves to pure ge-

---

Spinoza speaks of *infinite modes*.(See above, p. 122)

ometry, is the revolution of a straight line. But in analytical geometry it is otherwise. Although it is easy to show that this process will give a circle, the 'immediate cause' of a circle will not be any such graphical process, but the existence of a certain relation among the coefficients of the general equation of the second degree. For in analytical geometry the general notion of a curve of the second order is prior to that of any particular kind such as circle or ellipse: and from this general conception can be deduced not only the familiar geometrical properties of the circle, but others which are neither demonstrable nor intelligible except from the more general point of view.

We may also find more practical examples of that which (as I venture to suggest) Spinoza means to require in a definition. A chemical formula will give us a fairly good illustration. In this case the formula describes the thing exactly and in terms of its 'immediate cause,' namely, the elements by whose combination in definite proportions it is formed. And the definition itself leads to a scientific knowledge of the thing defined which is incomplete only by reason that our knowledge of the simple elements and of the dynamical laws according to which combination takes place is not complete. Or, to take another example from a science which is not physical, Savigny's definition of Agreement (*Vertrag)* as a legal term furnishes us with a perfect instance of what is sought by Spinoza. Most of the definitions found in our law books, and not least the definitions of Contract, are loose and unsatisfying. They are vague, insufficient, and redundant; they assume knowledge of other matters that have never been explained; they fail, in Spinoza's language, to expound the thing defined in terms of its *causa proxima.* But Savigny goes to the root of the matter and gives us a clear statement of the simple elements that make up the legal idea. His definition is accurate and exhaustive, and therefore fruitful. Or take, again, the minuter analysis by which the first chapter of the Indian Contract Act arrives at the more specific conception of contract. It builds up the *causa proxima* step by step in a series of elements, none of which, taken alone, would have any legal effect, but which combine to form the complex event whose legal significance is denoted by the technical term.

The last chapter of Spinoza's treatise now in hand, which however breaks off abruptly, shows that the way to a definition, as understood by him, was not to discuss the application of a word, but to consider what we know about the thing denoted by it. True it is that the greater part of the words and ideas in ordinary use are in the present state of our knowledge not capable of being defined at all in this sense. The definition of any 'natural kind,' to use J. S. Mill's term, would have to give us not only the specific characteristics of the kind in question, but their 'immediate cause,' in other words, to show how they come to be what they are: and it is barely conceivable that in this region of natural history we shall ever get beyond more or less probable conjecture. We have *verae causae* in natural selection, adaptation, and the like, but to assign the *proxima causa* of any existing type we should have to know exactly in what manner and proportions their effects took place in the particular instance. There is no reason to suppose, however, that Spinoza would have been afraid of saying that very few perfect definitions had been found or could be expected. The statement made earlier in the treatise (c. 4, § 22) that he had as yet been able to comprehend but very few things with the fourth or most perfect kind of knowledge, 'ubi res percipitur per solam suam essentiam vel per cognitionem suae proximae causae,' is indeed equivalent to this. I have little doubt that Spinoza believed his own definition of God, the sum and origin of all existence (to which we shall come afterwards) to satisfy the conditions here laid down by him; I am by no means sure that he did not consider it the only perfect definition attainable, except those of geometrical and other abstract conceptions, and possibly of the 'infinite modes.' It is impossible to see how his requirements can be strictly complied with in the case of any finite thing whatever: and it is equally impossible to suppose that he overlooked so manifest a difficulty.

Spinoza's next topic is 'the means of knowing eternal things.'[138] We must constantly derive our ideas, he says, from physical or really existing things, proceeding according to the series of causes from one really existent thing to another, and so as never to pass over into abstract and universal notions. So far there is not much difficulty in accepting his counsel; but we come upon an explanation which seems to unsettle everything. We are bidden to note that the series of causes and realities here

---

[138] Cap.14.

mentioned is not a series of particular and mutable things 'but only of constant and eternal ones.' It is beyond human powers to follow up the innumerable and complicated sequences of particular things: but it is also needless, for the actual train of events or 'order of existence' among finite things depends on external circumstances, and the 'very nature' *(intima essentia)* of things is to be sought in the 'constant and eternal things,' and the laws whereof those things are as it were the tables, and by which the course of all mutable things is governed. These 'constant and eternal' things are themselves particular *(singularia),* but, as they are present and operative everywhere, we must regard them as universal with regard to all mutable things, and as being the 'immediate causes' of all other particular existence.

What can these eternal things be? The interpretation that lies nearest at hand for a modern reader is to identify them with the constant relations among phenomena which we now call the laws of nature. But this is evidently not admissible. Spinoza, the downright enemy of abstractions and universals, knew the difference between relations and things far too well to confuse them in this way. Besides, he wanted no artificial way of describing laws of nature; the name was already familiar in his time, and he could speak of them, when he thought fit, just as we do. In fact, he does speak of the 'eternal things' as having laws of their own in some way attached to or involved in them, which pervade the whole world of phenomena. Clearly, therefore, the things in question are not themselves laws. Another explanation is offered by a writer who has done excellent work for the history of Spinoza's philosophical ideas, Professor Sigwart of Tübingen. He says with some confidence, on the strength of certain resemblances in language between our treatise and the 'Novum Organum,' that the 'eternal things' of Spinoza are identical with the Forms of Bacon's doctrine of Method. But surely this will not serve either. For the Baconian Forms are not things at all, certainly would not be recognized as such by Spinoza: and if we are to find a parallel in this treatise to what Bacon meant by the Form of a thing, it seems to me that it would be more hopefully sought in Spinoza's *causa proxima.* And Spinoza's nominalism, which we have always to bear in mind, is a sufficient warning against assuming that the 'eternal things' have anything to do with kinds, qualities, or classification.

My own opinion is perhaps too simple to be acceptable.[139] We have just found in the chapter treating of definition that Spinoza, for whatever reason, sometimes used general terms when his description was really meant to apply to very few instances or even to a solitary one. Accordingly we need not expect to find any great number of 'eternal things,' if we succeed in finding them at all. There would be nothing repugnant to Spinoza's habit of thought and discourse if there turned out to be very few of them. But when the illusory expectation of a large class of things, representing some such higher order of existence as the Platonic Ideas, is once done away with, the true solution presents itself, as I think, readily enough. The 'eternal things' are simply the 'infinite modes' which afterwards occur in the 'Ethics,' and which we have had occasion to mention in speaking of the influence exercised on Spinoza by the physical conceptions of Descartes.[140] These are, in the material world, in the first place Motion, which to a disciple of the Cartesian physics was a real, eternal, and constant thing; in the second place, as presupposing Motion, the material universe itself, taken as a sum of existence which is constant under all its changing aspects. In the world of thought we have, corresponding to Motion, a fact or process called 'infinite intellect;' what should answer in thought to the sum of material things, the 'facies totius universi,' we are not told.[141] We must also assume other corresponding facts without limit in other aspects of existence capable of being related to minds associated with them in ways analogous to the relation of the material universe to human thought; but these could be no part of human experience, nor imaginable by human faculties. This results from the theory of the Infinite Attributes, of which there is no mention in the present treatise.

The assertion that all particular things happen according

---

[139] It is not far removed from Trendelenburg's, *Histor. Beiträge zur Philosophie*, iii. 387. But he seems to identify Spinoza's 'eternal things' not with the infinite modes themselves, but with their laws or relations. See, too, Leibnitz's marginal note on this passage, ap. Foucher de Careil, *Leibniz, Descartes, et Spinoza*, p. 123. It consists of this list: *Deus, spatium,* materia, *motus,* potentia universi, intellectus agens, mundus. The words in italics are cancelled. The others, I suspect, were meant by Leibnitz, not for an interpretation of Spinoza, but for an improve, ment on him.

[140] P. 122, above.

[141] Ep. 66, *ad fin.*

to the laws of the 'eternal things' are on the view here taken equivalent, so far as concerns the material world, to saying that all physical events are ultimately explicable by dynamical laws. And to what could Spinoza more appropriately ascribe 'presence in all parts and unbounded operation' than to Matter and Motion? Again, a certain configuration of matter under dynamical conditions would be most naturally described in Spinoza's language as the *causa proxima* of every individual object.[142] But we are left without any farther light by Spinoza, for he goes into an auxiliary discussion of the nature and powers of the understanding: and with the chapter containing this the work breaks off. He enumerates the properties of the understanding, as the only practicable way of arriving at the full knowledge or definition of its nature. He speaks not of human understanding, but of the operations of human thought (nostras cogitationes) as depending on the nature of understanding in general: and I think there is room for more than a suspicion that the object of the definition which was never completed was to be not the human understanding as such, but 'intellectus absolute infinitus.' We shall here take note of only one of the propositions laid down as to the properties of intellect, which throws light on Spinoza's distinction between understanding and imagination, and is the first occasion of his using a phrase on which the difficulties of the last Part of the Ethics may in great measure be said to turn. 'It perceives things not so much under the head of duration, as *under a certain form of eternity* and without finite number; or rather it attends to the perception itself and not to number or duration. But when it imagines things, it perceives them as certain in number, and with a definite duration and quantity.'

This appears to mean that acts of pure intellect (such as the perception of a general truth in physics) are of universal validity and have no reference to particular events as such.

For example, the theoretical statement of the flight of a projectile in a resisting medium under the influence of gravity, and of the energy transferred to other bodies by its impact, is equally applicable at all times, everywhere, and to one or a thou-

---

[142] What Spinoza actually says, however, is that the 'fixa et aeterna' (instead of the particular configurations) are themselves the *causae proximae.* This is not exact, and the comparison of this passage with *Eth.* i. 28 goes to show that he afterwards perceived the inaccuracy.

sand experiences, assuming the laws of matter and motion to suffer no change. It is an affirmation 'sub quadam specie aeternitatis et numero infinito.' On the other hand the observation of the course and effects of a projectile in a particular experiment is the record of a specific event which happened at a given time and place, and otherwise under defined conditions: so much initial velocity, so much less at the end of successive seconds, so many foot-tons of striking energy, such and such fractures and displacements in the target. The facts are found 'sub certo numero, determinata duratione et quantitate.' I am not unconscious that interpretations of this kind are perilous; but I believe that the present one is near enough to the substance of Spinoza's meaning to be of some assistance until a better is found.

CHAPTER V

THE NATURE OF THINGS

Know in thyself and the world one selfsame soul:
Banish the dream that sunders the part from the whole.
ŚANKARA ÁCHÁRYA.

I am that which began;
Out of me the years roll;
Out of me God and man;
I am equal and whole;
God changes, and man, and the form of them bodily; I am the soul.
SWINBURNE, Hertha.

HAVING in foregoing chapters learnt to know something of Spinoza's habit of thought, we are now prepared to go up into the heart and citadel of his philosophy as we find it set forth in the 'Ethics.' I have endeavoured to make the philosopher himself in some measure smooth the reader's path to the difficulties of his great work: but it is not to be supposed that these difficulties can be wholly done away. Spinoza has cast his thought in singular and even startling forms, and we must be content to grapple with the form if we mean to grasp the substance. Yet it may not be useless to give at one's own risk a sort of free translation of the thought which, according to the view here taken of Spinoza's general purpose, may be apprehended as underlying the elaborate construction of his metaphysic. It seems to me that in modern language it may be rendered somewhat as follows.

Europe had for centuries been filled with the noise of scholastic discussion over questions incomprehensible to ordinary sense, of which the staple was furnished by such terms as *substance, attribute, essence, existence, eternity.* And these terms were the established stock in trade, as it were, not only of philosophical language but of philosophical thought. Such as they were, these were the tools with which Spinoza had to work. Even if he could have conceived the notion of discarding them altogether and inventing new ones, which however was in his circumstances not possible, it was only by keeping them in use that he had any prospect of inducing students of philosophy to listen to him. But the powerful and subtle minds which had exercised themselves on these ideas had troubled themselves but little as to their relation to actual things and man's knowledge of them. It was assumed that the foundations had been settled once for all, while the flood of new ideas, unseen and irresistible, was in truth advancing to break them up. The cunningly wrought structure of mediæval philosophy was doomed; and now that it has crumbled away philosophy goes houseless, though not despairing; for after all it is better to be a wanderer than to dwell in castles in the air.

But meanwhile what was a man in Spinoza's place to do? The terms were there to his hand, still the only currency of scholars; the ideas for which they had been framed were dead or dying, and the great scientific conception of the unity and uniformity of the world, often seen as in visions, but now unveiled in all its power by Descartes, had already begun to spread abroad, subduing everything to its dominion. A sincere and unflinching eye could already see that in the end nothing would escape from it, not even the most secret recesses of human thought. Only in the light of this conquering idea could the old words live, if they were to live at all. If any vital truth lay hidden in them from of old, it would thus be brought out and bear its due fruit; and what new life was wanting must be breathed into them through the new conception of the nature of things. This, I believe, was in effect the task Spinoza took upon himself. It cannot be maintained that it was altogether a possible one; and it is at least doubtful whether Spinoza himself was fully aware of its magnitude. I do not think he realized the extent of the revolution which was really involved in his use of philosophical terms. He seems to have been in perfect good faith shocked and surprised at the vehemence of the opposition excited by his opinions, though, from the point of view of the objectors, nothing could be more natural. He thought he was correcting erroneous interpretations when he was in truth abrogating the text. Thus we find almost everywhere in his work scientific and essentially modern thought clothed in the semblance of scholastic forms; and this creates for a modern reader an illusion which it is extremely difficult to shake off. It seems at first sight a mere paradox to say that Spinoza is not only more scientific than his predecessors, but, allowing for the unavoidable defects of his physical knowledge, as scientific as any modern philosopher whatever; that, so far from his metaphysical principles being repugnant or foreign to scientific thinking, it is just the thoroughly scientific cast of Spinoza's thought which has made his work a stumbling-block to the greater part of his readers; and that when he has been misunderstood, it has generally been because his interpreters have not had enough of scientific training or temper to understand him rightly. Nevertheless I hope to show that this apparent paradox is true.

In the exposition of his philosophy Spinoza follows a suggestion made by Descartes, and throws it into a highly artificial form borrowed from the usage of geometry. There is the same array of definitions, axioms, propositions, and corollaries, as in Euclid; and every step in the argument purports to be definitely warranted by something already demonstrated or claimed as self-evident. Only the diagrams are wanting to complete the external resemblance. Few readers will at the present time be found to doubt that this proceeding was on the whole unfortunate. It gives to Spinoza's work, in addition to its real difficulties, a needless air of abstruseness and technicality.

Probably many students have been thus frightened away before they had made any real acquaintance with his thought. The geometrical form of exposition has also led to much exaggerated language about the rigid consistency of Spinoza's system. Admirers have pushed their enthusiasm on this point into hyperbole, and critics, taking them at their word, have assumed that the whole system would be disposed of if they could succeed in picking holes in a few of the definitions. Again, critics have been misled in another way by the supposition that Spinoza's doctrines were intimately connected with the form in which they were stated; and no small ingenuity has been wasted on tracing his real or supposed mistakes to his reliance on the geometrical method. This oversight, though perhaps natural, might have been avoided by more careful consideration of Spinoza's other works, as we have already had occasion to point out. Lastly, it is very possible that in some ways this artificial mode of exposition had an unfavourable influence on Spinoza himself. I am disposed to think, in particular, that it materially disguised from him the nature and extent of the assumptions on which his work was really founded, and of the tacit appeals to experience contained in them. In geometry these appeals rest on a ground so broad and secure that, except for the higher geometry which involves discussion of the nature of geometrical truth itself, it does not matter whether they are recognized or not: but in philosophy it is otherwise.

It seems therefore not only permissible but desirable to depart considerably from the strict order of the original in the endeavour to give a generally intelligible outline of the 'Ethics.' But we cannot altogether leave the peculiar form out of sight: for much that is important and characteristic depends on Spinoza's use of particular expressions, which cannot be understood without reference to his definitions. And before we go farther it will be convenient to translate once for all the Definitions of the First Part. They are as follows: —

DEFINITIONS.

1. By *self-caused* (causa sui) I understand that of which the essence involves existence, that is, whose nature cannot be conceived otherwise than as existing.

2. A thing is called *finite in its kind,* which can be limited by another of the same nature. For example, a body is called finite, because we may always conceive another as greater. So a thought is limited by another thought. But a body is not limited by thought, nor a thought by body.

3. By *substance* I understand that which is in itself and is conceived by itself; that is, whose concept needs not the concept of another thing for it to be formed from.

4. By *attribute* I understand that which intellect perceives concerning Substance, as constituting the essence thereof.[143]

5. By *mode* I understand the affections of Substance, or that which is in somewhat else, through which also it is conceived.

6. By God I understand a being absolutely infinite, that is, Substance consisting of infinite attributes, whereof each one expresses eternal and infinite being.

Explanation. I say infinite absolutely, not in its own

---

[143] An earlier form of this definition is given in Ep. 27: 'I understand the same by *attribute*, except that it is called attribute with respect to the understanding, which attributes to substance such a determined nature as aforesaid.'

kind. For whatever is infinite only in its own kind may have infinite attributes denied of it; but if it is absolutely infinite, there belongs to its nature[144] whatever expresses reality, and involves no denial.

7. A thing is called *free*, which exists by the mere necessity of its own nature and is determined to action by itself alone: but *necessary* or rather *constrained,* if it is determined by something else to exist and operate in a certain determined manner.

8. By *eternity* I understand existence itself, so far as it is conceived to follow necessarily from the mere definition of the eternal thing.

Explanation. For such existence is conceived as an eternal truth, as well as the essence of the thing, and therefore cannot be explained in terms of duration or time, though its duration be conceived as without beginning or end.

Of these definitions the third, fourth, fifth, and sixth contain the fundamental ideas of Spinoza's metaphysic. The others may go without comment for the present except the first, which is remarkable rather for what it does not say than for what it says. Spinoza takes the current phrase *causa sui,* and defines it in a manner which leaves causation wholly out of account. In fact, his definition implies that the use of the word cause in this sense is really inappropriate: and except so far as we are left to assume the converse, namely, that everything which can 'be conceived otherwise than as existing' must, if it does exist, be said to be caused by something else, he does not tell us what he understands by the word Cause in any other use. In the axioms, indeed (ax. 4) he says 'the knowledge of an effect depends on the knowledge of the cause and involves it.' This must mean, if it is to give any acceptable sense, the knowledge of the effect *as such;* in that sense it is obviously true, but throws no direct light on Spinoza's conception of causation. Yet, when we couple it with the absence of any further definition, it does appear to suggest something very much at variance with the notions commonly formed about Spinoza's philosophy. This is that, so far from regarding causation as a kind of mysterious power which keeps together the order of nature, Spinoza regarded Cause and

---

[144] The Latin has *essentiam* in both places.

Effect as correlated terms framed by us to detach parts of the
order of nature from the whole for more convenient examination,
and nothing else. We know that he believed with an intense and
vivid belief in the continuity of all natural phenomena and processes. Several modern thinkers have independently come to the
conclusion that this same continuity does not suffer us to look
upon the notion of Cause and Effect as other than a convenient
artifice to keep our materials within manageable bounds. It is the
separation of that which is separable only in thought.[145] Spinoza
calls time and space, considered as measurable quantities, 'aids
of the imagination:' on this view causation would be an 'aid of
the imagination' too. But if we assume a real causal power or
nexus, the law of causation becomes the most universal law of
nature, prior even to that of uniformity; for we might conceive
the causal power to be universal but capricious in its operation.
Had Spinoza held this opinion, we might surely expect to find
causality prominent among the 'constant and eternal things'
which gave us some trouble to explain in the treatise on the
Amendment of the Understanding (p. 159 above). It would indeed hold a unique and supreme position among laws of nature
on Spinoza's system: for it would not only be universal in each
Attribute, but common to all the Attributes. But of all this there
is no hint, so far as I know, in any part of Spinoza's writings.

If the inference now suggested is correct, Spinoza would
have said that infinite intellect forms no idea of cause and effect,
except as being an idea present in finite minds.[146] For a mind
possessing infinite capacity and means of knowledge would perceive all things at once as being, and necessarily being, what
they are and not otherwise; but would not perceive the necessity
as distributed, so to speak, over the particular states and opera-

---

[145] G. H. Lewes, in *Problems of Life and Mind,* vol. ii.; Mr. Shadworth Hodgson, in his *Philosophy of Reflection,* 1878; *cf.* Mr. Carveth Read's
remarks in his *Essay on the Theory of Logic,* 1878; and see W. K. Clifford,
Aims and Instruments of Scientific Thought, in *Lectures and Essays,* Lond.
1879, vol. i. p. 149. *Cf.* also Trendelenburg's suggestion *(Histor, Beiträge,* iii.
275), that Causation in general (die abstracte Causalität) may be resolved into
the idea of Motion; Motion being considered as equally real on the subjective
and the objective side.

[146] The position suggested might be expressed in Spinoza's language
thus: 'In Dei infinito intellectu non dari obiective ideam causae singularis; sive
tantum eatenus dari, quatenus humanae mentis naturam constituit.'

tions of nature. To perceive things as necessary is to perceive them as they are, and the necessity of each thing is no other than the necessity of the universal order.[147] If it had occurred to any correspondent to put to Spinoza the particular question here proposed, we should possibly have had a decisive answer. As it is, we are left to conjecture, but not without probability to guide us. Spinoza does actually say that infinite intellect forms no general ideas. Therefore, in addition to what has been already said, there seems to be no alternative between holding that Spinoza regarded cause and effect as merely the machinery of finite conceptions, and that he thought causation as much a real thing as matter and motion.

What is it that Spinoza regards as 'self-caused' within the meaning of his first definition? The reply is given by the definition of Substance and by the chain of propositions formally showing that the two coincide. Substance is that which is 'in itself' or self-subsistent, and is conceived by or through itself, that is, without assuming anything else to exist.

In other words, it can be conceived as existing without any external reason for its existence. But we cannot seriously apply such a conception to anything short of the whole sum of being, within which we may seek for the reason of particular things, but outside which we cannot go. Explanation is of the relations between particular things; the universe in its entirety is inexplicable. And to say of the universe, in the scholastic language retained by Spinoza, that its essence involves existence, does not really import any greater assumption than that something does exist. It may indeed be asked what we mean by existence; and the question is not only a reasonable but an important one. But this way of considering the general problem of knowledge belongs to a later age than Spinoza's, and it is useless to complain of him for not having formally anticipated it. Anything, then, which is susceptible of explanation, derivation, or subordination to something outside it, is not Substance in Spinoza's meaning.

Attribute is that which is perceived as constituting the nature of Substance; and to understand Spinoza's view we must dismiss from our mind the common use of the term. If we think

---

[147] *Eth.* ii. 44.

of Spinoza's Substance as distinct from and underlying the Attributes, as being, so to speak, at the back of the Attributes and
guarded by them against any closer approach, we shall certainly
go wrong. Attribute is perceived, not as merely belonging to
Substance, but 'as constituting its nature.' Substance is indeed
manifested in the Attributes, but there is not an inaccessible reality behind the manifestations. The manifestations are themselves the reality; Substance consists of the attributes and has no
reality other than theirs. As for the suggestion that the perception
of the understanding in this respect may be illusory, in other
words that the reality of things is unknowable, it is one which
Spinoza was incapable of entertaining: it is wholly foreign to his
thought, and I submit that it ought so to be to all sound thinking.
This is not the place to enter on a general metaphysical discussion; but I may be permitted to say here shortly, by way of
clearing the ground, that to me it amounts to a contradiction in
terms to speak of 'unknowable existence' or 'unknowable reality' in an absolute sense. I cannot tell what existence means, if
not the possibility of being known or perceived. This position,
implicitly contained in Spinoza's definitions, was explicitly
taken up, and, as I venture to think, in the main conclusively established, by Berkeley. Since his time philosophy has done
something, and science much, to confirm his work. But I do not
know that the point will bear much labouring; it is too fundamental. One accepts it, or one does not, and the whole view of
the character and possibilities of metaphysic depends on this
primary decision. For the present, however, our chief concern is
not to defend Spinoza's conception, but to ascertain what it actually was. And I think there can hardly be a reasonable doubt that
for Spinoza to exist and to be intelligible were all one. Substance
is not an Unknowable, Noumenon, or *Ding an sich,* nor are the
Attributes forms imposed on it by the human mind. Yet, when
we have settled what the Attributes are not, there is no small difficulty in finding an unexceptionable term to describe what they
are. They are not forms of Substance, as we have seen; neither
are they operations or energies, for that also would make Substance prior to and distinct from them; and much less are we to
be misled by any false analogy to Neo-Platonic fancies of emanations and the like. The least unsatisfactory word I can suggest
is *aspect,* which has already been used by modern writers with

virtually the same meaning. Attribute, as Spinoza himself said in the earlier form of the definition, is Substance itself as known and identified by the understanding. The division of attributes, as far as human knowledge goes, is the ultimate division of experience into subjective and objective, or mental and material. We know a world of things extended in space, to the understanding of which, so far as we can understand them, the laws of matter and motion are our sole and sufficient guide. This is, in Spinoza's language, Substance perceived under the Attribute of Extension. Again, we know a world of thoughts, feelings, mental events, or however we may call its elements, to which the notions of space and extension are wholly inapplicable; we cannot ascribe mass to a sensation, or resolve a thought into atoms. And this is the domain of Substance perceived under the Attribute of Thought.

It is to be observed that, inasmuch as Attribute is defined by reference to intellect, and Thought is itself an attribute, Thought appears to be in a manner counted twice over. Likewise Extension and Thought, although they are the only Attributes we have anything to do with, are in Spinoza's view only two out of an infinite number. But the difficulties that arise on both these points are better postponed for a while.

As for the modes or affections of Substance, they are nothing else than particular things. Every material object is a mode of Extension, and every feeling is a mode of Thought. It will as a rule be found a help to the apprehension of Spinoza's meaning to read thing for mode; remembering that any aggregate whatever, within the limits of the same Attribute, may be taken as a single thing; and that this extends even to the whole material universe, and to the sum of all thought. The whole contents of any Attribute are regarded by Spinoza as an *infinite mode*. But his acceptance of motion as a real thing of constant quantity compelled him to regard Motion as an infinite Mode by itself, and more 'immediately produced by God,' or dependent on the very nature of the attribute of Extension, than Matter; since the sensible world, 'facies totius universi,' is not matter alone, but matter diversified by motion. This peculiarity has no sensible effect on the general bearings of Spinoza's philosophy.[148]

---

[148] The doctrine of the Infinite Modes is given in *Eth.* I. 21-23, but in

The definition of God as 'substance consisting of infinite attributes, whereof every one expresses eternal and infinite being,' brings us face to face with Spinoza's metaphysical imagination in the full extent of its daring. In the eleventh proposition of the First Part of the 'Ethics' he formally demonstrates that this 'absolutely perfect being' exists. Most people are content nowadays, when they set about explaining the nature of things, to assume that there is something to be explained; and if that were all, Spinoza's proof that the universe exists might be left aside as an historical curiosity. But there is more than one reason for dwelling on it. Spinoza follows in form, and even in language, the examples made familiar by theologians, and philosophers under theological influence or pressure, who had undertaken to prove the existence of a being apart from and above the universe. He does not simply break off from theological speculation and seek to establish philosophy on an independent footing; he seems intent on showing that theological speculation itself, when reason is once allowed free play, must at last purge itself of anthropomorphism and come round to the scientific view. Spinoza does not ignore theology, but provides an euthanasia for it; and there is every reason to believe that in so doing he faithfully reproduces the development of his system in his own mind. Hence his work has a peculiar fascination for liberal-minded theologians, and from the very first has excited the violent abhorrence of the more orthodox ones. There were similar grounds, as was remarked in our first chapter, for the exceeding bitterness of the opposition encountered by the 'Tractatus Theologico-Politicus.'

If Spinoza swallows up speculative theology in philosophy, he is equally determined not to confine the range of philosophical construction within the bounds of human experience. Rejecting the theological conception of the universe as created and governed by a magnified human despot, which indirectly makes man the measure of all things, Spinoza was not more willing to accept the contrary form of anthropomorphism which admits no reality of things outside what is known to ourselves. And he was determined withal not to give up the substance and reality of the knowledge we have in the search for some other

---

such general language that it would be unintelligible without the parallel passages in Ep. 66 and elsewhere. See p. 122, 161 above

imagined reality which might peradventure turn out a shadow. Thus encompassed with dangers, he escaped from them by a flight of speculation as daring and splendid as any that human intellect has achieved. The God of Spinoza is not merely Substance, but 'Substance consisting of infinite attributes.' The infinity of attributes is deduced from the perfection and reality of Substance. Perfection and reality are with Spinoza synonymous terms.[149] Whatever exists must exist as much as it can; and that whose nature is to exist, or which exists of itself, is under no possible restraint either internal or external which could set bounds to its existence. Therefore it will exist with infinite reality, in every possible way, and we must ascribe to it infinite attributes. The existent universe, though not the world accessible to a particular order of finite minds, must include every possible consequence of infinite being, and there is no real distinction between the actual and the possible.

Let us endeavour to put this in a shape more congenial to modern habits of thought. We know the world under the Attributes or aspects of extension and thought, and in each kind the sum of reality appears to be inexhaustible. Our world consists of modes of extension associated with modes of thought: the two orders of events being, as Spinoza sets forth later, strictly correlated and parallel. But we have no right to assume that this is the only world: for this would be to set bounds to infinite being. How can we tell what other aspects existence may not have to intelligence other than ours? We can conceive, though not imagine, relations of thought to other worlds analogous to those which we perceive between thought and extension. For all we can ever know there may be endless aspects of existence unimaginable to us. That which to the modern thinker appears as a speculative possibility, forbidding us to affirm that human knowledge is everything, appeared to Spinoza as a positive necessity, and he affirmed the infinity of Attributes as required by the perfection of Substance. Things must exist, not only after the manner in which they are manifested to us, but in every manner which infinite understanding can conceive. Yet that which we do perceive is not a part or fraction of the reality; for the Attributes unknown to us *express,* as Spinoza says, in infinite ways the very

---

[149] *Eth.* 2, def. 6.

same reality of things which we know, or may conceivably know, under the Attributes of Thought and Extension. In each Attribute the same order and sequence is repeated in the aspect or expression proper to that Attribute. Differing in kind, they are strictly homologous and parallel in form. A geometrical illustration may help us to understand Spinoza's conception. Let any one of the Attributes be likened to an infinite plane, and let figures be drawn all over the plane. The figures may then stand for the Modes, or particular things, comprised under that Attribute: and the whole plane itself, considered as a figured surface, will represent an infinite Mode. Now let us suppose an infinite number of other planes to be taken, and figures to be drawn on them similar and similarly situated to those drawn upon the first. Further, we suppose the figures to vary continuously, and the variations to be similar and correspondent in all the planes, so that at all times the configuration of all the planes is identical. Intelligent beings living on one of these planes and confined to two dimensions could have no imagination of any surface outside their plane, which however is to observers furnished with normal organs of sense in three dimensions only one plane arbitrarily selected out of an infinite number as the 'plane of the paper.' Yet such beings might conceive, though they could not imagine, the configurations of which they had experience as being repeated on infinite other planes inaccessible to their faculties. This is the sort of correspondence assumed by Spinoza to hold good between all the Attributes. But the illustration is imperfect in this, that there is no reason in the nature of the supposed case why the figures on different planes should not be dissimilar: whereas in Spinoza's view of the universe the corresponding modes in different attributes are not different things at all, but the same thing 'differently expressed.' Thus there is no room for divergence; there are not infinite and similar orders of things running parallel to one another, but one order in infinite manifestations. The order itself is the same in every aspect, somewhat as in the symbolical operations of mathematics the development of a function remains constant in form, whatever values we may give to the variables.

The parallelism of the Attributes includes as a particular case the exact correspondence of body and mind, to which the Cartesian school was already committed, though its founder tried to effect a compromise with prevailing notions by means of the doctrine of animal spirits: a doctrine which, as we have seen, was followed by Spinoza himself in his earlier essay 'Of God and Man.' By the time he wrote the 'Ethics' he was convinced that such a compromise was untenable; and there can be little doubt that his final and complete acceptance of the correlation of mind and body rested on grounds which we should now call scientific, the same in fact on which the most eminent of recent and living psychologists have come to the same conclusion. Hence, while the infinity of the Attributes was determined by a supposed necessity of speculation, the parallelism which constitutes the original and peculiar feature of this part of Spinoza's system appears to be an extension of the parallelism already fixed in Spinoza's view of the world of human experience as a necessity of scientific thought. It is to be observed that without this feature the Infinite Attributes would be a mere formless vision of unseen worlds, such as have abounded both before and since the time of Spinoza. So that even when Spinoza goes farthest in overleaping the bounds of experience, it is still the scientific element that gives consistence and definition to his work.

We may now see that although nothing outside Extension and Thought can affect human knowledge or impeach its reality, the Infinite Attributes are not merely ornamental. Spinoza's purpose is to keep a clear course between materialism on the one hand and subjective idealism on the other. He makes extension and thought equally real, and co-ordinate not only with one another but with infinite other aspects of existence. Thus the system is obviously not materialism.[150] It is no less remote from the subjective idealism which turns the universe into a phantom. It is proof even against the objections to which Berkeley's idealism is exposed. Professor Huxley, in his essay on Berkeley, supposes a piano to be conscious of sound and of nothing else. 'It would become acquainted with a system of nature entirely composed of sounds, and the laws of nature would be the laws of melody and of harmony;' and, having no conception of any other

---

[150] Except in the nomenclature of certain modern writers, who signify by *materialist* (as appears by their usage, though they do not give themselves the pains so to define it) any one who does not admit some dogma, generally that of free-will, affirmed by the particular writer to be essential to religion and morality.

sort of existence, it might reason thus: 'All my knowledge consists of sounds and the perception of the relation of sounds; now
the being of sound is to be heard; and it is inconceivable that the
existence of the sounds I know should depend upon any other
existence than that of the mind of a hearing being.' But we know
that the existence of these sounds requires, besides the mind of a
hearing being, the structure of wood and metal which makes the
visible and tangible piano, and a musician to play upon it.[151] So
that the Berkeleian piano would be mistaken, though by the hypothesis it could never have proof of its error. Now let us vary
the supposition and make it reason after Spinoza's manner. It
would then say something of this kind: Existence is manifest to
me in Thought and Sound: these are the Attributes under which I
perceive the reality of things, and each is infinite and perfectly
real in its own kind. But I may not assume that these are the only
possible aspects of existence, though they are the only ones that
fall within my apprehension. The fulness of things must be infinite in infinite kinds, and must be expressed in infinite ways besides these two of Thought and Sound. 'The auditory
consciousness of our speculative piano' would thus vindicate the
reality of its perceptions as far as they went, or the identity of
esse and *percipi* within the supposed limits of its faculties, and
yet its speculation would leave ample room for the existence of
the material piano, the musician, and the world in general. Substitute Extension for Sound in Professor Huxley's parable as thus
varied, and we have Spinoza's view of the relation of human
knowledge to the totality of existence.

The first remark on Spinoza's hypothesis that occurs to a
modern reader, being probably the last that would have occurred
to any of his contemporaries, is that by the nature of the case it is
incapable of verification. But perhaps that objection is not conclusive; for it is at least open to grave doubt whether any metaphysical hypothesis can be brought to this test, or can have, to
use the Kantian phrase, any other than a regulative value. Leaving this point aside, we have to see whether Spinoza's theory is
consistent in itself, and gives a consistent interpretation of our
actual experience. And, notwithstanding its apparent symmetry,
closer inspection shows that the difficulties are insuperable. Spi-

---

[151] *Critiques and Addresses*, p. 349.

noza found himself, indeed, unable to resolve the doubts propounded by Tschirnhausen, whose letters will compare very fa-
vourably with most of the modern criticism on the 'Ethics.' Man
is, as we know by all our experience, an extended and thinking
being, and nothing else. But, according to Spinoza, the reality of
everything is expressed in infinite ways. Mind and body are only
two expressions or aspects out of an infinite number: how then
do these two come to be exclusively associated? Why are the
other Attributes unknown to us? And are we to suppose those
Attributes to constitute other worlds perceived by finite creatures
who have no notion of Extension?[152] Such is the effect of
Tschirnhausen's first set of questions. The answer he received[153]
failed to satisfy him; and in truth it is not only obscure, but
seems to evade the main difficulty. Spinoza says that the human
mind knows only thought and extension, because it is nothing
else than a mode of thought associated with a particular body or
mode of extension (idea corporis actu existentis). But the difficulty is just to see how this dual association is to be reconciled
with the symmetrical co-ordination of all the Attributes.
Tschirnhausen returned, courteously but stoutly, to the attack.

'I well perceive,' he says, 'that in your system the universe is
one, and not many; but it is no less clear from the very passage to
which you refer me[154] that it is expressed in infinite ways, and therefore
that the being of every single thing is so expressed.

'Whence it seems to follow that though the modification constituting my mind and the modification constituting my body be one
and the same, yet that modification is expressed in infinite ways; once
under thought, again under extension, thirdly under an attribute of God
to me unknown, and so on to infinity; for the attributes of God are infinite, and the order and connexion of the modifications is, as I understand, the same in all. Hence arises this question: why the mind —
which embodies (repraesentat) a certain modification, which modification is expressed, not only in extension, but in infinite other ways —
why, I say, the mind perceives that modification only as expressed in
extension, (that is, the human body) and no other expression of it under
other attributes?'[155]

---

[152] Ep. 65.
[153] Ep. 66.
[154] Eth. ii. 7, schol.
[155] Ep. 67.

Spinoza's reply, apparently only a part of the letter in which it was given, is so brief that it may be translated in full.

'In answer to your objection I say that, although every particular thing is expressed in infinite ways in the infinite understanding of God, yet those infinite ideas whereby it is expressed cannot constitute one and the same mind of a particular thing, but constitute infinite minds; inasmuch as these infinite ideas have severally no connexion among themselves, as I have explained in the aforesaid scholium to Prop. 7, Part 2 of the Ethics, and appears from Prop. 10, Part 1. If you will sufficiently apply yourself to these, you will see that no difficulty remains.'[156]

Spinoza seems to say that every Mode of every Attribute other than Thought has a several mind or modification of thought to itself. Even the *intellectus absolute infinitus* appears to be manifold, so that each infinite mode of thought is appropriated to one Attribute only, and they are infinite in number. The result is that the modes of Thought are numerically equal to the modes of all the other Attributes together; in other words, Thought, instead of being co-equal with the infinity of other Attributes, is infinitely infinite, and has a pre-eminence which is nowhere explicitly accorded to it.[157] But if we go back to the definition we find that this pre-eminence has all the while been implied. For Attribute is '*that which understanding perceives concerning substance as constituting the essence thereof.*' Thus the ground is cut from under the apparent equality of the Attributes; and, though the system escapes the snares of subjective idealism, it does not escape idealism altogether. In order to judge Spinoza's attempt rightly, we must face the question whether such an escape was possible at all. If, as I think, his failure was due not to any want of philosophical power or ingenuity, but to the nature of the problem itself, it will be no mere exercise of historical curiosity to undertake a narrower scrutiny of his conception. Before we do this, one or two other difficulties may be mentioned. In a continuation of the correspondence already referred to, Tschirnhausen calls on Spinoza to show how the existence and variety of extended things is to be deduced *a priori* from the Attribute of

---

[156] Ep. 68.
[157] Cf. Erdmann, *Grundriss der Gesch. der Philosophie,* § 272, 5, 6 (vol. ii. pp. 55-61).

extension. It is not very clear whether Spinoza thought himself
bound to meet such a challenge or not; at all events he was not
ready with an answer.[158] If we regard his metaphysic as an attempt not only to interpret human experience as it is, but to demonstrate that it must be what it is, Tschirnhausen's question was,
as Trendelenburg says, a shot into the white. But it loses all significance if we treat the system as in truth resting on a foundation of empirical facts, and professing not to construct the world
a priori, but only to make the world intelligible. And this we are
entitled to do for our present purposes, though Spinoza himself
might hot have been content to accept such a limitation of his
aims. There are still, however, other stumbling-blocks. It is part
of Spinoza's theory that everything possible must actually exist;[159] and the objection that it ought all to exist at once, or else it
must be shown why one thing should exist before another, is not
adequately met by saying that duration in time is only a relative
conception in finite minds. The same principle has yet another
strange consequence. Spinoza had, of course, no suspicion that
the properties of Extension could be conceivably different from
those assumed in ordinary geometry, and verified in all our experience as far as verification has gone. But modern geometers
have shown that such differences are perfectly conceivable, and
that an indefinite number of consistent geometrical systems may
be framed with axioms contradicting in various ways those of
Euclid: and this in the range of three dimensions, without any
reference to the more knotty question whether space of more
than three dimensions is conceivable or not. So that a thorough-
going Spinozist, could such an one be found at the present day,
would have to believe that all conceivable geometries are realized in as many worlds of extension in three dimensions, presumably with varied dynamical laws to match; and if he believed
space of more than three dimensions to be conceivable, he would
also have to believe in infinite worlds of infinite dimensions as
actually existing. Besides all this, he would have to suppose corresponding modifications running through the infinite parallel
series of all the other Attributes. One may doubt if even the
boldest metaphysician of modern times, or the thinker most ea-

---

[158] Epp. 71, 72.
[159] *Eth.* i. 16.

ger to find room for the free play of a constructive philosophy untrammelled by the conditions of experience, would care to take upon himself such a burden of unseen worlds as this.

Let us now turn to the main point of Spinoza's implicit idealism. What is the conclusion to which it really points? What would Spinoza have done if he had not been unconsciously hampered by a remnant of Cartesian dualism? We have to observe that each Attribute is complete in itself: the possibility of mutual interference is rigorously excluded. The perception of things as extended is not a relation between the extended thing and the perceiving mind, for they are incommensurable. Every extended thing has its correlate in Thought, whether that correlate is part of a conscious mind or not; and when it is a perception in a conscious mind, the perception is a mode of Thought and nothing else. And the thing correlated to the perception is not the object perceived, but the organism of the perceiving subject. The series of *ideas* or modes of Thought is whole and continuous; no other Attribute has any part in it. How then can we say that Thought perceives Extension? or what ground have we for making Extension co-ordinate with Thought, and in some way, which nevertheless is not causation, necessary to its manifestations? Putting out of sight the supposed *a priori* necessity for an infinity of Attributes, let us assume Extension and all its modes to be blotted out of existence. Thought and its modes will by the hypothesis remain unaffected; every mental correlate of a material fact will be precisely what it was before; the psychical order of things, *ordo et connexio idearum,* will be unaltered. In other words, there will be no effect on the perceptions which take place in any mind, and though Extension be annihilated as an independent Attribute, no thinking being will miss it. The difference would be sensible only to an infinite intelligence placed as a spectator outside the universe and all its Attributes; but such an intelligence we are forbidden to suppose, for the universe can have nothing outside it. The same reasoning applies to all the other unknown Attributes. Hence all the Attributes except Thought are really superfluous: and Spinoza's doctrine, when thus reduced to its simplest terms, is that nothing exists but thought and its modifications. Feeling, or something commensurable with Feeling, is the only unit and measure of reality. The ultimate elements of thought are not merely correlated with the ultimate elements of things; they are the elements of things themselves. For, when the principle of continuity is once admitted, there is no need to assume any other. And this view, strange as it may seem at first sight, may be arrived at by divers ways. It may be reached even through the notion of a thing-in-itself or substratum of phenomena; and Kant was on the very point of thus reaching it, but left it aside. Accepting the alleged necessity for a substratum, noumenon, or whatever else it may be called, to support our phenomenal experience, we must admit that of the nature of this substratum, as it is in itself, we know nothing whatever. Therefore the substratum may as well be of the nature of mind as anything else. But mind is the one sort of real existence of which we have direct experience; it is that which is known in conscious feeling. And, seeing that a known kind of existence will satisfy the conditions required of the substratum, we have no occasion to postulate other unknown kinds. Indeed, the law of economy forbids us thus to multiply entities without need. Kant's authority, no doubt, is against this last conclusion; for he deliberately refused to proceed to it. His reasons, however, were not strictly scientific, as they are inseparable, historically if not formally, from his determination to reserve an inaccessible world of things-in-themselves as a field[160] for the exercise, assumed to be indispensable, of a Practical Reason whose demands could not be satisfied in the region of real knowledge. But Kant's own language on the subject is too important to be omitted: I give it accordingly in a free translation: —

'It has been proved that bodies are only phenomena of our outward sense, not things in themselves. Accordingly we may affirm that our thinking self is not bodily in this sense, that, being conceived as an object of the inner sense, it cannot, so far as it is a thinking thing, be an object of outward sense or a phenomenon in space. In other words, thinking things *as such* can never occur among outward phenomena; we can have no outward perception of their thoughts, consciousness, desires, &c.; for all this is the domain of the inward sense...

'But though extension, impenetrability, cohesion and motion, in short everything we obtain exclusively through the outward sense, cannot be or contain thought, feeling or the like, which in no case can be objects of outward perception; yet the *something* which underlies the

---

[160] Or might one say *playground*? *Spielraum,* at any rate, is an innocent term.

outward phenomena, and so affects our sense as to furnish it with the notions of space, matter, form, &c. — this something, I say, considered as noumenon, might well be the subject of thoughts, though we obtain from it through the outward sense no perception of ideas, will or the like, but only of space and its modifications. This something, whatever it be, has in itself none of the qualities of matter, such as extension, impenetrability and the like; for statements about these qualities are statements about our perceptions. But the qualities proper to the inner sense, namely, ideas and thought, may be ascribed to it without contradiction... Matter is complex as a phenomenon, but only as a phenomenon: and I am free to assume that it is in itself simple, and that the substance which to our outward sense is extended is in itself accompanied by thoughts capable of being represented in consciousness by an inward sense of its own. In this way the same thing that in one aspect is called bodily would in another be a thinking being, of which we could not perceive the thought, but could perceive the signs of it in the phenomenon. Then we should no longer say that only souls think, assuming soul to be a special kind of Substance; we should say, with common speech, that men think, in other words that *the same thing which as an outward phenomenon is extended is inwardly or in itself a Subject,* which is not composite, but which is simple and thinks.'[161]

Kant, however, threw out this hypothesis only for a special purpose, and did not pursue it. The closeness of the approach to Spinoza, of which Kant was probably not aware, is most striking; and the suggestion differs only in one point from the result which follows, as above pointed out, from developing the implicit idealism of Spinoza's theory of the Attributes. The difference is that Kant assumes the ideal or psychical thing-in-itself, or rather substitute for the thing-in-itself, to be a simple subject or monad. In Spinoza's system, on the other hand, as well as in the simplified form of it here proposed, the ultimate fact is not only represented, but adequately represented, by the phenomenon. The inward fact, or mode of thought, corresponds point for point with the outward fact, or mode of extension, and is complex in the same proportion. We must remember, however, that the inner and the outer world are not really different and parallel, but one and the same world under two aspects. This, indeed, is expressly and repeatedly stated by Spinoza. The process of criticism we have just gone through, supposing it to be legitimate,

[161] *Kritik der r. V.* 1st ed. *Kr. des zweiten Paralogismus der transsc. Psychologie*, pp. 287-8, Rosenkr., 304-6, Kehrbach (in *Universal-Bibliothek*).

does not affect the substantial and working value of Spinoza's metaphysic. The effect is only to strip it of brilliant but dangerous ornaments, and lay open the speculative ground on which it really stands. How Spinoza uses his metaphysical conception as a groundwork for psychology, and with what success, we shall see in due time.

Jacobi, who only half understood Spinoza, made the extraordinary statement that no man may profess to understand him so long as he finds a single line of the 'Ethics' obscure. The saying is one of those which produce a cheap effect by reckless disregard of the real difficulties. Lessing and Goethe knew better. And as to more recent philosophers and critics, it is hardly too much to say that no two of them have understood the metaphysical principles of the 'Ethics' in precisely the same manner. This being so, I am far from claiming or expecting general acceptance for the interpretation above given; I am content if I have made it intelligible. On the other hand the bearing of Spinoza's principles in their application to human nature is clear enough, and I do not know that his practical results have ever been found obscure except by those who were determined not to understand, though opinions differ as widely as possible as to their correctness and value. Whether the criticism of the purely speculative part be found interesting depends on one's belief or taste as to metaphysics in general. The reader who thinks metaphysics an impossibility or a useless luxury will probably have quitted me several pages back. For those who remain it may be worth while to sum up the criticism in a more technical form than I have yet allowed myself. Spinoza's Attributes are in effect defined as objects, or rather as objective worlds. But the general form of the definition disguises the all-important fact that the world of Thought, and that alone, is subjective and objective at once. The intellect which perceives an Attribute as 'constituting the essence of Substance,' itself belongs to the Attribute of Thought. Thus, if we push analysis further, we find that Thought swallows up all the other Attributes; for all conceivable Attributes turn out to be objective aspects of Thought itself. Spinoza does indeed return, but too late, to the double aspect of Thought:[162] and the formal part of his system remains a magnifi-

---

[162] *Eth.* ii. 20, 21, 43.

cent attempt at an impossible symmetry of the universe, in which thought vainly struggles to escape from its own fundamental conditions, and to conquer new worlds beyond the inexorable boundaries of experience.

It has been seen how great a part is played by infinity in the system; we have Attributes, infinite in number and in their several kinds, infinite Modes, and the like. It is evidently material to know what precise meaning was attached by Spinoza to the term. The explanation is partly given in the 'Ethics:' but we have to look chiefly to the letter to Dr. Meyer where, in answer to his friend's inquiries, Spinoza discusses the problem. He incidentally sets forth his view of other metaphysical conceptions which, though secondary and auxiliary, are of great importance. After a complimentary introduction Spinoza proceeds thus (Ep. 29): —

'The question of the infinite has always been considered very difficult, nay inexplicable, by those who have handled it, because they have not distinguished between that which is concluded to be infinite by its own nature, that is, by virtue of its definition, and that which is without limits by virtue not of its essence but of its cause' (in modern language, between that which cannot be conceived as finite, and that which as a matter of fact is indefinite in quantity); 'again they have not distinguished between a thing called infinite from having no limit, and a thing whose parts cannot be measured or expressed by any number, though a greatest and a least magnitude of the thing itself can be assigned; finally, because they have not distinguished between that which we can only understand but not imagine, and that which we can as well imagine as understand. Had they attended, I say, to these points, they would never have been overwhelmed by such a crowd of difficulties. For then they would have clearly understood what kind of infinite quantity is not capable of having or being divided into parts, and what without any contradiction is so. They would likewise have understood what kind of infinite may without any repugnance be greater than another infinite, and what kind may not be so conceived, as will plainly appear from what I shall presently say.'

He shortly recapitulates his technical use of the terms *substance, mode, eternity,* and *duration.* Duration, he says, is a term applicable only to the existence of particular things or modes. To substance belongs eternity, 'that is, infinite faculty (fruitionem) of existence or being.' When we consider the existence and duration of particular things with regard to those things only, and apart from the order of nature, we may freely conceive it as bounded, greater or less, and divided into parts, without in any way contradicting our conception of the thing. But eternity and substance cannot be conceived as limited: therefore if we seek to apply the conceptions of limit and measure to them the principal conception is already gone.

'Wherefore they talk idly, not to say madly, who think extended substance to be made up of parts or bodies really distinct from one another,... and all that heap of arguments with which philosophers commonly go about to show that extended substance is finite falls to pieces of itself. In the same case are others who, having persuaded themselves that a line is made up of points, have succeeded in finding many arguments to show that a line is not infinitely divisible.[163]

'Now if you ask why we are by nature so prone to treat extended substance as divisible, I answer, because quantity is conceived by us in two manners: to wit, by abstraction or superficially, as it is present to us in imagination through the senses, or in its quality of substance, which can be done only by the understanding. So that if we consider quantity as it is in the imagination (which is the common and easy way), it will be found divisible, finite, made up of parts, and manifold. But if we consider substance as it is in the understanding, and the thing is considered as it is in itself (*i.e.* as Substance; for only Substance is *in itself*) 'which is exceedingly difficult, then, as I have at former times sufficiently shown you, it will be found infinite, indivisible, and single.

'Again, from the fact that we can assign bounds to duration and quantity at our pleasure (that is, when we conceive quantity abstractedly, apart from Substance, and separate duration in our thought from the manner of its derivation from eternal things), there arise *time* and *measure;* time being conceived in order to determine duration, measure in order to determine quantity, so that we may most conveniently represent them in imagination. Then from the fact that we separate the affections of substance from substance itself and reduce them to classes for the like convenience of our imagination, there arises *number,* whereby we determine the same. Whence it is plainly to be seen that measure, time, and number are nothing else than ways of thinking, or rather of imagining.[164] Therefore it is no wonder that all

---

[163] Cf. *Eth.* i. 15, schol.

[164] Cf. *Cogit. Met.* part i. c. 1, § 4. 'Ad rem deinde explicandam etiam modos cogitandi habemus, determinando scilicet eam per comparationem ad aliam. Modi cogitandi quibus id efficimus vocantur *tempus, numerus, mensura,* et si quae adhuc alia sunt. Horum autem tempus inservit durationi explicandae, numerus quantitati discretae, mensura quantitati continuae:' and part ii. c. 4.

who have attempted to understand the course of, nature by means of notions of this kind, and those too ill understood, have so marvellously entangled themselves that at last they; could find no escape but by breaking all bounds and committing themselves to absurdities beyond measure.'

Hence the attempt to explain the ideas of substance, eternity, or the like, which belong purely to the understanding, by means of conceptions which are mere 'aids of the imagination,' is necessarily futile. It is like applying the intellectual tests of sanity and insanity to acts of pure imagination (nihilo plus agit quam si det operam ut sua imaginatione insaniat). Even finite things cannot be rightly understood if we confound their reality with these 'aids of the imagination.' For instance, if one confounds *duration* with measurable *time,* and goes about to divide it into parts, it is impossible to understand the lapse of time. To bring an hour to an end, half the hour must first pass, then half of the residue, then half of the next remainder, and so on without end:

'Wherefore many who are not used to distinguish abstractions from reality have made bold to assert that duration is compounded of instants, and so have fallen into Scylla in flying from Charybdis. For it is all one to compound duration out of instants and to make number by adding up noughts.'

We have here, it will be observed, Spinoza's answer to the standing puzzles as to the impossibility of motion, the difficulty of conceiving matter as either being or not being infinitely divisible, the contradictions implied in assuming time to have had or not to have had a beginning, and other catches of that sort. They are for the most part as old as philosophy itself. Some were brought into new prominence by Kant, who used them with extreme ingenuity to set an impassable barrier to the legitimate operations of human reason, and leave a world beyond the barrier, not accessible to reason and yet not inaccessible altogether. In our own time an elaborate misunderstanding of Kant has led to the waste of great powers on the invention of the so-called Philosophy of the Conditioned, which, having barely survived its inventor and first promoters, may be dismissed as past criticism.

Spinoza's meaning is clearly expressed, but in his own peculiar vocabulary, and it seems to call for a modern interpretation. The nature of things is really continuous; the further we push our inquiries the more we are compelled so to regard it. But in the common uses of life our imagination parcels it out for convenience. What we call *things* are persistent groups of our sensations and of relations between them: and the conception of a thing varies according to our knowledge and the purpose for which the conception is required. The identity and individuality of things is nothing but the persistence and similarity of relations, and is different as we take one or another set of relations. A living body is the same from day to day in one sense, not the same in another.

To common apprehension the common objects of sight and touch are unities complete in themselves and marked off from the rest of the world; they are conceived as whole until they are visibly divided. To the scientific apprehension they are composite structures built up of molecules, which again are built up of atoms. For common purposes and many scientific purposes we regard the internal parts of inanimate bodies as at rest; for other scientific purposes we regard them as in constant motion. If we take the separate things into which we have thus parcelled out the world, and try to reconstruct the unity of the world out of them, we shall naturally fail. For the unity was broken up in the act of imagining each thing as separate, and for the purpose of dealing with it separately. We cannot restore the unity without undoing the dividing work of the imagination.

As we divide the unity of the world materially by the conception of separate things, so we also divide it formally by those of measurable space and time. Extension is one and indivisible, but we measure out space by feet and inches, or by fractions of a millimetre, or by diameters of the earth's orbit, as may serve the matter in hand. Duration is continuous, but we first conceive time, as Newton said, to be something constantly and equably flowing, and then we take lengths of it, as it were, and mark them off into years, days, hours, and minutes. Number is involved in the possibility of things being conceived as separate.[165] If we perceive or conceive things and classes of things as

---

[165] Cf. *Cogit. Met.* part i. cap. 6, § 1: 'Nos autem dicimus *unitatem...* tantum modum cogitandi esse, quo rem ab aliis separamus, quae ipsi similes sunt, vel cum ipsa aliquo modo conveniunt.'

persistent, we can range them, in fact or in mental representation, side by side. And we find that they still persist, however we may alter the arrangement. As Sir James Stephen has excellently said, we are able to measure and count things because they stay to be measured and counted. We take matter occupying a definite part of space, and consider its motions and the transformations of energy therein involved apart from the general sum of matter and energy: in Spinoza's words, 'a modo, quo a rebus aeternis fluit,[166] separamus.'

That things do thus cohere and persist, so as to make measure and number possible, is a universal fact of experience; indeed there could be no experience without it. Why it should be so is an impracticable and barren inquiry (except so far as physical research may succeed in expressing the more complex properties of matter in terms of less complex ones), and Spinoza seems to pass it over. But he also seems to assume that it is not of the nature of understanding as such to perceive things by the 'aids of the imagination.' Extension, as we have seen, is for Spinoza only one of innumerable aspects of existence. Intelligences knowing Substance under other attributes would presumably have their own 'aids of the imagination,' corresponding to our spatial measurements. But we also find indications that existence and knowledge out of time were conceived by Spinoza as possible; in fact, he regards all scientific knowledge, the knowledge of things as necessary or 'sub specie aeternitatis,' as independent of time. Everything is eternal in its necessary aspect, or as part of the universal order, and the knowledge of it is eternal also. An unexpected use is made of this conception in the last part of the 'Ethics,' of which there is more to be said hereafter. In this point, I think, Spinoza was again striving to transcend experience. The knowledge that something is true at all times and in all places is not a knowledge out of time: for the act of knowing or feeling involves change, and change involves time. Without risking any transcendental proposition we may safely affirm that to the human mind, or to any mind similarly organized in the world we live in, existence out of time is not intelligible.

It is material to note that the 'aids of the imagination' are

---

[166] Res aeternae = infinite modes = in extension, Motion and Matter. See p.164, above

not represented by Spinoza as forms imposed by the mind upon things. They arise out of the relation between the reality of things and the finite mind which is unable to grasp it in imagination as an unbroken whole. Only the division and measuring is the work of the mind; that which we represent as divided and measured is perfectly real. We do not perceive things as extended in space because such is the constitution of our minds; we perceive them as extended because our bodies are extended, and we measure and divide extension for the purpose of comparing our perceptions. Thus Spinoza's doctrine of time and space cannot be called an anticipation of Kant's. He would never have admitted that the material world is extended only in respect of our perception. Kant assumes real existences which are unperceivable and unintelligible. Spinoza denies that any kind of existence is unintelligible, and also denies that the understanding makes existence what it is. The inner and outer aspects of the world are for him correlated, co-equal, and co-ordinate. Extension is made known to consciousness, Thought is made known in consciousness, but neither is derived from it. On the contrary, the conscious mind is a highly complex mode of thought, organized as the body, which is its outward aspect, is organized. Unorganized matter is correlated with proportionately simpler groupings of the ultimate elements of thought or feeling; and unorganized things are, in accordance with both common language and the inferences of science, regarded as unconscious. At the same time, thought being no less continuous than extension, or rather their continuity being the same, it is impossible to fix the point where life begins or leaves off. Why thought should become conscious and capable of reflexion when it attains a particular kind and degree of organized complexity is a question we have no means of answering, and Spinoza does not attempt to deal with it.

We are here partly anticipating Spinoza's psychology; but it may conduce to clearness to exhibit its principles in immediate connexion with their metaphysical foundation before we trace their application in the following chapter. It may also be permitted to anticipate the results so far as to observe that they show a remarkable coincidence with those of the modern English or empirical school. Spinoza starts from premises which are in appearance dogmatic and transcendental, and yet his conclusions are the same that have been independently reached by inquirers who acknowledged no source of knowledge but experience. At first sight the coincidence is perplexing, but it is not really very difficult to explain. The psychology of the 'Ethics' is founded in part on tacit assumptions of an empirical kind, in part on express ones which are in form universal and unqualified. But, in one way or another, much the same positions are assumed by Spinoza that are accepted by modern science and psychology as the basis of their work. And since a working hypothesis must be treated, so long as one works with it, as if it were absolutely true, there is no reason why the results and even the processes should not in great measure coincide. Thus we may well hold that all human knowledge is provisional, and yet receive as real additions to knowledge, and valid for practical purposes, doctrines arrived at and asserted in the first instance without any thought of such reservations.

NOTE TO CHAPTER V.

The doctrine of the Infinite Modes, one of the most difficult points in Spinoza's system, has been discussed piecemeal as it came up under one and another aspect. It may be useful to give a summary view of the results.

According to the explanation here proposed, the Infinite Modes are as follows: —

1. In Extension.

a. Motion, conceived after the Cartesian theory as a real thing and constant in quantity: 'quantity of motion' being the 'momentum' of modern usage.

b. The material universe or sum of extended things taken together as one Mode, 'facies totius universi.' This, being extension modified by motion and rest, is said to be produced by God not immediately but through the operation of motion ('mediantibus his primis,' Eth. i. 28, Schol.).

2. In Thought.

a. The sum of all the psychical facts or events corresponding to physical motion, 'intellectus absolute infinitus.'

b. There should be a sum of all particular modes of Thought taken as making up one Mode, to correspond to the 'facies totius universi.' But this is not specified by Spinoza. It might be the 'idea Dei in cogitatione' of Eth. i. 21, but there it seems not to be distinguished from 'intellectus absolute infinitus.'

We have then: —

	A.	Deus *(causa absolute proxima).*	
		Extensio.	Cogitatio.
Res aeternae seu modi infiniti (causae proximae)	B.	*Res a Deo immediate productae.*	
		Motus.	Intellectus absolute infinitus.
	B′.	*Modi qui et necessario et infiniti existunt, mediantibus his primis.*	
		Facies totius universi. (?)	Idea Dei in cogitatione.
	C.	*Res singulares quae finitae sunt.*	

There would also in theory be modes answering to these in each of the numerically infinite Attributes to us unknown.

This matter is fully and ably discussed by Ed. Böhmer

(Spinozana ii., *Zeitschr. für Philosophie u. philos. Kritik,* vol. 42, pp. 107-116, Halle 1863); his results agree to a considerable extent with mine, at which I had arrived before seeing his work. He takes Spinoza's 'facies totius universi' to cover Thought as well as Extension: a possible but, as it seems to me, not very probable interpretation.

CHAPTER VI.

BODY AND MIND.

Pensiti aver tu solo provvidenza,
  E 'l ciel, la terra, e l'altre cose belle,
  Le quali sprezzi tu, starsene senza?
Sciocco, d'onde se' nato tu? da quelle,
  Dunque ci è senno e Dio. Muta sentenza.
  Mal si contrasts a chi guida le stelle. — CAMPANELLA.

οὔτε βροτοῖς γέρας ἄλλο τι μεῖζον
οὔτε θεοῖς ἢ κοινὸν ἀεὶ νόμον ἐν δίκῃ ὑμνεῖν.

CLEANTHES, *Hymn to Zeus.*

OUR experience manifests to us a series of events in time. But we no sooner begin to reflect upon it than we find that the series is not single but double. We commonly speak of time and space as if they were on exactly the same footing; yet there is a distinction of some importance. Whatever happens in space can be perceived by several observers at once, so far as the conditions admit of their being conveniently placed. On the other hand, every one of us is aware of an immense number of events which can be perceived by nobody but himself, namely, his own thoughts and feelings. When I move my hand to write on this paper the motion can be seen by another person in the room full as well as by myself. The event is as much a part of his experience as of mine. But my will and sensations that accompany the act belong to me and to my experience alone. My companion can see my fingers on the pen, but he cannot feel the pressure which the pen exerts on them; he can follow the movements, but not the desires which direct them. He can form a notion of my feelings only by inference from what his own feelings have been in similar circumstances; immediate experience of them is wholly beyond his reach.

If we desire to use the word *unknowable,* we may find a harmless use for it by saying that the feelings of any one mind are in this sense unknowable for every other mind.

Each of us has a world of inner experience reserved to

himself alone, and a world of outer experience which he can share with other men. What is known by inward experience we call mind, or mental; what is known by outward experience is named matter, or material. Modern philosophers have stated the distinction in another form by the use of the terms Subject and Object. This has the advantage of fixing the attention upon the individual and incommunicable character of the mind's experience. The adjective derived from Subject, when taken in this technical sense, has passed into common use as an epithet for feelings or opinions resting on personal grounds, as distinguished from such as are due to causes found to operate in a similar way on great numbers of men under similar conditions. Its correlated term *objective* is not so familiar in England, but is freely used by German writers to denote absence of prejudice and distortion, faithfulness in reproduction, and the like. In this meaning it almost comes round to the earlier usage, where, as we have already seen in Spinoza's treatise on Method, a true idea is said to 'repeat objectively' the reality of the thing signified. Whether the terms have really done much good in philosophy is, I think, an open question. They have certainly led to much inelegance of language and some confusion of thought.

I have assumed that the division of Subject and Object is identical with that of Mind and Matter; but it may be needful to show cause for this, though it is in truth rather a matter of verbal definition than anything else. Let it be supposed that the two divisions do not coincide. Then Matter can be part of the Subject, or Mind part of the Object. The former is obviously impossible: for Matter, whatever it may be, is not part of my feeling. It is assumed to exist expressly as something outside my feeling. My own body and organs of sense belong to the objective world no less than any other bodies. Nor does it fare any better with the latter alternative. It is true I can reflect upon my own feelings, but that will not make them something outside me. Likewise I can think of other persons and their feelings; but that will not make their minds objects to me: for I think of their minds as trains of consciousness and feeling analogous to my own, but inaccessible to my direct knowledge. They are represented, in fact, as imaginary states of my own mind which it might assume under those other conditions which are actually present in the case of the other persons I think of. Therefore no part of Mind can be part of the Object. Thus we see that the division of individual experience by the conceptions of subject and object is the same which was applied to existence by the conceptions of mind and matter. Now this reasoning tends to show that the divisions are in themselves unsatisfactory. And we need not be surprised at it, having seen in the last chapter the metaphysical grounds for holding the ultimate distinction between mind and matter to be illusory.

The distinction in human experience is however quite real; and mankind, taking their experience as the measure of existence, have conceived the world of mind and the world of matter as two sharply defined regions set over against one another. But the same experience which suggested the division also shows us a constant connexion. The feelings which I cannot show to my fellow-man in any but a symbolic and representative manner, namely, by signs that he can interpret in terms of his own feelings, are paired with outward events which are parcel of our common experience. The gulf between the two worlds is bridged. How the bridge is possible is a problem which has exercised philosophers of all ages; and all their endeavours have failed so long as they have not perceived that the gulf itself is the creature of our own thought. It is an irrational and hopeless task to inquire how mind acts upon matter, or matter upon mind. We are trying to find a relation between things which have no common measure. The strength of an emotion cannot be expressed in foot-pounds, nor will our sensations of warmth help us to fix the mechanical equivalent of heat. Either we must give up the problem as a mystery, or we must invent another mystery to explain it, or we must say plainly that the common way of stating it is wrong, and that the distinction on which it is founded is wrong also.

The Cartesian school saw the difficulty, but still held to the conception of mind and matter as entities or substances distinct in themselves. The notion of mutual action was very nearly, but not quite, rejected by Descartes. He supposed a communication by means of the 'animal spirits,' the soul being able to change the direction though not the amount of their motion. His followers went further, and devised the theory of Occasional Causes, first propounded in its completeness by Arnold Geulinx. The correspondence of body and mind was kept up at every instant by a special operation of God's power. Material fire could have no effect of itself on the immaterial mind, but was the *occasion* of God's producing in the mind the sensations of light and heat. This was nothing else than postulating a perpetual miracle; and the Cartesians not only admitted as much, but made it a reason for recommending the opinion. Leibnitz put forward a simpler but not less arbitrary supposition. His famous doctrine of Pre-established Harmony, as applied to this particular question, likens mind and matter to two clocks constructed with absolute perfection of mechanism and set going at the same rate, so that, while each goes independently of the other, they keep exact time together. The metaphor of the two clocks is also found in Cartesian literature;[167] and we might perhaps liken the communication through the 'animal spirits' which is admitted in the earlier Cartesian theory to an electrical connexion such as is now sometimes used to regulate a distant clock by a standard timekeeper.

Spinoza's psychology takes the same view of the facts; but instead of seeking an artificial explanation for the correspondence of two such different things as body and mind, he boldly says that they are the same thing, and differ only as aspects. Their parallelism and mutual independence is thus not a mystery but an elementary fact. To ask why mind should correspond with matter is like asking why the convexity of a curve should answer to the concavity. Let us now proceed to consider Spinoza's work more in detail, giving to the reader who may not be acquainted with it the warning that the second part of the 'Ethics' is very difficult in form, and that many of the propositions become clear only by repeated consideration. The preliminaries however are less formidable in appearance than those of the first part, and we

---

[167] 'Sicut duobus horologiis rite inter se et ad solis cursum quadratis propter meram dependentiam qua utrumque ab eadem arte et simili industria constitutum est.' Editor's note to Geulincx's posthumous *Ethics* (ap. Bouillier, *Hist. de la Philosophic Cartésienne,* i. 305, 3rd ed.). With Leibnitz there is a universal harmony between the independent activities of the infinite monads or 'simple substances' which make up the sentient universe. Of this harmony the correspondence between the soul and the bodily organism is a particular case: *Monadologie,* §§ 78-81. 'Ce système fait que les corps agissent comme si (par impossible) il n'y avoit point d'âmes, et que les âmes agissent comme s'il n'y avoit point de corps, et que tous deux agissent comme si l'un influoit sur l'autre.' Leibnitz, like Spinoza, calls the mind a 'spiritual automaton.' *(Theodic.* § 403, and elsewhere.)

need not dwell much upon them. The specific assumptions as to the nature of man are simple appeals to common experience.[168] 'Man thinks;' 'we are aware of a particular body' — that is, each man is aware of his own body — 'as affected in many ways;' 'we are not aware, nor have we perceptions, of any individual things besides bodies and modes of thought.' Some further postulates are introduced at a later stage (after Prop. 13) concerning the composite nature of the human frame and the component parts themselves, and its powers of acting on and receiving impressions from external bodies.

The human mind, or man as a thinking being, is a mode of thought, and 'part of the infinite intellect of God' (Prop. 11, Coroll.). As such it must have its correlate or 'object' in extension; for the same reality of Substance is expressed in extension as in thought.[169] This object is nothing else than the human body, the existence of which is made known to us by our experience of its affections (Prop. 13). At this point occurs a note of great importance, the substance of which is best given in Spinoza's own words: —

'Hence we understand, not only that the human mind is united to the body, but what is to be understood by this union. But no one can understand this adequately or distinctly unless he first has adequate knowledge of the nature of our body. For the propositions hitherto established are very general, and apply no more to man than to all other individual things; which indeed are all endowed with mind, though in various degrees. For of every thing soever there is necessarily in God an idea, whereof God is the cause, in like manner as there is an idea of the human body: and thus whatever we have said of the idea of the human body must also be said of the idea of everything else. At the same time we cannot deny that ideas differ among themselves as their objects do' (the relations among modes of thought are parallel to those among the corresponding modes of extension) 'and that one is more excellent than another, and comprehends more reality; and therefore in order to determine wherein the human mind differs from others, and how it excels them, it is needful for us to know the nature of its object, that is,

---

[168] Spinoza himself attaches some importance to this: 'Omnia illa quae sumpsi postulata vix quicquam continent quod non constet experientia de qua nobis non licet dubitare.' — Prop. 17, Schol.

[169] Prop. 7. What becomes of the corresponding modes of the other Attributes? This difficulty, which is insoluble on Spinoza's principle of equal co-ordination, has already been discussed in the last chapter.

the human body. This however I cannot here explain, nor is it necessary for the purpose of my demonstration. But this much I will generally say, that the more any body surpasses others in its fitness for manifold actions or impressions, the more doth its mind surpass others in capacity for manifold perceptions; and the more the actions of a given body depend upon itself alone, and the less other bodies concur with it in its actions, the more capable is its mind of distinct understanding. Hence we can obtain knowledge of the excellence of one mind above others; and moreover see why we have but a very confused knowledge of our own body, and several other matters which I shall in the sequel deduce from these principles.'

There could not be a more distinct or positive declaration of the necessity that psychology, if it is to be a serious branch of scientific inquiry, should go hand in hand with physiology, and verify its results, as far as possible, by physiological observation. Persons who describe Spinoza as a mere dogmatic metaphysician have obviously never read as far as this Scholium. But to proceed to Spinoza's consequences. One of the first is that 'the idea constituting the human mind, as it is in itself, is not simple, but compounded of very many ideas.' For the human mind is the idea, or correlate in thought, of an extended body which is known to be very complex; and every part of the body must have its corresponding idea; so that the mind is composed of the ideas of the manifold parts that make up the body. In other words, the mind is complex precisely as the body is complex. Here at all events there is no metaphysical assumption in the popular sense of the term; nothing about a soul, or an Ego, or a simple substance, or an inward assurance of personality. We must complain of Spinoza, if we complain of him at all, for not being metaphysical enough. From this we are led on to the association of ideas, a topic in which Spinoza has anticipated not only the propositions laid down by modern psychologists, but the modern manner of handling them.

The perception of an external object is the state of mind corresponding to the modification of the bodily organism produced by that object. So long as that modification lasts, so long will the corresponding idea; in other words, the external body will be perceived or thought of as present. And this will be repeated if the parts of the organism concerned are again placed in the same disposition, whether by the presence of the same object or by any other accident. Hence we may imagine things as present when they are not. Here likewise it is observed that our notion of an external body is a function of our own organism, and has more to do with the nature of our own body than with that of the external one. Thus 'we understand what is the difference between that idea of Peter which constitutes the reality of Peter's own mind, and the idea of Peter which is in another man, say in Paul. For the former directly answers to (explicat) the reality of Peter's own body, and does not imply existence except while Peter exists; the latter *indicates rather the disposition of Paul's body than the nature of Peter,* and therefore while that disposition lasts Paul's mind, though Peter may not exist, will yet regard him as present to it.' Spinoza is fully conscious in this place of his double use of the overworked term *idea;* yet elsewhere, as we pointed out in a former chapter, he appears to mix up the two meanings; and in a later proposition (Part 2, Pr. 32) the verbal confusion reaches its climax. The proposition amounts to saying that every mental state is in one sense *true,* inasmuch as it really exists. But to return to the passage immediately before us: it is further noted that imagination is in itself not capable of error. If the mind imagines a non-existent thing as present, but also knows it not to exist, there is no error, but a pure activity of the imaginative power.[170] Again, 'if the human body has once been affected at the same time by two or more bodies, then when the mind afterwards imagines any one of them, it will thereupon remember the others also.'[171] This is the ground of memory and association. Memory is defined as 'An association (concatenatio) of ideas involving the nature of things outside the human body, which arises in the mind according to the order and association of the affections of the human body.'

'And hence we further understand why the mind should upon the thought of one thing fall into the thought of another thing which hath no likeness with the first. As for example, from thinking upon the word *pomum* a Roman will fall to thinking upon the fruit apple, which hath no likeness to that articulate sound, nor anything common with it, save that the man's body has often been affected by these two; that is, that the man often heard the word *pomum* when he saw the fruit itself; and thus every man will fall from one thought into another, as the habit

---

[170] Prop. 17, Schol'
[171] Prop. 18.

of each has ordered the images of things in his body. A soldier when he sees the footprints of a horse in sand will thereupon fall to thinking of a horseman, and thence into thoughts of warfare and the like. But a farmer will fall from thinking of the horse to thinking of ploughs, fields, and the like; and thus will every man fall into this or that course of thought, as he has been accustomed to join and associate the ideas of things in this or that manner.'

This contains, though only in outline, all the essentials of the modern doctrine on the subject.

The nature and limitations of human knowledge are then further discussed on the same psychological method. We know our own bodies only through our 'ideas of the affections wherewith the body is affected;' and we also have a reflective knowledge of these ideas, and this is the only knowledge which the mind has of itself.[172] Even in the most abstruse act of reflexion the mental operation is accompanied by the material series of changes in the organism; we cannot by any effort whatever transcend the organic conditions of thought, for they are the other side of thought itself. All our perceptions of external things consist in perceptions of our own body as modified by them; but this does not give us accurate knowledge of the constitution either of our own bodies or of the objects affecting them. For the things we actually perceive, whether due to the internal functions of our organism or to impressions on it from without, are but limited parts of extremely complex physical events extending far beyond our sentient organs. And on the whole, 'the human mind, whenever it perceives things after the common order of nature, has not an adequate knowledge either of itself or of its own body, or of external bodies, but only a confused and fragmentary one.' The mind is said to 'perceive things after the common order of nature' when its thoughts are determined by external circumstances, which with regard to the mind may be called accidental, and not by its own operation of reasoning.

Hence we have but a confused notion of the duration either of our own body or of external things, for this depends on the 'common order of nature;' and thus we regard all particular things as contingent and perishable; for to call a thing contingent

---

[172] *Eth.* ii. 19-23. As to Spinoza's pecular way of stating the doctrine of 'idea ideae,' cf. P. 173 above.

and perishable is as much as to say that we have no adequate knowledge of its duration. Error in general is explained as the privation of knowledge which accompanies inadequate or confused ideas.

'For example, men are mistaken in their opinion of their own freedom; which opinion consisteth only in this, that they are conscious of their own actions, and ignorant of the causes whereby they are determined. So that their idea of freedom is nothing else than their not knowing any cause of their actions. For when they say that human actions depend on the will, these are words for which they have no idea to answer them. What the will is, or how it moves the body, thereof they all know nothing; the pretensions of those who, feigning to know somewhat, devise houses and dwelling-places for the soul, are either ludicrous or disgusting.'[173]

Again, our visual impression of the sun's apparent distance is not altered by knowledge of the real distance. The error of the common sort is not in the visual impression itself, but in the ignorance that accompanies it. 'We imagine the sun as near us, not because we know not its true distance, but because the present affection of our body involves the nature of the sun only in so far as the same body is thereby affected.' It is to be observed that imagination here stands for the acquired interpretations of sensation which in ordinary adult perceptions are not distinguished from the sensation itself, but which really depend on the representation of many sensations experienced in the past and their various associations and consequences. The erroneous ideas in a finite mind, however are in themselves as necessary as the true ones, being part of the general order of nature. On the other hand there are ideas in the human mind which are necessarily adequate, namely ideas of those elements which are common to all perceptions, or, taking it from the objective side, to the human body and all bodies affecting it. 'Hence it follows that a mind will be fitted to perceive more things, and to perceive them adequately, as its body has more in common with other bodies:' in other words, the power of gaining knowledge from the outer world depends on the variety of the organs of sensation, and their adaptation to the physical influences by which they can be affected; a conclusion which must be admitted as very just,

---

[173] Prop. 35, Schol.

whatever we may think of Spinoza's way of demonstrating it. In
modern language, his position amounts to the now familiar
statement that sensation is a function of the organism as affected
by some external body. But the condition of the affected organism does not necessarily resemble the condition of the affected
body, except so far as they are both material systems in which
motion and transferences of energy are going on. Thus neither
our sensations nor the physical events in the organism immediately correlated with them can be said in any proper sense to resemble the external objects and events indicated by them.
Spinoza's argument seems to imply further that all men have an
adequate idea of matter and motion; for these are on his physical
principles the only constituents common to all bodies. This appears to be another consequence of the ambiguous use of the
word 'idea.' That which is feeling in itself, or to the inward
sense, would be to the outward sense, if it were accessible, a series of motions in a material organism. And motion, as such, is
everywhere the same, whether occurring in the organism or outside it. But this carries us no farther as to the correctness of the
information we derive from our senses concerning the outer
world, much less of the conceptions of matter and motion which
we may form by reflexion on our experience. Because my idea,
in the general sense of mental state, corresponds exactly to a series of physical events in my brain, it follows not that I shall
frame an adequate idea, in the sense of a consciously held conception, when I try to think what matter and motion are. All that
I can directly know is a state of my own feeling. It is only
through a long course of education and experiment that I can
interpret any such state in terms of other people's possible feelings, or, in other words, proceed from it to a statement about the
accompanying condition of my own organs or the dispositions of
external bodies determining that condition.

Spinoza, however, does not here explain what are the
notions common to all men, or the secondary maxims deducible
from them. He refers us for all this to another treatise, probably
the unfinished work on the Amendment of the Understanding, of
which an account has already been given, and he goes on to his
explanation of universals.[174] The limited resources of our organ-

---

[174] Prop. 40, Schol. 2.

ism permit us to form only a limited number of images. There is a point beyond which our senses become incapable of perceiving minute differences; the various organs of the human body, with all its delicacy of adaptation, are but rough instruments to observe the boundless variety of nature withal. We may observe in passing that Spinoza's statement, which is here partly modernized in form, is confirmed to the full by the results of modern physiology. The overlapping and confusion of many similar perceptions and the representations of them beget our generic or so-called universal notions. We have seen, for example, a great number of human beings in the course of life, and cannot remember all the differences of stature, complexion, features, and other matters. Every one carries a strong though not very distinct impression of the points in which all or most of the several perceptions have agreed, and the aggregate of these is called by the generic name of *man*. Thus one man's general ideas are not exactly like another's; they depend in each case on the individual's aptitude for perceiving and remembering this or that common feature in a multitude of objects. The crystallographer's idea of *diamond* is different from the chemist's, and that again from the jeweller's.

'Those who have often admired the stature of men understand by the name of *man* an animal of upright stature; while those who are accustomed to consider some other attribute will form some other general imagination of men, as, that man is an animal capable of laughter, two-legged, without feathers, or rational; and thus in other cases every one will form universal images of things after the habit of his body. Wherefore it is no wonder that so many controversies have arisen among philosophers, who have been minded to explain things as they are in nature by mere images of things.'[175]

This leads to a classification of knowledge in three degrees. The first is opinion or imagination, proceeding from one's own confused experience or the report of others. In this class are now included the first and second kinds of knowledge which we met with in the treatise on the Amendment of the Understanding (p. 139 above).

The second or reasonable kind is obtained by the posses-

---

[175] Prop. 40, Schol. 1. Compare Mr. F. Galton's recent paper on 'Generic Images,' *Nineteenth Century,* July 1879.

sion of common notions (which are necessarily adequate) and adequate ideas of particular properties of things.

The third, or intuitive kind, 'proceeds from an adequate idea of the absolute nature of some attribute of God to an adequate knowledge of the nature of things.' Our immediate perception that 6 is to 3 as 2 to 1 is given as an instance of it; but the formidable language of the general statement is not otherwise explained.

Knowledge of the first kind is precarious; the second and third kinds are certain, and are our only means of distinguishing truth from error. Then comes the proposition as to the ultimate test of truth which we have cited in a foregoing chapter (p. 141).

The rest of the second Part of the Ethics is mainly devoted to working out the theory of determinism. 'It is of the nature of reason to consider things not as contingent, but as necessary:'[176] it is the work of the imagination to regard them as contingent, and our notion of contingency arises from the confusion of many associations, in somewhat the same way that general notions arise from the confused impression of many particular experiences. Let a child on a given day see Peter in the morning, Paul at noon, and Simon in the evening; then at the beginning of the next day he will expect the day to run its course, and will also expect, if nothing occurs to counteract it, the sight of Peter, Paul, and Simon to be repeated in the same order; and the expectation will be strengthened by repetition of the experience. But if one evening James comes instead of Simon, the next morning's expectations of evening will bring with it conflicting images of Simon and James.

'For the boy is assumed to have seen at eventide only one or the other of them, not both together. With the coming eventide he will imagine now the one, now the other; that is, he will imagine neither of them as certainly, but both as contingently about to be present. Moreover the wavering of the imagination will be the same if it is an imagination of things which we consider in the same manner with reference to time past or present, and accordingly we may equally regard things as contingent, whether they be referred to a time present, past, or future.'

This passage suggests that determinists may turn the ta-

---

[176] Prop. 44.

bles on the maintainers of free-will in its popular sense of causeless choice by their own favourite device of an appeal to the common use of language. It is said that determinism reduces to an absurdity our ordinary feelings and forms of speech with regard to future events: but it is overlooked that we habitually apply the very same feelings or forms of speech to events which at the time are unquestionably determined. Nay, we may believe or positively know that they are determined, so long as we do not know which of the conceivable determinations is the one that has occurred. While we await the disclosure of a parliamentary division list, the result of an examination, the return of casualties in an action, the account of a friend's arrival in a distant country, or a hundred other things no less easily called to mind, our emotions of curiosity, hope, and fear are but little allayed by the thought that the matter itself is already decided; for the source of those emotions is not in the facts but in our ignorance of them, and we wonder, speculate, and form provisional imaginations of what we shall do in this or that event, just as if the event were still in the future. In familiar language we do not hesitate to couple hope or fear with the present and even the past tense. 'I hope you have enjoyed yourself;' 'I fear you have got wet:' it were mere pedantry to replace these by more accurate phrases. Again, the historian who investigates the actions and motives of men in the transactions of a past made obscure by distance, by the conflict of evidence, by the flattering or violence of partisans, or by the machinations of wrongdoers, is constantly driven to deal in surmise, contingency, and conjecture. Probably, he will say, this was the course of events; this was perhaps the reason for such or such a singular action; possibly this commonly received account is true, notwithstanding the difficulties attaching to it; now and then he will confess (unless he is a historian of the confident sort, who has a complete explanation for everything) that with his existing means of information he can only suspend his judgment. All statements of this kind are statements about our imperfect knowledge of matters which in truth have been settled once for all. The fact that events happened somehow and are past we know; the manner of it we do not know. Yet we constantly speak of them as uncertain, finding it useful and indeed necessary to do so. We say, for example, that Alcibiades was possibly concerned in the mutilation of the Hermæ, though it is most certain that either he was or he was not.

There does not appear to be anything in the nature of reason or of language that should compel one to suppose the notion of contingency as regards future events to be anything else than what it undoubtedly is as regards past and present events; that is to say, a fiction imposed on us by our limited means of knowledge. We hope and fear, not because the events are uncertain, but because we are uncertain; nor would a general belief that future events are as certain as past ones, at least if intelligently held, alter the expectations or conduct of mankind for any practical purpose. Assuredly it does not lead to the indifference of fatalism: for a little consideration will show that fatalism consists, not in believing all events to be the definite results of definite conditions, but in holding that the course of events is overruled by an arbitrary power which so constantly baffles all man's forethought as to make it not worth while to take thought for the future. Philosophical determinism is the opposite of this. The determinist holds, in accordance with common experience, that the deliberate action of men is among the conditions that shape the course of events, and is often the most important condition. If particular men or societies are foolish enough to think that their own acts or omissions count for nothing, that is a condition too, and its results will be greatly to their disadvantage. Determinism, in short, if only one applies it thoroughly, leaves all the common uses of life exactly where they were. For my own part, I hold that the choice I exercise in writing these lines is determined and in nowise arbitrary. But the sense of power involved in the conscious exercise of choice is none the less pleasurable for that. The schoolboy who runs, leaps, or swims knows mighty little of the complex mechanism that governs every action of his body. For all that English schoolboys could learn from their appointed teachers till within a few years past, he might fancy that his will acted immediately on his hands and feet. The student of riper years who seeks recreation in active exercise well knows that this is not so. He is aware that he cannot lift his foot from the ground, or adjust the balance of his oar, or shift the grasp of his ice-axe, without calling into play an apparatus exceeding in its intricate variety the staff and transport of a modern army. He knows that innumerable parts must work harmoniously together in their several functions to produce the desired motion.

Yet the physical delight of putting forth strength or skill is no less in the man than in the boy. This, as regards the body, is matter of common observation. I know not why it should be otherwise in the mind. But perhaps a much shorter answer should sufficiently meet the common objection that determinism robs life of its interest; for it is the experience of a reasonable number of persons who hold the doctrine, and who are not less competent than other men to bear witness to their own feelings, that it does nothing of the sort. In any case, it is time to return to Spinoza's own exposition.

The mind, he says, is a particular and determined mode of thought, and as such can have no absolute or unconditioned power of volition. Its state at a given moment, to whatever so-called faculty we may refer it, is the effect of some definite cause, which itself is the effect of a preceding cause, and so on without end.[177] The supposed faculties of the mind, and the will among them, are abstract terms having a merely verbal existence. 'Understanding and will have the same relation to this and that idea, or this and that volition, as *lapideity* to this and that stone, or *man* to Peter and Paul.' Spinoza does not mean to say that the desire which begets will is not a real and individual fact. How he treats desire we shall see later; here he explains that he distinguishes will from desire, and regards it as, in the abstract, a faculty, or, in the concrete, an act of affirmation or negation, or, as we should now say, of judgment. This appears to a modern reader to be a needless complication of his case. It is coupled with the doctrine that every idea involves a judgment,[178] which, if we take *idea* in Spinoza's larger sense as including all states of consciousness, is a paradox, and if we take *idea* in the restricted sense of conception, still remains difficult of digestion. Spinoza gives the affirmation that the angles of a triangle are together equal to two right angles as an example of a volition. Most people would deny that there is any volition concerned in such a judgment. What is implied in Spinoza's choice of such an example is that in his view the mind is quite as active in the formation of a necessary inference as in fixing on one conclusion or course of action out of several which may appear plausible. And who-

---

[177] *Eth.* ii. 48.
[178] Prop. 49, and Schol.

ever admits this cannot well refuse the corollary that 'will and understanding are one and the same.' In like manner perception is inseparable from judgment: to perceive a winged horse is to affirm that a horse has wings. So long as a winged horse or any-thing else is present to the imagination, and no other perception is present which contradicts its reality, we shall believe in the real existence of the object. This is the common experience of dreams, when the imagination is active and unchecked. And thus, if the objection is made that will differs in nature from un-derstanding, because we have it in our free choice to suspend our judgment whether we shall or shall not assent to a given percep-tion as corresponding to reality, the answer is that what we call suspense of judgment is our consciousness that the given per-ception is inadequate; in other words, it is itself a perception and belongs to the intellect. All this, it must be confessed, is a rather barren discussion, and at this day serves chiefly to show with what poverty of language, both in extent and in definition, psy-chology had to labour in Spinoza's time. But the manner in which he explains the strength of the common notions as to the relation of mind and body, of which the popular doctrine of free-will is really parcel, is of lasting interest. It occurs in a later place,[179] but it will be convenient to translate part of it here. Af-ter giving as a separate proposition the doctrine that the body can give rise to no operation of thought in the mind, nor the mind to any phenomenon of motion or otherwise in the body, he pro-ceeds to the difficulties of common sense on the subject: —

'I scarce believe, until I shall have assured myself of it by ex-perience, that men can be brought to consider this matter impartially: so firmly are they persuaded that 'tis from the mere decree of the mind that their bodies now move, now are at rest, and perform much else that flows from the pure will and faculty of invention in the mind. Certainly no man hath yet determined what are the powers of the body: I mean that none has yet learnt from experience what the body may perform by mere laws of nature, considering it only as a material thing, and what it cannot do without the mind's determination of it. For nobody has known as yet the frame of the body so thoroughly as to explain all its operations; not to say that in brutes much is noted which doth far sur-pass human cunning, and that men walking in their sleep often perform, so sleeping, that which they would never dare waking; which is proof

---

[179] *Eth.* iii. 2, Schol.

enough that the body may, merely by the laws of its own constitution, do much that its own mind is amazed at. Again, there is none can tell how and in what manner the mind moves the body, what measure of motion it can impart to it, or with what velocity.'

To say, therefore, that a particular action of the body is caused by the mind is only a grudging confession of ignorance as to its real cause. As for the appeal to common experience, it cuts both ways. If the body is helpless without the mind, so is the mind subject to be disabled by sleep, and otherwise limited in its operation by bodily conditions. If it be said that the existence of material works of art, such as houses, pictures, and statues, is inexplicable on the supposition that the human body is governed only by the physical laws of its constitution, and that the body could never perform such feats if it were not guided by the mind; the answer is, as before, that the objector knows not what the powers of the body really are. Moreover, the human body itself is infinitely more artificial than any work of human art. Men say they have experience that it is in the absolute power of the mind either to speak or to keep silence, and the like; to which Spinoza replies that if it were indeed as much in man's power to be silent as to speak, the world would be much happier. The argument is a little more fully illustrated in a letter (Ep. 62), which is partly identical with the passage in hand.

'I call a thing *free* if it exists and acts merely from the necessary laws of its own nature, but *constrained* if it is determined by something else to exist and act in a certain determinate way. Thus God exists necessarily, and yet freely, because he exists by the necessity of his own nature alone. So God freely understands himself and everything else, because it follows solely from the necessity of his own nature that he must understand everything. You see then that I make freedom consist not in a free decision of the will, but in free necessity...

'Imagine, if you can, that a stone, while its motion continues, is conscious, and knows that so far as it can it endeavours to persist in its motion. This stone, since it is conscious only of its own endeavour and deeply interested therein *(minime indifferens)*, will believe that it is perfectly free and continues in motion for no other reason than that it so wills. Now such is this freedom of man's will which every one boasts of possessing, and which consists only in this, that men are aware of their own desires and ignorant of the causes by which those desires are determined. So an infant thinks his appetite for milk is free; so a child in anger thinks his will is for revenge, in fear that it is for flight. Again, a drunkard thinks he speaks of his free will things which, when sober, he would fain not have spoken.'

That which we call choice in the mind is in truth exactly correlated, or rather identical, with some determined physical event in the body. Again, it must be conceded that our freedom of action depends on memory; we must remember a particular word, for example, before we can will to speak or not to speak it; and memory is not subject to the will. At best, therefore, the alleged power of volition can be exercised only within the limits fixed by the range of memory.

'But when we dream of speaking, we believe ourselves to, speak from a free decision of the mind, and yet we speak not, or if we do, it is by an independent motion of the body. We dream, again, of doing by the like decision sundry things which as waking men we dare not; and hereon I would fain know if there be in the mind two sorts of decisions, the one merely fantastic and the other truly free. But if we choose not to go that length in folly, it must needs be allowed that this decision of the mind which is believed to be free is not in truth distinguishable from the imagination or memory preceding it, and is nothing else than that affirmation which an idea, insomuch as it is an idea, doth of necessity include. So that these decisions of the mind arise therein by the same necessity as its ideas of really existing things. And they who believe themselves to speak or keep silence or do aught else by the free decision of their minds are men dreaming with their eyes open.'

So ends this characteristic and uncompromising exposition, which is too clear to need much commentary. Spinoza seems to assume rather confidently that no advocate of free-will would go so far as to maintain that there is a real operation of that excellent faculty in dreaming. As a matter of pure psychological argument, it is not easy to see what should prevent it. But the doctrine of free-will is never, so far as I know, maintained on a purely scientific footing: it is always rested, at least in great part, on the supposed necessity of having it as a foundation of moral responsibility. Therefore a disputant who, defending free-will on the usual grounds, should assert that free-will is really exercised in dreams, would find himself in an awkward position. For he must admit either that free-will and moral responsibility are not inseparable, or that we are morally responsible for all the crimes and follies which the best and wisest of us, as common experience abundantly shows, are liable to commit in our dreams. The first alternative deprives the volitionist of his principal interest in his cause; the second is too repugnant to common sense to be entertained, though something not unlike it was held by St. Augustine.

Let us return to the conclusion of the Second Part of the 'Ethics,' where Spinoza sets forth the advantages of the philosophical doctrine of necessity. It gives a marked foretaste of the manner in which the practical side of his teaching coincides with that of the Stoics. The attainment of happiness by man through realizing his intimate union with the whole nature of things; the distinction between things in our power and things not in our power; the avoidance of all disturbing passions, and the performance of social duties from rational desire for the common good: all these points occur in the paragraph I shall now translate, and all are not only present but conspicuous in the Stoic theory of morals. Spinoza's words are as follows: —

'It remains to show how much is gained for the uses of life by the knowledge of this doctrine, which we shall easily perceive from these considerations.

'First, it teaches us that we act only by the decree of God, and are partakers of the divine nature, and that in proportion as we are more perfect in our actions and more advanced in the understanding of God. Wherefore this doctrine, besides that it begets an absolute content in the mind, excels also in this, that it teaches us wherein our highest happiness or blessedness doth consist; that is, in the knowledge of God only, which leadeth us to do only such things as be commended by love and duty. Hence we clearly understand how far they go astray from a right judgment of virtue who look to be illustrated by God with extreme rewards for virtue and perfect actions, as for some extreme hardship of service; as if virtue and the service of God were not themselves very happiness and the extreme height of freedom.

'Secondly, it teaches us how to carry ourselves as concerning the gifts of fortune or things which are not in our power, I mean such things as depend not on our own nature; that is, that we should with an equal mind await and bear either countenance of fortune, seeing that all things follow from the eternal ordinance of God with the same necessity whereby it follows from the nature of a triangle that its three angles are equal to two right angles.

'Thirdly, this doctrine is good for civil conversation, insomuch as it teaches us to hold no man in hatred, contempt, or derision, and not to be angered or envious at any one. Further, because it teaches that every man should be content with his own and helpful to his neighbour;

not from womanish pity, favour, or superstition, but merely at the bidding of reason, according to the time and matter, as I shall show in the third part.[180]

'Lastly, this doctrine is of no small profit for the commonwealth in that it shows how citizens are to be governed and led, that is, not to make them do service, but to cause them to do freely whatsoever is best. Arid herewith I have finished that of which I purposed to treat in this Scholium, and so I make an end of this our second part; conceiving that therein I have explained the nature and qualities of the human mind at sufficient length, and as clearly as the difficulty of the thing admits; and that from that which I have delivered many conclusions may be drawn of excellent use and very necessary to be known, as in the sequel shall partly appear.'

With the second book of the 'Ethics' the general part, as we may call it, of Spinoza's philosophy comes to an end. The rest is concerned with the application to definite problems of the principles already laid out. Before we pass on to these we cannot but notice the one extraordinary defect which is conspicuous in Spinoza's psychology. One of the first things we expect from a psychologist nowadays is a systematic account of the processes of perception and knowledge. But Spinoza does not appear to have any theory of perception at all. He assumes, as we all assume, that there is some kind of correspondence between sensations in consciousness and things in the external world. But of the nature of that correspondence he has very little to say. We find the important proposition, which had already been given by Descartes, that sensation, being a function of the organism, depends not simply on the external object, but on the organism as affected by the object; we find also a marked appreciation of the advantages to be derived from studying the phenomena of sensation and thought under their physiological aspect. We do not find, however, any explicit handling of the problems which are started by the old Platonic question: What is Knowledge? The omission may be ascribed to several reasons. First, the aim of Spinoza's treatise is not to give a complete system of philosophy or psychology, but to show the way to human happiness. The philosophical introduction, elaborate as it appears, is subordinate to the ethical purpose. Next, these questions were not prominent

---

[180] Or rather the fourth. It appears from Spinoza's letters that the third and fourth part of the *Ethics* were originally meant to form one.

in Spinoza's time. They were put in the front rank of discussion by Locke, Spinoza's contemporary by birth, but in philosophy standing wholly apart from him and belonging to another generation. And I conceive that the psychological problem of knowledge was obscured to Spinoza's own mind by that ambiguous and distracting use of the word *idea* which has already been more than once noticed. Not that his metaphysical principles are in themselves unable to furnish means of dealing with the problem: on the contrary they very much simplify it. The puzzle of sensation, when considered in the usual way, is that there is a relation between the heterogeneous terms of consciousness and motion. Something happens in my optic nerves, physiology may or may not be able to say exactly what, and thereupon I see. Can my sensation of sight be said to resemble the thing seen, or the images on my two retinæ, or the motions in the optic nerves, and if so, in what sense? These questions are essentially insoluble on the common supposition that body and mind are distinct substances or orders in nature. If body and mind are really the same thing, the knot is cut, or rather vanishes. The problem of making a connexion between the inner and the outer series of phenomena becomes a purely scientific one. It is no longer a metaphysical paradox, but the combination of two methods of observing the same facts, or facts belonging to the same order: and the science of physiological psychology can justify itself on philosophical grounds, besides making good its claims by the practical test of results. But the people who cry *materialism* at everything they disagree with or cannot understand will doubtless cry out that this also is materialism. And they are very welcome to any good it can do them.

CHAPTER VII

THE NATURE OF MAN

Behold, I show you truth! Lower than hell,
Higher than heaven, outside the utmost stars,
    Farther than Brahm doth dwell,

Before beginning, and without an end,
    As space eternal and as surety sure,
Is fixed a power divine which moves to good,
    Only its laws endure.

Out of the dark it wrought the heart of man,
    Out of dull shells the pheasant's pencilled neck;
Ever at toil, it brings to loveliness
    All ancient wrath and wreck.

It slayeth and it saveth, nowise moved
    Except unto the working out of doom;
Its threads are Love and Life; and Death and Pain
    The shuttles of its loom.

EDWIN ARNOLD, *The Light of Asia.*

SPINOZA'S inquiry concerning the Passions, which forms the Third Part of the Ethics, is best introduced in his own words.

'THE PREFACE

'Most of those who have writ concerning the passions and man's way of life appear as if they handled not such things as belong to nature, and follow her common laws, but things outside nature; insomuch that they conceive man to be in nature as a kingdom within a kingdom. For they suppose that man rather confounds than follows the order of nature, and has an absolute power over his own actions, being no otherwise determined than by himself. As concerning men's weakness and unsteadfastness, they attribute these not to the common power of nature, but to some defect in the nature of man; which therefore they bewail, mock, despise, or (which for the most part happens) vituperate; and he passes for the best prophet who can most eloquently and shrewdly rebuke the human mind for its weakness. Not that most renowned authors have been wanting (to whose labour and ingenuity we do confess ourselves much indebted) who have written much and excellently on the right way of life, and have given to mankind precepts full of wisdom. But none of these, to my knowledge, hath determined the nature and strength of the passions, or what on the other part the mind can do in restraining them. I well know that the admirable Descartes (though he supposed the mind to have an absolute power over its own actions) yet endeavoured both to explain human passions by their immediate causes, and to show the road whereby the mind could come to a perfect mastery thereof. But, in my judgment, he hath shown nothing but the exceeding sharpness of his own wit, as I shall prove in the fitting place. But to return to those who choose rather to abhor or deride the passions and actions of men than to understand them; this sort will no doubt be amazed that I go about to treat of human defects and follies after the geometrical manner, and would fain demonstrate by certain reasoning that which, as they so loudly protest, is against all reason, idle, absurd, and abominable. But such is my way. Nothing happens in nature that can be ascribed to a defect of nature; for nature is always and everywhere one and the same, and her virtue and power of operation is the same: that is, the laws and rules of nature, according to which all things are made and change from one form into another, are everywhere and always the same; and therefore there should be but one and the same way of understanding things of whatsoever kind, to wit, by the universal laws and rules of nature. Thus the passions of hatred, anger, envy and the like, when considered in themselves, follow from the like necessity and virtue of nature as all other individual things; and accordingly they obey fixed causes, whereby they may be understood, and have their fixed properties, equally worthy of our knowledge as the properties of any other thing in the mere contemplation whereof we take delight. I shall treat therefore of the nature and strength of the passions, and the power of the mind over them, by the same method as I have treated of God and the mind in the foregoing parts; and I shall consider human actions and desires after the same sort as if the inquiry were concerned with lines, surfaces, or solids.'

This passage throws light, among other things, on the true significance of Spinoza's geometrical method. It is not that he thinks the geometrical method of exposition an infallible engine of discovery; but he is determined to conduct the investigation of human nature in a purely scientific spirit, and he chooses the geometrical form as the most perfect and striking type of scientific method. The scientific value of his results in this part of his work is not only recognized by modern criticism, but may be described as the one point on which almost all expounders and critics have agreed. Spinoza's account of the passions is universally spoken of as his masterpiece. I shall quote only one scientific testimony, which has a peculiar value as coming from a leading authority in physiology, being given in the course of his proper scientific work, and acted upon by him in an unmistakable manner. This witness is Johannes Müller.

'With regard to the relations of the passions to one another, apart from their physiological conditions, it is impossible to give any better account than that which Spinoza has laid down with unsurpassed mastery. In the following statement I shall therefore confine myself to giving the propositions of Spinoza on that subject.'[181]

And this he proceeds to do without further criticism or comment. We shall find that his view is indirectly confirmed by the work of more recent inquirers in both natural science and psychology.

The first spring of action, common to man with every creature, is self-preservation. We must not say the desire of self-preservation, for desire, as conceived by Spinoza, comes later. His leading propositions on the subject are thus expressed: —

'Each individual thing, so far as in it lies, endeavours to persist in its own being.

The effort wherewith everything endeavours to persist in its own being is nothing else than that thing's being what it is' (praeter ipsius rei actualem essentiam).[182]

In a former chapter we traced this fundamental proposition from its Cartesian use as a physical axiom or law of motion through Spinoza's repetition and extension of it in the exposition of Descartes which was his first published work. We also noticed that in a more extensive application it was current in the post-Aristotelian schools of Greek philosophy, and notably among the Stoics. In the middle ages, too, it appears to have been familiar in a scholastic form. Spinoza, however, probably knew nothing of its earlier history and meaning, and certainly did not concern himself with them. He took the statement from Descartes as a

---

[181] *Physiologie des Menschen,* ii. 543. Dr. Dühring's remarks on this are curious: 'In neuester Zeit hat auch ein Physiolog von einigem Professorruf, Johannes Müller, ungeachtet seiner engherzigen, religiös und politisch rückläufigen Denkweise, von seinem Standpunkt aus die von Spinoza gelieferte Statik der Leidenschaften für so gelungen erachtet,' &c.

[182] *Eth.* iii. pr. 6, 7; cf. *Cogit. Met.* pt. i. cap. 7, § 8.

general law of physics; and, as he extended without limit the scientific view of the world propounded by Descartes, so he extended the range of those principles from which the Cartesian
system undertook to explain all sensible phenomena, or at least
to show that they were explicable.

It is important to bear in mind the interpretation and
warning given by Spinoza himself. The statement that everything
endeavours to persist in its own being might seem to imply some
notion that the effort or tendency to self-preservation is a mysterious power implanted in things and antecedent to their existence. Such a power has been conceived in both ancient and
modern philosophies. Varieties of it are the *karma* of Buddhism,
which performs the singular teat of keeping up a chain of transmigration when there is no soul to transmigrate;[183] the supposed
ultimate activity symbolically called Will by Schopenhauer; and
the more elaborate version of it given as the Unconscious in
Hartmann's system. But Spinoza most carefully excludes all assumptions of this kind. The self-preserving effort is nothing else
than the thing's being what it is. Whatever the thing in question
may be, the mere fact of its existence means that it must be reckoned with. Great or small, there it is, and you cannot get it out of
the way without doing work upon it. Destruction is only a name
for processes of change which are peculiarly conspicuous to our
senses or important in their results. Every change implies motion, and every motion implies work, and signifies resistance
overcome. This resistance, as we call it from the point of view of
the worker overcoming it from the outside, is persistence or 'effort of self-preservation' if we shift the adjustment of the mind's
eye, and fix the centre of the field of imagination in the thing
operated upon. The use of the word effort *(conatus)* belongs to
the realistic habits of scientific language in Spinoza's time. He
speaks of effort in this relation, just as long afterwards mathe-
maticians were accustomed to speak of a force or power of inertia, which is indeed the same thing in its simplest physical
aspect. It might be rash to affirm that even now *vis inertiæ* and
other terms of the same kind do not survive in books which may
be put into the hands of students. But at that time the usage went
farther. Not only inertia was a force, but velocity was spoken of

---

[183] Rhys Davids, *Buddhism,* p. 118.

as the cause of a body's changing its place. Nay, in our own time Mr. Herbert Spencer has called momentum the cause of motion. We need not be surprised, then, that elsewhere Spinoza speaks of this self-preserving endeavour as a force (vis qua unaquaeque [res] in existendo perseverat).[184] In the case of living creatures he identifies it with life. In the less complex relations of the material world it would appear (as we have just seen) in the fundamental properties of matter — inertia, mass, and impenetrability. But the fact now assumed as ultimate for ordinary scientific purposes, that every atom of every element succeeds in preserving itself, would in Spinoza's view be no more than a striking illustration. The *conatus* is equally present in the most unstable as in the most stable of combinations. A molecule of water endeavours, in the peculiar sense here explained, not to be decomposed; and not less so, while it holds together, does the molecule of some of those transitory compounds which explode at a touch or vibration.

It will perhaps help us to understand Spinoza's meaning if we invert the order of his terms. Instead of considering whether things can be said to exercise a self-preserving effort, let us ask ourselves what we mean by a thing.[185] The question is not as easy as it seems; yet an answer may be given in few words. We take it from Mr. Herbert Spencer: existence, he tells us, means persistence. A thing is a group of phenomena which persists. Herein is its individuality, its title to be counted apart from the surrounding medium. We shall find that persistence for an appreciable time, in a manner obvious to sense, and against appreciable external force, is the test applied by the unconscious philosophizing of language.

The first requisite of a *thing* is that it should be apparently continuous in itself and not continuous with things outside it. It must be definite, or we should not want to name it; still

---

[184] *Eth.* ii. 45, Schol., with which cf. *Cogit. Met.* pt. ii. cap. 6, § 3; but he there says, 'Illa vis a rebus ipsis est diversa,' which is contradicted not only by the *Ethics,* but quite as strongly by a passage which stands earlier in the same work (pt. i. c. 6, §§ 8, 9). I have already suggested that the *Cogitata Metaphysica* may be made up of notes written at various dates.

[185] Spinoza gives a physical definition in Cartesian terms of *unum corpus sive individuum* in Part ii. of the *Ethics* (excursus after Schol. to Pr. 13). But it is not exactly to the present purpose, nor is it very lucid to the modern reader.

more must it be persistent, or we could not name it at all. What is more, the persistence must be conceived as depending on the thing itself, and not as a precarious result of external conditions. Take a cubical vessel full of water. The vessel is beyond question a thing. Is the water also a thing? Every molecule of it is assuredly represented as a real thing in the duly trained imagination, though it cannot be separately observed. But the body of water is not regarded as a *thing* either by a scientific or an unscientific observer. It is sensibly continuous, and it is persistent so long as it is confined by the walls of the vessel; but it will persist no longer. When the external restraint is removed it will flow away, assume other forms, and be dispersed. We refuse it the name of a thing because it is manifestly held together only by external forces. Take a cubic inch of water inside this vessel, or a cubic foot of air in the atmosphere: these again are not things in common speech, and for the like reasons. Cases may be put, however, so as to present all degrees of doubt. For example, is a pile of cannon-balls a thing? More work is required to dislodge one of the shot than to sever or destroy many things of undoubted *reality,* if we may use the term in a strictly scholastic sense; and the pile is not less continuous to the eye than many a rough stone wall or cairn which, like itself, is kept together merely by friction and gravity. Nevertheless, while nobody would hesitate to speak of the wall or cairn as a *thing,* I doubt whether any one would so speak of the pile of shot, unless as an object confusedly seen in the distance. I conceive that here we are determined by considerations of human use and intention. The normal use of stones is to be built into walls, and the possible uses of the individual stones are too trifling to be much thought of. Cannon-balls are made to be separately fired off, and the pile is in itself of no use whatever. In the case of the wall or cairn the parts are there for the sake of the whole, and are merged in it: in the case of the pile of shot the whole is there for the sake of the parts. Hence we regard the heap of stones as meant for one permanent thing, and the heap of shot as meant for a provisional arrangement of many things. In fine, the conception of individual things as such is an affair of our perceptions, and to some extent of our convenience. That such was Spinoza's view is pretty manifest from what he says in various places in the First and Second Parts of the Ethics, and this goes to support the reading now offered of his principle of self-preservation.

So understood, the principle is simple enough. How then does Spinoza connect it with the world of life and action? or what light can it throw on the intricate play of human passions? The connexion is made out by affirming that the impulse or desire of self-preservation which we know in our own feeling is a special manifestation of the universal principle involved in existence itself. The mind 'endeavours to persist in its being with a certain undetermined duration, and is conscious of this its endeavour.'[186] Such endeavour, considered with regard to the mind alone, is called will; considered with regard to mind and body together, it is called appetite; 'which is nothing else than the very being of the man, from whose nature those things of necessity follow which make for his preservation; and thus the man is determined to the doing of such things. Then betwixt appetite and desire there is no difference, save that for the most part desire is ascribed to men in so far as they be conscious of their appetite; and therefore it may be thus defined, that is to say: *desire is appetite with consciousness thereof.* From all which it appears that we have not endeavour, will, appetite, or desire for anything, because we deem it good; but contrariwise deem a thing good, because we have an endeavour, will, appetite, or desire for it.'

Whether this bold and far-reaching thought of Spinoza's can be justified in its whole extent I do not venture to say. But I entertain no doubt that, after all possible deductions, it contains profound and vital truth. It seems probable that the extreme complexity and the late development of distinct consciousness, and consequently of the emotions as they are known in the adult experience of mankind, were underrated by Spinoza. It may be that they were very much underrated, though we have already seen that the composite character of mind was most clearly asserted by him. He appears to jump from unconscious organic processes — which, let us again repeat it, are in his view mental as well as material, or rather both in one — to the facts of vivid consciousness. The love of life in man is more than an organic feeling; the finished ideas of memory and expectation, and even the highly wrought conceptions of our ethical and social nature, have their part in it. And in our active consciousness these more

---

[186] *Eth.* iii. 9, and Schol.

refined elements are predominant. But in the main it is enough for Spinoza's purpose that the organic feeling is there; and that such a feeling is in truth deeply rooted in us is a proposition which we need not waste time in establishing. We have already called in Mr. Herbert Spencer to help us to a modern reading of Spinoza's thought. We shall now for a like purpose appeal to his definition of life, which is especially valuable as an interpretation of scientific results framed in perfect independence of Spinoza's work, and proceeding on different lines.

According to this definition, life is 'the continuous adjustment of internal relations to external relations;' it 'consists in maintenance of inner actions corresponding with outer actions.' Now this adjustment or maintenance is precisely what Spinoza means by a thing's persistence in its own being. The organism endeavours to persist in the face of external conditions, converting them to its use when it can, or resisting them at need; and the success of this endeavour is life. It is observed by Mr. Herbert Spencer himself that the definition in this form is too wide; but, to whatever extent this may be a defect for the purposes of natural history or biology, from Spinoza's point of view it is a merit. The correlation of mind and matter being universal, and all things endowed with life in various degrees, philosophy is not concerned to draw a line anywhere to mark where life begins. Philosophically speaking, the attempt to draw one is illusory; and it is a question whether science itself may not ere long bring us the same report. We may confine ourselves for the present, however, to the undoubted manifestations of life. Spinoza does not profess to give a particular account of nature, or even the whole of animated nature, but of man. As regards life in its common acceptation, it will be seen that Mr. Herbert Spencer takes in a factor of great importance which is not marked by Spinoza. He speaks of continuous adjustment, thus implying that external relations are constantly changing and requiring adjustments to be effected. Nature commands the adjustment under the penalty of extinction. Now the striving of every creature to keep its own nature in harmony with the world around it is the fundamental fact whose consequences are traced in the modern doctrine of evolution. Natural history, as Mr. Darwin and Mr. Spencer have taught us to see, is the history of the never-ceasing effort of individuals and races to maintain a certain correspondence between the organism and its environment. The nearer this correspondence approaches to completeness, the more perfect and secure is the existence of the individual and the kind. Spinoza pointed to the law of persistence, but could not trace its working. We now know that in operation it becomes a law of development. Older by countless ages than conscious desire, older than anything to which we now grant the name of life, the primeval and common impulse — 'the will to live, the competence to be' — is at length in the sight of all men, as it was for Spinoza's keener vision, the root of all action and of all that makes the world alive. Not that we claim Spinoza as a forerunner of the theory of evolution. He had no materials for anticipating it; and even if he had seemed to prophesy it, the prophecy would have been a guess in the dark. His merit is rather to have abstained, with a singular philosophical tact or instinct, from any prematurely ambitious construction. As his work stands, one does not see that on the face of it his principle of self-conservation is sufficiently connected with the real world: there is a void space between the idea and the facts. But one also sees that the required connexion is wonderfully supplied by Mr. Darwin. The gap has been left open at exactly the right place, and Spinoza had the wisdom to leave it open rather than fill it up inadequately, and the courage to stand by the idea with such light as he had.

The practical value of Spinoza's analysis of the passions is, however, to a great extent independent of the general axiom from which he starts. All that is really necessary to be granted is that man has the impulse or instinct of self-preservation, and desires power and fulness of life: and this much it would need some boldness to dispute, however the fact itself may be explicable. Let us see how Spinoza reaches the cardinal definitions of Pleasure and Pain; cardinal because with him Pleasure, Pain, and Desire are the primary elements of which, according to the variety of objects exciting them, all human passions are compounded. It is stated as a direct consequence from the correspondence of body and mind that 'whatsoever increases or diminishes, helps or hinders, the active power (agendi potentiam) of our body; the idea thereof likewise increases or diminishes, helps or hinders, the sentient power (cogitandi potentiam) of our mind.' 'Thus we see,' adds the Scholium, 'that the mind may undergo great variations, and pass now to a greater, now to a lesser perfection; which effects explain to us the states of pleasure and pain. By *pleasure* I shall therefore hereafter understand an affection whereby the mind passes to a greater perfection; and by *pain* an affection whereby it passes to a lesser perfection.'[187] Here again there is a singular coincidence with modern scientific speculation. Mr. Herbert Spencer is led, on the one hand by the evidence of the actual conditions of pleasure and pain in their most conspicuous and regular manifestations, on the other hand by deduction from the hypothesis of evolution, to conclude that 'pains are the correlatives of actions injurious to the organism, while pleasures are the correlatives of actions conducive to its welfare.' But an action or event conducive to the welfare of the organism is precisely what Spinoza means by 'transition to a greater perfection;' conversely, an action injurious to the organism is in Spinoza's language a transition to less perfection. Pleasure marks the raising, pain the lowering, of the vital energies, and consequently the advance or depression of the creature in the scale of being, to a corresponding extent and in so far as the particular event is concerned. The results of the philosopher who still passes for a mere dogmatist agree in their full extent with those of the latest inquirer working by induction from the facts of biology. Spinoza's definition, it will be seen, implies that pleasure is not only normally but invariably beneficial in itself, and pain hurtful. Not that the normal indications of pain and pleasure may not be disturbed, so as to make them in particular cases blind or worse than blind guides. Experience of this kind is only too common; and the explanation of it is briefly touched on by Mr. Herbert Spencer, and has been more lately considered by others. But the pleasure which leads to ultimate harm is yet not an evil in itself, but a partial good bought at a ruinous price: the pain which brings healing is not by itself a good, but an evil submitted to that greater evil may be avoided. And we here use the terms good and evil as denoting the quality, not of the sensation as such (for that would only be to say that pleasure is pleasure and pain is pain), but of the events and relations in the organism immediately indicated by the sensation. Anæsthetics, for example, are useful not merely because pain is escaped for the moment, but because the shock and exhaustion which are the

---

[187] *Eth.* iii. 11.

direct consequences of pain are escaped with it. This view of the intrinsic utility of pleasure and hurtfulness of pain has been ingeniously maintained by Mr. Grant Allen, who thus completes the accordance between Mr. Herbert Spencer's doctrine and that of Spinoza. Accepting this view, we shall say that the action beneficial to the organism which, in Mr. Spencer's language, is correlated with pleasure, is not the antecedent or concomitant of the pleasurable sensation, but the corporeal or objective aspect of the sensation itself. The importance of the remoter consequences, and the weight of Mr. Spencers argument therefrom, remain, of course, unchanged. The individuals and races whose nervous system has been trained by experience to forecast impending good or ill at an early stage, and to report them by means of pleasure and pain to the centres of voluntary action, have an advantage in the struggle for life precisely like that of the prudent over the unthinking man, or of an army where sentinel and outpost duties are carefully performed over one in which they are neglected. But we must return to following Spinoza.

The special forms of Pleasure and Pain on which most of the passions depend are Love and Hatred. In Spinoza's language these include like and dislike; in fact the English language is alone, or nearly so, in marking a difference of degree in these emotions so sharply as it does. The mind seeks to retain in consciousness whatever increases its power, and to recall whatever may counteract the impression of such things as hurt or hinder it; these being simple manifestations of the self-preserving tendency. Hence arise Love, which is Pleasure accompanied by the idea of an external cause; and Hatred, which is Pain with the like accompaniment. And, by the law of association of ideas already given in the Second Part, objects in themselves indifferent may excite pleasure, pain, and desire by their casual association with other things which are of themselves apt to excite those emotions. Hence the obscure likings and dislikings which are commonly referred to an unknown cause called sympathy or antipathy. They depend on some association by resemblance which is known only in its effects.[188] Through association, again, a conflict of emotions is possible; for something which affects us with pain may at the same time call up memories of equal or

---

[188] *Eth.* iii. 12-15.

greater pleasure. But conflicts may be more directly produced, for the human body is exceedingly complex, and therefore may be variously affected at the same time and by the same object. External objects, too, are themselves complex, and may have complex effects on the same bodily organs. The emotions of hope, fear, confidence, despair, joy, and disappointment, are accounted for by the imagination working on the conception of pleasurable or painful events as future or past.[189] The effects of love and hatred in inducing emotions of pleasure and pain by sympathy are then set forth. We have pleasure in the welfare of a beloved object, and pain in its destruction; its pleasure and pain give rise to the like affections in us; we love that which we conceive as giving pleasure to it, and hate that which we conceive as giving pain; and hatred on the other hand produces the contrary effects (Eth. 3, 19-26). But the range and power of sympathy are yet wider. In addition to these causes the mere conception of anything as like ourselves is a source of induced emotion.

'When it happens that we imagine a thing like ourselves, and which we have not regarded with any particular emotion, to be affected with any emotion, we are thereupon affected with the like emotion'[190] (Pr. 27).

For, in so far as an external object conceived by us as affected in a particular way resembles our own body, so far will our representation of its condition include a representation or faint repetition of similar states of our own consciousness: or, under the physiological aspect, as Spinoza puts it, 'the idea of the external body imagined by us will imply an affection of our body like to that of the external body; and accordingly if we imagine any one like ourselves to be affected with any emotion, this imagination will be the expression in consciousness of an affection of our body like the said emotion.' Here, as often in Spinoza, the complexity and difficulty of the physiological side of the inquiry are apparently slurred or underrated. But the psychology is thoroughly sound in its main features, and we must

---

[189] Propp. 17, 18. I translate *conscientiae morsus* by 'disappointment,' as Spinoza warns us at the end of the book that his terms do not always bear their common meaning. Remorse is described later as *poenitentia*.

[190] The original *Affectus* is a wider term; not being confined to consciousness.

never forget that it was by keeping the physiological side constantly in view that Spinoza escaped the countless fallacies from which not even Kant has been able wholly to deliver us.

Varieties of these induced or imitative emotions of sympathy are pity, emulation or the pursuit of similar objects of desire, and benevolence, which is defined as a desire arising from pity, and seeking to liberate the object of pity from the evils of its condition.[191] Another result of this extended sympathy (which in modern language we may call the sympathy of race, or more shortly and exactly kindliness) is that 'we shall endeavour to do whatever we conceive men to look upon with pleasure, and shun the doing of that which we conceive them to shun' (Pr. 29). If we think we have succeeded in pleasing other men by our actions, the result is complacency; if we seem to have displeased them, it is shame. The belief that our affection towards any object is shared by others will strengthen that affection; if the disposition of another towards an object liked or disliked by us is contrary to our own, there ensues a fluctuation or conflict of emotion in us. Hence we endeavour to associate others with us in our emotions. This desire that others should agree with us has in its crude form the nature of ambition, and begets mutual hindrance and discord. Hence also arises envy: for another's enjoyment excites in us an appetite for the like enjoyment; and if it is such that it cannot be shared with our neighbour, we shall wish to deprive him of it.[192] How these effects of sympathy may be controlled to rational and social uses is not considered in the present part of the 'Ethics,' but will appear in due course. Spinoza throws out here, but without dwelling on it, the important hint that the psychology of the passions may be studied to advantage in children, their tender organism being as it were in a state of unstable equilibrium, and offering slight resistance to external impressions. We see that the laughing or weeping of others in their presence will make them laugh or weep; that they seek to imitate whatever they see others doing, and desire for themselves whatever seems to give pleasure to others.[193]

Other combinations and effects of the master passions of

---

[191] Benevolentia... nihil aliud est quam cupiditas e commiseratione orta. (Pr. 27, Schol. 2.)

[192] Pr. 30-32.

[193] Pr. 32, Schol.

love and hatred are worked out in a series of propositions which we shall not follow in detail. But it may be useful to translate a few of them as specimens of Spinoza's manner. The omitted demonstrations involve reference to other propositions without which they are not intelligible.

'*Prop.* 43. Hatred is increased by mutual hatred, and contrariwise may be abolished by love.

Demonstration. Whenever one conceives a person hated by him to be affected with hatred towards him, thereupon a new hatred arises while the first, by the supposition, is yet in being. But if on the other hand he conceive this person to be affected with love towards him, in so far as he conceives this he will regard himself with pleasure, and to that extent will endeavour to please that other; that is, to that extent he endeavours not to hate him and to do no displeasure to him. And this endeavour will be greater or less in proportion to the emotion whence it arises. Therefore if it be greater than that which arises from hatred, and through which the man endeavours to do displeasure to the thing he hates, it will prevail over it, and abolish the hate from his mind; which was to be proved.

Prop. 44. When hatred is wholly overcome by love, it passes into love; and this love is greater than if hatred had not gone before it.

Scholium. Though this be so, yet no man will endeavour to hate anything or undergo displeasure that he may enjoy this greater pleasure; that is, no one will desire harm to be done to himself for the hope of making it good, nor long to be sick for the hope of growing whole. For every man will always endeavour to preserve his being and to keep off pain as far as he can. But if it can be supposed that a man may desire to hate some one that he may afterwards be affected with greater love towards him, then he will constantly desire to hate him. For the greater the hatred has been, the greater the love shall be, and therefore he will constantly wish the hate to be more and more augmented; and for the like reason a man will endeavour to be more and more sick, that he may enjoy greater pleasure afterwards in the return of health; which is absurd.

Prop. 49. Love and hatred towards a thing which we conceive as free must both be greater, the occasion being otherwise the same, than towards a thing conceived as necessary.

Schol. Hence it follows that men, because they deem themselves free, are moved toward one another with greater love and hate than other creatures; besides which is to be considered the imitation of emotions above mentioned (Prop. 27, 34, 40, and 43 of this Part).'

A little farther on we have an important group of propositions concerning the active powers of the mind. When the mind contemplates itself and its own power, this gives rise to pleasure; while the contemplation of one's own weakness gives rise to pain.[194]

'This displeasure accompanied by the idea of our own weakness is called dejection *(humilitas);* the pleasure that arises from the contemplation of oneself is named self-love or self-complacency. And seeing this is renewed every time that a man contemplates his own faculties or active power, it likewise follows that every one is eager to recount his own doings and display his strength both of body and mind, and for this reason men are troublesome to one another. Also this oftentimes leads men to be enviously disposed, that is, to rejoice at the infirmity of their fellows, and be displeased at their excellence. For so often as this or that man conceives his own actions, he is affected with pleasure, and the more so as he conceives them more distinctly and as expressing a greater perfection; or in other words, the more he can distinguish them from others and contemplate them as individual things. Wherefore every one will most rejoice in the contemplation of himself when the quality contemplated in himself is somewhat he allows not in other creatures. But if that which he affirms of himself be ascribed by him to man or animals in general, he will not be so much delighted; contrariwise he will be displeased if he conceives his own actions as infirm in comparison of other men's. And this displeasure he will strive to put off, namely, by perversely construing the actions of his fellows, or dressing out his own as best he may. Thus 'tis plain that men are naturally prone to hate and envy, which last is also favoured by their bringing up. For it is the way of parents to urge their children towards excellence with the spur of ambition and envy. But peradventure some doubt remains, because we often admire men's excellence and do them honour. To remove this I shall add this following corollary.

No man is envious of excellence unless in one supposed his equal.

Demonstration. Envy is of the nature of hate or displeasure, that is, an affection whereby man's active power or endeavour is hindered. But man doth not endeavour or desire to do anything but what can follow from his own nature as he finds the same. Therefore a man will not desire any active power or excellence (for 'tis all one) to be attributed to him which belongs to some other nature and is foreign to his own. So his desire cannot be hindered, that is, the man cannot suffer displeasure, from his contemplation of some excellence in one unlike

---

[194] Propp. 53, 54, 55. Prop. 54 is a curious example of Spinoza's most artificial manner.

himself, and by consequence he cannot envy such an one. But his equal fellow he can envy, since he is assumed to be of like nature with him.'

So that when we admire men for singular foresight, courage, or other qualities, this is because we conceive their qualities, at least in that degree, as singular and above the common fortune of men. The hero is conceived as not of one mould with ourselves, and we no more entertain envy with respect to him than against the lion for his courage or against a tree for its height.[195]

It is to be observed that Spinoza is in this book concerned only with the play of the emotions when left to themselves. He does not mean to deny that rational and unselfish admiration of human excellence as such is possible and practicable. But this is the effect of right knowledge and the discipline of society, which have not yet been considered. It is next pointed out that pleasure, pain and desire, and therefore all the emotions derived from them, are of as many kinds and varieties as the external objects which are the occasion of them; and also that the emotions differ in every individual according to the difference of the internal conditions of his constitution. Thus the desires and appetites of animals are specifically different from the analogous desires and appetites in man, and the pleasure of a drunkard is by no means the same as the pleasure of a philosopher. Spinoza here approaches the question whether all pleasures are commensurable, which is prominent in modern discussions of the theory of ethics: but he does not pursue it. From his point of view it is at best superfluous, and I cannot help suspecting that, either in Spinoza's way or in some other not very far from it, we shall finally acquiesce in the same conclusion.

So far the discourse has been of the emotions considered as passions, or 'ascribed to man in so far as he is acted upon;' but there are also emotions of an active kind. Pleasure arises from the mind's contemplation of its own power; but such contemplation is present whenever the mind has a true or adequate idea (because true knowledge includes certitude or the consciousness of its truth, Eth. 2, 43, see p. 141 above). Therefore the conception of adequate ideas is a pleasurable activity of the mind; and activity as such includes the effort or desire of self-

---

[195] Scholia to Prop. 55.

maintenance. Hence there is a desire which is purely active. This active and reasonable desire is the source of virtue; which has two main branches according as desire is directed by reason to the welfare of the agent himself, or to doing good to other men and seeking their friendship. (Prop. 59, Schol.) Having thus brought the third part of the Ethics to an end, Spinoza recapitulates his definitions of the emotions with some few additions and new explanations. I shall make no apology for translating this piece at length.

THE DEFINITIONS OF THE EMOTIONS

1. DESIRE is the being of man itself, in so far as we conceive it as determined to a particular action by any given affection of it.

Explanation. We have said above, in the Scholium to Prop. 9 of this part, that desire is appetite with consciousness thereof; and that appetite is the being itself of man, in so far as it is determined to such actions as make for his preservation. But in that scholium I likewise noted that in truth I acknowledged no difference between the appetite and the desire of men. For whether a man be conscious of his appetite or not, yet the appetite is still one and the same; and thus, lest I should seem to fall into tautology, I would not explain desire by appetite, but have sought so to define it as to comprise in one word all those efforts of human nature which we signify by the name of appetite, will, desire or impulse. I might well have said that desire is the being of man itself, so far as we conceive it as determined to a particular action; but from this definition it would not follow (by Prop. 23, Part 2)[196] that the mind could be conscious of its own appetite or desire. Therefore, in order to include the cause of this consciousness, it was needful to add: *by any given affection of it.* For by an affection of human being or nature we understand every disposition thereof, whether it be innate, whether it be conceived purely under the attribute of thought or purely under that of extension, or be ascribed to both together. Here therefore I understand by desire man's efforts, impulses, appetites and volitions whatsoever, which after the manifold disposition of the

---

[196] 'The mind knows not itself, save so far as it perceives ideas of the affections of the body.'

same man be themselves manifold and not seldom contrary to one another, so that the man is dragged this way and that and knows not where to turn.

2. Pleasure is the passage of a man from less to greater perfection.

3. Pain is the passage of a man from greater to less perfection.

Explanation. I say passage: for pleasure is not perfection itself. For if the man were born with that perfection whereto he passes, he would possess the same without the emotion of pleasure; as more plainly appears from the contrary emotion of pain. For no man can deny that pain consists in a passage to less perfection, and not in lesser perfection itself, since a man cannot have pain in that he partakes of some degree of perfection. Neither can we say that pain consists in being deprived of a greater perfection; for deprivation is nothing. So the emotion of pain is an act, which can be no other than that of passing to a less perfection, that is, an act whereby the active power of man is diminished or hindered. See the Scholium to Prop. 11 of this Part. For the definitions of cheerfulness, merriment, melancholy and grief, I pass them over, because they have rather the nature of bodily affections, and are but kinds of pleasure or pain.

4. Wonder is the imagination of somewhat whereon the mind remains fixed because that particular imagination hath no sensible connexion with others. See Prop. 52 with the Scholium.

Explanation. In the Scholium to Prop. 18, Part 2, we have shown what is the cause that the mind from contemplating one thing straightway falls into thinking of another; namely because the images[197] of those things are mutually linked together in such order that one follows on the other. Which cannot be supposed where the image of the thing is novel; so that in such case the mind will be holden in the contemplation of the same thing till it be determined by other causes to think on other matters. Thus the imagination of a new object, if we consider it in itself, is of like nature with others: and for this reason I do not reckon wonder among the emotions, nor see any ground why I should, since this distraction of the mind ariseth from no positive cause that should draw the mind off from other things, but only

---

[197] In modern language we should say ideas or concepts.

from this, that a cause is wanting for which the mind should be determined to think on other things. Therefore I admit (as I have noted in the Scholium to Prop. 11) only three primitive or primary emotions, namely, of pleasure, pain, and desire; and I have mentioned wonder for no other reason than that it is our custom to call certain emotions derived from the three primitive ones by different names when they have regard to objects of our wonder. And for the same reason I am minded to add here a definition of contempt.

5. Contempt is the imagination of a thing which so little moves the mind that by the presence of the thing it is inclined rather to imagine the qualities which are not in the thing than those which are in it. See the scholium to Prop. 52.

The definitions of worship and scorn *(venerationis et dedignationis)* I here leave alone, since no emotions are to my knowledge named after them.

6. Love is pleasure accompanied by the idea of an external cause.

Explanation. This definition clearly explains wherein love consists. But that of the authors who define it as the will of the lover to unite himself to the thing loved expresses not the nature of love but a particular property thereof. And since the nature of love was not well understood by these authors, they could not so much as form a clear notion of that property; and hence their definition hath been generally esteemed pretty obscure. But it is to be observed that when I say that this property is in love, to have a will for union with the thing loved, I mean by will not an assent or conclusion, nor a free resolve of the mind (for this I have shown to be a fiction in Prop. 48, Part 2); nor yet the desire of being united to the thing loved when it is away, or of continuing in its presence when it is by; for love may be conceived without either of these desires; but by this will I understand the content which arises in him that loves upon the presence of the thing loved, whereby the pleasure of the lover is strengthened or at least encouraged.[198]

---

[198] Remembering that Spinoza's *amor* is taken in the widest possible sense, we may doubt if the property in question is universal. A statesman or philanthropist may do good to people hundreds or thousands of miles away who never heard of his existence. When he thinks of the good he has done them collectively, his feeling will be 'laetitia concomitante idea causae externae;' but

7. Hate (or dislike) is pain accompanied by the idea of an external cause.

Explanation. Whatever is to be observed here is easily collected from the explanation to the foregoing definition, and see the Scholium to Prop. 13.

8. Inclination is pleasure accompanied by the idea of something which is a casual occasion *(per accidens causa)* of pleasure.

9. Aversion is pain accompanied by the idea of something which is a casual occasion of pain. See as to these the Scholium to Prop. 15.

10. Devotion is love towards one whom we admire.

Explanation. Admiration or wonder ariseth from the novelty of the thing, as we showed in Prop. 52. If therefore it happen that we often imagine something we admire, we shall cease to admire it; and thus we see that devotion is apt to reduce itself to mere love.

11. Derision is pleasure arising from our imagination that something we contemn is present in something which we hate.

Explanation. So far as we contemn a thing which we hate, we deny existence of it (see Prop. 52, Schol.) and therefore (by Prop. 20) we are pleased. But since we assume that the man who derides a thing also hates it, it follows that such pleasure is unsubstantial. See the Schol. to Prop. 47.

12. Hope is an unconstant pleasure bred of the idea of a future or past thing, of the issue[199] whereof we are to some extent in doubt. See as to this Prop. 18, Schol. 2.

13. Fear is an unconstant pain bred of the idea of a future or past thing, of the issue whereof we are to some extent in doubt. See as to these Prop. 18, Schol. 2.

Explanation. From these definitions it follows that there is no hope without fear, nor fear without hope. For whoever is in hope and doubts of the issue of the matter, the same is assumed to imagine somewhat that excludes the existence of the thing hoped for; and so far, therefore, to receive pain (Prop. 19) and,

---

their individual presence may be indifferent or even disagreeable to him. Spinoza would say that even here there is some pleasure, but that it is overpowered by dislike arising from other causes.

[199] Or 'happening.'

while he is in hope, to fear that the desired thing may not happen. Again, he who is in fear, that is, doubts of the issue of a thing he dislikes, also imagines somewhat that excludes the existence of that thing; and therefore is pleased (Prop. 20), and so to that extent has hope that the thing may not happen.

14. Confidence is pleasure bred of the idea of a future or past thing concerning which our cause of doubt is removed.

15. Despair is pain bred of the idea of a future or past thing concerning which our cause of doubt is removed.

Explanation. Thus there ariseth of hope confidence, and of fear despair, when our cause of doubt as to the issue of the thing is taken away; which happens because a man imagines a past or future thing as present to him, and as such contemplates it; or because he imagines other matters which exclude the existence of those things which threw him into doubt. For although we can never be truly certain of the issue of particular things (by the Corollary to Prop. 31, Part 2),[200] yet it may so be that we have no doubt thereof. For we have shown (see the Scholium, Prop. 49, Part 2) that it is one thing to have no doubt of a matter, another to have the certainty of it; and thus it may come to pass that the imagination of a past or future thing may affect us with the same emotion of pleasure or pain as the imagination of the thing when present: as we have proved in Prop. 18 of this Part, which see, as well as its second Scholium.

16. Joy is pleasure accompanied by the idea of something past which happened beyond our expectation.

17. Disappointment or grief *(conscientiae morsus)* is pain accompanied by the idea of something past which happened beyond our expectation.

18. Pity *(commiseratio)* is pain accompanied by the idea of evil happening to another whom we conceive to be like ourselves. See the Scholia to Prop. 22 and 27 of this Part.

Explanation. Between pity and mercy *(misericordiam)* there seems to be no difference, unless perhaps that pity has regard to the emotion in particular, mercy to the disposition

---

[200] 'Omnes res particulares contingentes et corruptibiles esse.' The Proposition itself seems more in point: 'Nos de duratione rerum singularium quae extra nos sunt nullam nisi admodum inadaequatam cognitionem habere possumus.'

thereto.[201]

19. Approval *(favor)* is love toward some one who has done good to another.

20. Indignation is hate towards some one who has done ill to another.

Explanation. I know that these terms have a different meaning in common use. But my purpose is not to explain the meaning of words but the nature of things, and to signify the things by words whose accustomed meaning is not wholly repugnant to that in which I desire to use them. And so let it suffice to note this once for all. As to the causes of these emotions, see Coroll. 1, Prop. 27, and the Schol. to Prop. 22 of this Part.

21. Over-esteem *(existimatio)* is to think too highly of a man for love's sake.

22. Disparagement *(despectus)* is to think too meanly of a man for hate's sake.

Explanation. Over-esteem is thus an effect or property of love, and disparagement of hate; and so over-esteem may likewise be thus defined, that it is love, so far forth as it moves a man to think too highly of the thing loved, and on the other part disparagement may be defined as hate, so far forth as it moves a man to think too meanly of one whom he hates. See the Scholium to Prop. 26 of this Part.

23. Envy is hate, in so far as it disposeth a man to be sorry at another's happiness, and contrariwise rejoice in his misfortune.

Explanation. To Envy we commonly oppose Mercy, which accordingly may be thus defined, though against the usual meaning of the word:

24. Mercy (or Good Will) is love, in so far as it disposeth a man to rejoice in another's good fortune and contrariwise be sorry at his ill fortune.

Explanation. See more of envy, Prop. 24, Schol. and 32, Schol. in this Part. Now these be the emotions of pain, which the idea of somewhat outside us doth accompany as being their cause, whether of its own nature or by casual association *(per accidens.)* Hence I pass to those which are accompanied by the

---

[201] It is even more difficult to find in English the difference indicated by Spinoza. Auerbach uses *Mitleid* and *Mitgefühl.*

idea of somewhat within us as a cause.

25. Self-contentment is pleasure bred of a man's contemplating himself and his own active power.

26. Humility is pain bred of a man's contemplating his own impotence or infirmity.

Explanation. Self-contentment is opposed to humility, so far as we understand by it a pleasure that arises from contemplating our own active power. But so far as we also understand by it a pleasure accompanied by the idea of some act which we conceive ourselves to have performed by a free resolve of the mind, then it is the opposite of repentance, which we define thus:

27. Repentance is pain accompanied by the idea of some act which we conceive ourselves to have performed by a free resolve of the mind.

Explanation. We have shown the causes of these emotions in the Schol. to Prop. 51 of this Part, and Propp. 53, 54, and 55 and its Scholium. As to the free resolve of the mind, see Prop. 35, Part 2, Schol. But here it is also to be observed that 'tis no wonder that all acts in general which by custom are called *wrong* are followed by pain, and those which are called *right* by pleasure. For we may easily comprehend from what has been above said that this chiefly depends on education. Parents have so ordered it by reproving the one sort of actions and often rebuking their children therefor, and contrariwise commending and praising the other, that passions of pain are joined with the one, but of pleasure with the other. And this is likewise confirmed by actual experience. For custom and religion be not for all men the same; but what is holy with some is profane with others, and what is honourable with some is base with others. So that according as every man is brought up, he repenteth of a particular deed or maketh boast of the same.

28. Pride is to think too highly of oneself by reason of self-love.

Explanation. The difference of pride and over-esteem is that the latter hath regard to an outward object, but pride to the man himself, esteeming himself overmuch. Now as over-esteem is an effect or property of love, so is pride of selfishness, and may therefore be also thus defined, that it is self-love or self-contentment, in so far as it disposeth one to think too highly of himself. See Prop. 26, Schol. To this emotion there is none contrary. For no man thinks too meanly of himself through hating himself; nay there is no man thinks too meanly of himself, so far as he conceives that he cannot do this or that thing. For whatever a man conceives he cannot do, that he necessarily conceives, and by that notion he is so disposed that in truth he cannot do that which he conceives he cannot do. For so long as he conceives that he cannot do a thing, so long is his action not determined to that thing; and therefore so long is it impossible that he should do it. But now if we consider such things as depend merely on opinion, we can conceive how it may be that a man should think too meanly of himself. It may happen that a man in sorrow, while he considers his own infirmity, imagines that he is despised by everybody; and this while other men have nothing less in their thoughts than despising him. Again, a man may think too meanly of himself if he deny somewhat of himself with regard to a future time whereof he is uncertain; as if he should suppose that he can have no certain conceptions, or can desire and perform nothing but wicked and base things, and the like. Again we may say that a man thinks too meanly of himself when we see that for exceeding fear of shame he will not adventure what others being his equals will. Thus we have an emotion fit to be opposed to pride, which I shall call dejection. For as pride is bred of self-contentment, so is dejection of humility; and accordingly we define it thus:

29. Dejection *(abiectio)* is to think too meanly of oneself by reason of displeasure.

Explanation. Nevertheless pride is wont to be opposed to humility: but then we consider the effects of them rather than their nature. We call that man *proud,* who boasts exceedingly (see Prop. 30, Schol.), who talks of nothing but excellence in himself and faults in others, who would fain have precedence of all others, and who affects the dignity and apparel used by those whose estate is much above his own. Whereas we call him *humble,* who often blushes, who confesses his own faults and tells of other men's excellence, who gives place to all men, and who is of a downcast carriage and negligent of his apparel. Howbeit these emotions, I say humility and dejection, are very scarce. For man's nature, considered in itself, strives against them with all its power (see Propp. 15 and 54); and hence those who pass for being most downcast and humble are oftentimes the most self-seeking and envious.

30. Honour *(gloria)* is pleasure accompanied by the idea of some action of our own which we suppose to be praised by others.

31. Shame is pain accompanied by the idea of some action which we suppose to be blamed by others.

Explanation. As to these see the Scholium to Prop. 30 of this Part. I shall here observe the difference between shame and modesty. Shame is the pain following a deed whereof one is ashamed; but modesty is the apprehension or fear of shame, whereby a man is restrained from any disgraceful action. To modesty is commonly opposed shamelessness, which is in truth not an emotion, as I shall show in due place. But the names of the emotions, as I have already noted, go more to their application than to their nature. Thus much of the emotions of pleasure and pain, which I have now expounded as I purposed: and I go on to those which I ascribe to Desire.

32. Regret is the desire or appetite of possessing something, which is nourished by the remembrance of that thing, and at the same time checked by the remembrance of other things which exclude the existence of the thing so desired.

Explanation. When we remember anything, (as we have often said before), this of itself disposeth us to regard the thing with the same emotion as if it were actually present. But this disposition or effect, at least in waking hours, is mostly constrained by ideas of things which exclude the existence of the thing remembered by us. When therefore we remember a thing which affects us with any sort of pleasure, we at once endeavour to regard it with the same emotion of pleasure as if it were present; and this endeavour is thereupon restrained by the remembrance of things which exclude its existence. Wherefore regret is in truth a pain opposite to that pleasure which arises from the absence of a thing we hate, as to which see Prop. 47, Schol. But since the name of regret seemeth to have regard to desire, I reckon this emotion among those of desire.

33. Emulation is the desire of something excited in us by our conception that others have the like desire.

Explanation. When one runs away at seeing others run or fears at seeing others fear, or on seeing that another hath burnt his hand, draws in his own hand and moves as if his own hand were burnt, we say that he imitates the emotion of the other, but not that he emulates him: not because we know of any difference between the causes of emulation and of imitation, but because use will so have it that we speak of emulation only in him who imitates what he deems honourable, useful, or agreeable. As for the cause of emulation, see Prop. 27 of this Part and the Scholium. And why this emotion doth mostly go in couples with envy, see Prop. 32 with the Scholium thereto.

34. Thankfulness or gratitude is a desire or bent prompted by love, whereby we endeavour to do good to him who has conferred benefit on us in the like disposition. See Prop. 39, with the [first] Scholium to Prop. 41 of this Part.

35. Benevolence is the desire of doing good to one whom we pity. See Prop. 27, Schol. [2].[202]

36. Anger is a desire whereby we are impelled through hatred to do ill to one whom we hate. See Prop. 39.

37. Revenge is a desire whereby we are stirred up through mutual hatred to do ill to one who hath done ill to us with the like disposition. See Prop. 40, Coroll. 2, and the Scholium thereon.

38. Cruelty or barbarity *(saevitia)* is the desire whereby any one is impelled to do evil to one whom we love or pity.

Explanation. To cruelty is opposed clemency, which is not a passion, but the power of the mind whereby a man restrains anger and revenge.

39. Fear is the desire of avoiding at the cost of a lesser evil a greater one which we apprehend. See Prop. 39, Schol.

40. Daring is a desire whereby one is impelled to do somewhat attended with a danger which his peers are afraid to undergo.

41. Cowardice is ascribed to him whose desire is checked by the fear of a danger which his peers dare to undergo.

Explanation. Cowardice therefore is naught else than the fear of an evil which most men are not wont to fear; for which cause I reckon it not with the emotions of desire. Yet I have chosen to explain it here, because, in so far as we attend to the desire, there is a true opposition betwixt it and daring.

42. Consternation is ascribed to him whose desire to

---

[202] Quotred above, p. 229, note.

avoid evil is checked by amazement at the evil he fears.

Explanation. Consternation is therefore a kind of cowardice. But since consternation is bred of a double fear, it may be more conveniently defined as fear which holds a man in such bewilderment or distraction that he cannot remove the evil from him. I say bewilderment, so far as we understand his desire to remove the evil to be checked by amazement. And I say distraction, in so far as we conceive the same desire to be checked by the fear of another ill which equally vexeth him: whereby it comes to pass that he knows not against which of the two to defend himself. See the Scholia to Propp. 39 and 52. As to cowardice and daring, see Prop. 51, Schol.

43. Civility or deference *(humanitas seu modestia)* is the desire of doing what pleaseth men and omitting what displeaseth them.

44. Ambition is an immoderate desire for honour.

Explanation. Ambition is a desire whereby all the emotions are nourished and fortified (by Prop. 27 and 31 of this Part); and therefore this emotion can scarce be overcome. For so long as a man is holden by any desire, he is of necessity holden by this withal. 'The more a man excels,' saith Cicero, 'the more is he led by honour: yea the philosophers write books of despising honour and glory, and set their names to them.'

45. Luxury is unrestrained desire or love (which you will) of feasting.

46. Drunkenness is unrestrained desire and love of drinking.

47. Avarice is unrestrained desire and love of wealth.

48. Lust is in the like manner desire and love in bodily intercourse.

Explanation. Whether this last desire be restrained or not, it is commonly called lust. And these five emotions as noted in the Schol. to Prop. 56) have no contraries. For deference is itself a kind of ambition, as to which see Prop. 29, Schol. For temperance, soberness, and chastity, I have already noted of these also that they express not a passion but a power of the mind. And though it may be that an avaricious, ambitious, or timid man shall abstain from excess in these kinds, yet avarice, ambition, and fear are not contraries to luxury, drunkenness, or

lust.[203] For an avaricious man is oftentimes eager to stuff himself
with food and drink at another man's charges. An ambitious
man, so long as he hopes it may be hid, will stint himself in
nothing; indeed, if he live in drunken and debauched company,
his ambition will but make him the more prone to those vices. As
for the timid man, he doth what he would not. For though a miser should cast his wealth into the sea to escape death, yet he is a
miser still; and so if a lustful man is grieved that he cannot follow his bent, he ceases not thereby to be lustful. And in general
these emotions regard not so much the acts of feasting, drinking,
and so forth, as the inward appetite and liking. So that nothing
can be opposed to these emotions but high-mindedness and valour *(generositatem et animositatem),* whereof more presently.[204]

The definitions of jealousy and other perturbations of the
mind I pass over in silence, as well because they spring from the
compounding of the emotions already defined, as because they
mostly have no special names; which is a sign that for the uses of
life it sufficeth to have a general knowledge of them. And it is
established from tliose definitions of the emotions which we
have expounded that they all have their rise from Desire, Pleasure, or Pain; or rather that there be none beside these three, every
one whereof is wont to be called by divers names after the divers
presentments and tokens of them in outward operation. Considering these primitive emotions and that which we have above
said of the nature of the mind, we may now thus define the emotions, so far as they have regard to the mind alone.

GENERAL DEFINITION OF THE EMOTIONS

EMOTION, which is called a passion *(pathema)* of the
soul, is a confused idea whereby the mind affirms a greater or
less faculty of existence[205] in its body or some part thereof than it
had before, and on the occurrence of which the mind itself is

---

[203] *Castitati* in the Latin text by an obvious slip.

[204] Cp. Prop. 59 of this Part, Schol. *Animositas* and *generositas* are
the two species of *fortitudo.* 'Per animositatem intelligo cupiditatem qua unusquisque conatur suum esse ex solo rationis dictamine conservare. Per generositatem autem cupiditatem intelligo qua unusquisque ex solo rationis
dictamine conatur reliquos homines iuvare et sibi amicitia iungere.'

[205] *Existendi vis* really means neither more nor less than *existentia.*
See p. 221 above.

determined to think on one thing more than another.

Explanation. First, I say that emotion or passion in the soul is a confused idea. For we have shown (Prop. 3 of this Part) that the mind suffers only so far as it hath inadequate or confused ideas. Next, I say 'whereby the mind affirms a greater or less power of existence in its body or some part thereof than it had before.' For all ideas of [other] bodies which we have denote rather the existing disposition of our own body than the nature of the external body (Part 2, Prop. 16, Cor. 2). But the idea wherein an emotion really consists must denote or express the disposition of the body or some part thereof, because the body's active power or faculty of existing is increased or diminished, forwarded or hindered. It is to be observed that when I say 'a greater or less faculty of existence than before,' I intend not that the mind compares the present disposition of the body with a past one, but that the idea wherein the being of the emotion doth consist affirms of the body something which in fact involves more or less of reality than before. And since the nature of the mind consists in this, that it affirms the real present existence of its body (Part 2, Prop. 11 and 13) and we mean by perfection the nature of the thing itself; hence it follows that the mind passes to a greater or less perfection when it happens to it to affirm somewhat of its body or some part thereof which involves more or less of reality than before. When therefore I said above that the mind's power of thinking is increased or diminished, I desired to have only this meaning, that the mind formed an idea of its own body or some part thereof which expressed more or less reality than it had formerly affirmed of the same body. For the dignity of ideas and the present power of thinking are measured by the dignity of the object. Lastly I have added: 'and on the occurrence of which the mind itself is determined to think on one thing more than another,' that besides the nature of pleasure and pain, which the first part of the definition explains, I might also express that of desire.

CHAPTER VIII

THE BURDEN OF MAN

Denn alle Kraft dringt vorwärts in die Weite,
    Zu leben und zu wirken hier und dort;
Dagegen engt und hemmt von jeder Seite
    Der Strom der Welt und reisst uns mit sich fort;
In diesem innern Sturm und äussern Streite
    Vernimmt der Geist ein schwer verstanden Wort:
Von der Gewalt, die alle Wesen bindet,
Befreit der Mensch sich, der sich überwindet.
            GOETHE, *Die Geheimnisse.*

    Once read thy own breast right,
        And thou hast done with fears;
    Man gets no other light,
        Search he a thousand years.
Sink in thyself! there ask what ails thee, at that shrine.
        MATTHEW ARNOLD, *Empedocles on Etna.*

HAVING concluded his purely scientific analysis of the springs of action and passion, Spinoza proceeds to expound in the fourth Part of the Ethics 'the slavery of man, or the power of the emotions.' In a short preface he explains the notions of good and evil, as he conceives them.

'When a man hath determined to make something and brought the same to pass, not only that man himself will call his work perfect, but also every one that rightly knows or conceives himself to know the mind and aim which the author of that work had. For example, if a man shall see a particular work (which I assume to be not yet finished) and knows that the aim of its author is to build a house, he will call the house imperfect, but contrariwise perfect whenever he sees the work brought to the end which its author proposed to make of it. But if a man sees a work the like whereof he hath never seen, nor knows the mind of the workman, 'tis plain he cannot tell whether that work be perfect or not.'

A sentence, one may remark in passing, which deserves much meditation on the part of those who discuss natural theology, but has been before the world these two centuries without producing much result: and if we pause awhile to discuss the idea contained in it the digression will be less than it seems. For on this depends Spinoza's view of ethical good and evil, and consequently his whole theory of ethics.

The argument from design in all its common forms, and most of the obvious objections to it, proceed on the assumption that we have some independent knowledge of what the designs of nature are or may be expected to be. What we find in nature, especially animated nature, is fitness in various degrees for various purposes; organs of sense for example, ranging from a rudimentary state in the lower animals to the delicate and complex apparatus possessed by the highest. To say that this comes of design, and that the particular degree of fitness was designed in each case, is a pure assumption as far as the evidence of nature goes. I speak of degrees of fitness; for to talk of absolute fitness in nature, as popular teleology does or recently did, is merely to disregard the facts. Everything that exists is indeed in one sense the fittest possible; since if it were not so, it would not be the thing existing then and there, but the place would be filled by something else which was fitter under the given conditions. In other words, existence, is not a bare fact but a continuing process, and at every moment of the process the particular set of conditions lias one and only one possible result. This was long ago seen in a general way by Hume, and has been fixed as a distinct scientific conception by Mr. Darwin's discovery of it in a most important and striking concrete form. But if we assume a particular designed purpose, as seeing in the case of the eye, and inquire if the means are as perfect as they conceivably might be, we shall generally if not always find that they are not. Thus the human eye, considered as an optical instrument, has more than one grave defect: and the human ankle-joint is inconveniently weak in proportion to the strain thrown upon it by man's erect attitude in standing and walking. If, again, we say that the greatest fitness under given conditions is equivalent to absolute fitness, and is in fact the standard of perfection in human workmanship, it must be observed that in the case of human workmanship we know that the workman did not make his conditions: or, if there be conditions as to which we are uncertain how far they were within his control, we suspend our judgment as to the part of his work affected by them. Now in the case of the universe we have not this knowledge, and the suspense of judgment must needs be indefinite. We cannot separate the work from the conditions. In order to arrive at any final judgment we ought to know whether the conditions themselves were given with any and what design, and if so, whether or not subject to other conditions. And thus the inquiry would become endless, and we should never have anything solid to show for it. In short, the frame of nature is what it is, neither more nor less. If we believe it to be the work of an extremely powerful being, of intelligence and activities more or less analogous to our own, then we must also believe that it was and is intended to be just what it is. What inferences of any practical value could be drawn from that conclusion is rather too wide a question to be taken in the course of a digression. Some of those which might be drawn by an observer confining himself strictly to the evidence would be as follows: that if the being in question took any pleasure in his operations, it could only be the purely intellectual pleasure of working out a set of fixed rules, which he might possibly be supposed to have fixed by his own choice with that pleasure in view; that he had no conception of pain, and was therefore regardless of the amount of it that might be involved in executing the grand scheme of the universe (for one would not gratuitously ascribe malice to him); and that if that scheme had any ulterior object, it was not the happiness of living creatures generally or of any particular species of them. These inferences, however, are not such as expounders of natural theology either desire or profess to arrive at; and, as I do not myself attach any particular validity to the assumptions on which they would depend, it seems needless to dwell on them.

But now let us assume that we believe in design on independent grounds. Will this take us much farther? We still Cannot criticize the works of nature by the analogy of the productions of human art without knowing to what extent the objects and conditions are similar: we shall therefore still find ourselves in the same condition of absolute suspense. If we take it as known from other sources that the universe is a work of perfect wisdom and goodness, and perfectly adapted to fulfil some purpose which does not appear on the face of things, and which we can only partly understand, then we have after a sort an account of the whole matter. But it is an account which the witness of nature itself cannot either add to or confirm in any way. Detailed criticism and detailed apologies — for such is the tone of modern natural theology at times — are alike in the air, or rather *in vacuo*. It is not uncommon to speak of the wastefulness of nature as if it were something requiring an excuse. But why is it esteemed a merit in human operations to effect the desired result with the least possible expenditure of work and materials? Plainly because the available work and materials are limited. If the resources of the universe were at one's disposal, there would be no occasion for economy. So far as we can form any expectation in the matter, we might reasonably expect a magnified human intelligence commanding all the powers of nature to be at least as wasteful as nature actually is. The stability or instability of the existing order of nature cannot, in like manner, be judged perfect or imperfect unless we know whether or not the order was intended to be permanent. It was an accepted opinion till very lately that the solar system was a self-maintaining and self-compensating machine which, if left to itself, would go on for ever. And, strangely enough, it was commonly held by the same persons who extolled this as a perfection that the solar system, or at any rate the part of it inhabited by mankind, was intended to last only a few thousand years, and at the end of that time to be destroyed. On their assumptions the designer of the solar system acted like a builder who should put a stone house where a wooden shed would have done as well: unless, indeed, it were a mere display of magnificence like that of a barbaric prince at whose command whole palaces rise for the service of a day's festival, and are swept away with all their ornaments when the feast is over. For precisely the same reasons, it would be absurd to say that the instability now discovered by science in the constitution of the solar system is any mark of imperfection. And if we believe that we have evidence or presumption from other quarters of a design tending to the dissolution of the present state of nature, then it is quite fair to speculate on the physical means (imperfect vortex-atoms or the like) by which it might be carried out. Again, a designer may be limited in his choice of means either by external conditions or by some reason of his own; and of these conditions or reasons the spectator may know nothing. In the case of the sensible world and its order it is certain (apart from supernatural information) that we know nothing of them whatever. All our ideas of design and perfection are derived from the efforts of man, a finite being, working for definite objects and with such instruments as he can procure: and the attempt to find something answering to them in the constitution of the universe leads to nothing but insoluble perplexities. All this was most clearly seen by Spinoza, and the mastery of his conceptions, whether learnt from himself or from some other teacher, is the first condition of any free and rational treatment of the questions which beset the boundaries of our positive knowledge. I do not mean that it is necessary to accept Spinoza's ideas, but that it is necessary to know of their existence and to understand them.

The primary meaning of such terms as *perfect* and *imperfect* is according to Spinoza not only relative, but relative to the accomplishment of some particular design. But the formation of general ideas leads men to take their general idea of a species or kind as a standard, and regard every departure from it as an imperfection. And this way of thinking and speaking is applied indiscriminately to natural and to artificial productions, though we cannot ascribe design, or therefore apply any test of perfection in this sense, to nature as a whole.

'For that eternal and infinite being which we call God or nature acts by the same necessity wherewith it exists... so that the reason or cause why God or nature acts, and why he exists, is one and the same. As therefore he exists not for the sake of any end, so he acts for the sake of none; but hath as well of existing as of acting no beginning nor end. That which is called a final cause is nothing but the desire of man itself, considered as the origin or primary cause of anything. As when we say that to be inhabited was the final cause of this or that house, then 'tis plain we understand merely this, that a man having conceived in his mind the conveniency of dwelling in a house, was thereupon desirous to build it.'

Perfection and imperfection, then, are relative notions or ways of thinking, dependent on our classification and comparison of things. If we try to apply them on a universal scale, the only class-notion remaining with us for the purpose is the *genus generalissimum* of mere being, and we must measure perfection by amount of being or reality. Thus Spinoza explains his own former definition of perfection as identical with reality.[206] And apparently he regards it, or tends in this place to regard it, as only a particular aspect of things to finite minds that one should appear to have 'plus entitatis seu realitatis' than another. But on this he is not explicit.

The ethical notions of good and evil are the notions of perfection and imperfection, as applied to human character and conduct by means of a normal idea or standard of man. That the terms are in themselves relative is obvious.

'Music is good for a melancholic patient, bad for a man in grief; for a deaf man it is neither good nor bad. But though this be so, yet these words are to be kept in use. For since we desire to form an idea of man as a type of human nature to be set before us, it will be convenient to keep these words in the sense I have mentioned. By *good* I shall therefore understand hereafter that which we are assured is a means for approaching more and more nearly to the pattern of human nature we set before ourselves; and by *evil* that which we are assured is a hindrance to our copying of the same pattern. Further, we shall speak of men as more or less perfect, as they approach this pattern more or less nearly.'

Some definitions follow, of which we need only say that, by a distinction now first introduced, a *contingent* thing is defined as that which is not known to be necessary or impossible in respect of itself, or which we can equally well conceive to exist or not to exist; a *possible* thing as one not known to be necessary or impossible in respect of its conditions, or as to which we do not know if the conditions required for its production are fulfilled. There is a single axiom: 'No particular thing is found in nature which is not exceeded in power and strength by some other: but whatsoever thing be taken, another more powerful can be found, whereby the first may be destroyed.'

Man is a part of nature; his powers are limited and subject to be overmastered by external causes. On external causes, too, depends the strength of human passions; for passion is the modification of the mind under an external cause Hence flows a proposition of the first practical importance, that 'emotion cannot be controlled or removed, save by a contrary emotion

---

[206] *Eth.* ii. def. 6.

stronger than that which is to be controlled.'[207] Repeatedly one is led to marvel at Spinoza's critics, and ask oneself if they really have read him: and here one stops to doubt whether this most true and pregnant statement can ever have been considered by those who represent Spinoza as a framer of mere intellectual puzzles, having no root in the deeper part of man's feelings. It is not insignificant that the proof, which however would not add much to the conviction of a modern reader, is in form physiological. Hence knowledge, as such, is incompetent to restrain the passions: it can have that effect only in so far as it is an emotion.[208] And in fact knowledge of good or evil is in the nature of pleasure or pain; for it is by reference to supposed utility, which involves reference to pleasure and pain, that we determine any particular thing to be good or evil. Thus 'the knowledge of good and evil is nothing else than an emotion of pleasure or pain, in so far as we are conscious thereof.' Observe that this knowledge, or in English it would be better to say judgment, is not as yet assumed to be correct. Or, if we say that pleasure as such is always good, and pain as such always bad, which Spinoza does say later (Pr. 41 of this Part), we may affirm that an immediate judgment of good or evil is correct in itself, but not necessarily so with regard to concomitants and consequences. But even if we have a true judgment *(vera boni et mali cognitio)* the emotion produced by it may not prevail over other emotions conflicting with it. For emotion due to a present exciting cause is, other things being equal, stronger than that which proceeds from contemplation of something distant in time or place: and so memory and expectation are themselves more intense in proportion to the nearness of their objects; unless indeed the remoteness in time of the different objects compared be such that for our imagination both are practically infinite.[209] Again, that which we conceive as necessary affects us more strongly than that which is conceived as possible or contingent. In this and other ways the desires arising from a true knowledge of good and evil may be restrained or suppressed by others arising from divers contrary emotions. And in particular 'the desire arising from the knowledge of good and

---

[207] *Eth.* iv. 7.
[208] Prop. 14.
[209] Prop. 9, 10.

evil, so far as this knowledge has regard to the future, may easily be constrained or extinguished by the desire of things which are agreeable in the present.'[210] Hence the weakness of human nature and the difficulty of obeying the dictates of reason; hence the danger of wrong-doing in the face of knowledge, whereof the Preacher said, He that increaseth knowledge increaseth sorrow. We see that Spinoza felt profoundly and acutely the need of understanding being 'touched with emotion' before it can bring forth the fruit of good living. But his purpose is not to discourage men from well-doing.

'This I say not for any such purpose as to conclude that ignorance is to be chosen before knowledge, or that a fool and a man of understanding differ nothing as to the control of their passions; but because it is needful to know as well the power as the weakness of our nature, that we may determine what reason can and cannot do in controlling the passions. And in this part, as I have promised, I shall treat only of human weakness. For of the power of reason over the passions I am minded to treat apart.'[211]

Leaving it, then, for future consideration how the power of following reason is to be acquired, Spinoza proceeds to set forth what the precepts of reason are. He begins with a summary introduction which gives the leading ideas of his ethical system in a wonderfully short compass.

'Since reason demands nothing against nature, it therefore demands that every man do love himself, seek his own interest (I mean that which is truly so), and desire whatsoever truly leads a man to greater perfection; and generally that every man endeavour, so far as in him lies, to maintain his own being. And this is as necessary a truth as that the whole is greater than its part. Then forasmuch as virtue is nothing else than acting by the proper laws of one's own nature, and no man endeavours to maintain his own being otherwise than by those laws: it follows in the first place that the foundation of virtue is this very endeavour, and that happiness doth consist in a man's having power to maintain his own being. Secondly it follows that virtue is to be desired for its own sake, and nothing preferable or more useful can be found for whose sake it should be desired. And thirdly, it follows that men who kill themselves are infirm of mind, and merely overcome

---

[210] Prop , 16.
[211] Prop. 17, Schol.

by external causes repugnant to their own nature.[212] Again, it follows from the fourth postulate of the second Part[213] that we never can bring it to pass that we need nothing outside us to maintain our being, or live without any conversation with things that are outside us; and if moreover we consider our own mind, our understanding would surely be less perfect if the mind were alone and understood not anything beyond itself. Thus there be many things outside us, which are useful for us and therefore to be desired. Among these none more excellent can be thought of than such as wholly agree with our own nature: since if two individuals of the same nature are joined together, they make a new individual twice as powerful as either. Nothing, therefore, is so useful to man as man, nothing more excellent, I say, can be sought by men towards maintaining their being than that all should so agree in all things as that the minds and bodies of all should make up as it were one mind and one body, and all together strive to maintain their being to the best of their power, and all together seek the common interest of all. Hence it follows that men who are governed by reason, or who seek their own interest after the guidance of reason, desire nothing for themselves which they desire not for other men; and therefore also they be just, faithful, and honourable.'

This is given expressly as a short preliminary sketch, in order to obviate the prejudices of those who might be disposed to think 'that this principle, namely, that every man's duty is to seek his own interest, is the beginning of wickedness, and not of virtue and righteousness.' But the outlines of an ethical system are quite distinctly laid down; and we may conveniently pause here to notice the singular resemblance to Stoic doctrine. A life according to reason, which consists in following out the law of one's own nature, or self-preservation in the fullest sense, was precisely that which the Stoics aimed at. What they meant by following nature, however vague the phrase appears in itself, is the same that Spinoza means by *suum esse conservare*. It is the putting forth and maintenance of the activities proper to the individual and the species. With them no less than with Spinoza self-conservation was the ultimate spring of action.

For them, likewise, it is a fundamental axiom that only in the society of his fellow-men can man effectually preserve his

---

[212] It is difficult to see why a point of detail like this should be made so prominent. Can Spinoza have been thinking of Uriel Da Costa?

[213] 'The human body has need for its maintenance of many other bodies, whereby it is constantly as it were refashioned.'

being, fulfil the law of his specific welfare, or, as they said, 'follow nature.' Both the Stoics and Spinoza seem to treat the social character of man as a fact of common experience not open to contradiction and requiring no proof. Their morality is so far egoistic that they admit as a first principle that every man must seek his own welfare. But it is not selfish; for the very first of their mediate axioms is the contradiction of selfishness. The first condition of a man's welfare is the welfare of the society of which he is a part, or, as the Stoics said, a limb. Practical morality is therefore not individual but social, and the reasonable man can find his own weal only by pursuing the common weal and doing good to his fellow-men.

There are other points of coincidence, for example the determinism which is hardly less prominent in the Stoics than in Spinoza, and the stress laid on the active nature of virtue. On the other hand there are great differences in the general philosophical bases of the two systems. The Stoics were devoted adherents of teleology, which Spinoza wholly rejects; and to follow nature was to them the same thing as to follow reason, because they held nature, both in its general constitution and in specific forms, to be eminently reasonable. Spinoza could not speak of 'following Nature' as they did, though he speaks with them of following reason, and coincides with Stoic language even in the detail of ascribing freedom as a special honourable attribute to the wise or reasonable man. 'The wise man alone is free, and the fool is a slave' was one of the famous Stoic paradoxes: a paradox for this reason, that wisdom in the Stoic sense is an ideal state of passionless perfection which hardly anyone attains, and whoever has not attained this wisdom is yet in the outer darkness of folly. A form of speech like this might easily have been picked up by Spinoza from Horace or Cicero; but as to the deeper resemblances, I do not think they are to be ascribed to imitation, for the very reason that they go so far down. It is certain that Spinoza's acquaintance with Greek philosophy was superficial; anything he knew of the Stoics must have been at second-hand, and the resemblances in question have much more the air of being due to independent work on parallel lines than of being derived from second-hand information. One very characteristic point of Spinoza's ethical theory, the doctrine that emotion can be controlled only by emotion, is entirely absent from the teaching of the Stoics. They trust to pure reason to furnish not only light but heat and motive power, thus ignoring the strength and bondage of the passions, the 'affectuum vires' on which Spinoza so minutely and pitilessly dwells. The difference may not be of great practical importance if we compare the two systems as working systems of morality, in which point of view they seem almost identical. For the mental discipline and contemplation recommended by the Stoics are of a kind well fitted to produce the moral emotion required by Spinoza and all the best modern moralists as a necessary condition of righteousness, or rather the constant reserve of moral emotion which we call a moral temper. And, if the disposition be produced, it matters little for practical purposes whether it finds its due place in the scientific account of the process given by the teachers. This temper of moral devotion, if one may so call it, and the means of maintaining it, were indeed recognized as of importance; for example, they are not unfrequently considered by Marcus Aurelius; but these reflexions go side by side with positive statements that the mere knowledge of good and evil suffices to overcome evil impulses; or in other words that vice is nothing but ignorance.

The scientific advance of Spinoza's doctrine upon this is very great, and is of itself enough to establish his independent merit.[214]

The following propositions, in which Spinoza works out the doctrines briefly sketched in the passage last translated, fall into four groups.

The first deals with self-maintenance as the foundation of virtue (Prop. 19-25): the second with intelligence as the foundation of ethical judgment (26-28): the third, with the common nature and interests of men as the ground of social ethics (29-37): the fourth considers in detail what bodily and mental affections are good or bad with reference to man's common weal, and herein of the conduct and duties of the reasonable man (38-73): lastly, the ethical maxims are collected and restated in an Appendix.

First, the self-maintaining activity is the foundation of virtue. For virtue is active power, and power is the affirmation of

---

[214] On the resemblance and contrast between Spinoza and the Stoics, compare Trendelenburg, *Histor. Beiträge,* iii. 396-397.

the agent's existence. Living must come before living well, and
no man can desire a virtuous life without also desiring life itself.
'Virtuous action, as such *(ex virtute absolute agere),* is in us
nothing else than to act, live, or maintain one's own being (these
three are all one) according to reason and on the footing of
seeking our own interest.'[215]

Now the self-affirmation of the mind is understanding,
since the proper nature of the human mind is to understand: so
that the self-maintaining endeavour which is the beginning of
virtue is an endeavour after understanding. Hence good is whatever helps the understanding, evil whatever hinders it; and the
highest good is the knowledge of God, the most complete object
of knowledge and the condition of all other knowledge and existence. To know God (in other words to know the order of nature and regard the universe as orderly) is the highest function of
the mind: and knowledge, as the perfect form of the mind's normal activity, is good for its own sake and not as a means.

The attempt to reduce the proper nature and function of
the mind to pure intelligence, which is made in Pr. 26, is open to
much criticism. It depends on the doctrine that all real action is a
function of intellect (Part 3, Pr. 3): but even assuming this, the
self-maintaining effort of the mind 'quatenus ratiocinatur' is
briefly taken as equivalent to and involving the maintenance or
welfare of the whole man. The supremacy of reason is insuffi-
ciently explained and not proved at all. Spinoza's position here is
no doubt connected with the Peripatetic theory of the active intellect, and prepares the way for the peculiar developments of the
fifth Part of the Ethics.

The next group of propositions leads up to the social
grounds of morality by a chain of formal proof which is more
ingenious than convincing, and seems not even formally invul-
nerable. For instance, 'commune aliquid nobiscum' in Prop. 29
appears to be used in a different sense from 'cum nostra natura
commune' in Prop. 30: and Prop. 30 is difficult to follow. It is
easy to understand the position of Prop. 29, that we cannot be
affected for good or harm by anything which has not 'commune
aliquid nobiscum:' *e.g.* bodily hurt must be inflicted by a material body. But how then can we say with Prop. 30 that a thing is

---

[215] Prop. 24.

never hurtful 'per id quod cum nostra natura commune habet?' One human body may hurt another very much, by knocking it down or otherwise. If we say that this depends not on the assailing body being human, but on its being a solid body, the common properties of matter still remain: A runs against B and hurts himself: it is true he might have hurt himself as much or more by running against a post. But in any case the properties of mass and impenetrability are common to A's body and B's, and are of the essence of the hurt that follows. For if parts of A's body and B's could be in the same place at once, there would be no resistance, no violent compression of the colliding parts, and no hurt. Or if *natura* includes, as it probably does, the amount and distribution of energy in the particular material system affected (cp. Prop. 39), still the difference or incongruousness between the disturbed system and the external body is not of kind but of degree. There is still 'aliquid commune.' I think it must be allowed that Spinoza's way of talking of *natura* in this and similar passages is not free from residual entanglements of scholasticism.

Spinoza's object is to show that men disagree only in so far as they are swayed by passion, and agree in so far as they are governed by reason. Passion being an infirmity or negation, men cannot be said to agree in it; just as it is an abuse of language to say that white and black are similar in not being red. The counter-proposition that 'in so far as men live according to reason, they always and necessarily agree,' is supported by an appeal to experience which is more satisfactory than the formal reasoning.

'Experience likewise bears witness to our proposition every day, so clearly and abundantly that it is a common speech, that man is as a God to man. Yet it seldom happens that men live according to reason; but such is their fashion that they mostly bear ill will and do mischief to one another. Nevertheless they cannot endure a life of solitude, so that the definition of man as a social animal hath been in general approved: as indeed it is the truth of the matter that far more convenience than hurt arises from the common fellowship of men' (*i.e.* even when they do not live according to reason). 'Wherefore let the satirists make sport of human affairs as much as they will; let theologians decry them; let misanthropes do their utmost to extol a rude and churlish life, despising men, and admiring the brutes: yet men shall find that their needs are much best satisfied by mutual help, and that only by joining their strength they can escape the dangers that everywhere beset them; not to say how much more excellent it is and worthy of our knowledge to consider the actions of men than of beasts.'[216]

Passages of this kind give to Spinoza's system — strange as this may appear to such as know it only at second-hand — the character of a morality of common sense: and herein he shows an affinity to Aristotle's cast of thought which in this particular place is conspicuous. The position that good men are naturally friends, and that theirs is the best and only durable friendship, is dwelt upon with some fulness in the Eighth Book of the Nicomachean Ethics.[217] And Aristotle calls to witness the ordinary experience of reasonable men in very much the same way as Spinoza. In this case imitation or derivation is wholly out of the question: Spinoza knew Aristotle only in the distorted version given by so-called Aristotelian philosophy. The work of restoring Aristotle to his true place has hardly been effected even yet: in Spinoza's time it had not been begun.

Spinoza goes on to show that the highest good aimed at by virtuous or reasonable men is common to all and may be equally enjoyed by all, and that the virtuous man desires the same good for his fellows as for himself:[218] and he lays down in outline the foundations of civil society and law. His position, expressed in modern language, would be that society is antecedent to law; that legal right and wrong can exist only with reference to a government, and moral right and wrong only with reference to a community. The form in which he states it, however, is that 'every one exists by an absolute natural right,' and pursues by the same right whatever he supposes to be his own interest. If all men lived according to reason, their desires and pursuits would never clash, and the 'summum naturae ius' would suffice them without further definition. But, since in fact men are subject to passions, and one man's desires are incompatible with another's, they can live together and form a society only on the footing of mutual concession. This concession is guaranteed by the common authority of the society, operating not by reason (for the passions can be restrained only by stronger passion) but by the fear of penalties. The course of living prescribed by the community under the sanction of a penalty is law: 'and the

---

[216] Pr. 35, Schol.
[217] Cap. 3, sqq. I am indebted for this parallel to Prof. Land.
[218] Pr. 36, 37.

community thus established by laws and the power of self-maintenance is called a state, and those who are within its protection citizens.' Good and ill desert, justice and injustice, depend on the political order and exist only in the political or social state, 'where it is ordained by common consent what is good and bad, and every man is bound to obey the civil authority.'

'In the state of nature no man is owner of anything by common consent, nor does anything exist which can be said to be one man's more than another's; but all things are all men's, and thus in the state of nature we cannot conceive any purpose of giving every man his own,[219] nor yet of depriving any one of that which is his: that is, nothing done in the state of nature can be called either just or unjust. This becomes possible only in the civil state, where it is ordained by common consent what belongs to this and to that man.'

Here we have a first sketch of Spinoza's theory of law and politics, which coincides in the main with that of Hobbes, and so anticipates in its broad features the analysis adopted and developed by the later English school of jurisprudence. In this place however it is meagrely and not quite opportunely presented, and is not seen to advantage. One is struck by the capital omission to distinguish in any way between positive civil law, custom, and what we now call positive morality. The obvious fact that moral wrong-doing extends far beyond disobedience to the civil law, which leaves untouched many things commonly judged worthy of the strongest moral disapprobation, appears to be simply ignored. In order to make Spinoza's account complete even in outline on its own ground and from its own point of view, we need the conception of positive morality as a kind of informal law which aims at governing conduct in a particular society, and acts through the sanctions of collective approbation and disapprobation, being administered not by any set tribunal or officers, but by the members of the community at large. But on these points we need not dwell at present.

Next comes the consideration in detail of what things are useful and hurtful to man's common estate. In the first place, everything is useful which tends to preserve life, or, as Spinoza

---

[219] Voluntas unicuique suum tribuendi: alluding to the familiar definition of justice in the civil law (iustitia est constans et perpetua voluntas ius suum cuique tribuens, I. i. 1).

puts it in the language of his Cartesian physics and physiology, 'whatever tends to preserve the proportion of motion and rest subsisting betwixt the parts of the human body is good; and contrariwise that is bad which tends to alter the same proportion:'[220] the specific and individual character of any body whatever being considered as resulting from the mutual communication of motion among its particles in a certain definite proportion. The destruction or change of character consequent on the disturbance of this proportion in a living body is however not necessarily equivalent to death in the ordinary sense.

'I am not so bold as to deny,' adds Spinoza in the Scholium, 'that a human body, keeping the circulation of the blood and other properties which are esteemed the marks of life, may nevertheless receive another nature wholly different from its former one. For no reason compels me to hold that the body dies not unless it become a corpse; nay experience would seem to suggest the contrary. It sometimes befalls a man to suffer such change as that I would scarce call him the same, as I have heard tell of a Spanish poet, who having been seized with great sickness and recovered therefrom, yet was left so forgetful of his past life that he believed not the plays he had writ to be his own, and might indeed have been held for a grown-up child if he had forgotten his mother-tongue as well. And if this appear incredible, what shall we say of infants, whom a man of ripe age thinks to be so unlike himself in kind that he could never be persuaded he had been such himself, did he not apply to himself the analogy of other men? But lest I should afford occasion to superstitious persons for raising novel questions, I shall leave these matters alone.'

This is the whole of Spinoza's contribution to the vexed question of personal identity, which he seems to regard (and rightly so from the scientific point of view) as at best merely curious. In an equally general but simpler proposition which immediately precedes this one[221] it is laid down that such things are good as increase the capacity of the human body to receive impressions from without and to impress its own action on outward things. For the manifold and various adaptation of the body is likewise an adaptation of the mind and increases its power of knowledge. Pleasure as such is good, since it tends to increase of

---

[220] Pr. 39, referring to Def. in the Excursus after Pr. 13, part 2.
[221] Pr. 38.

active power, and pain as such is bad.[222] But localized pleasure
(titillatio) may be bad as interfering unduly with the activity of
other parts and of the body as a whole; and a pain which serves
to control this local excess of pleasure may be good. Love and
desire may, for the same cause, be excessive and unreasonable.
Hatred is never good; for it aims at the destruction of our fellow-
man; and the same consequence holds of all the emotions derived from it, such as envy, derision, contempt, anger. Here a
very interesting Scholium is added.

'Between derision and laughter I mark a great difference. For
laughter, like jesting, is mere pleasure; and therefore is in itself good,
so it be not excessive. Surely 'tis but an ill-favoured and sour superstition that forbids rejoicing. For why is it a better deed to quench thirst
and hunger than to drive out melancholy? This is my way of life, and
thus have I attuned my mind. No deity, nor any one but an envious
churl, hath delight in my infirmity and inconvenience, nor reckons towards our virtues weeping, sobs, fear, and other such matters which are
tokens of a feeble mind; but contrariwise the more we are moved with
pleasure, the more we pass to greater perfection, that is, the more must
we needs partake of the divine nature. Therefore it is the wise man's
part to use the world and delight himself in it as he best may, not indeed to satiety, for that is no delight. A wise man, I say, will recruit and
refresh himself with temperate and pleasant meat and drink, yea and
with perfumes, the fair prospect of green woods, apparel, music, sports
and exercises, stage-plays and the like, which every man may enjoy
without any harm to his neighbour. For the human body is compounded
of very many parts different of kind, which ever stand in need of new
and various nourishment, that the whole body alike may be fit for all
actions incident to its kind, and that by consequence the mind may be
equally fit for apprehending many things at once.'[223]

If at a former passage we were tempted to call Spinoza a
Stoic, we shall perhaps be tempted now to call him an Epicurean.
Here is none of the Stoic disdain for the common amenities of
life, no artificial striving to visit them with indifference or dis-
credit, no attempt to make a virtue of dispensing with them. Let
us remember that the speaker is one who did in his own person
largely dispense with them, and whose life was not only temper-

---

[222] Laetitia directe mala non est, sed bona; tristitia autem contra directe est mala. Pr. 41.

[223] Prop. 45, Schol.

ate, but quiet and frugal in the extreme. This is not the apology of a man of the world for his careless living, but the grave unrepining approval of innocent pleasures by a student debarred by his own circumstances from sharing in many of them. Nor does he approve them simply because they are pleasant, but as tending to a high purpose, the many-sided culture of body and mind. Yet the pursuits and enjoyments he mentions are simple and familiar ones, such as are more or less within the reach of every one above absolute poverty, and such as at this day naturally present themselves to an observer in most civilized countries. England, unhappily, is the one land where Spinoza's lesson falls most strangely on the ears of good and well-meaning men and is most sorely needed. In truth the need is a crying one, and we are only beginning to learn that rational recreation is a thing worth studying. But perhaps we shall hardly give ear to Spinoza in this matter while we refuse to profit by the living example of our nearest neighbours and kinsfolk. After all it may be best that we should go farther back yet and learn of the Greeks, who first and most perfectly discovered the worth and dignity of human life. We can say nothing better or greater of Spinoza's doctrine in this passage than that he unconsciously Atticizes.

There is something touching in the thought of this man, weak in body, of slender estate, living by sedentary toil and giving his leisure to philosophy, thus reconstructing for himself the Athenian ideal of a free and joyous life, in which the pursuit of beauty is chastened by wisdom and temperance, while wisdom itself is informed with the delight of a fine art, and contemplation goes hand in hand with the manhood and active fellowship of citizens. If it be said that this ideal fails to include the strenuous and self-denying aspects of virtue, the proposition is at least doubtful; but for the present it suffices to say that Spinoza at all events prescribes a canon of conduct as lofty and unselfish as any moral teacher of ancient or modern times. Not that in Spinoza's view any virtue is really self-denying: for the denial and restraint of the unruly passions and of all that we call selfish is the strengthening and affirmation of man's true self. But let us hear his next precept.

'He who lives according to reason endeavours to the utmost of his power to outweigh another man's hate, anger or despite against him with love or high-mindedness... He who chooses to avenge wrong by requiting it with hatred is assuredly miserable. But he who strives to cast out hatred by love may fight his fight in joy and confidence; he can withstand many foes as easily as one, and is in nowise beholden to fortune for aid. As for those he doth conquer, they yield to him joyfully, and that not because their strength faileth, but because it is increased.'[224]

The ethical value of the specific emotions is assigned on the principle that only those are good which spring from the active and rational part of man's nature. Hope and fear, since they involve pain, are good only so far as they may check the excess of other passions (Pr. 47). Pity, for the same reason, is in itself worse than useless, and will be shunned by the reasonable man (Pr. 50). Spinoza is careful to explain in what sense he means this, which in fact is the sense in which the Stoics laid down similar rules.

'A man who rightly knows that everything follows from the necessity of God's being and happens according to the eternal laws of nature will in truth find nothing worthy of hate, mockery, or contempt, nor will he pity any one; but, so much as human power admits, he will endeavour to do well, as they say, and be of good cheer. Moreover it is to be noted that he who is lightly touched with the passion of pity and moved by the distress or tears of another often doth somewhat of the which he afterwards repents; because as well we do nothing out of passion which we surely know to be good, as we are easily deceived by feigned lamentations. But[225] in this place I particularly intend a man who lives according to reason. For one who is moved neither by reason nor by pity to help others is justly called inhuman, since he acts as if he had no likeness to man.'

In like manner humility and repentance, though not part of the reasonable man's character, are relatively useful, and necessary for the government of mankind. Since men must err, it is better they should err on the side of submission than on that of pride and violence. This admission of a scale of relative merit as between passions and motives which in themselves are all alike unworthy of the reasonable man may remind us of certain features in the Stoic system, though the analogy is not exact. On the other hand the emotions which can be purely active, as goodwill

---

[224] Prop. 46, and Schol.

[225] Perhaps we should read *atqui* for *atque*. The Dutch version omits the con junction altogether.

(favor), self-contentment *(acquiescentia in se ipso)*, honour *(gloria)*, may have a reasonable origin and be positively good. And generally 'every activity to which we are determined by an emotion in the nature of passion may be determined in us by reason without such emotion' (Pr. 59). No particular action is in itself either good or bad, and therefore every particular action may in some conceivable circumstances be induced by reason. The act of striking, for instance, is in itself the lifting of the arm, closing of the fist, and forcible bringing down of the arm; and, considered as a physical action, it is a manifestation of the power or excellence proper to the human body *(virtus quae ex corporis humani fabrica concipitur)*. But the act may be performed for an infinite variety of purposes, lawful or unlawful, wise or foolish. The attitude and movements of Hamlet playing in good faith are the same as those of Laertes with his poisoned rapier. Cicero's hand wrote consummate prose with the same motion and characters as worthless verse.

'So, if a man that is moved with anger or hate is thereby determined to close his fist or move his arm, this happens (as we showed in the second part) because one and the same action may be joined with any sort of images of things; and thus we may be determined as well by images of things we conceive confusedly, as by those we conceive clearly and distinctly, to one and the same action. It appears therefore that every desire arising from an emotion of the passionate kind would be of no utility if men could be led by reason.'

In other words, reason and the active emotions related to it afford an adequate motive for every reasonably desirable act: but such motives will be effective only so far as the man to whom they are presented is reasonable.

One reason of desire being irrational, or not regarding the interest of the agent as a whole, is its proceeding from local pleasure or pain; and 'since pleasure is mostly referred to some one part of the body, we mostly exercise the desire to maintain our being without taking any thought of our health as a whole.' Another reason is the undue preponderance of the present over the future in our most common desires.[226] This however does not occur when the mind is guided by reason in its judgments; for then it conceives things 'under the form of eternity or necessity,'

---

[226] Pr. 60, and Schol.

and facts are regarded in their true relations and independent of their being past, present or future. Hence, in so far as we act reasonably, we choose not only the greater of two goods and the lesser of two evils, but a greater good in the future before a lesser in the present, and a lesser evil in the present which is to be outweighed by a greater good in the future.[227] In this group of propositions it is also pointed out that reasonable action is never produced by fear: 'under reasonable desire we seek the good directly and avoid evil indirectly... This is illustrated by the case of a sick and a healthy man. The sick man eats what he dislikes for fear of death; but the whole man enjoys his food and so hath better use of life than if he feared death and had an immediate desire of avoiding it. So the judge, when he sentences a criminal to death not from hate or anger, but merely for love toward the public weal, is led by reason alone.' (Pr. 63, schol. 2).

This part of the Ethics is now brought to a close by an enunciation of the qualities of the reasonable, or, as Spinoza now puts it with the Stoics, the free man. Here his propositions assume the nature of aphorisms; they cannot be considered strictly capable of proof, and that which stands first, one of the noblest and most weighty sayings ever uttered, seems to foreshadow the more daring flights of the succeeding book. Yet, if we regard it as a precept for use in life, it is on a scientific view of man's nature as just and reasonable as it is morally elevating; and the demonstration offered by Spinoza is extremely simple.

'A free man thinks of death least of all things, and his wisdom is a meditation not of death but of life.

Demonstr. A free man, that is, one who lives only by the bidding of reason, is not led by the fear of death, but immediately desires good; that is, to act, to live, and maintain his own being on the footing of seeking his true interest. And therefore he thinks of nothing less than of death, and his wisdom is a meditation of life; which was to be proved.' (Pr. 67.)

Again,

'If men were born free, they would, so long as they were free,

---

[227] Pr. 62, 65, 66. In Pr. 66, 'malum praesens minus quod causa est futuri [*futura* ed. Bruder by misprint] alicuius *mali*' is obviously corrupt. The contemporary Dutch translator appears to have read *maioris boni,* which may be accepted as a practically certain correction *(Nagel. Schriften,* p. 244).

form no notion of good and evil.' (Pr. 68.)

This depends on a foregoing proposition (64) that the knowledge of evil is necessarily inadequate; and it seems to be a direct reminiscence of Maimonides, who says (More Nebuchim, c. 2) that Adam before the Fall had a true 'intellectual comprehension' and knew nothing of probable opinion, to which the categories of good and evil belong. By the unfallen intellect things were distinguished not as good and evil, but only as true and false. Spinoza gives in a Scholium a not dissimilar interpretation of the Mosaic history, and endeavours incidentally to find authority in it for various points of his psychology. To what extent he was serious in this must be left to every reader's conjecture; but it is quite possible that he was really disposed, after the example abundantly set by Maimonides and others, to regard the legends of Genesis as elaborate philosophical allegories.

The statement that 'only free men are perfectly grateful to one another,' which has already been thrown out in general terms, is now given as a formal proposition (Pr. 71): there seems to be a play on the meaning of the adjective which is rather more natural in Latin than in English. On the other hand (Pr. 70), a free man whose conversation is among the ignorant will avoid receiving favours from them; for he cannot please them except by requiting them after their own manner with such things as are good in their conceit. But the desire of the free man is to seek both for himself and for other men only that which is pointed out as good by reason. 'Therefore the free man, that he may neither come into ill repute with the ignorant, nor follow their appetites instead of holding to reason only, will endeavour, so far as he may, to eschew favour from them.' But Spinoza is careful to add a word of explanation to show that he does not counsel a cynical and unsociable reserve. 'I say *so far as he may.* For though men be ignorant, yet they are men, and in our necessary occasions can give a man's help, than which nothing is more excellent. And therefore it often happens to be of necessity to receive some favour from them, and by consequence to return thanks to them after their own fashion. Moreover a certain caution must be observed in the act of declining favours, lest we seem to despise men, or to be so avaricious that we fear having to recompense them, and thus fall into giving ground of offence by our very care to avoid it. So that in declining favours regard must be had to expediency and good manners.'

Again 'the free man never acts fraudulently, but always in good faith;' and this is laid down as an universal proposition applicable even to extreme cases (Pr. 72). Lastly the reasonable man finds true and perfect freedom not in a solitary independence but in living in society and under a common law with his fellow-men (Pr. 73). It is considered unnecessary to follow out in detail the character of the wise or, as he is now called, the strong man. That he will hate no man, have no anger, envy, or contempt for any one, and be free from pride, easily follows from the general propositions already given as to the conditions of social and reasonable life. Spinoza now proceeds to collect the precepts of right living already stated or implied in various parts of his argument into a more compact form. This appendix is as follows.

'Cap. 1. All our endeavours or desires so follow of necessity from our nature that they may be understood either by that nature alone as their immediate cause, or only by regarding ourselves as a part of nature, which cannot be adequately conceived by itself apart from other particular things.

C. 2. The desires which follow from our nature in such wise that they may be understood by it alone are those which are ascribed to the mind in so far as it is conceived as consisting of adequate ideas; but other desires are ascribed to the mind only in so far as it conceives things inadequately, and their strength and increase must be defined not by the power of man but by the power of things outside us. And therefore the former are justly called *actions,* the latter *passions.* For the former ever denote our power, the latter our impotence and maimed knowledge.

C. 3. Our actions (that is, those desires which be determined by man's power or by reason) are always good; the rest may be either good or bad.

C. 4. It is therefore of exceeding use in life to perfect, so far as we can, the understanding or reason, and herein alone consisteth the highest happiness or blessedness of man. Blessedness, indeed, is nothing else than the contentment of mind arising from the intuitive knowledge of God. And to perfect the understanding is nothing else than to understand God and the attributes of God, and the actions that necessarily follow from his nature. Wherefore the final aim of a man led by reason, that is, the chief desire whereby he seeks to govern all others, is that which makes for the adequate conception both of himself and of all things which be subjects of his intelligence.

C. 5. There is therefore no reasonable life without intelligence, and things are good only in so far as they help man to enjoy that spiritual life which the name of *intelligence* doth signify. And those things which hinder man from perfecting his reason and enjoying the rational life are alone by us called evil.

C. 6. Now because all things whereof man is the sole efficient cause are necessarily good, no evil can happen to man save by outward causes; to wit, inasmuch as man is a part of nature, whose laws his nature is bound to obey, and he to accommodate himself to her in almost infinite ways.

C. 7. And it cannot be otherwise than that man should be a part of nature and follow her common order; but if his conversation be with such creatures as agree with his own nature, thereby man's active power will be holpen and fostered. Contrariwise if he be among those whose nature agrees not with his own, he will scarce be able to accommodate himself to them without some great change in himself.

C. 8. Whatsoever is found in nature which we judge to be *evil,* or to be capable of hindering our existence and enjoyment of life in reason, that we may repel from ourselves by whatever way seems the safer. And whatever is found on the other hand which we judge *good* or *useful* for the maintenance of our being and enjoyment of life in reason, that we may take and convert to our own use as we will. And generally every one hath an absolute natural right of doing what he judgeth to make for his own advantage.

C. 9. Nothing can agree better with the nature of any particular thing than other individuals of the same kind. Therefore (by cap. 7) there is nothing more useful to man for the maintenance of his being and enjoyment of rational life than a man who governs himself by reason. Again, since among particular things we know of none more excellent than a man who governs himself by reason, therefore a man can in no way better show the power of his skill and understanding than in so training up men that at last they may live as true subjects under the dominion of reason.

C. 10. So far as men bear to one another envy or any emotion derived from hate, they are contrary to one another; and are therefore to be feared in proportion to the excess of their power over that of other creatures.

C. 11. Yet minds are conquered not by force of arms, but by love and highmindedness.

C. 12. It is of exceeding use to men to enter upon acquaintance and so bind themselves together that they may the better make themselves all one power, and generally to do such things as are fitted to establish friendship.

C. 13. But for this they need skill and vigilance. For men be of many minds (seeing few of them live as reason prescribes), and yet are mostly envious and more prone to revenge than to pity. So that to endure every man's humour and restrain oneself from copying their passions is a matter of no small resolution. Yet those who rather chide men and rebuke their faults than teach them virtue, and can break their spirits, but not strengthen them, are grievous both to themselves and others. Thus many have been driven by their overmuch impatience or misguided zeal for religion to live with brutes rather than men; as boys and lads who cannot quietly bear to be scolded by their parents will go for soldiers, and choose the hardships of war and a tyrannical discipline rather than convenience at home and a father's counsel withal, and suffer any burden to be put upon them if only they may spite their parents.

C. 14. Therefore although men for the most part carry everything after their own fancies, yet from their common fellowship there ensues far more convenience than harm. So it is the better part to bear wrong from them with an even mind, and be diligent in whatever is fitted to bring about concord and friendship.

C. 15. That which begetteth concord is that which belongs to justice, equity, and good report. For, besides what is unjust and iniquitous, men are also displeased with what is in ill repute, or when a man doth reject the usage received in their commonwealth. And for winning their love those things be chiefly necessary which have regard to *religion* and *piety.*

[Reference is made to previous propositions as to these terms. Religion is the sum of desires and actions proceeding from the idea or knowledge of God, *i.e.* from the conception of the order of nature as one and uniform. Piety is the desire of well-doing produced by living according to reason. Pr. 37, Schol. 1.]

C. 16. Concord is also commonly produced by fear; but this is treacherous. Also fear ariseth from a weakness of the mind and therefore belongs not to the exercise of reason; and the same holds of compassion, though it hath on the face of it a certain show of piety.

C. 17. Men are likewise overcome by liberality, chiefly those who have not wherewithal to buy the necessaries of life. But helping every one in need is far beyond the means and convenience of any private person. For a private man's wealth is no match for such a demand. Also a single man's opportunities are too narrow for him to contract friendship with all. Wherefore providing for the poor is a duty that falls on the whole community and has regard only to the common interest.

C. 18. In receiving favours and the return of gratitude there is a material distinction, as to which see the Scholia to Pr. 70 and 71.

[That is, the reasonable man endeavours to decline favours from the ignorant which would place him under embarrassing obligations; but between free men there is a free and unrestrained affection, apart from and above any question of returning or recompensing favours.]

C. 19. Meretricious love, that is, the lust of generation which ariseth from outward beauty, and in general every kind of love that hath any cause beside freedom of mind, doth easily pass into hate, unless (which is worse) it be a kind of madness; and then more discord than concord grows of it. See the Coroll. to Pr. 31, Part 3.

C. 20. As concerning marriage, 'tis certain that it agrees with reason if the desire of bodily union is bred not merely of outward sense but of the desire to beget children and bring them up in wisdom; and also if the love of both parties, namely the man and the woman, has not outward sense alone for its cause, but freedom of mind in the chief place.

C. 21. Concord is also produced by flattery; but this is at the cost of vile slavishness or falsehood. None are more easily taken with flattery than the proud ones, who fain would be first, and are not.

C. 22. Dejection hath a false show of piety and religion. And though dejection be contrary to pride, yet is the downcast man very near being proud. See Schol. to Pr. 57.

C. 23. Likewise concord is advanced by shame, but only in things which cannot be hid. Also because shame is in itself a kind of pain it belongs not to the exercise of reason.

C. 24. The other emotions of pain towards men are plainly against justice, equity, good report, piety and religion. And though indignation hath on the face of it a show of equity, yet life is but lawless where any man may pass judgment on another's deeds and vindicate his own or another's right.

C. 25. Civility *(modestia)*, that is, a desire of pleasing men which is determined by reason, is referred (as we said in the Schol. to Pr. 37) to piety. But if it arise from passion[228] it is ambition, a desire whereby men do mostly stir up strife and tumults under the pretence of piety. A man who desires to help others by counsel or deed, so as they may together enjoy the chief good, will be very forward to win their love to him, but not to draw them into admiration of him, that a doctrine may be called after his name, nor in any manner to give cause of offence. Also in common talk he will eschew telling of men's faults, and will speak but sparingly of human weakness. But he will speak at large of man's virtue and power, and the means of perfecting the same, that thus men may endeavour, not from fear or disgust, but wholly in joyfulness, to live, so far as in them lies, after the commandment of reason.

C. 26. Except men we know of no particular thing in nature, in whose mind we may take pleasure and which we may join to ourselves

---

[228] *Affectu*: but Spinoza must mean *affectu qui passio est.*

by friendship or any manner of society; and therefore whatever there is beside men in the world the reason of our convenience doth not require us to preserve, but persuades us according to the divers uses thereof to preserve, destroy, or adapt it to our own use as we will.

C. 27. The utility we derive from things outside us is (besides the experience and knowledge we acquire from observing them and changing them from one form into another) in the first place the conservation of our body. And in this regard those things are chiefly useful which can so feed and nourish the body as to make all its parts fit for their proper offices. For the better fitted the body is to be impressed and to impress outward bodies in divers ways the more fit is the mind for thinking. (See Propp. 38 and 39.) But of this kind there seem to be very few things in nature. Wherefore for nourishing the body as it needs we must use many foods of different kinds: the human body being indeed made up of very many parts of different kinds, which be in need of constant and manifold nourishment, that the body may be equally fit for performing all things which are within its natural power, and consequently that the mind may also be equally fit for perceiving many different things.

C. 28. Now for achieving this the strength of every man would scarce avail unless men lent one another their help. But money has given us a token for everything. Whence it happens, that the imagination thereof doth mainly busy the minds of the common sort; for they can scarce imagine any kind of pleasure without having withal the idea of money as its cause.

C. 29. This is the fault only of them who seek money not from poverty nor for their needs, but because they have learnt arts of gain and make a mighty show with them. 'Tis true they tend their bodies by habit; but scantily, since they esteem themselves to be losing so much of their goods as they spend on maintaining their own bodies. But they who know the right use of money and fix the measure of wealth only according to need can live contented with a little.

C. 30. Since then those things are good which assist the members of the body to perform their office, and pleasure consists in this, that the power of man, in so far as he is composed of body and mind, is advanced or increased; therefore all things be good which bring us pleasure. Yet since things operate not for any such purpose as to give us pleasure, nor is their power of action limited according to our convenience, and also because pleasure is mostly related to some one part of the body above the rest; therefore most emotions of pleasure are subject to excess, unless reason be on guard, and consequently so are the desires engendered of them. Besides all which emotion leads us to count that first which is agreeable in the present, and we cannot consider things future with a proportionate liveliness. See the Scholia to Pr.

44 and Pr. 60.

C. 31. But superstition seemeth contrariwise to hold that for good which brings pain, and that for evil which brings pleasure. But, as we have said, (Schol. to Pr. 45) only an envious man can take any delight in my weakness and inconvenience. For the greater is our pleasure the more do we pass to greater perfection, and therefore the more do we partake of the divine nature; nor can pleasure ever be bad, when it is governed by a just regard for our interest as a whole. But he who is led by fear and doth good only to avoid toil is not led by reason.

C. 32. Now man's power is very much confined, and is infinitely surpassed by the power of external causes; and therefore we have not any absolute power of converting to our own use things outside us. Yet we shall bear with an even mind that which happens to us against the conditions of our own advantage if we are aware that we have done our part of the business, and that the power we possess could not have gone so far as to avoid those evils; and that we are a part of the whole order of nature and bound thereby. Which if we clearly and distinctly understand, that part of us which is described as *intelligence,* that is, our better part, will therein be wholly contented and will endeavour to persist in that content. For so far as we understand, we can desire nothing but what is necessary, nor can we rest content in aught but the truth; and therefore so far as we understand these things rightly, the endeavour of our better part agrees with the universal order of nature.'

This summary does not appear to call for any particular explanation. The equivalence of action, intelligence, and virtue, which stands out in the leading enunciations, has already been remarked on: the description of intelligence as 'our better part' at the conclusion is of some importance as leading up to the doctrine of the following Part. Attention may be called to the moral elevation of the precept given in cap. 25. It is a lofty refinement of the fundamental duty of good will to men which is not to be found, so far as I know, in any other moralist. The tone is very like that of Marcus Aurelius, but I have not met with an exact parallel to the matter either in M. Aurelius or elsewhere.

CHAPTER IX

THE DELIVERANCE OF MAN

Nec pietas ullast velatum saepe videri
vertier ad lapidem atque omnis accedere ad aras
nec procumbere humi prostratum et pandere palmas
ante deum delubra nec aras sanguine multo
spargere quadrupedum nec votis nectere vota,
sed mage pacata posse omnia mente tueri.

LUCRETIUS: v. 1198

Je croi, dist Pantagruel, que toutes ames intellectives sont exemptes des ciseaulx d'Atropos. — RABELAIS: *Pantagruel,* book iv. ch. xxvii.

La raison triomphe de la mort, et travailler pour elle, c'est travailler pour l'éternité. — E. RENAN: *Discours de réception,* 3 avril, 1879.

WITH the fourth Part of the 'Ethics' it might appear at first sight that Spinoza's task was ended. He has laid bare the constituents of human motives and passions; he has explained the working of these passions in the various circumstances of life; he has contrasted the slave of passion with the reasonable or free man, and has declared the precepts of righteousness and goodwill. But he esteems his work only half done, and goes on to that which remains as to something he has been longing to take in hand.

'At length,' he says in the Preface to Part V., 'I pass on to the other division of my Ethics, concerning the method or path which leads us to freedom. And in this I shall treat of the power of reason, and show what is its native strength against the emotions, and thence what is the freedom or blessedness of the mind. Whence we shall see in how much better case is the wise man than the ignorant. But by what means and method the understanding is to be perfected, and by what skill the body is to be tended that it may truly do its office, pertains not to this inquiry; for the latter of these is the concern of medicine, the former of logic.'

The fact is that Spinoza's aim has throughout been practical. He has undertaken the scientific analysis of the passions, not without the pure curiosity of the man of science, but mainly to the end of showing how they may be mastered, and the conditions of man's happiness assured. In this he is at one with the Greeks, and particularly, as in many points before, with the Stoics. But Spinoza explicitly denies the Stoic assumption that the will has an absolute power over the emotions: a denial which, on comparison of his express contradictions of Descartes, might be taken to imply an admission that in other ways the Stoic doctrine appeared to him profitable and worthy of respect. In the same passage he goes on to controvert the Cartesian theory of a connexion between the mind and the body through the pineal gland, by which Descartes endeavoured to show 'that there is no soul so feeble but that, being rightly trained, it may acquire an absolute dominion over its passions.' Spinoza points out that the hypothesis of the pineal gland being the seat of consciousness, transmitting impressions to the mind from without, and receiving orders from the mind which are sent on to the nerves of motion by means of the animal spirits, is contrary to Descartes' own principles of scientific work; introducing as it does assumptions more baseless and occult than any of the scholastic occult qualities which Descartes rejected. He also remarks that Descartes did not and could not assign any mechanical measure of the alleged power of the mind to initiate or control the motions of this gland: 'in truth, will and motion being incommensurable, there is no comparison betwixt the power or force of the mind and the body: and therefore the force of the latter can in no wise be determined by that of the former.' The physiological difficulties of the hypothesis are lightly touched on, but so as to show that Spinoza did not overlook them. In its actual form this preliminary discussion is now chiefly interesting as a monument of the extraordinary hold the Cartesian philosophy must have acquired on that generation to make Spinoza thus go out of his way to refute the most fantastic and untenable point of it. But the substance of Spinoza's argument remains applicable to the various quasi-materialist attempts that from time to time have been made, in the supposed interest of spiritual truth, to establish or make plausible some kind of physical communication between the mind and the brain.

When we examine in detail what Spinoza has to say 'of

the power of the understanding, or of Man's freedom,'[229] we find that it consists of two independent parts. The first (Part V. of 'Ethics' to Prop. 20) is a consistent following out of the psychological method we have already become familiar with. The condition of mastering the emotions is shown to be a clear and distinct understanding of their nature and causes; and the love of God — which is nothing else than the rational contemplation of the order of the world, and of human nature as part thereof — is described as the greatest happiness of man in this life, and the surest way of establishing the rule of the understanding over the passions. Here again one might suppose, and with more reason than before, that nothing more remained to be set forth. But it is not so: Spinoza proceeds to lay before us a theory of intellectual immortality, or rather eternity, the perfection whereof consists in an intellectual love of God which is likewise eternal, and 'is part of the infinite love wherewith God loves himself.' This exposition, which takes up the fifth Part of the 'Ethics' from Prop. 21 onwards, presents great difficulties. It is by no means obvious, in the first place, what is Spinoza's real meaning; nor can we feel sure that any explanation is the right one until we have some probable account of the manner in which Spinoza reconciled the doctrine, as we may propose to read it, with the rest of his own philosophy. And this latter problem is a yet harder one.

The question has been evaded, as it seems to me, by most of those who have written on Spinoza. Critics who regard him as a transcendental dogmatist naturally feel no particular difficulty at this point: why should not Spinoza dogmatize about the eternity of the mind as well as about Substance and Attributes? So they are content to give some abridgment or paraphrase of Spinoza's argument which in truth explains nothing. Others, led by their own prepossessions to disregard all the rules of historical and critical probability, have sought, in the face of Spinoza's express and repeated warnings, to make out that his theory is a doctrine of personal immortality in the ordinary sense, or some sense practically equivalent to it, only stated in an unusual way and supported by artificial reasoning. Some few, taking a view of the general meaning of Spinoza's philosophy similar to that which has been maintained in the foregoing chap-

---

[229] Title of Part V.

ters, have manfully striven to reduce this apparently eccentric part into scientific conformity to the main body. But they are forced to say either that Spinoza did not clearly know his own meaning, or that he did not succeed in saying what he meant, or that he deliberately said things he did not mean: none of which suppositions can be entertained by any serious and impartial reader of the 'Ethics' except as a desperate remedy. For my part, I would rather confess myself baffled than help myself out by any one of them, especially the last: and in fact I long thought the obscurity of the last portion of the 'Ethics' all but hopeless.

The explanation I shall now put forward with the hope of throwing some light upon the historical affinities of this speculation, and its logical connexion with Spinoza's psychology, is one that has occurred to me almost at the last moment, and after repeated consideration.

It may be observed here, as a matter independent of any particular interpretation of Spinoza's thought, that there is some reason to believe that he was himself conscious of not standing on the firmest ground in this place. The propositions concerning the eternity of the mind seem to be carefully isolated from the rest: the love of God arising from clear and distinct self-knowledge (Prop. 15) is kept apart from the intellectual love which is the privilege of the mind in its eternal quality (Prop. 33), though on almost any possible reading of Spinoza's theory the two must coincide; and at the end Spinoza guards himself by showing that the validity of ethical motives and precepts is independent of the exalted doctrine he has just been setting forth (Prop. 41). In a writer so careful and subtle indications of this kind are not to be neglected. I believe that Spinoza's argument was to himself satisfactory; but it hangs, as I read it, on a very special point in his theory of knowledge, and it may well be that he saw the danger of its not being satisfactory to other people. Moreover I am inclined to think that Spinoza wished emphatically to disclaim any intention of relying on a supernatural or supersensible world for the foundations of ordinary virtue and morality. He puts his eternity of the mind as a kind of supplemental speculation; if we accept it, so much the better; if not, the rest of his work will not be impaired. It might perhaps be suggested that this series of propositions was in fact an afterthought. But conjectures of this kind are too uncertain to be worth pursuing.

Let us now turn to a connected survey of the book; taking first in order, as it comes, the practical and fairly obvious part. The opening propositions, in which the conditions of the mind's power of self-control are laid down, run as follows:

1. As particular thoughts and ideas of things are arranged and connected in the mind, exactly so are bodily modifications or images of things arranged and connected in the body.

(This is an immediate inference from the complete parallelism of mind and body.)

2. If we separate a disturbance or emotion of the mind from the thought of its outward cause, and associate it with other thoughts, then love or hatred towards that outward cause, as likewise the agitations arising from those emotions, will be destroyed.

(For love and hate depend on the idea of the external cause being present.)

3. That emotion which is a passion ceases to be passion as soon as we form a clear and distinct idea thereof.

(For passion as such is a confused idea.)

4. There is no modification of the body whereof we cannot form some clear and distinct conception.

(For all bodies and affections of bodies have some properties in common, and our conceptions of these are adequate.)

Hence it appears that it is more or less in every one's power to attain a clear understanding of his own nature, and to that extent to be superior to passion. So that the first precept of freedom may be thus expressed: Understand the passions that you may be master of them. Nay, the very emotions and desires that otherwise would be pernicious are converted to beneficial uses by the government of the understanding. For example, 'we have found man's nature to be such that he desires others to live after his own plan. And in a man not governed by reason this desire is the passion called ambition, which is little removed from pride; whereas in the man who lives according to reason it is a virtue or activity, and is called piety.' Such is the nature of the mind's power over the emotions. Of course it might equally be expressed in terms of the attribute of Extension, as a power of the body over the particular modifications of the organism which correspond to the emotions in consciousness. But, as Spinoza is here considering the emotions in their mental aspect as states of feeling, he naturally follows both convenience and common use in regarding the facts on the psychical rather than the physical side. This does not the least imply, as a hasty reader might think, that he loses sight of the physical side. If there is one canon of interpretation more important than another for the right understanding of Spinoza, it is that the physiological correlations of mental action are never overlooked by him for a moment, whatever his language may be.

Next, how may this power of the mind be strengthened? By conceiving all things as necessary; for the knowledge of a thing as determined by definite causes tends to prevent us from fixing any emotion upon it (Pr. 5, 6).

'The more this knowledge of things as necessary is applied to particular things where of we have a distinct and lively imagination, the greater is this power of the mind over the emotions, as experience also doth bear witness. For we perceive sorrow for any possession that is lost to be abated whenever the man who hath lost it adviseth with himself that this possession could in no manner have been saved. So likewise we see that no man pities a child because it cannot speak, walk, or reason, or because for so many years its life is in a manner unconscious. But if the more part of us were born grown up, and one here and there as a child, then who but would pity children? since then we should regard the state of infancy not as a thing natural and necessary, but as a defect or fault in nature. And after this sort we might mark several other instances.' (Pr. 6, Schol.)

It is further pointed out that an emotion arising from rational contemplation, since it depends on constant and ever present facts in the order of nature, will be stronger, other things being equal, than emotions directed towards a particular absent object; and that emotion is stronger in proportion to the number of distinct exciting causes acting together to produce it. Then comes a proposition in the nature of practical application: —

'So long as we are not disturbed by emotions contrary[230] to our nature, we have the power of ordering and connecting the affections of the body in pursuance of the intellectual order.' (Prop. 10.)

---

[230] *Contrarii* is omitted in the text of the *Opp. Posth.* It is tacitly supplied by the Dutch translator, and replaced in the text of Gfrörer's and Bruder's edd.

Spinoza comments on this in a Scholium, which seems to mark a period in the discussion. It is of a very practical kind, and may strike the reader as not being original: in which case I would ask him to reflect that we have much reason to be thankful that in moral precepts intended for real use no great originality is either needful or practicable. The scientific discussion and explanation of morality is the task of philosophers. But morality itself is made by the community of right-minded men, whether they happen to be philosophers or not: and when we come to speak of the actual contents of morality and the conduct of life, the philosopher has little or no advantage over any other right-minded man beyond the habit of expressing himself in accurate language. No system of ethics can do more than organize the common moral sense of good men. Let us hear Spinoza, therefore, as one speaking to us in the name of us all. That which is spoken with the common voice and in the common name of man's conscience may well be common; if it is not, we should strive to make it so. But it can never be commonplace.

'By this power of duly ordering and linking together the affections of our body we may bring it to pass that we be not easily wrought on by evil passions. For greater force is needed to control emotions ordered and linked according to the intellectual order than those which are uncertain and loose. Wherefore the best we can compass, so long as we have not a perfect knowledge of our emotions, is to lay out a method and settled rules of life, to commit these to memory, and constantly[231] to apply them to such particular cases as do commonly meet us in life, that so our imagination may be penetrated therewith, and we may ever have them at hand. We laid down, for example, among the precepts of life, that hatred should be conquered by love or high-mindedness, not repaid in kind. Now that this command of reason may always be ready for us at need, we should often think upon and consider the wrongs commonly done by men, and in what manner they are warded off by a noble mind. For thus we shall knit the image of a wrong done us to the imagination of this precept, and the precept will always be at hand when a wrong is offered us... But we shall note that in ordering our thoughts and imaginations we are ever to attend to that which is good in a particular thing, that we may always be determined to action by an emotion of pleasure. For example, if one sees that he exceedeth in the pursuit of honour, let him think of the right use

---

[231] *Continuo:* Spinoza was probably not ignorant of the classical usage of the word, but it would not suit this context.

thereof, and for what purpose it is to be pursued, and by what means to be acquired, not of the misuse and vanity of it, the inconstancy of mankind and the like, of which no man thinks except for infirmity of spirit. For with such thoughts do ambitious men most plague themselves, when they despair of attaining the station they are bent upon; and so venting their anger they would fain be thought philosophers. 'Tis certain that they are most greedy of honour who are loudest concerning the misuse of it and the vanity of the world. Nor is this peculiar to the case of ambition, but it is common to all who meet with ill fortune and lack strength of mind... So he who endeavours to govern his emotions and desires purely by the love of freedom will strive, as best he may, to know the virtues and their causes, and to fill his mind with the joy which arises from the true knowledge of them; but in no wise to study men's faults, nor to flatter them and make merry with a false show of liberty. And whoever will diligently observe and use these precepts (for they are not difficult), assuredly in a short space of time he will be able for the most part to guide his actions after the rule of reason.'

We are next introduced to the exercise of contemplative reason described as the love of God, which consists in the distinct understanding of one's own nature. There is no form or mode of knowledge which cannot be made to some extent clear and distinct; in other words, 'referred to the idea of God,' since without God nothing exists or can be conceived. Clear and distinct understanding of one's own nature involves pleasure, and this is accompanied by the idea of God; and therefore the resulting emotion is love of God, and, being associated with every act of understanding, must hold the chief place in the mind that entertains it. God, on the other hand, is not subject to passion, not capable of pleasure or pain, and cannot properly be said to love or hate any one. Therefore, since we cannot desire that God should contradict his own nature and perfections, 'he who loves God cannot endeavour that God should love him in return.' And this love of God is the chief good which men can seek under the guidance of reason; it may be common to all men, and we can wish it for others as much as for ourselves. Thus it is not liable to be marred, like the common affections of men, by envy or jealousy.[232]

Here again there is a pause and a summing up.

'I have now collected,' we read, 'all the remedies against the

---

[232] Propp. 11-20.

emotions, that is, everything that the mind considered in itself is capable of doing against them. Whence it appears that the power of the mind over the emotions consists, — 1. In actual knowledge of the emotions (see Schol. to Pr. 4 of this Part). 2. In the separation of the emotions from the thought of the external cause of which we have a confused imagination. 3. In respect of time, wherein those affections which have regard to things we understand overmatch those that have regard to things we conceive confusedly or brokenly (Prop. 7). 4. In the number of causes by which those affections are fostered that have regard to the universal properties of things or to God. (Prop. 9 and 11.) 5. Finally in that order in which the mind can arrange and link together its own emotions.'

Spinoza goes on to say that the mind's power consists in knowledge, considered not as freedom from error but as its natural and proper activity. Not absence of inadequate ideas, but preponderance of adequate ones, is the condition of mental health. Clear and distinct knowledge, more especially the third or intuitive kind, gives us the means of controlling the passions to such an extent that they have but an insignificant part in the mind: —

'Likewise it engenders love towards an immutable and eternal being, truly within our reach; which therefore can be sullied by none of the defects common to other kinds of love, but may constantly increase, and may possess the best part of the mind and thoroughly penetrate it. And herewith I have finished what concerns this present life... And so it is time for me to pass on to other matters which belong to the duration of the mind without regard to the body.'

We are now on the threshold of the singular and difficult part of Spinoza's exposition. I shall begin by stating as clearly as I can what I conceive his meaning to have been. Next I shall point out what I believe to be the historical ancestry of his doctrine. Then I shall give the leading points of the argument in Spinoza's own words, or as nearly so as may be, and at the same time exhibit in detail, for any reader who cares to follow me so far, the manner in which I justify my interpretation.

Whatever is known as part of the necessary order of nature, in other words exactly or scientifically, is said by Spinoza to be known 'under the form of eternity.' And this is eminently true of the immediate knowledge which he calls the third kind. Now in every act of knowledge the mind is (in Spinoza's technical sense) the *idea of* a certain state of its own body; and if we regard this as a knowledge of its own body (which I shall show that Spinoza does), the mind in contemplating things as necessary knows its own body 'under the form of eternity.' But the knowing mind has a consciousness or knowledge of itself which exactly corresponds to its knowledge of the body; in Spinoza's language, it is the *idea* of itself as well as of the body. Therefore in all exact knowledge the mind knows itself 'under the form of eternity:' that is to say, in every such act it is eternal, and knows itself as eternal. This eternity is not a persistence in time after the dissolution of the body, for it is not commensurable with time at all. And there is associated with it a state or quality of perfection called the *intellectual love of God.* This is not an emotion, since the emotion of pleasure involves transition to greater perfection, and therefore a finite time; but it is related to the emotion of love as the eternity of the mind is related to its existence in time in a particular act of knowledge. The intellectual love of man for God is part of the infinite intellectual love wherewith God loves himself; and the mind, together with whatsoever it knows 'under the form of eternity,' is a link in an infinite chain of eternal beings, which all together make up the infinite mind of God. Reserving the discussion of difficulties and the critical analysis of Spinoza's argument, let us endeavour to seize the points which stand out most distinctly in this daring flight of speculation. The eternity of the human mind is a function of pure intellect, and depends on the mind's power and habit of exact knowledge. Its perfection goes along with the attainment of the most perfect kind of knowledge, and its degree is different in different individuals. It has no relation to time, and therefore is not a future life or continuance of personal consciousness in the ordinary sense. At the same time it is in some sense individual; the active and understanding mind is an 'eternal mode of thought' which is part of the infinite intellect, but is not lost in it.

It seems to me that we cannot but trace in this a direct connexion with the Aristotelian doctrine of immortality taken up and developed by the Averroists in the middle ages. M. Renan's warning is before my eyes:[233] but it is M. Renan himself who

---

[233] 'Rechercher si Averroes peut revendiquer quelque chose dans le système du penseur d'Amsterdam, ce serait dépasser la limite on doit s'arrêter, dans les questions de filiation de systèmes, une juste curiosité: ce serait vouloir retrouver la trace du ruisseau quand il s'est perdu dans la prairie.' — *Averroès*

supplies us with the links that complete, as I submit, a sufficient chain of evidence.

In various passages of Aristotle a doctrine of intellectual immortality is indicated rather than worked out. The passive or receptive elements of the mind are perishable; only the active intellect (νοῦς ποιητικός), and the individual mind so far as it partakes thereof, are eternal and immortal. Whether this active intellect is only the sum of similar elements in individual minds, that by virtue of which the mind is rational in each case, or is to be regarded as having a permanent existence beside and beyond the minds of individual men, is a point not altogether free from doubt in Aristotle himself. The commentators resolved and developed the question in various ways. Ibn-Roshd (Averroes) appears to have considered the active intellect as being independent of this and that man's individuality, and of one substance in all men, but existing only in individual men: a unity realized and reflected in the multiplicity of finite minds. In any case, the personal immortality of the individual is excluded by the Averroistic doctrine. The active intellect is immortal, either in itself or as embodied in the human race which is mortal only as regards individuals: this and that soul can be immortal only so far as they have part in the active intellect; not as individual, but as rational and belonging to universal reason.[234]

When the Mussulman fanaticism which took alarm even in Averroes' lifetime had effectually suppressed the cultivation of philosophy within the bounds of Islam, the light was kept alive by a series of Jewish scholars of whom Moses ben Maimon, the contemporary of Averroes, was first in time and in renown. The various problems of the Peripatetic system, and this particular one among them, were taken up and eagerly discussed. It was not fully entered upon by Maimonides, but he inclined to go with Ibn-Roshd in holding that immortality was not individual. Levi ben Gerson dealt with it at length, and after elaborately criticizing the opinions of Ibn-Roshd and others, concluded in favour of an immortality which was intellectual but also individual. Rejecting the notion of union with the universal reason, and retaining the Aristotelian theory that contemplative knowledge is

---

et l'Averroisme, 2d ed. p. 199.
[234] Renan, op, cit. pp. 122-158.

the only proper function of an eternal mind, he held that the individual mind is immortal in respect of the knowledge possessed by it at the time of its emancipation from the body. It has a fuller and freer possession of this knowledge, but not having the organism and senses by which alone new experience can be acquired, it cannot in any way extend it.[235]

We are fairly entitled to assume that Spinoza was not unacquainted with the writings of Gersonides; through them he would have become acquainted with the Peripatetic doctrine of intellectual immortality as understood by the commentators, and with the Averroist modification of it, as well as with Gersonides' own speculations. And if this knowledge is admitted, no supposition is more natural than that Spinoza's own doctrine was suggested to him from this quarter. The leading ideas are the same, only worked into formal agreement, as we shall presently see, with Spinoza's metaphysics and psychology. His insistence on the eternity of the mind being wholly independent of time, and incommensurable with existence determined in time, appears to be peculiar to himself; and in the transfiguration of contemplative knowledge as the 'intellectual love of God' there is perhaps a reminiscence of the Neo-Platonic influence which was still predominant when he wrote the 'Treatise of God and Man.' In that work, it may be not amiss to observe here, we find little or nothing to throw light on the part of his mature system now under consideration. The theory of immortality is but vaguely sketched out, and, so far as we can assign it to any generic type, is decidedly Neo-Platonic rather than Aristotelian; the soul's capacity for immortality being represented as depending on its detachment from the body and union with God. But it is worth noting that in the 'Cogitata Metaphysica' some space is given to denouncing the error of those who 'consider eternity as a form of duration.' And on the point of eternity having to do with *essentia* not *existentia,* it is said: 'Nobody will ever say that the being of a circle or a triangle, so far as it is an eternal truth, hath endured longer at this day than it had in Adam's.' — 'Cogitata Metaphysica,' Part 2, c. 1.

---

[235] Joël, Levi ben Gerson (Gersonides), als Religions-philosoph (in *Beiträge zur Gesch. d. Philosophie):* 'Der von Seele und Leib befreite Geist denkt alle seine Erkenntnisse auf einmal und als Einheit. Nur neue Erkenntnisse zu erwerben ist er ausser Stande,' p. 45.

I proceed to the fuller statement of Spinoza's argument. The leading propositions are as follows.

Prop. 21. *The mind cannot imagine anything or remember things past except while the body endures.*

It will be sufficient to observe, without reproducing Spinoza's proof and references, that in the Second Part memory has been treated as dependent on association, which involves a material mechanism in the brain; and in like manner imagination cannot be exercised without a material organ of thought and storehouse of impressions.

Prop. 22. *There nevertheless necessarily exists in God an idea which expresses the being of the individual human body under the form of eternity.*

Again let us pass over the formal demonstration, and look back to Prop. 44 of Part 2. There we find that 'it is of the nature of reason to perceive things under a certain form of eternity,' which is the same thing as perceiving them as part of the necessary order of nature. The human body, like everything else, is part of the necessary order of nature, and can therefore be thought of 'under the form of eternity,' as determined by natural laws whose operation is always and everywhere the same. The *essentia* of a result of given conditions, or *what* it shall be, has nothing to do with the tract of time or portion of space in which the conditions are found: for Spinoza, like most if not all writers down to our own time, assumes that the laws of nature can be exactly known, and are known to be absolutely and universally valid. The *existentia* of a particular result — *when* and *where* it shall be, if at all — the fact that it does occur at a given time and place — this cannot be expressed in terms of the eternal laws of nature alone, and therefore cannot be determined in thought by pure intellect, but only with the help of the imagination. Thus the 'idea which expresses the essence of this and that human body under the form of eternity' would seem to be nothing else than the knowledge of the human body as a necessary part of the order of nature. Further, it seems a fair extension of Spinoza's language to say that everything known 'under the form of eternity' is to that extent eternal. We shall presently see that he all but says it in so many words. What Spinoza has really arrived at, then, is that in a certain sense the human body may be called eternal. We must carefully observe that this eternity has nothing to do with the persistence in time of the ultimate elements of the organism after the organism is dissolved. Let us now see what follows.

'Prop. 23. *The human mind cannot be wholly destroyed with the body, but somewhat of it remains which is eternal.*

Demonstr. There is necessarily in God, by the foregoing proposition, a concept or idea which doth express the being of the human body. This accordingly must needs be something which pertains to the being of the human mind (by Prop. 13, Part 2).[236] But we do not assign to the human mind any duration that can be described by time, except so far as it doth express the actual existence of the body, which is explained by duration and may be described by time; that is (by Coroll. Prop. 8, Part 2)[237] we assign not existence to it except while the body endures. But seeing there is nevertheless somewhat which by a certain eternal necessity is conceived through the being of God, this somewhat which belongs to the being of the mind will necessarily be eternal.

Schol. This idea which doth express the being of the body under the form of eternity is, as we said, a determined mode of thought which belongs to the being of the mind and is necessarily eternal. Yet it cannot come to pass that we remember anything of an existence before the body, since neither can there occur any traces thereof in the body, nor can eternity be described by time, nor have unto time any proportion. But none the less we do feel and are aware that we are eternal. For the mind feels not less those things which it conceives by the understanding than those which it doth hold in memory. The eyes of the mind, wherewith she sees and observes things, are no other than demonstrations. So that although we remember not that we existed before our body, yet we feel that our mind, in so far as it involves the being of the body under the form of eternity, is eternal; and that this manner of its existence cannot be described by time or explained in terms of duration. Thus our mind can only so far be said to endure, and its existence be described by a determined time, as it involves the actual existence of

---

[236] 'The object of the idea which makes up the human mind is a body or certain actually existing mode of extension, and nothing else.'

[237] 'So long as particular things do not exist, save so far as they are contained in the attributes of God [*i.e.,* so long as they exist potentially but not actually], the objective being or ideas of them do not exist, save in so far as the infinite idea of God exists.' This is a case of the universal parallelism. Whatever can be said to exist potentially in the order of extension must also be said to exist potentially in the order of thought. The universe as a whole, which on the side of thought is 'infinita Dei idea,' involves the whole history of things and every possible consequence of the laws of nature.

the body; and it hath only so far the power of limiting the existence of things by time, and conceiving them under the category of duration.'

Observe, again, how distinctly the notion of persistence in time is cut off from that of eternity. Spinoza's eternal life is not a continuance of existence but a manner of existence; something which can be realized here and now as much as at any other time and place; not a future reward of the soul's perfection but the soul's perfection itself. In which, it is almost needless to remind the reader, he agrees with the higher and nobler interpretation of almost all the religious systems of the world. Whether it is called the life eternal, the kingdom of God, wisdom, liberation, or *nirvána,* the state of blessedness has been put forward by the great moral teachers of mankind as something not apart from and after this life, but entering into and transforming it.[238] The after-coming generations of dull and backsliding disciples have degraded these glories of the free human mind into gross mechanical systems of future rewards and punishments.

But we must return to the critical study of the argument. A difficulty presents itself at first sight, which has weighed much with those who have thought that Spinoza's only real meaning (notwithstanding his express declaration that eternity is out of relation to time) must be that the ultimate elements of body and mind alike persist in other forms after the living organism is broken up. It looks as if too much had been proved, though not stated; as if what is asserted of the human mind were by implication asserted of all things whatever. Spinoza would then be saying aloud: 'The human mind is in a certain sense eternal' — and adding in a whisper, for the few who could penetrate his secret: — 'and everything else too.' This reading was long ago put forward (still with a certain amount of reserve) by Boullainvilliers in his so-called 'Refutation of Spinoza,' 1731, a title which thinly disguises a popular exposition; and it has been suggested in our own day in Holland by Dr. Van Vloten, and lately propounded with some confidence by Mr. Lotsy. The objections are however insuperable. Either Spinoza gratuitously gives an involved and obscure demonstration of a consequence which on his metaphysical principles is perfectly simple, or his argument

---

[238] I fear this cannot be said of Mahomet, and moral enthusiasm is precisely what the religion founded by him seems to be most wanting in.

is from beginning to end a piece of deliberate duplicity. The first alternative is repugnant to Spinoza's intellectual character, the second to his moral. And then, even if he were capable of throwing dust in his readers' eyes, what possible motive had he? To save appearances, it is suggested. If that were so, it would be a curious thing that he began to think of saving appearances after he had written nine-tenths of the Ethics without the slightest regard to any such prudential economy. There is nothing of the kind in his treatment of popular theology, of final causes, of free-will, of current ethical notions, of dominant Cartesian theories. Nay, the allusions to common opinion in this very series of propositions are as far from disguise and conciliation as anything in the earlier Parts. If Spinoza's design was to save appearances, he has gone about the work with incredible clumsiness and want of tact. Besides all this, it is hopeless to reconcile the proposed interpretation with Spinoza's express words. In short, I do not see how any careful reader can on full consideration so understand him, unless he is steadfastly minded not only to find in the Ethics a complete modern doctrine of physiological psychology, but to find nothing else.

Let us consider Spinoza's reasoning more narrowly. The human body may be known as part of an eternal order, 'under the form of eternity,' and so may any other body; that must be allowed. The human mind, as strictly corresponding to the body, point for point and element for element, may be known in like manner; and so may the mind or complex of mental facts corresponding to any other aggregate of matter. Is there nothing more to be said then? and is there no prerogative left for man? Yes, and a great one, the prerogative of knowledge. If the atom of matter and the primitive cell of organic life may be called eternal, yet their eternity is only in the thought of the higher intelligence which knows them as part of the immutable order. The knowledge of the material atom 'under the form of eternity' is not in the mind-atom that is paired with it. But the knowledge of the human body 'under the form of eternity' need not be in some separate thinking being: it may be in the mind of that body itself. The mind can know its own body 'under the form of eternity'; and in knowing the body it knows itself. The knowing and self-conscious mind is, as we saw in the Second Part, *idea ideae* as well as *idea.* Thus it is eternal in the strength of its own knowledge, and is conscious of its eternity. It is the clear consciousness accompanying every act of knowledge, not any such vague sentiment or presentiment as is relied on by the popular doctrine of immortality, that Spinoza calls to witness when he says: *Sentimus experimurque nos aeternos esse.*

But what is the mind's knowledge of the body 'under the form of eternity'? To know under the form of eternity is to know rationally or exactly. In modern language what we mean by having a rational knowledge of our own body is being able to give a scientific account of its structure and functions: and if we carried this conception into Spinoza's propositions we should make the eternity of the mind depend on one special kind of knowledge, and reduce the way of salvation to a course of human physiology — a conclusion too grotesque to dwell upon. In fact the mind's eternal knowledge of the body, as understood by Spinoza, is not a knowledge of the human body generically, but a relation between the particular mind and the particular body which we should not now think of calling knowledge at all. The key to this part of his argument is the ambiguous use of the word *idea* on which we have already commented in the Second Part of the Ethics. The word is sometimes used in the common sense, as meaning a concept in the mind referred to some object of knowledge outside it: sometimes in the sense peculiar to Spinoza's metaphysical system, as meaning the mode of thought (which may or may not be in a conscious mind) corresponding to a given mode of extension. In the first sense *idea* is the image or concept, *ideatum* the thing perceived or conceived; in the second *idea* and *ideatum* are one and the same thing 'expressed' in the attributes of Thought and of Extension. To take a concrete instance, Peter thinks of Paul. The thought in Peter's mind is in the first sense *idea Pauli;* in the second sense it is *idea affectionis corporis Petri,* that is, Peter's thought about Paul is strictly parallel to a certain definite state of the material machinery of imagination in Peter's brain. So if I think of a geometrical proposition, the *ideate* of my idea is in the one sense a set of geometrical relations in space, in the other sense my own body (and especially my brain) as modified in that particular act of thought. Now Spinoza, as we have already pointed out, habitually carries over statements and inferences from the one meaning of the term *idea* to the other, apparently without the least suspicion that his

procedure is open to any objection. When I know an external
fact, the state of my mind which is my knowledge is the *idea* of
the external fact in one sense. But it is the *idea* of a certain state
of my own body in the other sense. Accordingly Spinoza affirms
that the mind in every act of knowledge also knows its own
body; though so long as it perceives things 'after the common
order of nature' its knowledge of itself and the body is not adequate.[239] Now when the mind is in the act of rational or scientific
knowledge of anything whatever — in other words, when it perceives things 'under the form of eternity,' — Spinoza says, trans-
ferring to the relation between the mind and its own body what
belongs to the relation between the mind and the object of
knowledge, that the mind knows its own body 'under the form of
eternity.' So knowing its own body and consequently itself, it is
eternal, and depends only on its own activity for this eternity. As
Spinoza says farther on, 'the mind conceives nothing under the
form of eternity, save so far as it conceives the being of its own
body under the form of eternity, that is, save so far as it is eternal.' (Eth. V. Pr. 31, Demonstr.; cp. Pr. 29). The verbal confusion involved in Spinoza's way of stating his doctrine is no
doubt surprising at the present day. But it has not been assumed
here to explain this particular doctrine; we could not help taking
note of it, on quite independent grounds, in going through the
Second Part.[240] And when we remember that in Spinoza's time
psychology was really in its infancy, and hardly any serious attempt had been made to work out the theory of perception, our
surprise may be considerably abated.

      Apart from the peculiar form of his argument, Spinoza
falls in this place into a metaphysical difficulty of which he was
so far aware that he made a distinct effort to escape it. The eternity of which the mind is conscious in the act of rational knowledge is wholly out of relation to time. Also it is distinctly stated
to be a kind of existence.[241] Here, then, we have existence out of
time, and a knowledge or perception of it in consciousness. Now
it is at least a serious question whether existence out of time is
conceivable. We cannot think of existence except in terms of

---

[239] Eth. 2, Pr. 24-29.

[240] P. 201, above.

[241] Hanc eius existentiam tempore definiri sive per durationem explicari non posse. Prop. 23, Schol.

actual or possible experience. But experience involves consciousness or at least feeling. And it is not a metaphysical speculation, but an established fact of science, that change of some kind is the necessary condition of all feeling and experience. Every feeling of which we know anything or can form a notion is a feeling of transition, of an event, of something happening: which on the physical side is motion of some kind in the sentient organism.

Even an apparently continuous sensation is a series of many rapidly succeeding nervous shocks. The more we analyse feeling, the more we find change and motion to be its constant form: and these involve time. It would seem, therefore, that without making any transcendental or universal affirmation, but as a matter of human experience as far as it has gone, we must say that existence out of time is a combination of words to which we can attach no real meaning. The position involves more consequences than can be here discussed; as for instance the total rejection of all attempts, however powerful and ingenious, to set up an Absolute, Unconditioned, Unknowable, or any form of unapproachable reality supposed to be somehow more real than the things we feel and know. For the present it is enough to beg the reader to believe that such a position is philosophically tenable, notwithstanding that (as he can see for himself) it is in no way repugnant to common sense. If, being valiant in speculation and disregarding objections of this kind, we begin to talk about something alleged to exist without relation to time, the objection will be forced upon us in a practical shape by the extreme difficulty we shall soon find in pursuing our discourse without manifest contradictions. Probably the objection did not occur to Spinoza in the shape in which it is here put: for that shape is the result of modern inquiries. But he felt the logical difficulty of discussing eternity in the language of time; and he endeavoured to secure himself by the following characteristic remark.

'We shall here note that, although we be now certain that the mind, so far as it doth conceive things under the form of eternity, is eternal; yet, in order that our ensuing exposition may be the easier and the better understood, we shall consider the mind (like as we have done thus far) as if at a given moment it began to be, and to understand things under the form of eternity; and this we may safely do without any risk of error, so that we use care to conclude nothing except from evident premisses.'[242]

Having laid down this caution, Spinoza sets forth the 'intellectual love of God' which is the crown of the mind's perfection. It has already been stated that the most perfect activity and excellence of the mind is to understand things with the third or intuitive kind of knowledge; and that this begets the highest degree of contentment attainable by human nature.[243] Again, this knowledge implies the knowledge of God; hence the delight of the highest intellectual activity is a pleasure accompanied with the idea of God as its cause. That is, it is love of God; 'not in that we conceive him' adds Spinoza 'as now present, but in that we understand God as eternal, and this is what I call the intellectual love of God.'[244] Like the knowledge from which it springs, it is eternal; on which there is another curious remark.

'Although this love toward God hath had no beginning, yet it hath all the perfections of love in the same manner as if it had arisen in time, as we feigned in the corollary to the foregoing proposition. And herein there is no difference but that the mind hath eternally had the same perfections which (as we feigned) accrued to it at a particular time, and that accompanied by the idea of God as the eternal cause thereof. And since pleasure consisteth in a passage to greater perfection, 'tis plain blessedness must consist in this, that the mind hath perfection in full possession.'

Here, the reader will observe, we are required to form the idea of an eternal causation; and this lands us in an impossibility if we regard the cause as an antecedent of the effect, as in that case we have to conceive a relation which is in time and out of time at once. But this difficulty would probably not touch Spinoza. There is nothing to show that he conceived cause and effect as being necessarily antecedent and consequent; on the contrary, it is pretty clear from the First Part of the Ethics that he did not. God, as the absolute first cause, is the immediate cause of motion and matter, and they of all material things; and similar relations hold in the other Attributes. But there is here no question of priority in time.

Freedom from the passions, though not itself perfection,

---

242 Prop. 31, Schol.
243 Propp. 25, 27.
244 Pr. 32, Coroll.

is a condition of perfection: hence the mind, so far as it partakes of eternity, must enjoy this freedom, and Spinoza naturally proceeds to show that 'the mind is not exposed, except while the body endures, to those emotions which are reckoned as passions.' Whence it follows that none but the intellectual love is eternal. And here for the first time Spinoza takes distinct notice of the common opinion of immortality.

'If we consider the general opinion of mankind, we shall find that they are indeed aware of the eternity of their own mind; but confound the same with duration, and ascribe it to the imagination or memory, which they suppose to remain after death.'[245] This explains why Spinoza throughout this part of his work avoids the use of the term *immortality,* and it exposes more fully than any comment could do the hopelessness of attempting to represent him as maintaining the immortality of the soul in the ordinary sense: yet the attempt has been made.

One more surprise remains: the philosopher is determined to outdo the theologians with their own vocabulary. 'God loves himself with an infinite intellectual love:' the intellectual love of human minds towards God is part of this infinite love, and in it God may be said to love men; in which there is no contradiction of the foregoing statement that God neither loves nor hates any one, since this intellectual love is not an emotion. It is perhaps difficult to remember that the substance of the propositions thus expressed is still purely and simply the human mind's contemplation of itself and its own certain knowledge as part of the infinite and necessary order of the universe; that for Spinoza the divine love is nothing else than conscious acceptance of universal law, the 'welcoming every event' of the Stoics; and that the secret of blessedness and glory (for those titles are expressly claimed and justified) is none other than a mind steadfastly bent on the truth.

It seems a poor and barren conclusion to bear up the solemnity of language: so strong is the prejudice bred of our inveterate custom of hungering after dreams and neglecting the realities under our hands. After all, if we turn Spinoza's thought into a guide for action, if we translate his speculative propositions into a practical imperative, what is the outcome? Even that

---

[245] Pr. 34, Coroll. and Schol.

which true and fearless men have preached through all the generations to unheeding ears. Seek the truth, fear not and spare not: this first, this for its own sake, this only; and the truth itself is your reward, a reward not measured by length of days nor by any reckoning of men. This lesson assuredly is not an idle one, or unworthy to be set forth with fervent and solemn words. And if any man ever had a special title so to repeat the lesson, that man was Spinoza, whose whole life was an example of it.

On the strength of these passages Spinoza has been called a mystic; and, while they have perplexed philosophical inquirers, they have exercised a sort of fascination on many readers. As to the actual contents of them, their author is no more a mystic than Aristotle, if, as I have endeavoured to show, the groundwork of his doctrine is the Aristotelian theory that contemplative knowledge is the highest and most proper function of the mind, in respect of which alone it can be said to partake of eternity. Moreover the form chosen by Spinoza may be partly due, as I have already hinted, to the desire of encountering theologians with their own weapons. But there is unquestionably something of an exalted and mystical temper in his expressions; and it seems possible enough that, but for his scientific training in the school of Descartes, he might have been a mystic indeed. If this be so, Descartes has one claim the more to the gratitude of mankind.

But these seemingly transcendental propositions are not left without practical application. The intellectual love, being a quality of the mind 'inasmuch as it is regarded as an eternal truth depending on the nature of God,' is indestructible. And the greater is the activity in a particular mind of the clear understanding described as the second and third kinds of knowledge, the more does the man partake of eternity, the less is he exposed to evil passions, and the less does he fear death (Pr. 38, 39). And then there is a sudden return to the physical aspect of things, as if to show that it has never been forgotten. 'He that hath a body of most various capacities hath also a mind whose greatest part is eternal' (Prop. 39). For the 'power of ordering and connecting the affections of the body according to the intellectual order' is a perfection of the body. Naturally the body includes the special organs of thought and reflexion; the outward and apparent excellence of the human body is not asserted to be the necessary index of contemplative power. At the same time Spinoza would no doubt have said that, other things being equal, the commonly recognized qualities of health, strength, comeliness, activity, and the like, are all in themselves good and desirable; and that whatever makes for the health of the body must in some degree make for the health of the mind. In this place his meaning is defined by himself in a Scholium.

'Since human bodies possess various capacities, there is no doubt they may be of such a character as to be attached to minds that have much knowledge of themselves and of God, and whose greatest or chief part is eternal, and this to such apoint that they scarce fear death. But for the better understanding of this it shall be observed that we live in perpetual mutation, and are called *happy* or *unhappy* according as we change for the better or the worse. Thus one who from being a child or a youth becomes a corpse is said to be unhappy, and contrariwise it is accounted happiness if we have been able to run the full course of life with a sound mind in a sound body. And in truth he who (like a child) hath a body of very few capacities and largely subject to outward influences, hath a mind which, if we take it in itself, is little or not at all aware of itself, or God, or the nature of things; and contrariwise he that hath a body of many capacities hath a mind which, if we take it in itself, is very well aware of itself, of God, and of the nature of things. Therefore it is our chief endeavour in this life to change the infant's body, so far as its nature admits and is convenient, into another which shall have many capacities, and shall belong to a mind as fully aware as may be of itself, of God, and of the nature of things; and so that everything that belongs to its memory or imagination shall in comparison of the understanding be of hardly any weight.'

Here Spinoza seems to regard education, both physical and mental, as a process of organic development not differing in kind from the purely natural processes of growth; a guiding and training of the possibilities of variation already given in the organism. Though the point is but slightly touched, there is enough to show a striking approximation to our most recent discoveries in this branch of the science of human nature, the most important and perhaps the most neglected of its practical applications.

It has already been incidentally stated that the eternal part of the mind is greater in some individuals and less in others. But however this proportion may be, the eternal part is in every case the more perfect: for this is the only truly active part of the mind, and perfection consists in and is measured by active power. And here Spinoza adds, rather abruptly, a final meta-physical conclusion: namely, 'that our mind, so far as it under-stands, is an eternal mode of thought, which is determined by another eternal mode of thought, and that again by another, and so on to infinity; so that all together make up the eternal and in-finite understanding of God.' The other eternal mode of thought by which the mind is immediately determined would seem to be the thing known by the mind 'under the form of eternity,' and the infinite chain in which these are links to be the whole order of the universe under the attribute of Thought. But, it may be said, this will be only the order as existing at a given moment, since the thing known 'under the form of eternity' must be a particular thing. Spinoza might reply that it is only the infirmity of human imagination that compels us to conceive the order of things as fixed at a particular time, and even as it is we can con-ceive that the state of the universe at a given moment includes potentially the whole history for an infinite past and future. This would involve holding that the difference between potential and actual existence is only in respect of human imagination, besides the assumption (made as a matter of course by Spinoza) that our knowledge of the laws of nature is or may be exact and univer-sal. However, the speculation is not pursued, and we are brought back to a more practical ground.

'Though we knew not that our mind is eternal, we should still put in the first place piety and religion,[246] and gener-ally everything which in the Fourth Part we showed to belong to valour and high-mindedness.' (Pr. 41).

The proof is simply that the virtues and the reasons for practising them have already been established on a footing-independent of the mind's eternity.

'But the belief of the common sort,' it is added, 'seemeth to be otherwise. For they mostly seem to hold themselves to be free in pro-portion as they may do after their own lusts, and to be deprived of their right in proportion as they are bound to live after the commandment of God's law. So they hold piety and religion, and generally everything that belongs to firmness of mind, to be burdens, and hope after death to cast them off and have the reward of their service, that is of piety and

---

[246] These terms have been defined in Eth. 4. 37, Schol. 1. Religion is all desire and action prompted by knowledge of God, *i.e.*, by rational knowl-edge: piety is the desire of well-doing produced by a life according to reason.

religion. But not merely this hope, but likewise (and chiefly) fear, to wit of being punished with grievous torments after death, doth move them to live after God's law, so far as their poverty and weakness of spirit doth admit. And if men had not this hope and fear, but held that the mind perishes with the body, and no longer life remains for poor mortals (worn out forsooth with the burden of pious living), they would go back to their own desires, guide their actions by the desire of the moment, and be ruled rather by hazard than by themselves. Which to me seemeth no less absurd than if a man, because he knows he cannot with wholesome food sustain his body for all time, should choose to cram himself with poison and deadly things; or because he perceives that the mind is not eternal, I mean not immortal, would therefore live as one demented and without aid of reason. But things of such absurdity are scarce fit to be mentioned.'

The vulgar notion of virtue having a reward to claim is further contradicted in the next and final proposition.

'Blessedness is not the prize of virtue, but virtue itself; nor have we the gifts of virtue through controlling our desires, but we can control our desires because we have the gifts of virtue.

'...Herewith I have finished all that I purposed to set forth of the power of the mind over the emotions, and of her freedom. Whence it is evident how great is the wise man's power and his advantage over the ignorant man who is driven by blind desire. For such a man is distracted by external influences and in many other ways besides, and doth never attain true contentment in his soul; he lives as it were without sense of himself and God and the nature of things, and no sooner ceases to suffer than he ceases to be. Whereas the wise man, if we take him as such, is of a constant mind, and, being aware of himself and God and the nature of things in a way of eternal necessity, doth never cease to be, but is ever in possession of true contentment. And if the way I have shown to lead hither seems exceedingly hard, yet it may be discovered. That truly must be hard which is so seldom found. For if salvation were so easy and could be found with little trouble, how should it come to pass that nearly all mankind neglect it? But every excellent work is as difficult as it is rare.'

These are the last words of Spinoza's Ethics; words of gravity but not of discouragement. In their literal sense they are not quite consistent with what he has said in a former proposition; for we have there read that it is not difficult to pursue the life of reason and freedom: and such a life must lead ere long, on Spinoza's principles, to wisdom and true knowledge. Perhaps he contemplated a practical standard of righteous living and happiness attainable by ordinary men with a good will, and a higher kind of satisfaction accessible only by strenuous thinking and the habit of contemplative science. He seems to have thought it at least improbable that the great bulk of mankind should ever be able to dispense with the external coercion of human laws and ordinances, or even with the belief in supernatural rewards and punishments, as a guide of conduct. Once more we note how near he comes to the Stoics. The wise man is thoroughly possessed of the knowledge that virtue is self-sufficient, and therein finds his happiness, whatever his external conditions: but the perfect ideal of wisdom can scarcely be realized by man. The philosopher nevertheless makes this his aim, and comes as near it as he can. The way is open to everyone alike: but as it is, the bulk of mankind are governed by the coarser motives which alone they appreciate, and which experience has shown to be necessary for the maintenance of society. Such is the Stoic position as well as Spinoza's. In so far as this is a statement of fact, we have no right to ask whether it is agreeable or flattering to human pride, but only whether it is true; and, whether we consider Spinoza's time or our own, we shall find it not easy to deny. So far as it implies the absence of hope that the description may some day cease to be true, at least as regards the commonwealth of civilized nations, we may regret that Spinoza did not see his way to believing in the improvement of mankind. But before we pass any intellectual or moral censure upon him for this, we should ask ourselves whether, his circumstances and his knowledge of history and institutions being such as they were, he had reasonable grounds for expecting any continuous improvement. He wrote in a time which on the whole was one of reaction, and in which the blessings of a far distant past, partly by the legendary bias common to all ages, partly under the special influence of the Renaissance, were vastly exaggerated. The movement of free thought seemed arrested; in politics everything was confusion; the growth of science was only beginning. Spinoza was not the man to win a cheap reputation for largeheartedness by facile promises of a golden age.

In this last Part of the Ethics we have traced a curiously involved and artificial argument, and have tried to show to what extent it turns on Spinoza's peculiar use of language which modern criticism cannot allow to pass current. Yet his doctrine of the eternity of the mind must remain one of the most brilliant endeavours of speculative philosophy, and it throws a sort of poetical glow over the formality of his exposition. We have already said that it has a sufficiently certain practical lesson. But still we linger over it, seeking for some expression which may so give us the central idea that we can accept and use it for ourselves, some concentration of the commanding thought without the precarious dialectical form in which it is clothed. If the task were still to attempt, it might be a hard one; but there is no need for any such attempt. The essence of Spinoza's thought is already secured for us by a master who combines delicacy of perception and the intellectual tact which is the flower of criticism with consummate power over language. M. Renan has expressed it in the perfectly chosen words which I have placed at the head of this chapter, and with which, so far as I can preserve them in translation, I shall now end it: *Reason leads Death in triumph, and the work done for Reason is done for eternity.*

CHAPTER X

THE CITIZEN AND THE STATE

Ond' egli ancora: Or di'; sarebbe il peggio
Per l'uomo in terra, se non fosse cive?
Sì, rispos' io: e qui ragion non cheggio.

DANTE: *Paradiso*, 8, 115

Whatsoever therefore is consequent to a time of war, where every man is enemy to every man; the same is consequent to the time wherein men live without other security than what their own strength and their own invention shall furnish them withal. In such condition, there is no place for industry, because the fruit thereof is uncertain: and consequently no culture of the earth; no navigation, nor use of the commodities that may be imported by sea; no commodious building; no instruments of moving, and removing, such things as require much force; no knowledge of the face of the earth; no account of time; no arts; no letters; no society; and which is worst of all, continual fear, and danger of violent death; and the life of man, solitary, poor, nasty, brutish, and short.

HOBBES: *Leviathan*, ch. 13.

THE metaphysical parts of Spinoza's philosophy are expressed, it must be allowed, in a manner not congenial to English habits of thought: and in studying his 'Ethics' the English reader may be at some disadvantage as compared with those who have been trained in a Continental school. When we come to Spinoza's theory of politics the balance is redressed. Though not actually a disciple of Hobbes, Spinoza so closely follows him that the philosophy of law and government which appears in the 'Tractatus Theologico-Politicus,' is just indicated in the 'Ethics,' and is worked out in the 'Tractatus Politicus,' distinctly belongs to the general doctrine characteristic of the English school of jurisprudence. This doctrine was first clearly given out by Hobbes, then taken up after a long interval by Bentham, then carried on with additions into a new generation by Austin; it has in our own time been endowed by the work of Sir Henry Maine and others with the breadth and flexibility that were wanting in its earlier stages, and is now accepted, with more or less development and modification, by nearly all English writers who pay any serious attention to the scientific study of law.

Hence the leading ideas of Spinoza's treatise on Politics ought to have for an English reader nothing very strange in them. The treatise was the latest work of his life, and is unfinished; but that which remained to be added would have been concerned mostly with points of detail. The editors of the 'Opera Posthuma' have given in the preface an extract from a letter of Spinoza's written while he was engaged on this work.

'I should not miss this opportunity were I not already engaged by a matter I judge more to the purpose, and which I think will also please you better, that is, the composition of a treatise on Politics, which on your persuasion I began some time ago. Of this treatise there are six chapters now finished. The first contains a kind of introduction to the body of the work. The second treats of the law of nature; the third, of the right of the supreme magistrate; the fourth, what affairs of state be in the supreme magistrate's discretion; the fifth, what is that last and chief good which a society may contemplate; and the sixth, by what method a monarchical government ought to be established that it may not slide into a tyranny. At present I am on the seventh chapter, wherein I formally prove all the heads of the foregoing sixth chapter touching the institution of a well ordered monarchy. After this I shall proceed to aristocracy and popular government, lastly to legislation and other particular questions regarding political science.'

Neither the date, the occasion alluded to in the first sentence, nor the correspondent's name is disclosed. The chapters on aristocracy were afterwards added, and one on democracy was begun, in the middle of which the treatise breaks off. There is another letter of Spinoza's to Jarig Jellis (Ep. 47), dated February 17, 1671, which seems to throw some more light on the matter. In this he says: —

'A friend of mine sent me a while ago a book entitled "Homo Politicus,"[247] whereof I had heard much talk. On perusal of it I found it as mischievous a book as can be devised or composed by man. To this author's mind the chief good is rank and wealth, and thereto he directs

---

[247] Presumably the work catalogued by Barbier in his *Dictionnaire des ouvrages anonymes* (No 20,602 in ed. 1824). 'Homo politicus, hoc est, consiliarius novus, officiarius et aulicus secundum hodiernam praxin, auctore Pacifico a Lapide (Christophoro Rapp, Cancellario Electorali Borussiæ). *Cosmopoli,* 1665, in-4.'

his teaching... For the rest, he mightily recommends deceit, promising and breaking one's promise, lying, false swearing, and much else of the same kind. When I had read all this I fell to thinking how I might indirectly controvert this author by a book in which I should treat of the chief good, then show the distracted and wretched state of those who seek office and fortune, and lastly prove by convincing reasons and abundant examples that commonwealths must needs perish, and have perished, through men's insatiable appetite for these things.'

It is possible that we have here the germ of the 'Tractatus Politicus,' though the plan sketched out is very different from that which Spinoza began to execute. All that is left of it is the problem, treated in a purely scientific manner, of determining the conditions of stability in political institutions. Spinoza's unfinished treatise cannot be said to hold a place in political science at all comparable to that which is held by the 'Ethics' in philosophy. So far as I know, it has been but little studied and has had no marked influence on Continental thought. In England, where it might have had a better chance, the general prejudice against Spinoza prevented it from obtaining the attention it deserved. Thus the political theory of Spinoza has been left as it were stranded between the two main currents of speculation. We shall find, however, that the examination of it is no waste of time. The 'Tractatus Politicus' is much more than what it appears to be at first sight, a mere adaptation of Hobbes to the terminology of the 'Ethics.' Hobbes is nowhere expressly mentioned by Spinoza, save once in answer to a correspondent, and once in a note to the 'Tractatus Theologico-Politicus.'[248] But the departures from his method and conclusions involve a good deal of tacit criticism; and this implied criticism takes a strikingly modern line on some points. For substantial anticipation of modern constitutional doctrines it would be unreasonable to look in a writer of Spinoza's time. Occasional remarks occur, however, which make us regret that Spinoza never wrote his chapter on the theory of legislation. He points out with perfect clearness the futility of

---

[248] Cap. 16, § 34, *n*. 'In whatever commonwealth a man is, he may be free. For certainly a man may be so far free as he is governed by reason. But reason every way persuadeth to peace (N.B. Hobbes is otherwise); but this cannot be secured unless the laws of the commonwealth are kept.' There is an oversight here, for Hobbes makes peace the first object of rational desire. *Leviathan*, c. 13, *ad fin.* and c. 14.

sumptuary laws, and assigns the true ground of it, namely, that society has no interest in enforcing them. 'Laws which can be broken without any wrong to one's neighbour are made light of; and so far from such laws restraining the appetite and lusts of mankind, they rather heighten them. *Nitimur in vetitum semper, cupimusque negata.*[249] Men who have the leisure will always find the wit to evade laws made to regulate such matters as cannot be wholly forbidden, banquets, games, apparel, and the like; wherein excess only is evil, and that to be measured by the particular citizen's fortune; so that it cannot be defined by statutes of general application.'[250] Spinoza has been charged, and still is charged by some of his critics, with preaching absolutism. The whole scope of the 'Tractatus Theologico-Politicus,' which is an elaborate plea for liberty of thought and expression, is a refutation of this: and there also occur in the 'Tractatus Politicus' many sentences and maxims which show a very different temper. Such are the following: — 'It makes for slavery, not peace, to deliver all power to one man.' 'It is better that the just counsels of a realm should be laid open to enemies, than that the wicked secrets of tyrants should be concealed from citizens.' With this last saying we may contrast one of Hobbes: — 'In deliberations that ought to be kept secret, whereof there be many occasions in public business, the counsels of many, and especially in assemblies, are dangerous.'[251]

It may be convenient, before entering upon details, to give a general view of Spinoza's plan, and of the extent to which he agrees with and differs from Hobbes. They both aim at the construction of a science of politics on the basis of the known facts of human nature; and the assumptions they make about average human nature are much the same. But Hobbes, writing with a view to immediate controversies, does not adventure himself to any length on the path of speculative construction. The practical bearing of his argument may be summed up in one sentence: Every monarch ought to be absolutely supreme in matters both spiritual and temporal; England is a monarchy; therefore the king of England is absolute. Spinoza, on the other

---

[249] 'We spurn at rule, and seek forbidden joys.' — Ovid, *Amor.* iii. 4. 17.

[250] *Tract. Polit*, c. 10, § 5.

[251] Leviathan, c. 25.

hand, undertakes the ideal construction of the most stable types of institutions for monarchy, aristocracy, and democracy respectively. He goes nearly as far as Hobbes, but not quite, in his dislike and distrust of revolutions; and, probably taking from Hobbes his notions of the English Constitution and of contemporary English history, gives the English civil war as an instance of a rebellion which had ended in complete failure. He thinks it must be almost always a fatal mistake to attempt a fundamental change in an existing government, of whatever type it may be. But in the abstract his preference is for democracy, a preference more distinctly expressed in the 'Tractatus Theologico-Politicus' than anywhere else. Democracy is defined, however, in such a way as to include most of the governments commonly called aristocratic or constitutional. It is also remarkable that Spinoza's ideal monarchy is on the whole a more popular government than his ideal aristocracy. His theory of sovereignty is essentially the same as that of Hobbes. But he does not carry it out into the same unqualified consequences. According to Hobbes the origin of the State is a covenant of mutual concession prompted by the mutual fear of men in a lawless condition, and by the rational desire of peace which is the first law of nature; where a law of nature means a rule discovered by reason as a means toward self-preservation. The sovereign, whether he be one man or an assembly of men, bears the person of the united multitude who 'reduce all their wills, by plurality of voices, unto one will,' and in this union become a commonwealth. The collected power and authority of every citizen is transferred to him by the common mandate, to be used at his discretion for their peace and common defence. Further, the mandate is irrevocable, since it is not several from each citizen to the sovereign, but depends on the social covenant of all the citizens. Every subject has covenanted with every other that their natural right shall be and remain transferred to the sovereign. Hobbes admits that the unanimous assent of the sovereign and all the subjects (not of the subjects without the sovereign) may determine the sovereign's right; the result of which would be a total dissolution of government and return to the natural state of war. Whether the whole commonwealth, including the sovereign, might change the form of government without passing through anarchy is a question which, so far as I know, he left untouched. At all events, the sovereign is an agent whose powers cannot be effectually recalled or renounced in any practically possible circumstances: and no subject can complain of acts of state done by the sovereign, because every such act has been authorized by the subject and must be deemed his own. Modern readers cry out, of course, that all this scheme of covenants and mandates is the purest fiction. But Hobbes is not altogether unprepared even for this. He catches the objecting individual in a dilemma. Either you have agreed, he says, to transfer your power to the sovereign or you have not. If you have, then you are estopped from disputing the acts of the sovereign. If you have not, you declare yourself a stranger to the State, and therefore the State has no duties towards you and may treat you as an enemy. Apart from these particular turns of dialectic, Hobbes' argument always comes round to offering the choice between submission and war; and war is for him so clearly the worst of evils that the choice cannot be doubtful. Whether the argument is not equally good to establish (as Dante long before had actually sought to establish) the necessity of an universal monarch to keep the peace between sovereign states, as the sovereign in each state between individuals, is another question to which Hobbes does not seem to have applied himself.

In Spinoza we do not find these rigorous extremes. He describes government as founded on the common consent of the governed, but there is no elaborate analysis of the supposed contract. Again, he regards the power of the State not as swallowing up the natural power or right of the individual to act as he thinks best for his own interest, but as holding out effectual motives to the citizens to agree in exercising that right or power in a particular way, namely, by living peaceably under the laws. Further, although he nowhere expressly says that rebellion is right even in an extreme case, he does say quite plainly that no government is really absolute, since in the last resort its power is limited by the endurance of its subjects, and there are some things which no community will endure. Thus a supreme government, though it cannot offend against its own civil laws, may in a certain sense offend against the law of nature. Rulers who so carry themselves as to invite the contempt or hatred of their subjects run the risk of committing political suicide. 'Such deeds turn fear into indignation, and the state of civil society into a state of war.' As far as the theory of the English constitution goes, Parliament might pass an Act forbidding people to perform their contracts. But in that case Parliament would cease to be obeyed, and Englishmen would have to find some other form of government. Moreover Spinoza holds it competent to the sovereign power not only to interpret but to alter the fundamental laws of the commonwealth, provided that it can be done without provoking a revolution that would in fact, not only by the constructive dissolution of a supposed covenant, dissolve civil society; which Hobbes does not seem to contemplate. There is indeed one natural right which Hobbes holds to be inalienable, the right of personal self-defence; and consequently the right of inflicting punishment 'is not grounded on any concession or gift of the subjects,' but is part of the natural right of self-preservation exercised by the sovereign on behalf of the commonwealth. 'For the subjects did not give the sovereign that right; but only in laying down theirs, strengthened him to use his own, as he should think fit, for the preservation of them all: so that it was not given, but left to him, and to him only.'[252] Spinoza's exceptions are much larger. His language on this point in the 17th Chapter of the 'Tractatus Theologico-Politicus' is particularly explicit. In the foregoing chapter he has laid down the theory of absolute sovereignty as founded on a concurrent cession of individual rights, without even Hobbes' reservation of self-defence. But he now points out that absolute sovereignty is an ideal never completely realized. No man can ever put himself wholly at another's discretion; nor have there ever been rulers who did not stand in some fear of their subjects.

'In truth, if men could so far lose their natural right, that for time to come they might do nothing without the will of them that held sovereign right, then governors might without remedy use all extremities of violence towards their subjects: which opinion I think no man can entertain. Wherefore it must be allowed that every man reserveth to himself much of his own right, which therefore dependeth on no other man's resolution, but on his own alone.'[253]

In fine, the right of a government over its subjects is

---

[252] *Leviathan*, ch. 28.

[253] Cf. Hume, in the Essay on the Origin of Government. 'In all governments there is a perpetual intestine struggle, open or secret, between Authority and Liberty, and neither of them can ever absolutely prevail in the contest.'

really its power of commanding their obedience: but this does not mean only commanding by force or threats, for it is the fact of obedience, not the motive, that makes men subjects. The subject fulfils the law whether he obeys from hope, fear, both together, or any other cause.

'A man is then most under another's government when he determines of full consent to observe all that other's orders; and it follows that the prince who hath most dominion is he that reigns over his subjects' minds. But if they had most dominion who be most feared, then that eminence would manifestly belong to the subjects of despots, who by their despots are most greatly feared.'

And though governments cannot control men's thoughts and affections directly, they may do it indirectly. This again looks like a reflection on Hobbes, who is emphatic on the point that governments can control nothing but overt acts.

We may now understand Spinoza's answer to his correspondent in Ep. 50: —

'As concerning the politics, the difference betwixt Hobbes and myself of which you ask consists in this, that I ever save natural right harmless, and hold that the sovereign magistrate in any state hath no more right over his subjects than is measured by the excess of his power over the subject, which' *(i.e.* the identity of right and power) 'always takes place in the state of nature.'

It would appear that altogether Spinoza attached decidedly less importance than Hobbes to the question of the origin of government. What he regarded as the main thing was the fact of a government existing and being able to maintain itself. In Hobbes' view it is difficult to see how a government once established can ever lose its title: the Leviathan once framed not only exists *de jure,* but is knit together by a *vinculum juris* which nobody can undo. He is driven to admit in some measure the principle of allegiance to *de facto* governments: but all he will say is that, if the rightful government becomes unable to protect any of its subjects, these subjects are remitted to their natural right of self-preservation, and may give their allegiance to any power from which protection can be had. His greatest aversion and contempt is for the doctrine of mixed government; and his logical triumph over the fallacy of divided sovereignty is hardly distinguishable from his practical dislike of all attempts to shift the centre of power or divide the substance of it from the form. While Hobbes expressly admits that an aristocracy or democracy may exist under monarchical appearances, he utterly refuses to consider whether there is anything to be said for holding the constitution of England to be of this kind. The name of monarchy seems enough to dazzle his judgment when he comes to the specific case. Spinoza does not share this temper. His theoretical analysis does not prevent him from having regard to the convenience of mankind, and he is no more an absolutist than Bentham. In his ideal commonwealths he makes elaborate provision for checks and balances, which in their spirit almost anticipate the constitutional publicists of the eighteenth century.

The point on which Hobbes and Spinoza are most thoroughly in accord is the total rejection of all claims, on grounds of religion or otherwise, to set up a jurisdiction equal or superior to that of the civil power. They both denounce ecclesiastical pretensions at every opportunity; and, while they both admit that if a private man has a special revelation he must obey it even against the State, they give it to be understood, in almost identical terms, that the possibility of a special revelation need not be practically considered. No man can have immediate assurance of its truth except him to whom it is actually revealed, and therefore no private citizen is bound to take notice of anything alleged for revealed truth by another, 'who, being a man, may err, and, which is more, may lie.'[254] One who sets up for a prophet is at the very least bound to prove his office by miracles; Hobbes adds as a no less indispensable test of a true prophet that he must not preach any religion but the established one. Spinoza suggests that even if a real prophet appeared in a modern commonwealth there would be no strict obligation to receive him. So that 'in a commonwealth, a subject that has no certain and assured revelation particularly to himself concerning the will of God is to obey for such the command of the commonwealth.'[255] The State is supreme over all persons and in all causes, ecclesiastical and temporal, except in hypothetical events which cannot happen.

We have seen that Spinoza first gives the theory of sov-

---

[254] *Leviathan*, ch. 32.

[255] *Leviathan,* ch. 26; cp. Spinoza, *Tract. Polit.* c. 3, § 10; *Tract. Theol.-Pol.* c. 16, §§ 61 sqq. and 19, passim.

ereignty in unqualified terms, and then states in another chapter the qualifications which he sees to be needful in applying it to existing facts. This deserves a word of special notice. The faculty of clearly grasping an abstract doctrine, and withal remembering that it is an abstraction, and not a complete account of the actual phenomena, is by no means a common one. In our own day it has been reserved for Sir Henry Maine[256] to point out with accuracy the ideal character of the conception of sovereignty and positive law developed by Hobbes and his followers, and thus to furnish the means of assigning its real philosophical and practical value. That Spinoza should have seriously attempted a similar process, and to a certain extent succeeded, is perhaps not the least of the circumstances that show the independence of his thought even where there is the strongest appearance of his following others.

Having thus indicated the general nature of Spinoza's political theory, we may proceed to a more detailed view of the 'Tractatus Politicus.' In the introductory chapter Spinoza announces his intention of dealing with the subject in a purely scientific manner. On this point he repeats in substance what he had said in the Preface to the Third Part of the Ethics. One remarkable passage betrays how strangely he underrated the extent and complexity of the problem.

'I am firmly convinced that all the kinds of commonwealths which can be devised for men's living together in harmony, and likewise the means whereby a multitude should be guided and kept within settled bounds, have been shown by experience; so that I do not think there is anything not repugnant to experience and practice which we can discover by meditation on this topic, but hath before now been known and put to trial. For such is the temper of men that they cannot live except in some common bond of laws; and the laws of commonwealths and affairs of state have been founded and considered by men of the greatest wit (whether by policy or by craft); wherefore 'tis hardly credible that we should be able to devise anything fitted to be of use to society which opportunity or accident hath never offered, and which men busied on public affairs and mindful of assuring their own interest have not discerned.' (c. 1, § 3).

Yet this only seems strange to the eyes of us who have

---

[256] Lectures on Sovereignty in *The Early History of Institutions*.

learnt by fairly trying scientific methods how complex the world is. We have already seen that Spinoza's belief in a comparatively short road to certain and complete knowledge of everything was the belief of almost all the aspiring minds of his time. Not only Descartes before him, but Leibnitz after him, sought and expected to find universal methods, and looked forward to the consummation of the sciences within a few generations. And here we may be allowed to put in a word for Bacon, who has been both praised and blamed more inconsiderately than almost any philosophical writer. Bacon's belief in a general art of scientific discovery which would go near to equalize men's intellects is now easily seen to have been erroneous. But it was not a singular or a perverse belief at the time. If we ridicule Bacon on this score, we must ridicule him for not having known more than Leibnitz did a century later. So too in the present case of politics, Spinoza's opinion that no experiment of importance remained to be tried was the opinion generally held by the most competent persons of his time. The variety of constitutions then existing in the remaining Italian republics, the free cities of the Empire, and the Swiss cantons, appears to have suggested that all possible variety was exhausted rather than to have stimulated curiosity. Certainly Hobbes never dreamt of the great experiment impending in England, which has been directly and indirectly the parent of so many more.

Again, the writers of the eighteenth century treated the English constitution as having reached its final development; and they regarded a state which Hobbes would have called anarchy as the highest actual and theoretical perfection of government. Nor had they any clear notion of the distinction between the outlines of positive constitutional law and the great body of informal constitutional usage which clothes the legal skeleton with full and various life. Hume's political essays, though full of brilliant remarks, are still in the main unfruitful. His 'Idea of a Perfect Commonwealth' is not unlike the 'Tractatus Politicus' in design and arrangement, allowance being made for the difference of scale, and it has about as much or as little practical value. In Montesquieu we find the true forerunner of the modern historical method. But to pursue this here would be to go too far astray.

It may be well to translate the next following paragraph

of the introductory chapter of the 'Tractatus Politicus,' as it contains a phrase (italicized in the translation) which is often and deservedly quoted by modern writers on Spinoza.

'In applying myself therefore to the science of politics, I pretended nothing new or unknown, but only to prove by certain and undoubted reasons, or to deduce from the constitution of man itself, the propositions most agreeable to practical use. And in order to inquire of the matters of this science with the same freedom of mind we are wont to use in the mathematics, I have made it my especial care *neither to mock, to bewail, nor to denounce men's actions, but to understand them:* and to this end I have considered men's emotions, such as love, hate, anger, envy, honour, pity, and other agitations of the mind, not as defects of human nature, but as properties which belong to it in like manner as to the nature of air there belong heat, cold, storms, thunder, and the like; which though they be inconvenient, yet are necessary and have constant causes whereby we endeavour to understand their nature, and the mind rejoices in the right contemplation of them no less than in the knowledge of such things as are pleasing to the senses.'

Political science is to concern itself with human nature not as it ought to be, but as it is. It must not be assumed that men will act in public affairs according to the true dictates of reason unless it is made their obvious interest not to do otherwise. For the welfare of the State it is all one from what motive men obey the law and perform the duties of their station, so that good government be secured. 'Freedom and strength of mind are virtues in private men; but the virtue of governments is safety.' Spinoza proceeds to consider the fundamental principles of government, starting from the facts of average human nature (cap. 2). We translate the paragraph in which the philosophical grounds of his theory are laid down.

'Any particular thing in nature may be adequately conceived, whether it existeth or no. And as the beginning of existence of particular things in nature cannot be deduced from their definition, so neither can their continuance in existing. For the thing itself, as it is in our conception,[257] remains the same after it has begun to exist as before. As therefore the beginning of their existence cannot follow from their essence' (*.i.e.* the knowledge of *what* a thing is differs from the knowledge *that* such a thing is), 'so neither doth their continuance in

---

[257] *Essentia idealis;* a term which does not, I think, occur in the *Ethics.*

existence: but to go on existing they need the same power which they need for beginning to exist. Whence it follows that the power of all things in nature, whereby they exist, and therefore whereby they have effects, can be no other than the eternal power of God himself. For if it were any other created power, it could not maintain itself, nor by consequence other things, but would need for its own continuing in existence the same power that was needed to create it.

'Now from this conclusion, that the power of things in nature, whereby they exist and work, is identically the power of God, we easily understand what is natural law or right.[258] For since God hath right to everything, and the right of God is nothing else than the power of God, so far as it is regarded as absolutely free, it follows that everything in nature hath of nature so much right as it hath power to exist and work; seeing the power of each several thing in nature, whereby it doth exist and work, is no other than the free and absolute power of God. Therefore I understand by the law of nature the statutes or rules of nature according to which all things happen, that is, merely the power of nature. And thus the natural right of the whole of nature, and by consequence of each several individual, doth extend so far forth as its power; consequently whatever every man does by the rules of his own nature, that he does by perfect natural right, and hath right over nature so far as by his power he prevails.'

This statement of Spinoza's, and the corresponding passages in Hobbes, appear to us at this day far-fetched if not perverse. It is so much easier to say at once that such phrases as law of nature, natural right, have no meaning in jurisprudence and political science; that laws conferring rights can exist only in a society; and that, so far as we can conceive man as not a member of society, we must conceive him as not subject to any law. But a dominant set of phrases, however inappropriate to a particular writer's purpose, is not thrown aside without struggles. In Spinoza's time the Law of Nature was not only still commonly spoken of and appealed to, but the idea had received an important revival and extension at the hands of Grotius and his contemporaries. To discard the term would have been simply impossible. Both Hobbes and Spinoza could only strive to fix a new meaning of their own upon it. It may help us to understand the meaning sought by Spinoza if we here shortly recapitulate the position assumed by his philosophy with regard to the fundamental ideas

---

[258] Spinoza uses the one term *ius naturae*. The double meaning cannot be given by any single word in English.

of ethics and law.

The notions of *good* and *bad* arise as soon as we consider an individual whose existence and welfare are distinguishable from the existence of the universe as a whole. For every creature some things are good and others bad. But the same things need not be good and bad for different individuals, or for the same individual in different circumstances.

When we have a society composed of individual men capable of independent action, that which is *good* or *bad* for the society becomes *right* or *wrong* for the individuals composing it. What is esteemed good or bad by the society at large, or by the opinion prevailing in it, is prescribed or forbidden to the individual members as being right or wrong. This is what modern English writers have called Positive Morality.

When in a particular society there has been formed an organized government provided with definite means of making itself obeyed, and that government prescribes, permits, and forbids particular kinds of conduct, then conduct falling under these rules acquires further special qualities. What is prescribed is legal duty or just; what is allowed is legally right; what is forbidden is legally wrong or unjust. This is, in modern language, Positive Law.

Again, certain rules of conduct may be discovered by reflection on the general conditions of human nature, and these rules are independent of particular social systems. They may be regarded either as scientific statements about the conduct men actually pursue, in so far as their reason is not disturbed by passion, error, and prejudice, or as moral precepts setting forth an ideal to which, as reasonable men, we shall endeavour to conform in our way of life. Such propositions or precepts are given in the fourth part of Spinoza's 'Ethics,' and answer in a general way to the rules of conduct given by Hobbes as laws of nature.[259] So far as a man follows these precepts, he is said to live according to reason.

It is true that Spinoza does not clearly recognize the distinction between Positive Morality and Positive Law, or rather

---

[259] *Leviathan,* c. 14. Hobbes distinguishes between *ius* and *lex,* and defines *lex naturalis,* in effect, as a rule of conduct discovered by reason, and tending to the self-preservation of the agent.

omits to take note of the existence of Positive Morality. Indeed the conception is a modern one. But it fits well enough into Spinoza's scheme, and the statement would have been so incomplete without it that I have felt justified in adding it. Now it will be observed that in this scheme *right* and *wrong* are terms of civil or social morality, not of the natural morality which is concerned with the self-maintenance of the individual. For the individual, as such, there is only good and bad. Nevertheless most things which are good or bad for the individual are also right or wrong, in other words good or bad for society. Hence most things which are first regarded as simply good or bad come to acquire a certain value in the social scale of rightness and wrongness; and ethical associations derived from the community are at last carried over to the general notions of goodness and badness themselves. A similar association takes place, but to a less extent, between the ethical and legal notions of right and wrong. Hence the intellectual analysis is difficult, and is apt to excite in the moral sense a kind of jealousy bordering on repugnance.

On the other hand there are elements of possible conflict. We have at least two distinct sources of rules of conduct, or, according to the developed statement here presented, three. One set of rules is propounded by reason as *good;* another by the community as *right;* another by the civil power as *law.* Now it may be that all these rules coincide, so far as they cover the same ground; but we are not entitled to assume that they will. Indeed there could not be a complete and universal coincidence unless all societies and all governments were guided by right reason; which is not the case. Positive Law may conflict with Positive Morality; both Positive Law and Positive Morality may conflict with the dictates of reason. If this happens, which are we to follow? Spinoza does not explicitly discuss questions of this kind. All he has to say on the matter is that reason bids man to live sociably with his fellow-men, and prescribes obedience to the civil law as being, in general, the surest way to that end. And when reason says, 'obey the law,' we follow reason in obeying the law, though the particular law may be one that we disapprove. This general indication of the relation of Ethics to Politics is perhaps as much as can be expected in a political treatise. It is also proper to observe that although Spinoza constantly implies that the ethical conceptions of *right* and *wrong* are of a quasi-legal character, and are not applicable except to men living in society, this is not necessary to his political theory as such. Having premised this much, we resume the order of the treatise.

Every man does what he thinks most for his own interest: and whatever he actually does, whether reasonably or foolishly, he has, in Spinoza's terminology, a *natural right* to do. Men have conflicting interests in so far as they are subject to passion; and man is more formidable to man than any other creature. But men are subject to passions; therefore men left to themselves would be in frequent conflict, or in other words the state of nature is a state of war. On the other hand, a state of life in which every man must fight for his own hand is too precarious to be tolerable. Man cannot exercise his faculties with any pleasure or convenience except in society, where his strength is multiplied by union: and in this sense it may justly be said that man is a social animal. When a multitude of men live together in society, each individual, being powerless as against the united will of the rest, has no more right than the society chooses to leave him. The right which arises from and is determined by the power of the society over the individual is called government or dominion *(imperium),* and is vested in the person or persons, be they many, few, or one, who are appointed to the supreme charge of public affairs.

The body of men subject to one government is a State.[260] Its members are called citizens in respect of their franchises and privileges, subjects in respect of their duties. No citizen can be free to do whatever he pleases; for if he were, he would be above the State. Neither can the citizens be free to interpret the laws of the State as they please; for this would make every man judge in his own cause, and virtually independent of the State. It is for the State to determine what is just and unjust, and for the citizen to obey the law; the will of the State must be the will of every citizen. If it be said that it is against reason thus to give up one's own judgment, the answer is that reason exhorts to peace and a secure life, which cannot be had except in a well-ordered State. The advantage of living under settled laws is far greater than any hardship which we may feel in a particular case from having to

---

[260] Cap. 3.

obey a law which we think unreasonable. This leaves it quite open to citizens to suggest amendments in existing laws, and endeavour by all peaceable means to procure them; which is expressly mentioned in the 'Tractatus Theologico-Politicus' as not only allowable but commendable.

Next the limits to the power of the State are considered. As the free or reasonable man is the strongest among men, so that State is strongest whose institutions are most according to reason. For the strength of the State depends on the union of the citizens; and union cannot be unless the laws of the State are directed to the general good. Again, the subjection of the citizen to the State consists either in fear of the power of the State or in love of civil society and order. Therefore the State has no jurisdiction over things to which men cannot be induced by reward or compelled by punishment. No man can abandon, for example, his own power of judgment. Nobody can be compelled to believe that the whole is not greater than its part; that God does not exist; that a finite body before his eyes is infinite, and the like. Further, there are matters so repugnant to human nature in other ways that no power can compel obedience in them; as, to produce evidence against oneself, to kill one's parents, not to attempt saving one's life, and the like. 'If we say notwithstanding that the commonwealth hath right or power to command such things, we can no otherwise conceive this than as one might say that a man has a right to be mad. For what else than madness would be a rule of law to which no man can be bound?' In applying this test, however, we must consider the ordinary temper of men. There may always be some perverse or insane persons inaccessible to the motives upon which most men in most circumstances obey the law. But this does not prevent the law from being in general efficacious. As for the particular individual who sets himself against the State, as one having nothing to hope or fear from it, Spinoza says (in this point agreeing with Hobbes) that he may be considered as an enemy. Again, the power of the State is limited by public opinion; 'such matters are not within the right of the State as excite a general opposition.' For if a government issues commands which provoke many citizens to resistance, it thereby deprives itself at once of a certain measure of its power.

As for the rights of independent States against one another, they are the same as those of individuals in the imaginary state of nature. Peace between States corresponds to society between individuals in so far that it rests upon consent. The obligation of treaties lasts as long as the reasons for which they were made, and no longer: a proposition which may be unacceptable to some theorists, but which has been abundantly verified in the history of Europe, and not less since Spinoza's time than before it. Indeed it seems impossible, on any political or ethical principles whatever, to lay it down as an absolute proposition that the obligation of treaties is perpetual. Whence can governments derive the right of binding their subjects and successors for all time by improvident undertakings?

It follows from the view already given of the functions of a commonwealth that the sovereign authority alone has the direction of public affairs, and that for any one to meddle with them unauthorized is a usurpation of government.[261] If it be asked whether the sovereign power in a commonwealth is bound by law, and capable of doing wrong, the answer is that civilly it is not so, but naturally it is. 'For if a commonwealth were bound by no law or rule, without which it would not be a commonwealth, then we should have to regard a commonwealth not as a thing existing in nature but as a chimæra. Thus a commonwealth does wrong when by action or sufferance it brings in causes of its own destruction.' Power is always limited by the capacities of the thing acted upon as well as the faculties of the agent. 'If I say, for instance, that I may of right do as I will with this table, I suppose not thereby that I have a right to make the table eat grass.' So the commonwealth cannot compel its citizens, being men, to a kind or extent of submission contrary to human nature. 'Therefore that the commonwealth may maintain its right, it is bound to maintain the motives of fear and respect; otherwise it ceases to be a commonwealth.' Nevertheless fundamental changes can be regularly effected only by the sovereign authority itself. Revolutions may in extreme cases be necessary, but they are extra-legal and in the nature of acts of war.

Spinoza then considers what is the best condition or ideal, as we should now say, of a government,[262] without regard to its particular form. This is a question of fact, not of right; it is

---

[261] Cap. 4.
[262] Cap. 5, De optimo imperii statu.

one thing to govern by law, another to govern well. The object of a commonwealth is peace and protection; the excellence of a commonwealth consists therefore in men's living in amity and observing the law. For since men are by nature much the same everywhere, habitual discord and law-breaking are more the fault of institutions than of the particular offenders. And the peace here meant is a cheerful and rational acquiescence in the law, not a submission compelled by force.

'A commonwealth whose subjects rise not in arms because they are overcome by terror is rather to be spoken of as being without war than as enjoying peace. For peace is not mere absence of war, but an excellence proceeding from highmindedness; since obedience is the constant will to perform that which by the common ordinance of the State ought to be done. Moreover a commonwealth whose peace depends on the dulness of its subjects, and on their being driven like cattle, to learn nothing but slavery, is more fitly called a wilderness than a commonwealth.[263] When therefore we say that the government is best under which men lead a peaceable life, I mean that life of man which consisteth not only in the circulation of the blood and other properties common to all animals, but whose chief part is reason and the true life and excellence of the mind.'

In the same spirit he says again in the following chapter:

'If slavery, rudeness, and desolation are to be called peace, then is peace the most wretched state of mankind. Truly there are more and sharper disputes between parents and children than between masters and slaves; and yet it were no good housekeeping to make the father into a master, and hold the children for slaves. It makes for slavery, not for peace, to confer unlimited power on one man.'

Reference is made to Machiavelli in terms of great respect, and Spinoza conjectures that his real purpose in elaborately showing 'what means a prince who has no other motive than the lust of power should use to strengthen his government' may have been to point out the futility of removing a despot when the causes are left untouched which impel the ruler, whoever he may be, to reign despotically; and perhaps also to warn free communities against putting themselves in the power of any one man. The true intention of Machiavelli's treatise has been a

---

[263] 'Rectius solitudo quam civitas dici potest:' with obvious allusion to the well-known 'solitudinem faciunt, pacem appellant.'

standing puzzle to modern critics, and Spinoza's guess is perhaps as good as any other.

Before we leave the general part of the treatise, we may observe that if there be anything illiberal or tending to an apology for despotism in Spinoza's marked dislike to violent changes in affairs of State, the fault is shared by him with one of the most thoughtful of English Liberal statesmen of recent times. At the end of his 'Dialogue on the best form of government' Sir George Cornewall Lewis puts the following sentiment in the mouth of Crito, an impartial bystander whose opinions may fairly be taken as corresponding with those of the author himself.

'Looking back upon the course of revolutionary movements and upon the character of their consequences, the practical conclusion which I draw is that it is the part of wisdom and prudence to acquiesce in any form of government which is tolerably well administered and affords tolerable security to person and property.'

And we may add that, as matter of fact, the most successful revolutions have been either re-assertions of ancient rights (as in England in 1688), or not merely domestic revolutions, but risings against a dominion which was actually or virtually foreign; as in the struggle for the independence of the Netherlands, and the liberation of Italy in 1860. Cases of this kind are not considered by Spinoza, and, though not uncommon in history, scarcely belong to the theory of municipal politics.

In the remainder of the 'Tractatus Politicus,' as far as it goes,[264] the ideal institutions appropriate for the different forms of government are sketched out and justified. It is not worth while to follow Spinoza minutely through this part of his work; we may be content with fixing our attention on a few salient points. Under the head of Monarchy it is repeated with some emphasis (and it would seem with implied criticism of Hobbes) that no one man can really be sovereign. A monarch must in practice be guided by counsellors, and thus a nominally absolute monarchy is a covert and therefore bad form of aristocracy. Accordingly Spinoza's ideal monarchy is limited in various ways. There is a great council roughly corresponding to the Parliament of a modern constitutional system: it is however not elective, but appointed by the Crown, subject to fixed conditions as to age and

---

[264] Capp. 6-11: cap. 11 is unfinished.

otherwise. The Crown must take the advice of this assembly, but is free to act upon any opinion supported by a certain number of votes. A smaller standing Council is to take charge of executive business and the routine of administration. The army is to consist only of citizens, and to receive pay only in time of war; and military commands are to be annual. Although this is to modern eyes one of the most unpractical points in Spinoza's scheme, it probably did not seem so at the time. Not only then, but throughout the eighteenth century, a standing army was the bugbear of constitutional theorists: and to this day the forms of the English constitution treat it as a temporary necessity rather than a constant part of the appliances of an independent State. As to ecclesiastical affairs, no particular religion is to be established by law, but the king may have a private chapel.

Next comes the ideal aristocratic constitution, which is not unlike the monarchical in its general features; the precautions and checks being however more elaborate. Aristocracy is defined as the government in which the sovereign power belongs to a select number of the citizens who themselves fix the terms of admission to the governing body. The number may be either small or large: indeed according to Spinoza's definitions the governing body might bear a larger proportion to the whole adult population in some aristocracies than in some democracies. There must be an established religion, for the sake of unity among the governing body, but of the simplest possible kind as to doctrine. Others are to be tolerated, but may not compete with the established one in public display. A conjecture is made as to the historical origin of aristocracies (c. 8, § 12) which comes remarkably near what is now known or presumed to be the truth from the results of later researches. We have originally a homogeneous community of free men founding, let us suppose, a new city. As between themselves they are equal, and willingly recognize their equality. But strangers will gather round the original stock, attracted by various motives: and to these strangers equal rights will not be allowed, nor indeed will they seek them in the first instance. In course of time the new comers increase, and become assimilated to the original stock of the founders in everything but civil status and rights: till at last the difference between them appears conventional, and the community of free men with its outskirt of dependents has become a people governed by a favoured class. A few words are given by Spinoza to the subject of public instruction; with a promise, unhappily not fulfilled, of resuming it in a future chapter. He expresses a decided opinion against official endowments, holding that State universities 'are established not for the cultivation but for the repression of understanding' and that every citizen should be free to teach in public at his own charges and his own risk.

The polity for which an aristocratic government is best adapted is that which consists of several confederated cities of approximately equal power (c. 9); and further rules are given for this special case. One of them, namely, that the permanent scat of the federal government must not be in any one of the united commonwealths, is in effect identical with the precaution observed by the founders of the United States in providing a seat of government exempt from the jurisdiction of any particular State, and subject to the exclusive authority of Congress.

The general aim of all institutions, as well those expressly recommended as others 'which may be devised in each several government agreeably to the nature of the country and the temper of the inhabitants,' should be to lead men to obedience rather than compel them.

'A government which aims at nothing else than to guide men by fear will be rather free from defects than possessed of merit. Men are to be so guided as that they may deem themselves not to be guided, but to live after their own mind and of their own free resolve; and that they be kept to allegiance by love of freedom, care for increasing their substance, and the hope of attaining honourable places in the government. But for statues, triumphs and other such whets to valour, they be tokens rather of slavery than of freedom. Rewards are ordained for the valour of servants, not of free men. I do confess that by spurs of this kind men are extremely quickened; but such things, which at first are awarded to notable men, yet afterwards, as envy increaseth, are given to worthless fellows that are puffed up with wealth, whereby all honest people are in great indignation. Likewise those who can make a show of their ancestors' triumphs and statues think themselves to be wronged if they have not precedence over others. And lastly, to say no more, 'tis certain that equality (which once being cast off, the liberty of a society must needs perish) can by no means be preserved when especial honours are awarded as of common right to any one man of illustrious excellence.'

Passages like this are interesting as showing how very

modern a good deal of our political experience is. Spinoza does not seem to contemplate the possibility of a social aristocracy being combined with a system of equality before the law, and coinciding only in part with political eminence: nor does it occur to him that evils which now appear to us obvious enough are likely to result from concentrating human ambition and vanity on the one object of official power and distinction.

Having explained his federal aristocracy, Spinoza declares with some confidence that a State framed on this model would be as stable as it is possible for a government to be, and could be dissolved only by some overwhelming external violence. He then passes on to democracy (c. 11). The definition of democracy is peculiar; the criterion of a democratic government, as understood by Spinoza, being a franchise fixed by law. By franchise we do not mean a representative franchise in the modern sense (for of representative government Spinoza seems to have no notion) but simply the right to take part, in some way or other, in the government of the country, which however would include the voting power of modern constitutions. Thus there may be a qualification by age, by primogeniture, or by payment of taxes to a certain amount, and it matters not whether the actual governing body thus constituted be large or small in proportion to the whole number of inhabitants. Even though the qualified citizens be fewer than the sovereign council might be in an aristocratic commonwealth of the same size, the government is still to be classed as democratic, 'because the citizens appointed to rule the commonwealth are not thereto chosen by a sovereign council as the fittest, but are appointed merely by the law.' This definition includes, it is obvious, the most widely different political systems. To begin with, every form of representative government is a democracy in Spinoza's sense; the French monarchy under Louis Philippe, with its restricted *pays légal,* no less than England since the Reform Act of 1867, or the French Republic since 1871 with universal suffrage. But Spinoza announces it as his intention to treat only of one form of democracy, that namely 'in which all men indifferently who owe undivided allegiance to the State, are in other respects of legal capacity, and are of good conversation, are entitled to vote in the sovereign assembly and to undertake the offices of government.' This is intended to exclude, as Spinoza explains, aliens, women, infants, serfs, and criminals. On the point of excluding women from political power he gives reasons in a separate paragraph, the last of the unfinished chapter. He puts it simply on the ground that men are the stronger; not merely with their physical strength as individuals, but intellectually and in social combination.

'If women were by nature the equals of men, and equally endowed with firmness of mind and intellect, wherein chiefly consists human power, and consequently right, then surely among so many and various nations there should be found some where both sexes ruled equally, and others where men were ruled by women and so brought up as to be inferior to them in intellect.'

(This anticipates the topic much insisted on by some recent advocates, that the general inferiority of women to men is entirely the result of education.)

'And seeing this hath nowhere come to pass, we may clearly affirm that women have not by nature an equal right with men, but must needs give place to them; and hence that it is not possible the two sexes should bear rule equally, much less that men should be ruled by women.'

Further, a little consideration of human passions and jealousies will show that 'equal rule of men and women cannot have place without great prejudice to peace.' It is open to supporters of female suffrage either to disregard Spinoza's objections as frivolous, and dismiss him, like other opponents, as a narrow-minded person, or to distinguish him on the ground that he was considering the question, not of a vote for representatives, but of a direct and active participation in public affairs. It is more to our present purpose to remark that the objections, whatever may be thought of their merits, are not at all of the kind we should expect from a man answering to the popular notion of Spinoza. They are far from being appropriate to a man who sits in a garret and spins metaphysical cobwebs. Indeed, with the exception of a reference to the fable of the Amazons in the pedantic manner of the time (which I have thought it needless to translate), they are such as might well be used at this day in the House of Commons.

Here the treatise comes to an untimely end. It is not probable that Spinoza's account of an ideal democratic State would have contributed much to the science of politics, but we may still regret not having it. Some light might have been thrown on the question, at present obscure, what was the extent of Spinoza's familiarity with the public affairs of his own country. In dealing with a subject-matter more apt to be illustrated by domestic examples and, it would seem, more after his own heart than the discussion of monarchical and aristocratical institutions, he would have had a better occasion of showing his knowledge and opinions on matters of present interest. That he did not neglect the political writings of the time we know from a reference in the discussion of aristocracy (c. 8, § 31) to an author mentioned by Spinoza as 'prudentissimus Belga V.H.' This V.H. is Pieter de la Court[265] (1618-1685), an eminent publicist who wrote under the initials D.C. (De la Court) V.H. (Van den Hove, the Dutch equivalent). He was a friend of John de Witt, and opposed to the party of the Stadtholders. The terms in which Spinoza, who is not lavish of praise, refers to De la Court are not without significance as to his own political sympathies. If, as divers excellent persons have maintained, Spinozism is in politics a doctrine of absolutism, we are driven to conclude that Spinoza did not understand his own philosophy, and in fact that he was the first anti-Spinozist. But the reader will now be in a position to judge this question even without referring to Spinoza's text. It sufficiently appears, I venture to think, not only that Spinoza was a firm and consistent supporter of political liberty, but that he was disposed to go much farther in letting individual thought, habits, and enterprise alone than the majority of statesmen of his own time. His condemnation of sumptuary laws must have appeared rash, his mistrust of State endowments pedantic if not suspicious, and his notions of religious toleration wildly extravagant. Even his contention that in a monarchical State the monarch should be subject to the law was likely to be received with doubtful favour in some quarters. For various reasons his work has been eclipsed by that of Hobbes; and in the actual history of the theory of politics it can hold only a rank subordinate to the 'Leviathan.' But the judgment of history is not always the judgment of philosophy. Hobbes' power of reasoning and mas-

---

[265] I owe identification (so far as I know hitherto unpublished) to Dr. Campbell.

tery of English command and deserve an admiration which it would be difficult to exaggerate. But Spinoza's doctrine rests on a wider and more generous view of human life; it is less encumbered with fictions; it aims at a higher mark. It is the work, not of a powerful mind which has espoused the cause of a party and makes philosophy a partisan, but of a philosopher who is proud of being a free citizen.

CHAPTER XI

SPINOZA AND THEOLOGY

> One knocked at the Beloved's door; and a voice asked from within, 'Who is there?' and he answered, 'It is I.' Then the voice said, 'This house will not hold me and thee.' And the door was not opened. Then went the Lover into the desert, and fasted and prayed in solitude. And after a year he returned and knocked again at the door. And again the voice asked, 'Who is there?' and he said, 'It is Thyself!' and the door was opened to him.
>
> E. FITZGERALD, from JELALADDIN.

> Rends-toi compte de Dieu. Comprendre, c'est aimer. —
> VICTOR HUGO: *Les Contemplations,* livre 3me, no. 8.

IN various parts of Spinoza's work there are incidental discussions of prevailing theological conceptions, not so much by way of direct attack as for the purpose of explaining Spinoza's own different point of view. We have hitherto not noticed these passages. Their interest is perhaps more historical than philosophical, and moreover the consideration of Spinoza's metaphysical theory gave us quite enough to do without attending at the time to his controversial digressions. But Spinoza's bearing towards the current theology of his time is an element of some importance in our knowledge of the man, and his position as regards religion in a wider sense excites questions which, even if it be impossible to answer them to our satisfaction, it is impossible to leave untouched. It has already been pointed out that Spinoza nowhere professes to attack theology in general, but only to refute the erroneous philosophical doctrines attached to theology by particular Churches and theologians. He leaves no room, however, for a technical system of theology standing side by side with philosophy, whether as claiming to control it or merely to belong to a distinct and independent sphere of thought. Natural religion is identical with philosophy, and the power of revealed religion consists not in adding new philosophical truth, or systematic truth of any kind, to that which reason can discover, but in showing men a way of salvation independent of philosophy.

So far as theology is distinct from philosophy it is not a body of doctrine but a rule of life. Obedience is within every man's power, but not wisdom. This is the burden of the 'Tractatus Theologico-Politicus,' and the severance of faith from philosophy there spoken of does not mean that what is disbelieved as matter of reason may be believed as matter of faith, but that when the distinct objects of the two are rightly understood no collision is possible. The whole scope of revelation is practical, and the claims of revealed religion to be accepted by mankind rest not on demonstrative but on moral certainty. We further collect that, apart from speculative questions as to the actual truth of particular doctrines, it was in Spinoza's view a practical necessity that the great majority of mankind should have a dogmatic religion of some sort, but that he also thought it possible and desirable that the fundamental dogmas should be very few and simple.[266] Similar assumptions are made in the treatise on Politics, as we saw in the last chapter.

Now we cannot expect to learn the whole mind of Spinoza from the writings in which these statements occur. In the 'Tractatus Politicus' he professes to take men as he finds them; in the 'Theologico-Politicus' he is to a great extent conducting a hypothetical argument on premises which he is content to assume by way of concession. He is addressing himself as a citizen to citizens and statesmen, not as a philosopher to philosophers. On the other hand we cannot assume that the position taken by him for this purpose is to be set aside as merely occasional and hypothetical. The philosophical criticism of the 'Ethics' does not justify us in disregarding it: for, as Spinoza himself would have been the first to point out, the subject-matter of the two arguments is not the same. The 'Tractatus Theologico-Politicus' affirms that a plain man who does not enter upon philosophy may without harm, or even with profit, believe whatever he finds most edifying, provided that he believes it sincerely and allows the like freedom to others. But it is clear enough that the author himself does not accept popular theology or the popular interpretation of Scripture; and the discussion of current theological philosophy in the 'Ethics' is only the development of what is already suggested in the earlier work. Then we have a curious

---

[266] *Tract. Theol.-Pol.* cc. 13-15.

correspondence with Oldenburg on special points, belonging to the last year or two of Spinoza's life. Here, again, one cannot tell exactly how much allowance is to be made for Spinoza's desire to accommodate his expressions of unwelcome opinions to his friend's habits of thought and language.

There are two distinct things to he considered. The general discussion of propositions in theology, or in mixed theology and metaphysics, has a speculative value independent of the conclusions we may form about Spinoza's exact personal relations to historical theology. But the place which religion and the religious sentiment held in Spinoza's individual life cannot be estimated without some endeavour to ascertain those relations, however difficult it may be. It will be best to take first that branch of the subject where we are on firmer ground, and the matter is of wider interest. We turn back, then, to the First Part of the 'Ethics.'

Spinoza maintains, as we have seen, the doctrine of a universal necessity which is identical with freedom when we consider the universe as a whole. And he says (Pr. 17) that 'God acts merely by the laws of his own nature and without constraint;' and in this sense God alone can rightly be called a free cause. In other words, the order of the universe as a whole is self-contained and self-determined. Discussion follows in a Scholium.

'Others hold that God is a free cause, forasmuch as (in their opinion) he can bring it to pass that the things which, as we have said, follow from his nature or are in his power, do not happen or be not produced by him. But this is as if they should say that God could make it not to follow from the nature of a triangle that its three angles should be equal to two right angles; or that from a given cause its effect should not follow, which is absurd. Also I shall prove below, without the help of this proposition, that neither understanding nor will belong to the nature of God. I know there are many who think they can prove that free-will and the height of understanding belong to the nature of God; since, as they say, they know no greater perfection which they can attribute to God than that which is the highest perfection in ourselves. Again, though they conceive God as having in act the perfection of understanding, yet they believe not that he can make all those things to exist which he doth in act understand; for thus they conceive the power of God would be taken away. If, they say, he had created all things that were in his understanding, then he could have created nothing more, which they hold repugnant to God's omnipotence. And so they have chosen to describe God as every way indifferent, and creating nothing else but what by a supposed absolute will he hath determined to create.'

But we have shown, Spinoza continues, that all things follow by the same necessity from the infinite nature or power of God; so that the omnipotence of God is always and eternally in act: whereas the other opinion really denies his omnipotence, for it is assumed that God cannot or must not create everything he has conceived, lest he should 'exhaust his omnipotence and make himself imperfect.'

'Therefore in order to affirm God's perfection these men are driven to affirm at the same time that he cannot bring about everything to which his power extendeth; than which I see not what can be devised more absurd, or more repugnant to the omnipotence of God.' As for understanding and will in God, they must be wholly different from ours, and resemble them only in name. Human understanding is conditioned by the things understood; the divine understanding is the cause and origin of them. It is also the cause of human understanding, and for that very reason must be different from it, as Spinoza proves by a curious piece of formal argument. But this is not all. Farther on he points out that both understanding and will are in every case particular determined modes of thought, having particular finite causes. They belong to *natura naturata,* not to *natura naturans.* And accordingly 'will and understanding are related to the nature of God in the same way as motion and rest[267] and generally all things in nature, which must be determined by God to exist and act in a particular manner. For will, like all other things, needs a cause to determine it to exist and act. And though any particular act of will or understanding hath infinite consequences, yet God cannot therefore any more be said to act out of freedom of will than because of the consequences of motion and rest (which be likewise infinite) he can be said to act out of freedom of motion and rest. Wherefore will belongeth not to the nature of God more than other things in nature, but standeth with respect to it no otherwise than motion and rest and all other things, which we have shown to follow from the necessity of God's nature, and thereby

---

[267] As to Spinoza's theory about 'motus et quies,' see pp. 123-128 above

to be determined to exist and act in a particular manner' (Pr. 32, Coroll. 2).

The next proposition affirms that 'things could not have been produced by God in any other manner or order than they have been produced.' And it is maintained (Schol. 2) that this doctrine, so far from detracting from the perfection of God, as many persons may hastily suppose, is required by it. Assume with the objectors that will belongs to the nature of God: it will be admitted that all things depend on his will for being what they are, and that his decrees are eternal; for his mind cannot be supposed variable. 'But since in eternity there is not any *when,* or *before,* or *after,* it follows merely from the perfection of God that God never can or could decree otherwise than he doth; or that God was not before his decrees, nor can be without them.' To say that God might have made things otherwise than he did is to say that his will and understanding might have been otherwise than they are. But this leads to inadmissible consequences. It is agreed by all philosophers (Spinoza possibly is thinking of the Schoolmen as well of the Jewish Aristotelians) that the divine understanding is never *in potentia* but always *in actu.* But since the will and understanding of God are indistinguishable from God himself, as is likewise admitted, it follows that if God's will and understanding had not been what they are, he must have been other than he is. That is, in order to make things otherwise than they are God himself must have been other than he is. But some will say that perfection itself depends on the will of God, and that what is now perfection might have been imperfection if he had thought fit so to make it. But this would amount to the assertion 'that God, who must needs understand that which he wills, can by his will bring it to pass that he shall understand things otherwise than he doth understand them. Which (as above shown) is an exceeding absurdity.'[268] Then follows a very characteristic remark.

'I confess this opinion, which doth subject all things to an alleged indifferent will of God and holdeth everything to depend on his pleasure, is less wide of the truth than the opinion of those who hold that all God's actions have regard to a rule of good (Deum omnia sub

---

[268] With the whole passage compare and contrast St. Thomas Aquinas, *Summa Theologiæ* Part i, Quaest. 19, artt. 2-5.

ratione boni agere). For such men seem to affirm somewhat outside God, and not dependent on him, which God keeps before him as a pattern in his works, or at which he aims as at a fixed mark. This plainly is naught else than to make God subject to fate; than which nothing more absurd can be propounded of God, whom we have shown to be the first and singular free cause of all things, both as to their essence and as to their existence.'

Spinoza here repudiates two popular conceptions of the Deity in one breath; one which makes him an absolute ruler whose only law is his own will, and another which regards him as constantly fulfilling a moral law conceived as in some way independent of him. In the one view he is a despotic monarch, in the other a governor bound by an unchangeable constitution. The world is his plaything, or an inscrutable something is his master. In the latter case, the only evidence we have of the ultimate sovereignty of the moral law is in the human conscience: and hence it would seem that conscience must be the judge of God as well as of man. And this may really be the view obscurely held by a large number of the right-minded persons who accept theology in its ordinary forms, even those who would verbally assert the other opinion, namely, that the moral law is what it is because God has chosen to make it so. For though many say that moral commandments are binding because they express the will of God, few of those who say so would not also say that the will of God is always good; where the meaning of *good* might indeed be vague, but at any rate would be something more than the name of that which God wills.

A more philosophical variety of this opinion is to go so far with Spinoza as to say that the order of nature, and the moral law as part thereof, belongs to the nature of God itself; and then to add that the moral law appertains in some peculiar and eminent way to the nature of God, so as to make him the proper object of a feeling similar in kind to that which we entertain for good men, but infinitely magnified in degree. This position, or something like it, is adopted by divers modern theologians. It is free from the metaphysical absurdity pointed out by Spinoza in the cruder form of moral theology, but raises difficulties of another kind. The objects of morality being particular and relative to man, there appears to be no convenient mean between refraining from the application of moral ideas to the order of nature as a whole, and asserting that the universe exists for the sake of man. This last position was formerly thought acceptable or even obvious, but for several reasons there is a growing disinclination to defend it. Again, it is not impossible to deny in terms that morality is relative to human society. But those who do this must be prepared to show us the universal morality of which human morality is only a particular case, or at least to bring forward some probable evidence of it. They should be able to explain, for instance, in what sense morality existed in the world before any human society was formed. So far, however, from feeling any difficulty on this score, they would in general be the first to proclaim the dignity of man as the only moral creature, and to exalt him above all other finite beings precisely on that ground. On this point also it is hard to be sure whether people really accept everything they profess. The universality of the moral law may be asserted in words, while the real meaning is only that there are permanent elements in human nature and society to which there correspond permanent moral relations, or that the broad groundwork of morality could not be different from what it is unless human nature were also different. But this is a proposition which at the present day nobody will dispute, least of all anyone who has apprehended the lessons of Spinoza's 'Ethics.' In the same way the principles of right and wrong may be called eternal and immutable in a sense to which no serious exception can be taken, namely, that these principles are necessary consequences of the constitution of man, which itself is part of the universal order of nature, and that they are as permanent as mankind itself. It is possible that some of those who speak as if they thought the scientific discussion of ethical theories dangerous to morality may imagine that these last-mentioned propositions are attacked, and may wish only to defend them when they put forward statements of apparently wider scope. Certainly it is not an uncommon mistake to fancy that everyone who does not accept some transcendental theory of ethics must regard morality as casual and conventional, and variable in every new set of circumstances: whereas if it were possible to regard morality as casual and conventional, it would be by means of the assumption that moral law is nothing but the commandment of a being who gives no reason for his commands, but will crush us if we disobey.

But we cannot here attempt to pursue this topic farther, and indeed the task might prove endless. There are no harder illusions to get rid of than anthropomorphic ones (or perhaps it would be better to say anthropocentric); and there is no reason to suppose that the possible and more or less plausible forms of such illusion are either exhausted or exhaustible. As to the modern transcendental theories of superhuman morality which claim to be founded on a strictly philosophical method, it may be a sufficient excuse for saying nothing of them that they have no point of contact with Spinoza. But one may observe that a transcendental theory is by its very nature a kind of *deus ex machina.* Disproof may be impossible; in fact, I should be disposed to say that if any transcendental theory is capable of actual disproof, it can only be the result of bad workmanship. But the burden of proof lies on the transcendentalist to show that his *deus ex machina* is necessary; at least that is the opinion of people who have not the transcendental faculty.

We have now seen that according to Spinoza the actions of God are not directed by a will that can even be supposed mutable, by anything that can be called choice, or towards a moral end. But he further says that they are not directed towards ends at all. In more technical words, he wholly rejects Final Causes. To most English minds it may possibly seem that the exclusion of deliberation and choice from the order of the universe would of itself imply the exclusion of final causes. But recent speculation in Germany has shown that it does not: and Spinoza's appendix to the First Part of the 'Ethics' is not only a vigorous piece of controversial exposition which as a work of art one would be sorry to lose, but it is by no means philosophically superfluous. His professed object is to expose the prejudices which lie at the root of most confused thinking about the order of nature. 'All the prejudices,' he says, 'which I here mean to lay bare depend on this point only; to wit, that men commonly suppose all things in nature to act as themselves do for a purpose; insomuch that they make sure that God himself orders all things for some fixed end (for they say that God made all things for man's sake, and man to worship him).' The origin and the groundlessness of this belief are accordingly to be explained. Men think themselves free, and act with a view to some desired end. Thus they come to regard the purpose of an action as a necessary and sufficient explanation of the action. If in a particular case they can get no positive information of the purpose, they form a conjecture from the analogy of the motives by which they have themselves on other occasions been determined to actions of the same kind. Then, finding so many things in nature useful for man's life, they regard all things as instruments for man's use; and knowing that they found and did not make these conveniences, they infer that some ruler of the world, having freedom like that of human agents, must have made them of set purpose for the benefit of mankind. Proceeding to guess at this ruler's motives from the analogy of their own, they form the opinion that the Gods ordered the world for man's use that so they might acquire men's gratitude and have honour and worship of them.

'And so this prejudice hath grown to a superstition and struck root deep in their minds; which was a reason moving every one to extreme diligence in considering and explaining the final causes of all things. But whereas they sought to show that nature doth not anything in vain (that is, without regard for the use of mankind) they have shown nothing, as it seems, but that nature and the Gods, if this were so, should be as distraught as themselves. Mark, I pray you, to what a pass the matter comes at last. Among so many conveniences of nature they must needs find not a few things contrary, as storms, earthquakes, plagues and the like, and these they affirmed to happen for that the Gods were angered for wrongs done them by men, or faults in performing their rites; and though experience did every day protest, showing by numberless examples that good and ill turns befall the obedient and the disobedient indifferently, nevertheless they ceased not from their confirmed prejudice.' For it was easier to assume that mischievous things had unknown uses than to reconstruct their habits of thought: and so the further assumption was made that the counsels of the Gods were beyond human understanding: 'which cause would have alone sufficed to hide the truth for ever from mankind, had not the mathematics, which are concerned not with designed ends, but only with the nature and properties of figures, made manifest to them another pattern of truth.'

Spinoza then argues, in his usual concise manner, that the doctrine of final causes is in itself untenable: among other reasons, it is inconsistent with the perfection of God: 'for it God

acts for a designed end, it must needs be that he desireth something which he hath not.' And it is observed that a common way
of defending final causes is by a method otherwise unknown of
'reduction, not to impossibility but to ignorance.' For example, a
tile falls from a roof on a man's head and kills him. It shall be
proved by this method that it fell on purpose to kill him: for if
that had not been God's design, how could all the conditions for
the event concur then and there? You may answer, it happened
because the wind blew and the man was passing that way. They
will stand to it with another question: why did the wind blow,
and why was the man going by just then? If you assign fresh reasons, they will again ask new questions, as they always can,
since of questioning there is no end: 'and so they will never
cease asking for the causes of causes, until you take flight to that
sanctuary of ignorance which they call the will of God.' And
thus it happens that to seek out the causes of what seems wonderful, and to aim at understanding the operations of nature instead of staring in dull amazement, is to incur the suspicion of
heresy. For those who are commonly esteemed the sole expounders of divine truth well know that the destruction of ignorance is the destruction of fear, on which their power is built.

It is then explained how current notions of beauty, ugliness, and the like, are relative to men's organs and dispositions.
This part of the appendix is a rapid sketch in anticipation of what
is given at large in the following books of the 'Ethics,' and we
therefore need not dwell upon it: some expressions, however, are
remarkable for their affinity to recent psychological theories independently worked out from the side of physical science. 'If the
motion impressed on the optic nerves by the objects that the eyes
perceive be such as promotes health, the objects which cause it
are named beautiful; those which excite the opposite kind of
motion are called ugly.' Hence appears the answer to the common difficulties touching the perfection of the world. If, it is
asked, everything is the result of God's perfection, whence come
the many imperfections of nature, corruption, ugliness, disorder,
evil, sin? But this is to confuse the nature of things with human
imaginations of them.

'The perfection of things is to be reckoned only from their
own nature and power; and things are not therein more or less perfect
that they delight or offend the sense of men, or that they are convenient

for the nature of man or repugnant thereto. If any ask, why God hath not so created all men that they should be governed only by reason? I give them no answer but this: Because he lacked not matter for creating all things, even from the highest degree of perfection unto the lowest. Or more exactly thus: Because the laws of his own nature were so vast as to suffice for producing all things which can be conceived by an infinite understanding' *(ab aliquo infinito intellectu:* a hypothetical infinite mind which must be distinguished from the infinite intellect which we have met with as one of the things 'immediately produced by God.')

From the universal point of view perfection is fulness of being, and has nothing to do with the perfection that is relative to man's use or convenience.

So far Spinoza's general criticism of theological ideas. It enables us to say with reasonable certainty, up to a certain point, what the God of Spinoza is not. He is free, but not exercising choice; for all his works are necessary, and the law of their necessity is the law of his own being. His acts do not spring from design; where there is no choice there can be no deliberation, and a being which embraces the universe is sufficient to itself. He is not a moral being in the sense of having preferences; for he with respect to God all things are perfect in their kind. Even understanding and will cannot be said to belong to his nature. In short, the God of Spinoza is not the personal God often said to be required by the innate religious sentiment of man. But if he is thus impersonal, it would be misleading, and not in accordance with Spinoza's turn of thought, to say that he is unconscious. It is true that understanding, as a determined mode of thought, belongs only to determined things. Even the infinite intellect which includes all thought and consciousness is a particular thing. The object of these distinctions, however, is partly to secure the equality of all the Attributes, of which we have already spoken. It remains a cardinal point of the system that God is a thinking being who can think infinitely in infinite ways (Eth. 2, Pr. 3). This does not involve, it is true, the supposition of a consciousness analogous to human consciousness. Such a supposition is quite inadmissible on Spinoza's principles; for human consciousness is a state of a mental organism, answering in the Attribute of thought to a state of the human body in the Attribute of extension. And God's consciousness could be like man's only if the material universe were organized like a human body; which some enthusiasts have indeed in later times been found to affirm. It is stated however in one of the latest propositions of the Ethics, already cited (Pt. 5, Pr. 40), that the human mind 'so far as it understands' is an eternal mode of thought which together with endless other such modes 'makes up the eternal and infinite understanding of God.' All human knowledge, then, is not only contained but in some manner united and as it were incorporated in this 'infinite understanding.' The mind of God gathers up into an eternal unity the true ideas of all finite minds in all time. And also, since every idea or mode of thought is said to be 'true with respect to God,' in that it really exists and corresponds to a really existing mode of Extension,[269] it would seem that every finite mode of thought whatever, whether in a conscious finite mind or not, must have its due place somewhere in the infinite chain. All this will doubtless appear obscure. I can only say that Spinoza has left it so, and that it does not seem to me worth while to attempt to force an illusory definiteness upon that which is incapable of definition. The difficulties of Spinoza's theory of the eternity of the mind, which of course would recur here, have already been pointed out.

It is clear, on the whole, that the real difference between Spinoza and the common forms of orthodox philosophy is not that he denies consciousness to God, for this he never does; or that he denies God's consciousness to be like man's, for this many orthodox philosophers would also deny, and theologians of the weightiest authority have in fact denied it as strongly as Spinoza himself. The point of his heterodoxy is that he will not call God exclusively or eminently a thinking being. To say that God is a spirit is in Spinoza's view just as inadequate and misleading as to say that man is a spirit. Man is a thinking being, but he is also a corporeal or extended being; and thought is only one of the infinite Attributes of God. But here there recurs another point of which we have already treated, namely the latent idealism of Spinoza's metaphysical system, which may have coloured his thought on this subject almost without his knowing it. Perhaps he regarded the infinite variety of the universe (including as it does in his view countless forms of existence to us wholly unimagin-

---

[269] See p. 201, above.

able) as reflected and redoubled, and at the same time grasped as a single whole, in the 'infinite intellect of God.' But all this, again, comes perilously near to a mere playing with words.

The discussion of Spinoza's metaphysic in its bearing on theology is much complicated by his having no philosophical term equivalent to the modern *consciousness,* and generally not regarding things from that point of view. In one passage of his early work, the 'Cogitata Metaphysica' (Part 2, c. 8, § 1) he does mention the term Personality as being used by theologians to explain their distinction of qualities or attributes (in the common sense) in God. He adds that the term is as mysterious to him as the mystery it is intended to explain, and that further light is to be hoped for only in the beatific vision ('quamvis constanter credamus in visione Dei beatissima quae fidelibus promittitur Deum hoc suis revelaturum').

Now an appeal to revelation, either here or hereafter, for enlightenment on a philosophical question is a thing utterly contrary to Spinoza's later principles, as abundantly appears from the 'Tractatus Theologico-Politicus.' And this passage occurs in a work where Spinoza is not expressing his own opinions, except so far as he can suggest them in a professedly Cartesian commentary without actually contradicting Descartes. Either the passage is ironical, hinting to the disciple of Descartes that his master has brought him to a theologico-philosophical deadlock whence nothing but a revelation will help him out: or (as I think more probable) it was written by Spinoza at a very early time, when he was still disposed to believe in mysteries. At the date of the 'Essay of God and Man' he seems to have thought it possible that new Attributes might become known to man by revelation; for in one place (Part I, c. 7, note) he speaks of Thought and Extension as the only Attributes *as yet* known to us.

It is remarkable that the theological colouring of Spinoza's philosophy becomes fainter as we proceed in the 'Ethics,' and in the third and fourth Parts *Deus* appears more and more like a bare synonym for *natura.* But then, just as one might begin to think that the verbal disguise has been completely thrown off, we come upon the intellectual love of God in the fifth Part. After all God has not been reduced to Nature, but Nature exalted to God. Spinoza begins and ends with theological terms; and yet, when we translate his doctrines into modern language, we find a view of the world standing wholly apart from those which have been propounded or seriously influenced by theology. His earlier writings help us to understand the seeming riddle. He started with the intention of making theology philosophical, but with the determination to follow reason to the uttermost. Reason led him beyond the atmosphere of theology altogether, but his advance was so continuous that the full extent of it was hardly perceived by himself.

Those to whom names are important may be left to settle as best they can by what name Spinoza's doctrine shall be called. Most people call it Pantheism. There is no particular harm in this, except that Pantheism is so vague a term as to be applicable and applied to diametrically opposite theories. For example, the Hindu philosophers of the orthodox Brahmanical schools are in a general way pantheists, and are commonly so named. But they hold that all finite existence is an illusion, and life mere vexation and mistake, a blunder or sony jest of the Absolute. We need hardly repeat that Spinoza holds nothing of the kind. So that when somebody talked a while ago of 'Pantheism from the Vedas to Spinoza,' he might as well have talked of the law of evidence from Manu to the Indian Evidence Act, as far as any logical connexion went: to say nothing of the circumstance that the Vedas are many centuries earlier than systematic Hindu philosophy, and the earliest parts of them are not pantheistic. Again, the Stoics were also pantheists: only they went to the other extreme and held that the universe was the product of perfect reason and in an absolute sense good. A description which includes these opinions as well as Spinoza's cannot be of much use for conveying exact information. And then it is difficult to say how far Theism does or does not overlap Pantheism. Lately Mr. Fiske of Harvard has written a very lucid and systematic work, setting forth a view of the nature of things identical in the main with Mr. Herbert Spencer's and he calls his view Cosmic Theism. Now it is certain that Mr. Spencer's and Mr. Fiske's doctrine excludes the belief in a so-called Personal God, and the particular forms of religious emotion dependent on it. Whether any large number of people will agree to use the name of Cosmic Theism for the doctrine I do not know, and cannot pretend to care very much. But it is evident that Spinoza must be called a Theist by such persons, be they many or few; since his ideas are not less theological than Mr. Fiske's, and his language more so. Then there is the facile and once frequent name of Atheism, which however polite and intelligent persons have lately shrunk from using. This is just as well, as it is not only an ugly name, but has no intelligible meaning. At least the nearest approach to a definition that I can suggest is that an atheist means anybody who disagrees with one on any theological question of importance; the speaker being, of course, the judge both of what questions are theological, and whether they are important enough to call names about. Probably the historical meaning is definite enough, namely, a citizen who refuses to worship the Gods appointed to be worshipped by the authorities of his city. But to apply this in England at the present day would obviously lead us into great incivility towards classes of persons who are not only respectable and influential, but quite orthodox as orthodoxy has been understood ever since the Act of Toleration.[270] As for Agnosticism, we may be allowed to put off any discussion of this last addition to the vocabulary of sects and persuasions till some one has called Spinoza an Agnostic. In fine, we conclude that to dwell on these matters of nomenclature is unprofitable: and we decline, for similar reasons, to enter on the question, on which chapters if not volumes might be spent, whether Spinoza's way of looking at the world and man is to be called a religion or not. If it is fitted (with allowances and additions according to the state of knowledge for the time being) for the use of reasonable men in the conduct of life, sooner or later reasonable men will find it out and use it, under whatever name. If it is not, reasonable men will not be persuaded to use it by the most positive and formal proof that it satisfies at all points the best possible definition of a religion.

We may now go on to consider Spinoza's utterances as to the particular revelations on which the claims of Judaism and Christianity, the only historical religions with which he was acquainted, are commonly made to stand. It is needless to say that the materials for a comparative study of religions were not accessible in Spinoza's time. The religions of the East were known

---

[270] Yet the term *atheist* appears to include even now, in the borough of Chelsea and at the time of a general election, a member of the Society of Friends.

only by loose and superficial report, and this was especially the case with Buddhism, the most important of all. Spinoza probably knew of its existence (in his letter to Albert Burgh he specifies India as the seat of divers religions); but of its origin, its fundamental doctrines, and the personal character of its founder as preserved by tradition, he can have known nothing. Indian Buddhism, indeed, remained a sealed book to European scholars long after his time.[271] This has to be borne in mind if we undertake to reduce Spinoza's judgments to the measure of our own time. In the first chapter of the 'Tractatus Theologico-Politicus,' where the nature of prophecy is discussed, the revelation of the Decalogue occurs as a question to be specially dealt with. It is the opinion of some Jewish authors, Spinoza says, that the words of the commandments were not actually pronounced by God, but the Israelites heard an inarticulate noise, while at the same time the commandments were inwardly perceived by them.

'And this' (he proceeds) 'I myself once thought, since I found the words of the decalogue in Exodus different from those in Deuteronomy; whence it seems to follow (since God spoke but once) that the decalogue was to lay down not the very words of God but only the meaning. However, if we are not to do violence to Scripture, it must certainly be allowed that the Israelites heard a real voice.'

This voice we must suppose to have been created for that occasion. But this supposition is by no means free from difficulty: for how could this finite and created voice give the Israelites any rational certainty of the existence or nature of God beyond what they had before? And moreover the whole narrative suggests not only that there was a real voice, but that God himself spoke in the fashion of a man. 'Wherefore I doubt not,' Spinoza concludes, 'that herein lies a mystery, of which we will speak more at large afterwards.' Are we to infer that Spinoza thought it proper on this point to follow the example set by Ibn Ezra on other points of historical criticism? By talking of a mystery does he simply mean, as Ibn Ezra meant beyond question, that he does not choose to explain himself further? Certainly he has brought together precisely the kind of evidence, and

---

[271] The Buddha appears in Montesquieu (doubtless through Jesuit accounts of Chinese Buddhism) as 'Foé, législateur des Indes.' *Esprit des Lois,* book 14. c. 5. Cp. note B to Bayle's article on Spinoza.

suggested precisely the kind of considerations, which a modern critic would bring forward to show that the whole narrative is an anthropomorphic myth. The hypothesis he actually gives is a sort of rationalized miracle: since God does not speak like men, he must have specially ordained that the Israelites should hear certain words pronounced as by a magnified human voice. It is extremely difficult to believe that this really commended itself to Spinoza. Again, it sufficiently appears from other parts of the treatise that in Spinoza's eyes the pre-eminence of the Jews as the chosen people was a fact to be studied and explained on the ordinary principles of historical and political reasoning. The divine election of the Hebrew nation is identified, as we should now say, with natural selection. Again, the whole and only scope of revelation, in the view set forth by Spinoza in various parts of the treatise, is to assure men that there is a way of salvation by obedience without speculative knowledge. And this obedience does not consist in following any particular set of precepts, but in the exercise of justice and charity. The only necessary and really catholic faith is summed up in this: 'that there is a supreme being, loving justice and charity, whom all men are bound to obey that they may be saved, and to worship by showing justice and charity to their neighbours.' (c. 14, § 24). Philosophical questions as to the nature and attributes of God are indifferent to faith.

'Whether he be fire, spirit, light, thought, or otherwise, is of no account to faith; nor yet in what manner he is the type of the right life, for example, whether because he hath a just and merciful mind, or because by him is the being and operation of all things, and through him therefore we also have understanding, and through him perceive that which is true, just, and good: to faith it is all one what every man holds touching these things. So again it is indifferent to faith whether one believe that God is everywhere essentially or potentially; that he governs nature freely or by the necessity of his own nature; that he dictates laws as a prince, or shows them as eternal truths; that men obey God from absolute free will, or by necessity of the divine ordinance; that the reward of good and punishment of wicked men is natural or supernatural.'

Thus, too, it is not the business of revelation to give rational demonstrations but to move men to obedience. And here is the answer to the difficulties formerly raised about the voice from Sinai.

'Although the voice which the Israelites heard could not have given them any philosophical or mathematical certainty of the existence of God, yet it sufficed to ravish them with amazement at God's power (such as they already knew him), and to impel them to obedience; which was the purpose of that display. For God's will was not to show the Israelites the attributes of his nature as they are in themselves (seeing he did not as then reveal any), but to break their stubborn mind and draw it to obedience; and so he went to work with them not with arguments, but with the blast of trumpets, thunder, and lightnings.'

This, it will be observed, removes only half the difficulty. The other half is not touched either in the chapter on miracles or elsewhere. Remembering that the 'Tractatus Theologico-Politicus' is a work of conciliation, we may conclude without much hesitation that Spinoza did not himself regard the circumstances of the Mosaic revelation as historical.

When in the following chapter he speaks of the necessity and authority of revelation, he passes over the thunders of Sinai, and only adduces in general terms the testimony of the prophets. And the prophets he regards (herein pretty much following Maimonides) as men gifted with a particularly strong and vivid imagination, which became the instrument of a kind of special insight; the prophet's individual character, education and habits colouring all his visions and determining the form in which they were recorded. On this point also the question occurs whether Spinoza is giving his own opinion, or only aims at giving the most rational theory within the limits of certain assumptions he has imposed on himself for a special purpose. It is almost impossible to draw the line between these two positions in the 'Tractatus Theologico-Politicus,' and I doubt whether Spinoza always drew it himself.

The passage on the general necessity of revelation to which attention has just been called deserves further consideration. It has been seen that the foundation of theology and the sum of faith is that men can be saved by mere obedience without knowledge. Not that obedience is the only way; for knowledge leads to the same life and the same salvation, as Spinoza is careful to explain. But this efficacy of obedience is not demonstrated: it may be asked then, why do we believe it? If blindly and without reason, then we act foolishly; if on the other hand we say it is capable of proof, theology is absorbed in philosophy.

'Now to this I answer, I clearly hold that this fundamental doctrine of theology cannot be discovered by natural reason, at least there hath no man been found to demonstrate it, and therefore revelation was highly necessary; but nevertheless we may so use our judgment as to accept the revelation once made with at least a moral certainty. I say moral certainty: for we cannot look to have greater certainty herein than the prophets themselves to whom it was first revealed, and whose certainty was yet but moral, as we have already shown. Wherefore those go clean astray who endeavour to prove the authority of Scripture by arguments of the mathematical kind... And we may reasonably embrace this fundamental position of theology and Scripture, though it cannot be mathematically proved. It is folly to reject merely for this cause that which is confirmed by the witness of so many prophets, from which flows great comfort to men who do not excel in understanding, and to the commonwealth ensues no small advantage; and which we may believe without any hurt or danger: as if for the rational conduct of life we could admit nothing as truth which on any plausible ground may be called in doubt, or as if the greater part of our actions were not uncertain and hazardous.'

Once more, at the end of the chapter Spinoza repeats that he attaches the highest value to revealed religion in the sense we have just explained.

'Since we cannot perceive by the light of nature that mere obedience is a way to salvation, but only revelation teaches that this is brought to pass by the singular grace of God, which our reason cannot attain, it appears by consequence that the Scriptures have brought exceeding comfort to mankind. All men without exception can obey, and there be but a very few, compared with the whole of human kind, who acquire a virtuous disposition by the guidance of reason: so that if we had not this witness of Scripture, we should doubt of the salvation of nearly all men.'

Two points of some interest are left unexplained by this statement, namely, the precise meaning of salvation or being saved, and how, if at all, the facts of revelation or the truth revealed can be expressed in philosophical language. In the first question there is nothing to detain us. For Spinoza salvation cannot mean anything else than that deliverance from the passions to which the other way, the clear but arduous way of reason, is shown in the 'Ethics.' But of revelation what are we to understand? How can God as conceived by Spinoza, the being in whom is the infinite reality of infinite worlds, whose freedom is the necessity of the universe, to whose nature neither understanding nor will must be specially ascribed, reveal particular truths or duties to men by particular acts of grace? Again, the alleged contents of revelation are hardly adequate to the machinery. It seems paradoxical, or at least not consistent with Spinoza's general way of thinking, to call in the Law and the Prophets to assure us that the reward of a tranquil mind may be earned by righteousness and goodwill without philosophy: for this is what the message of Scripture seems to come to, when we substitute for the term salvation the meaning almost certainly attached to it by Spinoza. Is this a matter to learn from signs and wonders? or, thinking and saying what he does of signs and wonders in general, can Spinoza really mean to assert the supernatural communication of this one point of practical knowledge? On the other hand, the words are express and even emphatic: and we have no right to sacrifice Spinoza's good faith to the dogma of his rigid consistency, which has arisen, as I have already had occasion to point out, from attaching exaggerated importance to the geometrical form used in the 'Ethics.' Perhaps we are free to suppose that Spinoza regarded revelation as the manifestation of a particular kind of human genius, the disclosure of moral truth by an insight natural in its presence and operation, but occurring only in a few men. But if prophecy be simply a kind of genius, why should it have ceased? And why does Spinoza lay so much stress on the necessity of the true prophet's doctrine being confirmed by a sign? In order to dispose of modern impostors, one might think at first sight. But he must have well known that professing prophets are never at a loss for a sign; and moreover he has a much shorter way with new propounders of revelations, as we saw in considering his theory of politics. Altogether the difficulty remains considerable. There is an unexplained gap between the rationalizing criticism of the 'Tractatus Theologico-Politicus,' which goes a long way, but refuses to go all lengths, and the thorough-going speculation of the 'Ethics.' Difference of dates will not account for it, since we know that Spinoza's philosophy was matured long before the Theologico-political Treatise was published.

The difficulty, however, applies only to our estimate of Spinoza's personal opinions. For philosophical criticism the

'Tractatus Theologico-Politicus' may be taken by itself, and anything propounded or suggested by it may be adopted or left aside on its own merits. And the view of revelation there put forward seems to contain at least this truth: that the appearance of a religion which puts a moral law before ceremonies, and organizes morality instead of merely organizing sacrifices, processions, penances, miracles, indulgences, is a capital fact in the history of the world. The religion which reaches this height, whether gradually or by the first impulse of a founder, is vital and has the means of victory. Judaism, Buddhism, Christianity, to some extent Mahometanism, possess or have possessed this power. It is true that religion always tends, in the hands of its ordinary ministers (who cannot as a rule be more than ordinary men), to revert to the ceremonial stage. It is also true that the opposite danger of mysticism is ever present. But when a religion has once been or become moral, there is always room for men of moral genius to arise within it and revive the latent power. This they do at the risk of being misunderstood and disowned; in some cases they find themselves cut off altogether, and found a new religion or communion; in others the Church is wise in time, and their work is openly or tacitly accepted. Thus Judaism underwent a great moral transformation in the hands of the prophets, but not without great struggles; and again, at the very time when the Jewish polity was doomed to final destruction, the moral side of Jewish religion received a further development the results of which have never been lost. On the other hand Buddhism owes its independent existence to Brahman jealousy and exclusiveness; it appears, at least, that the Buddha had for himself no intention of going outside the very large bounds of Hindu orthodoxy. In our own country Wesley, who elsewhere might have become the founder of a new cosmopolitan order, was driven to leave his name to a sect. And in Christianity we have the greatest of all examples (though as to its actual scale and extent not greater than Buddhism) of a religious movement not originally aggressive assuming an entirely new character under the stress of opposition, and becoming at last a power of the first magnitude. It is curiously parallel with Buddhism in the circumstances that it has been reduced to insignificance in the scenes of its early conquests, and has found its strength in distant lands and among men of alien races and traditions.

What has Spinoza to say of the power of Christianity and the person of its founder? His own words shall presently be given. But we must attempt to find an equivalent for them in the language of our own time: and, leaving aside the question of revelation in the abstract, I think we may say that Spinoza looked on Jesus as a man of transcendent and unique moral genius, standing out above Moses and the prophets in some such way as Moses was conceived by the Jewish doctors to stand above all other prophets.[272] But he did not regard him as otherwise of a different mould from mortal men. The mysteries propounded by Christian theologians appeared to him scarcely to deserve express contradiction: they were not so much untrue as unintelligible. In discussing the nature of prophetic vision (Tract. Theol.-Polit. c. 1, §§ 22-24) Spinoza says: —

'Though we clearly understand that God can communicate immediately with men (for he communicates his nature to our mind[273] without any bodily instrument); yet that a man should purely in his mind perceive matters which be not contained in the first principles of our knowledge, nor can be deduced therefrom, his mind must be of surpassing excellence and beyond man's capacity. Wherefore I believe not that any man ever came to that singular height of perfection but Christ, to whom the ordinances of God that lead men to salvation were revealed, not in words or visions, but immediately: so that God manifested himself to the apostles by the mind of Christ, as formerly to Moses by means of a voice in the air. And therefore the voice of Christ may be called, like that which Moses heard, the voice of God. In this sense we may likewise say that the wisdom of God, that is, a wisdom above man's, took man's nature in Christ, and that Christ is the way of salvation. But here it is needful to explain that of those things which sundry churches determine concerning Christ I have naught to say, neither do I deny them; for I am free to confess I comprehend them not. What I have now said I collect from Scripture alone.'

And again in the chapter on God's laws (c. 4) it is said that even Moses received and understood his revelations not as declarations of eternal truth but as positive laws or precepts, and regarded God under the human attributes of a prince and lawgiver.

'This, I say,' adds Spinoza, 'is to be affirmed only of the

---

[272] Cp. *Tract Theol.-Pol.* c. 1, § 21.
[273] That is, in our ordinary knowledge.

prophets who deliver laws in the name of God; but not of Christ. Of Christ, though he too appears to have delivered laws in the name of God, we are yet to think that he perceived things truly and adequately. For Christ was rather the very mouth of God than a prophet; since (as we showed in the first chapter) God gave revelations to mankind by the mind of Christ, as aforetime by angels, that is, by particular voices and visions.'

And if Christ ever declared after the fashion of a law-giver the truths which he perceived in their eternal necessity, it must have been from regard to the ignorance of his hearers. Spinoza thus appears to ascribe to Christ not only a surpassing power of moral intuition, but a corresponding strength and clearness of understanding in relation to the truths thus perceived. The reader may already have observed, what is still more plain in reading the 'Tractatus Theologico-Politicus' at large, that Spinoza takes no account of the historical development either of morality or of religion. It was hardly possible that he should; the omission is simply to be noted and borne in mind.

These opinions of Christ's office and character were naturally unacceptable even to moderately orthodox readers. In 1675 Oldenburg asked Spinoza (Ep. 20) to explain himself farther on this and other points. The answer on this head is as follows (Ep. 21): —

'I say that it is by no means necessary to salvation to know Christ after the flesh; but of the eternal Son of God, that is, the eternal wisdom of God, which has shown itself forth in all things, and chiefly in the mind of man, and most chiefly of all in Jesus Christ, we are to think far otherwise. For without this no one can attain the state of blessedness; since this alone teaches what is true and false, good and evil. And because, as I have said, this wisdom was chiefly shown forth through Jesus Christ, his disciples preached the same as by him it was revealed to them, and showed that in that spirit of Christ they could exalt themselves above others. As for the proposition added by sundry churches, that God took on himself the nature of man, I have distinctly stated that I know not what they mean. To speak plainly, they seem to me to speak as improperly as if one should tell me that a circle had assumed the nature of a square.'

Oldenburg is unsatisfied, and insists on the necessity of keeping a certain amount of miracle and mystery as the foundation of Christianity (Ep. 22). This leads to an answer where Spinoza comes very near to the specific conclusions of modern theological criticism, and (what is more remarkable) by much the same road (Ep. 23).

'As to my opinion of miracles, I have sufficiently expounded it, if I mistake not, in the theologico-political treatise. I now add but this much: if you consider these matters, to wit that Christ appeared not to the Sanhedrin, not to Pilate, nor to any of the unbelieving, but only to the saints; that God hath no right or left hand, nor is naturally in any one place, but everywhere; that matter is everywhere the same, and that God cannot display himself outside the world in the imaginary space men feign; lastly, that the fabric of the human body is restrained by the mere weight of the air within certain bounds: you will then easily perceive that the appearance of Christ after his death was not unlike that in which God appeared to Abraham, when Abraham saw men and asked them to dine with him. You will say, surely all the Apostles believed that Christ had risen from the dead and in truth ascended into heaven; which I deny not. For Abraham likewise believed that God had dined with him, and all Israel believed that God had come down from heaven in fire to Mount Sinai and spoken to them in his proper person; whereas these and sundry other matters of the like sort were appearances or revelations adapted to the capacity and conceit of the men to whom God was minded thereby to reveal his counsel. I conclude therefore that the resurrection of Christ from the dead was in truth spiritual, revealed only to the faithful, and to them after their capacity; consisting in this, that Christ was gifted with eternity and rose from the dead (the dead, I mean, in that sense in which Christ said: let the dead bury their dead), in that by his life and death he gave a singular example of holiness; and he raises his disciples from the dead in so much as they follow this example of his life and death. And it were no hard matter to explain the whole doctrine of the Gospel according to this hypothesis. Nay, the fifteenth chapter of the first Epistle to the Corinthians can be explained by no other, or Paul's arguments understood, for on the common hypothesis they are evidently weak and may be confuted with little pains; not to mention that in general the Christians have interpreted spiritually what the Jews have interpreted materially.'

Oldenburg again rejoins that the narrative of the passion and resurrection is continuous, lively, and circumstantial, and cannot be taken otherwise than literally throughout. Spinoza replies (Ep. 25) by repeating his opinion yet more explicitly.

'With you I take the passion, death and burial of Christ literally, but his resurrection I take allegorically. I admit that this also is told by the Evangelists with such circumstances as that we cannot deny that the Evangelists themselves believed Christ's body to have risen and ascended into heaven, there to sit on the right hand of God; and that he might have been seen by unbelievers, had any such been in the places where Christ appeared to his disciples: but in this they might well be mistaken without prejudice to the Gospel doctrine, as happened to other prophets also, whereof I have given instances in my former letters. But Paul, to whom also Christ appeared afterwards, boasts that he knows Christ not according to the flesh but according to the spirit.'

Oldenburg was not content with this, but once more protested (exactly as an English Broad Churchman might now protest if he fell into a similar correspondence with a Dutch theologian of the liberal school) that the literal historical fact of the Resurrection is the indispensable foundation of Christianity. So far as we know, he had the last word. It is needless to dilate on the wonderfully modern character of Spinoza's criticism; it speaks for itself.

As regards the practical problem of religion considered as a guide of life, Spinoza seems to make a distinction between philosophers and the majority. For the philosopher religion is acquiescence in the order of nature, with the delight in knowledge thereby engendered, and living a righteous life at the bidding of reason. Questions about particular revelations and supernatural narratives are for him nothing else than historical and critical questions of more or less interest in themselves, but not affecting the conduct of life. God and the world stand sure for him without miracles or prophecies. But for the majority religion is obedience to a revealed rule; a rule which can and ought to be reduced to the simplest terms, and almost or entirely freed from requirements of belief in specific supernatural events. And it is pretty clear that Spinoza is not only describing what he deems practicable for his own time, but deems that it must be so for all time. Now that we have come to regard human thought as the result of a continuous process of growth, we cannot think distinctions of this kind maintainable. We cannot hold it a permanent necessity of human nature, however inevitable it may seem for a long time to come, that there should be one creed for the few and another or others for the many. The state of things contemplated by Spinoza is an artificial compromise which could not last even in the most favourable conditions. In what manner religion will be transformed in the future we cannot tell:

whether by the gradual widening and purifying of existing forms, or by some new manifestation of individual genius, or by the diffused working of strong and subtle thought, dissolving forms and leaving no vocation for prophets. It has hitherto been the aim of religions to fix man's ideal in life once for all. We now find that man's life and thought will not be fixed, that our ideals themselves are shifting and changing shapes, figures of 'the shade cast by the soul of man.' One after another the advancing tide reaches them, rises above them, and they disappear. Must we simply acquiesce in this perpetual flux of our aspirations? or may we suppose that some new form will emerge which, if not absolutely permanent, may be as constant for us and our children as the ideals of bygone generations were for them? It is conceivable, as it once seemed in a kind of vision to the clear-headed and truth-loving friend to whose memory I have dedicated this book, that the sense of natural law might become an organic intuition and fill the world with a new beauty that would leave no room for questioning; or, to express it in Spinoza's language, that the 'intellectual love of God' should become a constant power and delight in the daily life of our successors. It is not long since a leader in science uttered in a scientific meeting the hope that one day, through the continued evolution of human powers, 'light may stream in upon the darkness, and reveal to man the great mystery of thought.' Of this also, if we may not now say that it will be, we must not say that it will not be. Difficulties one can see with ease; and it is always unlikely that the first expression of a great hope should closely correspond to the fulfilment. But difficulties are made to beget daring, not to nourish despair. Such visions and hopes as these are not to be lightly deemed of, shadowy though they may appear. For men will not seek without high longings; and if seeking they find not what their imagination longed for, still they find, and the search itself is worthy.

But howsoever light is to come, or we are to be enlightened to see it, no cry or complaint will hasten it: we must work and wait, but above all work. Least of all must we listen to those who would entreat or command us to go backward instead of forward. Neither the stars in their courses nor the working of man's thought will go back for any man's word, or for prayers, or for threatenings. To those who have not the temper of intellectual enterprise, whose feelings are indissolubly entwined with the traditions of the past, and who would fain recall for the world the days of peaceful belief, we can only say, sorrowing for them but steadfast and hopeful for ourselves, that so it must be. But to those who chide and reproach we shall show, if need be, a bold and even a warlike front, answering to their denunciations with Haeckel: *Impavidi progrediamur.* Science, they cry, is irreverent; she has laid hands on mysteries and made the world profane and common. In the face of such language it is not for those who bear the lamp of knowledge to apologize and speak humbly. They need no excuse and have no occasion to do their work by the good leave of the letter-worshippers and article-makers. Nay, but it is the makers of articles and dogmas who are irreverent. They have desecrated the glory of the world with dark habitations and dwellings of idols, not enduring to live in the open light; and when their tabernacles are broken down, and the sun in his strength quells at last the unclean fumes of their censers and their sacrifices, their eyes are blinded with that splendour, and they cry out that the world is darkened. *Contaminata est in operibus eorum, et fornicati sunt in adinventionibus suis.* Reverence will never be wanting from those who study nature with a whole heart; reverence for the truth of things, and for all good work and love of the truth in man. And for the great leaders of men who have conquered them not with the sword but with the spirit, who, seeing above their fellows what man's life is and might be, have given their own lives to make it worthier, for these chiefly shall our reverence be unfailing. Whether such an one was named among his people Socrates the son of Sophroniscus, or Gautama who is called the Buddha, or Jesus who is called the Christ, he shall have endless honour and worship of free men, and not least of those who have learnt most from Spinoza for their thoughts of man and the world.

Forward, then, we must ever go, finding what light we may; and he that most surely finds will be he that least fears danger and loss. The old Northern tale tells how Brynhild lay on the enchanted mountain, cast in a deep sleep and clad in mail of proof, with a wall of fire round about her. But Sigurd came and rode through the fire, and cut through the armour, and delivered her; for he was fearless of heart, and rode Odin's horse, and bare Odin's sword, wherewith he had slain the worm that guarded the great treasure. And now men, being afraid to look on the living face of truth, have charmed her asleep and, for that she was not strong enough by herself, have imprisoned her in a grievous weight of armour, clothing her with creeds, and confessions, and articles. And the great and deadly serpent Superstition, bred of fear and ignorance, keeps watch on the treasure of knowledge. Only he who has slain the serpent and knows not fear can bestride Odin's horse and ride through the wall of fire; only he who wields Odin's sword can draw near to that sleeping might and beauty, and sunder the stifling links of mail, and show the divine face to men.

CHAPTER XII

SPINOZA AND MODERN THOUGHT

For such men as these death is not the end of life. They live on in our remembrance of them and in their works. Their thought animates others who come after them, and again others who come after these. Were not that the true immortality?

P. A. S. VAN LIMBURG BROUWER: Akbar

I saw the body of Wisdom, and of shifting guise was she wrought,
And I stretched out my hands to hold her, and a mote of the dust they caught;
And I prayed her to come for my teaching, and she came in the midnight dream —
And I woke and might not remember, nor betwixt her tangle deem:
She spake, and how might I hearken? I heard, and how might I know?
I knew, and how might I fashion, or her hidden glory show?

WILLIAM MORRIS: Sigurd the Volsung

To give an account of the reception and fortunes of Spinoza's thought; to trace the signs of its acceptance by a few in the time when it was for the most part rejected with indignation or contempt; to follow its working in the various fields of literature and speculation where, having at last risen to the due height of its worth, it has more lately made itself felt: — this would be an undertaking equivalent, if fully performed, to writing the history of modern philosophy. We should not go beyond the truth in saying with Auerbach, one of those who have in our own time done most to make Spinoza's work better known and understood, that Spinoza's mind has fed the thoughts of two centuries. And we should much err if in considering Spinoza's influence in Europe we confined our view to the marks which his system has left in the formal theories or discussions of later philosophers. It has more than once been remarked that, while much recent philosophy is in divers manners and degrees pervaded by Spinozism, there has never been a Spinozist school as there has been a Cartesian and a Kantian school. The truth is that the strength of Spinozism is not in the system as such, but in its method and habit of mind. Hostile critics have attacked the system ever since it was made known, some with real power, some with desperate captiousness; but even when they are successful the spirit eludes them. Not only will it not be driven from philosophy, but in like manner it works its way into regions where formal philosophy is unwelcome or unknown. Religion and poetry become its carriers unawares, and it might not be too fanciful to trace its presence even in the fine arts. It is more or less true of every great philosopher, but it is eminently true of Spinoza, that the history of his philosophy is interwoven with the general history of culture. What has been written about Spinoza or directly adopted from him represents but a part of his power in the world, and a still less part of the activity and power of the ideas which Spinoza clearly discerned and firmly grasped when they were as yet too hard even for strong men.

All that I can attempt here is to show in outline how it has fared with Spinoza's philosophy in the world of science and letters down to our own time. The reader who is curious enough in the matter to wish for critical and bibliographical information will find references in the introductory chapter which may help him to seek further for himself. We may conveniently begin, as we shall have to end, with Spinoza's own country. The first effect of his writings in Holland was to raise a storm of controversial indignation, chiefly against the 'Tractatus Theologico-Politicus;' not that it was more obnoxious to orthodox criticism than the 'Ethics,' but it had more general and practical interest. Books and pamphlets were poured forth in abundance by writers of various degrees of notoriety and ability, and were esteemed at the time — so at least we are told by Colerus, who gives the titles of several of them — to have accomplished the refutation of Spinoza with all the success that could be desired. I suppose there is nobody now living who has read them; and perhaps there is no enormous presumption in suspecting that the reading of them would not now be found profitable, though it might possibly be amusing now and then. This zeal for refuting the blasphemous, atheistic, deceitful, soul-destroying works of Spinoza — such were the epithets with which the authors garnished their arguments, in the usual taste of the time — was by no means confined to the theological faculty. Several of these writers were laymen; at least one, Spinoza's correspondent Blyenbergh, had no pretension to be a scholar. Medicine produced its champions too. The Jewish physician Isaac Orobio was in the field in good time with a tract against Spinoza and his apologists; and Dr. Bontekoe, in the course of an extremely quaint work on the numberless virtues of tea, published only two years after Spinoza's death, took occasion emphatically to renounce Spinozism. Some one had accused him, it appears, of atheism. 'I will one day show the world,' he exclaims, 'what sort of an atheist I am, when I refute the godless works of Spinoza, and likewise those of Hobbes and Machiavelli, three of the most cursed villains that ever walked this earth.'[274] The variety of Dr. Bontekoe's other pursuits and quarrels (which were many) appears to have prevented him from fulfilling this rather comprehensive promise. It happened afterwards, curiously enough, that the career of the greatest of Dutch physicians, and the leader of European medicine in his time, was in a manner determined by the blind fury of orthodox company against Spinoza. Blind it was in the particular case at least, as the story will show. Boerhaave was in his youth intended for the ministry. While he was a theological student, he was travelling one day with a person who abused Spinoza in violent language, something like Dr. Bontekoe's, we may suppose. Boerhaave, though himself no follower of Spinoza, could not refrain from asking the speaker if he had read any of Spinoza's writings. This was enough to fasten on Boerhaave the name of Spinozist: and accordingly he betook himself to medicine, seeing himself cut off from all prospect of advancement in the Church.[275] Only one writer, so far as we know, Abraham Cuffeler, had the courage to stand forth in open defence of the 'Ethics.'[276]

So many were the refuters of Spinoza that before long they fell out among themselves, and two or three of them incurred the suspicion of being no better than Spinozists in disguise. Such accusations are familiar in theological controversy, the more zealous champions seeing an enemy in every one who

---

[274] *Tractaat van het excellenste Kruyd Thee* &c. In's Gravenhage, MDCLXXIX. p. 349, cp. p. 199.

[275] H. J. Betz, *Levensschets van Baruch de Spinoza,* (The Hague, 1876), p. 25; Van der Aa, Biographisch Woordenboek der Nederlanden, *s.v.* Boerhaave. It appears that he had actually disputed against Spinoza in an academical thesis.

[276] *Specimen artis ratiocinandi,* &c., 1684. Van der Linde, *Bibliografie,* nos. 151a, 151b, 151c.

fails to go all lengths with them; and the grounds were probably as slight in this case as they generally are. At the same time undoubted manifestations of Spinozism arose within a generation after Spinoza's death in the most unexpected quarter, the Reformed Church of the Netherlands itself. The local disturbance produced by the movement was considerable; and it is said that traces of it remain even now in small isolated societies who find their spiritual comfort in mystical doctrines once formally condemned by the church as Spinozistic heresies. One of the first leaders was Pontiaan van Hattem of Bergen-op-Zoom, whose works soon acquired fame enough for Hattemist and Hattemism to become current terms of vituperation. Van Hattem had several disciples of more or less note, among whom we may here mention the female enthusiast Dinah Jans, and Jacob Bril, who pushed his master's mysticism to extremes. Probably the movement came at this stage under the influence of Böhme and the earlier German mystics; and we must remember, as M. Janet has pointed out, that apart from Spinoza's writing a certain mystical and pantheistic tendency already existed in the theology of the Low Countries. Cartesianism, too, had its mystical developments. But the original connexion of Hattemism with Spinoza seems to be free from doubt. Hattemism, in fact, was an exaggeration of Spinozism on its apparently mystical side. Faith was defined as the knowledge of man's absolute union with Christ, who is God conceived in his full perfection, to which this union belongs; while the foundation of sin is the error of regarding God's being as separate from or opposed to that of man. The true Christian is the man who has attained beatitude by the consciousness of this identity. Evil is regarded, with Spinoza, as a negative and relative conception; nay, the sin against the Holy Ghost is explained to consist in attributing any positive existence to evil and sin. Van Hattem's only criticism on Spinoza was that he arrived at his results by speculation instead of finding them in Scripture. His doctrines were elaborately condemned in a kind of official syllabus by the ecclesiastical authorities of Middelburg. Part of the declaration required of suspected persons ran as follows: 'Especially I renounce the doctrine taught by P. van Hattem in his writings, and account the same blasphemous and soul-destroying. I testify that I hold in abomination these Spinozistic opinions, in what words or language soever they may be expressed.' At the same place, and I presume at or about the same time, a number of anonymous works were burnt by order of the authorities of Middelburg as being 'full of the abominable and blasphemous sentiments of the Libertines, modern Spinozists, Hattemists, and Freethinkers.'[277] Another conspicuous figure in this episode appearing somewhat later than Van Hattem is Frederick van Leenhof, a minister of Zwolle. His offence consisted in the publication of a book entitled 'Heaven on Earth; or a short and clear account of true and constant blessedness' (1703); which was in fact an attempt to construct a rationalized system of Christian ethics embodying most of Spinoza's doctrines. Leenhof accepts from Spinoza not only determinism (in itself an orthodox doctrine enough) but the ethical condemnation of sorrow and all passions involving it. He expressly adopted Spinoza's definition of pleasure, and justified this in an apologetic work on the ground that Spinoza's ethical definitions were an improvement on those of Descartes. He also set forth in language closely copied from Spinoza's the doctrine that painful feelings cease to be painful in so far as we form adequate ideas of them and contemplate them as part of the eternal order of the world. Withal he steadily protested that his opinions were not amenable to the charge of heterodoxy; but the authorities of the Reformed Church thought otherwise, and continued to denounce the Leenhoffian heresy all through the eighteenth century.

For the rest, this theological strife in the Netherlands had no effect, so far as appears, on the knowledge or criticism of Spinoza's doctrine elsewhere: and it was soon so much forgotten that it escaped the notice even of historians of philosophy till, towards the beginning of the most recent period of Spinozistic criticism, it was opportunely brought to light by Dr. van der Linde in a monograph which he has since corrected and completed in certain particulars in his Bibliography of Spinoza. The light he now throws upon this episode makes no direct addition to our understanding of Spinoza's philosophy; but it is interesting to know that the immediate effect of his work was so much greater than had been supposed. I do not know how far Spinoza may have been similarly taken up by readers of a mystic turn at other times and places. An attempt has been made to show that

---

[277] Van der Linde, no. 169, note. This was in 1714.

Swedenborg, the most illustrious of modern mystics, borrowed considerably from him. On this ground, however, nothing is more deceptive than general resemblances.[278]

Let us turn to the reception of Spinoza's work by the larger world of European thought. It is quite possible to exaggerate the neglect of it which prevailed for about a century after his death; it is quite possible also to exaggerate the misunderstanding which accompanied and partly caused this neglect. Spinoza was rejected, but never forgotten; and rejected not so much because his ideas were wrongly apprehended as because few of his readers were educated up to the point of tolerating them. The rejection, however, was complete. Spinoza was for the time thrown clean out of the stream of European speculation, and philosophers in all countries went their way without taking any serious account of him. A variety of circumstances combined to produce this result. First and most obvious is the enmity of orthodox theologians of all denominations. But Spinoza had also incurred the hatred of the philosophical party which, itself recently under the ban of the churches, had now won for itself a respectable position, and in many seats of learning was supreme. The Cartesians could never forgive Spinoza for his independence. To have improved on Descartes and gone the length of openly contradicting him was in their eyes the worst heresy of all. On the other hand, the affinities of Spinozism were plain enough to give a handle for ugly-sounding accusations of Descartes' teaching in its tendency if not in its actual contents: and thus it became almost necessary for Cartesians, anxious to vindicate their new-fledged orthodoxy, to be zealous in denouncing this strange growth which seemed to many to be of their own stock. Spinoza's philosophy had to contend with the whole weight of the Cartesian school as well as with the power of the churches. There was one man who perhaps had the power, if the will had been present, of doing justice to Spinoza and seeing it done by others. Leibnitz was certainly capable of understanding Spinoza; he had held correspondence with him, seen and talked with him. We know that he read his writings with some care. His own philosophical conceptions were probably fixed before they

---

[278] See Van der Linde, no. 331; R. Willis, *Benedict de Spinoza*, p. 187.

could have been much affected by anything in Spinoza's: but a serious recognition of Spinoza's importance by Leibnitz, however much criticism had accompanied it, would have made it impossible for Spinoza to be treated with contempt.

Leibnitz, however, not only failed to do justice to Spinoza, but encouraged injustice. It is difficult to believe that his conduct in this matter was sincere. The references to Spinoza in his published works are in a tone of systematic depreciation. It was Leibnitz who started the shallow dictum, since repeated and expanded by many imitators, that Spinoza did nothing but cultivate some of the seed sown by Descartes. His personal intercourse with Spinoza, which could not be denied, is extenuated as much as possible. But in general Spinoza is simply ignored, even where one would most expect to find reference to him, as in the theory of pre-established harmony. Not that I can regard the pre-established harmony of Leibnitz as borrowed from Spinoza.[279] But when Leibnitz is professedly reviewing the various attempts already made to explain the relation of mind and matter, it is surprising to find all mention of Spinoza's theory omitted. There would be no great cause for surprise if the theory were mentioned without Spinoza's name; that would be only in the manner of the time. But the omission is total, and cannot well be an accident. Then Leibnitz's saying already quoted, and still more, his other epigrammatic judgment that 'Spinoza begins where Descartes ends, in naturalism,' have very much the air of being ingeniously contrived to disparage in one breath Spinoza for having only developed the philosophy of Descartes, and the philosophy of Descartes for being capable of such a development. They point the way to the charitable sentiment uttered in perfect good faith by a modern French writer after a careful study of both systems: 'Let us forgive Descartes for having raised up Spinoza!' Whether Leibnitz had the deliberate intention of exalting his own originality at Spinoza's expense, or was misled by an unconscious bias, it is certain that his action had a considerable share in keeping Spinoza out of his rightful place. So, as we have said, philosophy went its way without giving ear to Spinoza, and sunk in the hands of Leibnitz's successors into dogmatic formalism.

---

[279] See p. 197 above.

Meanwhile a new school was arising in England who might possibly have recognized in Spinoza's teaching the voice of a friend if not of a master. But it fell out otherwise. The English philosophical school grew up in perfect independence, and perhaps it was better so. Locke, Berkeley, Hume all make some little mention of Spinoza; but in every case it is so slight and desultory as to show plainly that they had never thought of Spinoza as a writer deserving to be seriously considered. Locke brackets him with Hobbes in loose condemnation as 'those justly decried authors.' Berkeley speaks of 'those wild imaginations of Vanini, Hobbes, and Spinoza;' and of 'modern Atheism, be it of Hobbes, Spinoza, Collins, or whom you will:' and he seems to have accepted the popular view of Spinozism as a merely formal system. The following passage from 'Alciphron' (Seventh Dialogue, § 29, Works, ii. 334, ed. Fraser) is worth quoting: —

'I have heard, said I, Spinosa represented as a man of close argument and demonstration.

'He did, replied Crito, demonstrate; but it was after such a manner as one may demonstrate anything. Allow a man the privilege to make his own definitions of common words, and it will be no hard matter for him to infer conclusions which in one sense shall be true and in another false, at once seeming paradoxes and manifest truisms. For example, let but Spinosa define natural right to be natural power, and he will easily demonstrate that 'whatever a man can do' he hath a right to do. Nothing can be plainer than the folly of this proceeding: but our pretenders to the *lumen siccum* are so passionately prejudiced against religion, as to swallow the grossest nonsense and sophistry of weak and wicked writers for demonstration.'

It appears, however, that Berkeley had really read Spinoza; which is more than can be said of either Locke or Hume. It is possible that Locke, taking the general Continental estimate on trust, set down Spinoza as a kind of erratic Cartesian; and we know that from Cartesianism in any form he expected no solid profit. As to Hume, Professor Huxley has pointed out that he was pretty uniformly indolent in making himself acquainted with philosophical literature even on points that immediately concerned his work. If he ever did take up Spinoza, it is unlikely that he had the patience to pierce through the rind of definitions and axioms. Indeed it has been the common fate of many readers and critics of Spinoza to stick fast in the First Part of the Ethics. But it is also possible that if Hume had looked far enough into Spinoza to find other things more to his mind, as would have been, for example, the appendix on Final Causes, and the pitiless onslaughts made in various places of the Ethics on the current logical doctrines of universals and the like, he would not have cared to leave any evidence of it in his work. The open defence of opinions commonly reprobated was not at all consistent with his attitude of pure scepticism. Besides, to profess any particular interest in Spinoza was at that time equivalent to throwing oneself into the troubled waters of theological and sectarian polemics, which was exactly what Hume wanted to avoid.

For the misapprehension of Spinoza's philosophical importance was not only consistent with his making a great stir in the theological department of the world of letters, but was to a great extent the natural consequence of the repulsion excited by the theological bearings of his doctrine. Divines filled with horror at the impious writer who denied an extra-mundane Deity, final causes, and free will, had not the time or temper to examine his contributions to the science of human nature. Moreover, the 'Tractatus Theologico-Politicus' had already made it impossible for the 'Ethics' to be fairly dealt with. We have already seen how it was received in the Netherlands when it first appeared. In England it does not seem to have been much known till some time after Spinoza's death; though as early as 1678 Cudworth gave a contemptuous paragraph to it in his 'True Intellectual System of the Universe' (p. 707). Cudworth declares that 'as for that late theological politician' who contended that 'a miracle is nothing but a name which the ignorant vulgar gives to *opus naturæ insolitum,* any unwonted work of nature, or to what themselves can assign no cause of,' he finds his discourse 'every way so weak, groundless, and inconsiderable, as not to deserve a confutation.' A translation was published in 1689, not very elegantly written, and not disclosing either the translator's or the author's name. Either in this form or in the original Latin the treatise must have obtained a good deal of currency, as in 1697 we find one Matthias Earbery coming forward to demolish it with more valour than wisdom ('Deism examin'd and confuted in an answer to a book intitled, Tractatus Theologico-Politicus'). Earbery admits with a sort of apology that Spinoza had some scholarship. 'Nor am I ignorant,' he says in his Preface, 'that the author of this book was very well versed (pardon the expression) in the writings of Moses and the Prophets.' But he soon makes up for any excess of civility he may have been guilty of: 'I thought it would be at least some punishment, as it were, to the very shades and Manes of this author to show the world that he, who so long has found a place in the libraries and hands of very learned men, has scarce for his stupidity, and trifling way of arguing, merit to obtain a place amongst the lowest forms of inferior animals.' In course of time other champions of weightier metal attacked the 'Ethics' also, but still in distinctly theological interests. John Howe, a great light of English nonconformity, devoted a chapter of his book, 'The Living Temple,' to 'animadversions on Spinoza.' His refutation of Spinoza's metaphysical principles is a fair specimen of the dry and windy jangling over verbal definitions which then passed muster for philosophical discussion with the help of the reader's foregone conclusion. No doubt it was much esteemed at the time, and may be so still by readers who are able to reproduce in themselves the mental condition of Howe's original audience. He never gets beyond the definitions of Substance and Attribute, and shows no sign of really understanding Spinoza. My own impression is that he had not so much as read beyond the First Part. But the most serious and capable polemic against Spinoza was that of Clarke in his Boyle Lectures, otherwise known as the Discourse concerning the Being and Attributes of God. He is little more courteous, if at all, than Earbery and Howe. Spinoza is described as 'the most celebrated patron of atheism in our time;' his 'vanity, folly, and weakness' are exposed; and his argument against final causes is dismissed as hardly fit to be gravely refuted: 'I suppose it will not be thought that when once a man comes to this he is to be disputed with any longer.' It is nevertheless clear from the prominence given to Spinoza, as to Hobbes, that Clarke practically thought both of them more formidable than he was willing to admit. Clarke's criticism turns on the conception of Substance, the doctrine of final causes (on which, as just mentioned, he is curt and supercilious), and free will.[280] The Discourse was translated into French in 1717, and into Dutch as late as 1793, I

---

[280] Cp. L. Stephen, *English Thought in the Eighteenth* Century, 120; and as to Toland, *ib.* 104.

presume as a counterblast to the German revival of Spinozism.[281]
A less famous divine, by name Brampton Gurdon, likewise formally attacked Spinoza in a later series of Boyle Lectures, in
1721 and 1722. 'Spinoza,' says Mr. Gurdon, 'is the only person
among the modern Atheists, that has pretended to give us a
regular scheme of Atheism; and therefore I cannot act unfairly in
making him the representative of their party.' Two whole sermons and several passages in others are given to demolishing so
much of Spinoza's philosophy as is supposed by the preacher to
be still in need of demolition.

Unorthodox writers, as a rule, either neglected or affected to neglect Spinoza for reasons which may easily be di-
vined. Toland, however, speaks of him with considerable
respect, and justifies himself for so doing. Criticizing Spinoza's
physics, which he seems to have understood very superficially,
as 'undigested and unphilosophical,' Toland maintains his right
to say that 'yet Spinoza was for all that a great and good man in
many respects, as may not only be seen by his works, but also by
the account of his life since that time publish'd by Colerus, a
Lutheran minister, though as contrary to some of his sentiments
as any man breathing.' Such language from Toland would only
confirm Spinoza's general reputation as an atheist of the worst
kind, or perhaps a deist (it mattered little which), among orthodox readers. The popular judgment of the religious world on him
is given with amusing crudeness in a little dictionary of religions
and sects, for the most part written with fairness and moderation,
which was published about the beginning of this century and
went through many editions. In this book we read under the head
of Atheism, that 'Spinoza, a foreigner, was its noted defender.'
So far as I know, there was no serious philosophical consideration of Spinoza in England until it was brought in by Coleridge
along with his general stock of German literature and philosophy. Thus the modern study of Spinoza in England depends ultimately on the restoration of his fame by Lessing in Germany,
of which we have presently to speak.

Meanwhile we must turn to the fortunes of Spinoza in
France; on which ground the reader who wishes for more detail
than we can here give will find an excellent guide in M. Paul

---

[281] Van der Linde, *Bibliogr.* nos. 292, 293.

Janet. Refutations of Spinoza were prepared by theologians in France even before the appearance of the 'Opera Posthuma.' Afterwards Massillon declaimed against him as a monster of impiety, and two Cardinals, De Polignac and De Bernis, published versified refutations of him, the one in Latin, the other in French:[282] De Bernis's performance is commended by Ste.-Beuve as combining vigour with discretion. But perhaps the two cardinals should rather count as showing that the name of Spinoza was the centre of a certain excitement in the general world of letters. It appears on the whole that Spinoza was more written and talked about in France than in England during the eighteenth century; but he was no less completely excluded from the order of seriously recognized philosophers. As in this country, he was rejected with abhorrence by the orthodox, and, with few exceptions, slighted by freethinking writers. Bayle gave a long article to Spinoza in his Dictionary, which is a curious and unequal mixture of anecdote, gossip, and criticism. Little of it is now of any value; but it was for a long time the only accessible and comparatively readable account of Spinoza's system. The alleged affinities of Spinozism with other ancient and modern systems, including Súfism and Chinese Buddhism (known to Bayle and his authorities as *Foe Kiao)* are traced with an enormous display of learning. Spinoza is called an atheist all through, and the philosophy of the 'Opera Posthuma' described as a most absurd and monstrous theory, contradicting self-evident truths. It is surmised that most French philosophers of the eighteenth century had no other knowledge of Spinoza than they could derive from this article, which was closely copied by Diderot in the Encyclopædia. Condillac, in his 'Traité de Systèmes,' first published in 1749, criticizes in some detail the First Part of the Ethics. He thinks Bayle's criticism superficial, but arrives at a result quite as unfavourable to Spinoza. He writes from an antimetaphysical point of view and under the geometrical fallacy, if I may so call it, which has misled so many of Spinoza's critics. Spinoza is treated as a dogmatic trifler who deceives himself with an unintelligible scholastic jargon. What Condillac undertook to do and thought he had done was (nearly in his own

---

[282] Specimens of both are quoted in Voltaire's notes to his poem, *Les Systèmes.*

words) to show that Spinoza talked about things of which he had no clear conception, that his definitions are loose, his axioms far from being true, his propositions fantastic and barren. He challenges the followers of Spinoza — as if there was at that time supposed to be some considerable number of them — to choose between abandoning the system as having no real meaning, and providing a distinct explanation of the meaning they profess to find in it.

Voltaire discusses Spinoza more or less deliberately in various places. Of his person he speaks with high respect; in the criticism of his philosophy he goes in the main with Bayle, though his language is not wholly consistent. Like Bayle, he seems to find a certain pleasure in the paradoxical contrast between Spinoza's supposed impious doctrines and his moral life. 'Il renversait tous les principes de la morale, en étant lui-même d'une vertu rigide.' Again, he speaks of 'le sophiste géométrique Spinosa, dont la modération, le désintéressement, et la générosité ont été dignes d'Epictète.' Elsewhere Spinoza is used by Voltaire as an example of virtue apart from belief in supernatural dogmas. The mixture of personal generosity with philosophical narrowness in Voltaire's estimate is at first sight strange, but ceases to be so when we bear in mind that the form of pure theism strongly and even vehemently maintained by Voltaire made him a champion of natural theology and final causes. The 'Tractatus Theologico-Politicus,' where Spinoza's opinions on these points are not developed, seems to have been read by Voltaire with attention and something like approval; at least his expressions of dissent are of the most faint and formal kind, and coupled with marked and specific praise.[283] As to the 'Opera Posthuma,' Voltaire had probably not read them; he calls Spinoza's Latin dry, obscure, even bad; and when he wants to discuss Spinoza's metaphysics he quotes from the so-called refutation by the Count de Boulainvilliers.

This work is curious enough to deserve special mention, and may be introduced by Voltaire's significant remark that under the title of 'Refutation of Spinoza' Boulainvilliers gave the

---

[283] *Lettre sur Spinosa,* in *Méianges Littéraires*: 'Get ouvrage est très-profond et le meilleur qu'il ait fait; j'en condamne sans doute les sentimens, mais je ne puis m'empêcher d'en estimer l'érudition,' &c.

poison and forgot to give the antidote. The book is a popular exposition of the 'Ethics,' in which little is preserved of the arrangement or the language of the original. Some passages appear
to be inserted from the 'De Intellectus Emendatione,' and occa-
sionally we meet with terms and lines of argument which are not
in Spinoza at all. It was not published till after Boulainvilliers'
death; but he left with it an apologetic preface which thinly disguises the real purpose. He professes to have met with the 'Opera Posthuma quite by accident, and bought the book for the sake
of the Hebrew grammar: then, he says, having nothing else to do
in the country, he made acquaintance with the philosophical
writings, and, thinking it of high importance that they should be
properly refuted, conceived the plan of expounding their contents in a more generally intelligible form: 'afin que le système
rendu dans une langue commune, et reduit à des expressions or-
dinaires, pût être en état d'exciter une indignation parcille à la
mienne, et procurer, par ce moyen, de véritables ennemis à de si
pernicieux principes.' The volume also contains, I presume to
save appearances, reprints and extracts of sundry controversial
publications relating to Spinoza and Spinozism. It further includes the life of Spinoza by Colerus, with large interpolations
from the untrustworthy work of Lucas, which Boulainvilliers
knew only in manuscript. In that form Lucas's biography appears
to have had some currency in freethinking society on the Continent, and it oddly enough became associated with a certain
'Traité des trois imposteurs,' which occurs together with Lucas,
and also alone, under the title 'L'Esprit de Monsieur Benoit de
Spinoza,' or 'L'Esprit de Spinoza.'[284] As for this last-mentioned
production, it has nothing whatever to do with Spinoza, nor yet
is it a translation of the Latin book 'De tribus impostoribus,' of
which the true date and origin have long been a standing puzzle
of bibliographers. For us the only interest of it is that the circumstances show Spinoza's name to have become a sort of catchword for anti-theological as well as theological polemics, and
with about equal ignorance on both sides of what his philosophy

---

[284] MSS. in the Royal Library at the Hague. The combination had
been printed in 1719, but was shortly afterwards called in. See Van der Linde,
Bibliogr. nos. 99-104. The MSS. are in neat French handwriting of the first half
of the eighteenth century. There is another in the British Museum. See Introduction for more detail.

really was.

It would be difficult to say to what extent Spinoza may have been read in a more judicial spirit by people who kept themselves clear of polemics altogether. Montesquieu, having ventured to treat historical and political problems in a scientific manner, was accused as a matter of course of Spinozism. He had no difficulty in showing that the charge was absurd.[285] There is pretty strong internal evidence, however, that Montesquieu had read the 'Opera Posthuma;' not in his great work indeed, but in the 'Lettres Persanes,' a place at first sight less likely. In the fifty-ninth Letter the following sentence occurs: 'On a dit fort bien que, si les triangles faisoient un dieu, ils lui donneroient trois côtés.' This appears to be an unmistakable allusion to a passage we have already quoted in a former chapter from Spinoza's letters.[286] For the rest, the 'Lettres Persanes' are much less guarded in other respects than the 'Esprit des Lois.' To discuss what they entitle us to conclude as to Montesquieu's real opinions would take us too far.

While Voltaire and the Encyclopædists were still at the head of European thought, and happy in the conviction that Spinoza might be left alone as an enthusiast who had the personal merit of being a virtuous heretic and odious to orthodox authorities, but was philosophically quite hopeless, the movement had begun in Germany, as yet unobserved, which was to restore him to his true place. If a date is to be fixed for the birth of modern Spinozism, it must be Lessing's conversation with Jacobi in 1780. But many years before that time Lessing had been in correspondence with Moses Mendelssohn about Spinoza, and, what is of more importance, had thoroughly assimilated Spinoza's ideas and used them in his own work. Still earlier he had written thus of Mendelssohn, then quite a young man, to another friend: 'His sincerity and philosophic turn of mind make me look on him as one that will be a second Spinoza. To make him altogether like the first nothing but his errors will be wanting.'[287] It is clear that Lessing had carefully studied Spinoza, and under-

---

[285] *Défense de l'Esprit des Lois*, ad init.

[286] P. 83, above.

[287] Letters to J. D. Michaelis, Oct. 16, 1754; to Mendelssohn, April 17, 1763. Cp. Dr. Karl Rehorn, *G. E. Lessing's Stellung zur Philosophie des Spinoza,* Frankfurt-am-Main, 1877; J. Sime, *Lessing,* vol. ii. p. 296, &c.

stood him better than many later philosophers and critics; it is also clear that Lessing never fully accepted Spinoza's point of view as applicable to the theory of human nature and the conduct of life. Not only do the words just quoted show this, but it appears from Lessing's statement and indications of his own philosophical opinions, unsystematic as they are. There were points on which he came nearer to Leibnitz. But his intellectual sympathies were all with Spinoza, both as against the common orthodox denunciation and as against the half-intelligent criticism of the free-thinking French school. A man thus disposed, and standing at the head of German literature, if indeed he may not be called the founder of modern German culture, was eminently fitted to render to Spinoza's memory the justice that had been so long delayed. It was not done, it is true, by openly preaching Spinoza's merits. That was left by Lessing to the coming generation who had learnt from him; and he taught them much better than he would have done by direct preaching. It is but one example, if I mistake not, of the characteristic method of his work.

After Lessing's death a discussion arose between Jacobi and Moses Mendelssohn as to what Lessing's opinions had been. Mendelssohn was preparing a memoir of Lessing, and Jacobi communicated to him, as a matter of interest he might perhaps not know, that Lessing had been a Spinozist. Mendelssohn declined to accept the statement, and there ensued a correspondence, long, desultory, and now sufficiently tedious to follow, which ended in a personal controversy. The part of it which is still interesting is Jacobi's account of his talk with Lessing about Spinoza. He wrote it down for Mendelssohn, apparently from memory, three years after it took place: but the impression it had made was obviously deep, and his report may be taken as in substance correct. It was on the 5th of July, 1780, that Jacobi paid a long desired visit to Lessing: they talked much and of many things, and the next morning they fell into more talk over Goethe's 'Prometheus,' which Jacobi had with him, and Lessing saw for the first time. 'You have shocked so many people,' said Jacobi as he gave it him to read, 'that you may as well be shocked for once yourself.' 'Not at all,' replied Lessing after reading the lines: 'I know all that at first hand.' Let us interpose a warning before we follow up the dialogue as given in dramatic form by Jacobi. Judicious readers have before now observed that

Lessing seems to have had a mind to disport himself with Jacobi, to put things paradoxically, to shock him a little, and never to let him fully see if he were serious or not. Jacobi, however, took it all seriously and solemnly. The conversation proceeds thus: —

Jacobi. You know the poem?

Lessing. I never read the poem before, but I like it.

Jacobi. So do I in its way, or I would not have shown it you.

Lessing. That is not what I mean. The point of view of that poem is my own. The orthodox conceptions of Deity will do no longer for me; I cannot stomach them; ἓν καὶ πᾶν — I know no more than that. Such is the drift of this poem too; and I am free to confess it is much to my mind.

Jacobi. Why, that makes you pretty much in accord with Spinoza.

Lessing. If I am to call myself after any master, I know of no other.

Jacobi. Spinoza is good enough for me: but 'tis a sorry kind of salvation one can find in his name.

Lessing. Well, so be it. But, after all, do you know of any better?

Before Jacobi had time to recover from his astonishment, they were interrupted. Lessing renewed the conversation the next morning. Jacobi explained that he had rather hoped to get some help against Spinoza from Lessing.

Lessing. Then it seems you know him.

Jacobi. I think I know him as very few can have done.

Lessing. Then there is no help for you: you had better make friends with him for good and all. There is no other philosophy than the philosophy of Spinoza.

Jacobi is then drawn into a pretty full exposition, Lessing only putting in a stimulating question every now and then. At one point Lessing suggests that the eminently respectable Leibnitz was in truth a Spinozist. 'Do you mean it seriously?' cries Jacobi. 'Do you doubt it seriously?' answers Lessing. Presently Jacobi comes back to the suggestion and develops it at some length.

Lessing. I shall leave you no peace till you come out with that parallel — to think that people go on talking of Spinoza as if he were a dead dog!

Jacobi. They would do just the same afterwards. To grasp

Spinoza requires a mental effort too long and too stubborn for them. And no one has grasped him to whom a single line in the 'Ethics' has remained obscure.

Notwithstanding this brave saying, Lessing appears to have had his doubts whether Jacobi really understood Spinoza, and modern critics have certainly not taken his mastery of the 'Ethics' at his own valuation. The general purport of Jacobi's rather long-winded observations is that Spinoza's philosophy is logically unanswerable but morally unacceptable; Spinozism, he says, is atheism. For practical purposes he takes refuge in an act of faith, *salto mortale* as he calls it in the conversation with Lessing, who with a certain irony declined at his age to follow in any such adventures; being unable, he said, to trust his old limbs and heavy head for such a leap.

The strife of Jacobi and Mendelssohn over Lessing's body could not fail to concentrate attention on Spinoza and his doctrines. Some notion of the effect that was produced is given by Herder's preface to the second edition of his dialogues on Spinoza's system, published in 1800. It is there said that the edition might have been ready several years earlier, but was delayed for various reasons. In particular, Spinoza had become so popular (being taken up by some even with extravagance) that an unpretending attempt to remove the common misapprehensions about him seemed to have lost its point.

'Since 1787, when these dialogues were first printed, much had been changed in the philosophical outlook of Germany. The name of Spinoza, which used to be mentioned with a shudder of abhorrence, had since then risen so high with some persons that they could never name it except for the disparagement of Leibnitz and other excellent authors.'

We may take it, then, that some ten or twelve years after Lessing's death the tone of educated German society with regard to Spinoza had undergone a complete change. Herder's dialogues themselves give a version of Spinoza's doctrine, or rather of what it might have been, which may be described as a sort of idealized naturalism. Their general aim is curiously like that of some writers of our own day who, accepting the theory of evolution as established by science, but not content with its purely scientific aspect, have endeavoured to make it the vehicle of new and refined forms of teleology. Some of Herder's points and phrases might still be found suggestive.[288] The general tendency of his reading of Spinoza is thus opposed to Jacobi's, and not unlike that which has on the whole prevailed among later German critics. An undercurrent of anti-Kantian polemic is traceable in many parts of the dialogues.

Kant himself was unaffected by the rising influence of Spinoza. Either he never considered Spinoza seriously, or he came to the consideration of him too late. What mention there is of Spinoza in Kant's philosophical writings is but slight and occasional. In one place he is criticized on the one point of final causes, but not lucidly or adequately.[289] The reader of Kant may indeed find here and there curious approximations to Spinoza's lines of thought. One such has been pointed out in a former chapter. But these are on the face of them accidental; they are such that if Spinoza's corresponding work had been present to Kant's mind the resemblance must have been less or more. It is hardly needful to add that Kant's way of approaching the problems of philosophy is entirely different from Spinoza's. Only the generation succeeding Kant felt the full power of the revived Spinozism in philosophy; for the time its work was more in the semi-philosophical regions of literature and poetry. Lessing's mantle fell in a great measure upon Goethe; and for Goethe, as for Lessing, Spinoza was a living and eloquent guide. By Goethe even more richly and variously than by Lessing the ideas put forth by Spinoza were refashioned in less technical forms, endowed with new life, and spread abroad among the educated public. Goethe too, like Lessing, was not altogether in speculative agreement with Spinoza, but nevertheless assimilated and used him. The direct, one may indeed say decisive, influence of Spinoza on his mind — for it is his own word — is no matter of conjecture: it is told by Goethe himself. He had long sought un-

---

[288] For example, he meets the objection that Spinoza does not account for the individuality of things by saying that when Spinoza is rightly understood this is a specially strong point in his system. The *principium individuationis* is identified with life, and is capable of degrees which depend on the degree of organization attained. 'Je mehr Leben und Wirklichkeit, d. i. je eine verständigere, mächtigere, vollkommnere Energie ein Wesen zur Erhaltung eines Ganzen hat, das es sich angehörig fühit, dem es sich innig und ganz mittheilet, desto mehr ist es Individuum, Selbst.'

[289] *Kritik der Urtheilskraft*, § 73.

satisfied for guidance and sustenance; at last he came on the 'Ethics' of Spinoza, and there found something he could repose in.

'What the book may have given to me, or what I may have put into it of my own, it is impossible for me to say: enough that I found here that which stilled the emotions: a wide and free prospect over the physical and moral world disclosed itself before me. But what chiefly drew me to Spinoza was the boundless unselfishness that shone forth in every sentence. That marvellous saying: 'Whoso truly loves God must not expect God to love him in return,' with all the propositions that support it, all the consequences that flow from it, was the burden of all my thoughts. To be unselfish in everything, most of all in love and friendship, was my highest pleasure, my rule of life, my exercise, so that my foolhardy saying of a later time, If I love you, what is that to you? — was truly felt by me when I wrote it. I must not forget to acknowledge in this case as in others the truth that the closest unions are the result of contrast. The serene level of Spinoza stood out against my striving endeavour in all directions; his mathematical method was the complement of my poetical way of observation and description, and his formal treatment, which some could not think appropriate to moral subjects, was just what made me learn from him with eagerness and admire him without reserve.'

In another passage, less quoted but not less remarkable, Goethe tells how the sight of an old attack on Spinoza (it seems to have been Kortholt's 'De tribus impostoribus magnis') led him to take up the 'Opera Posthuma' again, after a long interval. He well remembered the effect of the first reading, and this time again he seemed to attain an extraordinary clearness of intellectual vision.[290] He goes on to say what was the lesson he found in Spinoza. The whole of our education and experience bids us to renounce and resign: 'Dass wir entsagen sollen.' The problem of man's life is to reconcile himself to this. One ready way is the superficial way of the many, to proclaim that all things are vanity. But the path of wisdom, sought only by a few, is to cut short the pains of resignation in detail by a resignation once for all; to rest one's mind on that which is eternal, necessary, and uniform,

---

[290] 'Ich ergab mich dieser Lektüre und glaubte, indem ich in mich selbst schaute, die Welt niemals so deutlich erblickt zu haben.' — *Aus meinem Leben*, book xvi. *ad init*. The passage above translated is towards the end of book xiv.

and possess ideas which remain undisturbed by the contemplation of a transitory world. This was the secret of Spinoza for Goethe. Not that he ever assented in detail to the letter of his doctrine. He knew too well how difficult it is for one man to enter into another's thoughts, how easy misunderstandings are, even to flatter himself that he thoroughly understood Spinoza. For some time he meant to introduce a visit to Spinoza into his unfinished poem on the Wandering Jew. The scene was much thought over, but never written.

Against Jacobi's reading of the Ethics Goethe protested in emphatic language. 'My own way of looking at nature,' he wrote, 'is not Spinoza's; but if I had to name the book that of all I know agrees best with my view, I could only name the Ethics. I hold more and more firmly to worshipping God with this so-called atheist, and gladly leave to you and your allies everything to which you give, as you needs must, the name of religion.' He returned again and again to Spinoza for spiritual light and strength, and the 'Ethics' continued to be the companion of his old age.

But, though Goethe's purpose of paying an express poetical tribute to Spinoza was not executed, the place filled by Spinoza in his thoughts makes itself known in his writings in manifold ways. In dramatic and lyrical poetry, in romance and in proverbs, in 'Faust' and in epigrams, the same presence meets us. In fact Spinozism is so widely spread and pervading an element in Goethe's works, that for that very reason it is useless to give specific instances: if one were to begin, one would be launched into a commentary on Goethe. The series of poems entitled 'Gott und Welt' may be referred to as showing Goethe's speculative tendencies in a concentrated form. It was Lessing and Goethe more than the philosophers by profession who secured the place of Spinoza in modern German thought and literature. The work of tracing his influence and recognition down to the present time would need a monograph to itself. Novalis, Schleiermacher, and Heine may be mentioned as leading names among those who from divers quarters and on divers occasions have celebrated Spinoza's memory. Heine in particular has given to Spinoza some of his most charming pages. More lately, a thorough philosophic study of Spinoza has, in one remarkable instance, been united with great powers of literary expression.

Auerbach, the translator of Spinoza's works, also stands in the
first rank of German novelists. One book ('Spinoza, ein
Denkerleben') he has given expressly to a story of Spinoza's
early life, in which the outlines of fact we possess are filled in by
a skilled and sympathetic hand. For those who can read German,
but fear to attack technical works on philosophy, there can be no
better introduction to Spinoza. More than this, Auerbach's other
work is full of Spinozism; and at least one of his books carries
on the face of it the purpose of showing the value of Spinoza's
philosophy as a working view of life.

In philosophy Spinozism, to which Kant remained a
stranger, was largely taken up by his successors. Fichte's teaching is widely different from Spinoza's in its method and conclusions, but it is evident that he had studied Spinoza and felt his
power. Some of Fichte's metaphysical interpretations of theology have all the appearance of being taken from Spinoza with
but little alteration. We find in him also a short criticism on Spinoza's theory of Substance.[291] Hegel and Schelling were more
explicit. They both spoke of Spinoza with high admiration. To be
a philosopher you must first be a Spinozist; if you have not Spinozism you have no philosophy at all: such were Hegel's repeated sayings. To the same effect Schelling said that no one can
attain true and full knowledge in philosophy who has not at least
once plunged into the depth of Spinozism. But when Schelling
and Hegel had occasion, in expounding their own systems, to
show how much they had improved on Spinoza, they not only
became critical, but their criticism was hardly respectful. Hegel
even allowed himself a bad pun on the manner of Spinoza's
death.[292] Their chief objection to Spinoza's philosophy, so far as
it can be made briefly intelligible, is that his system of the world
is lifeless, rigid, motionless. Schelling compares it to Pygma-
lion's statue before life had been breathed into it. Nevertheless it
is admitted that Spinoza was the founder of modern philosophy;
and this has been confirmed by the general voice of German

---

[291] *Werke,* i. 121, ed. 1845. For resemblances see especially *Religion-
slehre,* 10te Vorlesung.

[292] 'Abgrund der Substanz... in dem Alles nur dahin schwindet, alles
Leben in sich selbst verkommt; Spinoza ist selbst an der Schwindsucht gestor-
ben.' Hegel's and Schelling's criticisms are collected and discussed in C. von
Orelli's *Spinoza's Leben und Lehre,* Aarau, 1850.

criticism ever since. The continuance of philosophical interest in Spinoza among German thinkers down to this time is sufficiently shown by the amount of discussion which has been specially given to him. One school, indeed, which just now is popular, regards Spinoza with considerably less favour. This is the school of Pessimism, founded on the brilliant extravagances of Schopenhauer and the more methodical system of Hartmann. Schopenhauer could not abide Spinoza, first, it would seem, for being a Jew, and next for being an optimist; the charge of optimism being established by the simple assertion that 'pantheism is essentially and necessarily optimism.' Yet Spinoza neither maintains that the universe as a whole is to be called good or the best possible (for these with him are purely relative conceptions), nor does he anywhere commit himself to any opinion as to the actual balance of pain and pleasure in the world. Schopenhauer does not trouble himself with these distinctions. He makes an end of Spinoza in three or four pages of dashing criticism, calls him an unconscious materialist, among other names, and goes out of his way to cast a gross insult on Spinoza's race.[293] Hartmann deals with Spinoza much more soberly, neither vituperates nor misrepresents him, and sometimes quotes him with approval. But Spinoza's general habit of mind is of course as entirely opposed to dogmatic pessimism as to dogmatic optimism; and those who find their philosophic satisfaction in pessimism cannot be expected to have much sympathy for him. On the other hand, this estrangement, whatever its amount may be, seems likely to be compensated or more than compensated by increased appreciation of Spinoza from the scientific side. Müller's testimony as to his account of the passions has already been quoted. Even more important is the striking likeness between Spinoza's results and those reached in our time by workers who, like Wundt and Haeckel in Germany, and Taine in France, have come to psychological questions through physiology, or taken the equivalent precaution of informing their philosophic judgment with competent physiological instruction. It may be safely affirmed, I think, that Spinoza tends more and more to become the philoso-

---

[293] *Die Philosophie der Neueren*, in *Fragmente zur Gesch. der Philosophie* (vol. V. of works, ed. Frauenstädt). The almost incredible piece of bad taste referred to, which I do not care to repeat, is on p. 95.

pher of men of science.

The German restoration of Spinoza was yet new when Coleridge, foremost in transplanting hither the fruits of the great revival of German culture, began to speak and write of him in England. The immediate effect, it is true, was nothing conspicuous; nevertheless the present appreciation of Spinoza in this country must be ascribed to Coleridge more than to any other one man. For the bulk of readers he spoke in parables; but (in this resembling Lessing) he did something even better than teaching the public; he taught their teachers. His written and spoken words were treasured by a select circle of those who formed the literature and literary habits of the next generation. At one time he talked much of Spinoza with Wordsworth, as we know from a droll anecdote told by Coleridge himself. It was in the first fever of the great war with France, when the minds of loyal subjects were haunted by red spectres of Jacobin clubs and corresponding societies. Coleridge and Wordsworth were staying peaceably enough in Somersetshire, with no manner of treason in their thoughts. But at that time whoever was not a Tory was held little better than a Jacobin, and they fell under suspicion. The rest shall be told in Coleridge's own words.

'The dark guesses of some zealous Quidnunc met with so congenial a soil in the grave alarm of a titled Dogberry of our neighbourhood, that a spy was actually sent down from the government *pour surveillance* of myself and friend. There must have been not only abundance but variety of these "honourable men" at the disposal of Ministers; for this proved a very honest fellow. After three weeks' truly Indian perseverance in tracking us (for we were commonly together) during all which time seldom were we out of doors but he contrived to be within hearing (and all the while utterly unsuspected; how indeed *could* such a suspicion enter our fancies?) he not only rejected Sir Dogberry's request that he would try yet a little longer, but declared to him his belief that both my friend and myself were as good subjects, for aught he could discover to the contrary, as any in His Majesty's dominions. He had repeatedly hid himself, he said, for hours together behind a bank at the sea-side (our favourite seat) and overheard our conversation. At first he fancied that we were aware of our danger; for he often heard me talk of one *Spy Nozy,* which he was inclined to interpret of himself, and of a remarkable feature belonging to him; but he was speedily convinced that it was the name of a man who had made a book and lived long ago.'[294]

What Coleridge thought of Spinoza's importance as a philosopher is to be gathered from various scattered notices. A pencil note made by him in a copy of Schelling's philosophical works runs as follows: —

'I believe in my depth of being that the three great works since the introduction of Christianity are — Bacon's "Novum Organum," and his other works, so far as they are commentaries on it; Spinoza's "Ethics," with his letters and other pieces, as far as they are comments on his Ethics; and Kant's "Critique of the Pure Reason," and his other works as commentaries on and applications of the same.'[295]

At the same time Coleridge was neither a Spinozist nor a Kantian. His position as regards Spinoza was not altogether unlike Jacobi's, though he would never have expressed himself so crudely as Jacobi did on the consequences of the system. While he admired Spinoza both intellectually and morally, he could not fully accept his way of thinking. Even at a time when he was all but convinced by Spinoza, he was not satisfied. 'For a very long time, indeed,' he writes, 'I could not reconcile personality with infinity; and my head was with Spinoza, though my whole heart remained with Paul and John.'[296] Crabb Robinson tells in his Diary[297] of an interview with Coleridge at which he spoke of the 'Ethics' as a book that was a gospel to him, explaining at the same time that he nevertheless thought Spinoza's philosophy false. 'Spinoza's system has been demonstrated to be false, but only by that philosophy which has demonstrated the falsehood of all other philosophies. Did philosophy commence with an *it is* instead of an *I am,* Spinoza would be altogether true.' But somehow this particular utterance of Coleridge's does not seem quite so genuine as the others. It is difficult to think the little scene reported by Crabb Robinson altogether free from affectation. There is a touch of deliberate display in Coleridge's kissing the frontispiece of the 'Opera Posthuma;' it is almost theatrical. The occasion was his borrowing the book of Crabb Robinson. Had he then no copy of his own?

---

[294] *Biographia Literaria*, ch. x.

[295] *Ib.*, note 17 to ch. ix. ed. 1847.

[296] *Ib.* ch. x.

[297] Vol. i. p. 208, 3rd ed.

However, there can be no doubt that Coleridge's feeling about Spinoza was in itself deep and constant. We may be sure that when he spoke of him to Wordsworth, it was with earnestness and eloquence. And this, when we consider Wordsworth's position in English literature, is a matter not without importance. It seems not too fanciful to suppose that Coleridge's expositions of Spinoza may have counted for something in the speculative strain that runs through so much of Wordsworth's works, and thence, at one more remove, in the study and reverence of nature which most cultivated persons now accept as a matter of course, but which in Wordsworth's time was new, and to not a few of his critics appeared ridiculous. The impulse of artistic nature-worship, derived mainly from Wordsworth, has been the source, in one way or another, of nearly everything that has had real life and power in the English art and poetry of this century. Let it not be supposed that in saying this we claim Wordsworth as a Spinozist. The views of man and the world more or less systematically expressed by him are wholly different from Spinoza's, though it would not be difficult to find apparent parallels in detail;[298] and on the other hand, there are only the slightest hints in Spinoza himself of the possible artistic bearings of Spinozism. But here we are considering not opinions or propositions which can be followed or discarded, nor even an intellectual habit, but an æsthetic temper which may be induced in imaginative minds by contact with forms and systems of thought aiming in the first instance at quite other ends. This kind of influence is consistent with indifference or even opposition in other regions. And, whatever may be thought of the influence on Wordsworth of Coleridge's modified Spinozism, it is certain that Coleridge and Wordsworth, above all others, so transformed the intellectual atmosphere of England as to make it possible that Spinoza should in due time be studied with care and intelligence even by those who did not go with him in his conclusions.

Another foremost poet of that time is now known to have been an eager student of the 'Tractatus Theologico-politicus,' if not of the metaphysical part of Spinoza's work. A quotation from the Tractatus appears in the notes to the original

---

[298] Compare, for instance, Spinoza's 'omnia, diversis tamen gradibus, animata sunt,' with Wordsworth's *Lines written in Early Spring*.

edition of Shelley's 'Queen Mab,' and he began an English translation of it. A fragment of the MS. came by some means into the hands of Mr. C. S. Middleton, the author of a book on 'Shelley and his Writings' (London, 1858). Mr. Middleton took this for an original work of Shelley's, one of the 'school-boy speculations alluded to by Medwin,' and considered it 'too crude for publication entire'![299] In the winter of 1821-2 Shelley was at work on this translation, and obtained a promise from Byron to write a life of Spinoza by way of preface to it.[300] The 'Tractatus Theologico-politicus' translated by Shelley and introduced by Byron would have been a striking addition to the philosophizing of poets. But the plan was soon cut short by Shelley's death; and though he seems to have made some way in the translation, none of it has been found, save the fragment above mentioned (perhaps a rough draft), which he had probably left with other papers in England.

Nearly half a century passed from the time when Coleridge was overheard talking of the mysterious 'Spy Nozy' before Spinoza was taken up in a serious way by English philosophical criticism. Among the first to draw attention to him were two men of extremely different habits of thought, F. D. Maurice and G. H. Lewes. They approached Spinoza from their diverse points of view, the one holding a transcendental philosophy which almost merged in theology, the other thinking (at least when he first wrote of Spinoza) that philosophy was impossible. They naturally criticized Spinoza's system on widely different grounds; but they nevertheless agreed in something really more important, for they vied with one another in appreciating his moral and intellectual grandeur. Lewes's work on this subject ranges over a long time, and in its latest form is still recent; many English readers must owe to it their first conception of Spinoza's worth, and have been determined by it to study him at first hand. Two English writers who are still living, and distin-

---

[299] The true source of the fragment was pointed out by Mr. J. Oxenford. Mr. Middleton, in acknowledging the correction, suggested that Shelley had used not Spinoza's Latin, but a French version *(Athenæum,* Jan.-June, 1858, pp. 211-243). But Shelley cites the Latin in his notes to *Queen Mab*; and I find his English distinctly nearer to the Latin than to the old French translation of 1678, the only one then in existence.

[300] See Introduction, p. 10.

guished in other fields of literature, Mr. Matthew Arnold and Mr. Froude, have made brilliant contributions to the knowledge of Spinoza in this country. But as to Mr. Arnold's essay on the 'Tractatus Theologico-politicus,' I find one serious ground of complaint, that he has not written another on the 'Ethics.'

In France the study of Spinoza was taken up from Germany by the school of philosophical criticism of which Victor Cousin was the chief. The tendency of the school was hostile to Spinoza's philosophy and all ways of thinking allied to it, and remains so to this day so far as its traditions have been kept up. Nothing else could be expected from a philosophy which was in effect a revival of French Cartesianism and was proud of its ancestry. But if Spinoza met with little sympathy from French philosophers of the official school which, as a school, may be now considered extinct — he met with careful discussion. The introduction to Saisset's translation of his works is about the best adverse criticism of Spinoza with which I am acquainted. More lately Spinoza has been handled by M. Paul Janet in the candid and impartial spirit of the scientific historian, and by M. Renan with delicate insight and sympathy, and the eloquence of which he is an unrivalled master. Meanwhile philosophy is being more and more followed in France, as well as elsewhere, in a spirit of disinterested earnestness and with a faithfulness to scientific method of which much may be expected in no distant future. In this movement there is yet another assurance that Spinoza will not fail to receive his due from the best and most vigorous thought of modern France.

M. Taine, who stands at the head of the French scientific school, has given in his principal work, 'De l'Intelligence,' a discussion of the relations of mind and matter which is thoroughly in accordance with the spirit of Spinoza's doctrine. I refer especially to his development of the thesis, 'la nature a deux faces,' where the coincidence is complete, or all but complete.[301]

Turning our eyes again to Spinoza's own land, we find in the last twenty years a revival of interest in him which, though late in its beginning, has already obtained considerable importance. The way was led by Dr. van Vloten, to whom is due the first publication of Spinoza's 'Essay of God and Man,' and of

---

[301] *De l'Intelligence,* Part I. Bk. 4, ch. ii., and Part II. Bk. 2, ch. i.

several letters and parts of letters which had been withheld by the original editors of the 'Opera Posthuma.' Other scholars and critics have followed him with good effect, and the two-hundredth anniversary of Spinoza's death, which fell in 1877, gave occasion for a sort of concentration of their activity. It was decided to invite subscriptions from all civilized countries in order to erect a statue of Spinoza at the Hague, in sight of the spot where he passed the latter years of his life. This project could not be carried out in time for the anniversary itself, which was nevertheless fitly celebrated, M. Renan contributing a discourse of which something has already been said. At the same time Professor Land of Leyden gave a special lecture on Spinoza's philosophy in the regular academic course, which has been printed with illustrative and critical notes, and in this form constitutes one of the most valuable monographs we now possess on the subject. Altogether, Spinoza has fared better in his own country in the last few years than he ever did before. Neither has reaction been wanting to prove the solidity of the movement, if more proof were needed. There was a pretty sharp recrudescence among orthodox journalists, critics, and theologians of the old polemic against Spinoza. Some of these criticisms were able and dignified, but the greater part copied with little alteration the violence and ignorance exhibited by their predecessors two centuries ago. I had the advantage of seeing a set of articles from a certain Flemish ultramontane journal, which not only pronounced Spinoza a second-rate sophist, but would not allow M. Renan to be capable of writing French. His style was gravely described as 'flasque et énervé.' It would be difficult to decide whether this remarkable judgment proceeded from the imbecility of impotent rage, or from the impudence of a dogmatist assured that his audience would accept anything.

However, the plan formed by a committee of Dutch scholars to do honour to Spinoza in his dwelling-place met with no serious obstacle beyond a certain amount of unavoidable delay. Subscriptions came in gradually indeed, but in sufficient amount to ensure ultimate success; and it is worth noting that, next to the Netherlands, Great Britain bore the chief part in this work. But of the designs for a statue which were furnished by several competitors, that of M. Frédéric Hexamer, a young Parisian sculptor, was chosen by the Committee. The bronze casting was completed in the course of the present year, and on September 14 the monument was unveiled and handed over to the municipal authorities of the Hague. Meanwhile, by a happy coincidence, the house in the Paviljoensgracht where Spinoza lodged had been identified beyond doubt, though the fabric has been rebuilt since his time. The spot is now marked by a tablet let into the wall, and inscribed with a short record. But a word must be said of M. Hexamer's work: it presents the philosopher in a sitting posture, his head bending down on one hand as if making a pause in his writing to think over some new question. The figure, as befits the subject, is dignified, not by idealised features or any conventional pose, but simply by being natural and unaffected. The pedestal bears for all inscription the one word: SPINOZA. This is as it should be, for thus the beholder has no particular gloss on Spinoza's teaching thrust upon him, and may rest undisturbed in that way of regarding Spinoza's worth which suits him best. Thus, too, it is made manifest, as was from the first the earnest desire of all concerned, that the homage paid to Spinoza is not that of any particular school or sect. There have appeared as fellow-workers in this cause men whose general philosophical opinions, whose readings of Spinoza's doctrine, and whose estimate of its value as a finished system of thought, are widely different. For like reasons the assistance of students of philosophy in other lands was invited, not so much in the hope of obtaining large contributions as for the sake of showing that Spinoza's fame belongs not to one country, but to every place where men are found to think seriously on the deepest problems of life. The names of men illustrious in philosophy and literature in England, France, and Germany, men otherwise separated from one another in their occupations, pursuits, and beliefs, were inscribed side by side on the roll of supporters. And thus the nature and the power of Spinoza's work are most fitly symbolized; thus he would himself have desired to be commemorated. His aim was not to leave behind him disciples pledged to the letter of his teaching, but to lead men to think with him by teaching them to think freely and rightly for themselves. We said at the beginning of this chapter that Spinozism, as a living and constructive force, is not a system but a habit of mind. And, as science makes it plainer every day that there is no such thing as a fixed equilibrium either in the world without or in the mind within, so it becomes plain that the genuine and durable triumphs of philosophy are not in systems but in ideas. Wealth in vital ideas is the real test of a philosopher's greatness, and by this test the name of Spinoza stands assured of its rank among the greatest. We who have thus far endeavoured, however imperfectly, to follow the working of Spinoza's mind, and to explain his thoughts in the language of our own time, honour him even more for that which he suggested, seeing the far-off dawn of new truths as in a vision, than for that which his hands made perfect. Not even from those whom we most reverence can we accept any system as final. A speculative system is a work of art; it is an attempt to fix an ideal, and in the very act of thought which marks it off with individual form the ideal is transformed and drawn up into a still unexplored region. Experience and science combine to warn us against putting our faith in symbols which should be but aids to thought. The word that lived on the master's lips becomes a dead catchword in the mouth of scholars who have learnt only half his lesson. And therefore it will still be in time to come that when men of impatient mind cry out for systems and formulas, demanding to possess the secret of all wisdom once for all, there will be no better answer for them than was given long ago by the son of Sirach: *The first man knew her not perfectly; no more shall the last find her out. For her thoughts are more than the sea, and her counsels profounder than the great deep.*

APPENDIX A

THE LIFE OF SPINOZA

BY COLERUS

The English version of Colerus is an indifferently printed small octavo of 92 pages. I do not know that it has ever been reprinted. In the present reprint obvious errors and misprints in English words, such as *absur'd* for *absurd, Jugdment, Preson,* for *Judgment, Person,* and the like, as well as obvious errors of the press in punctuation, have been tacitly corrected; but all genuine peculiarities of spelling, punctuation, &c., have been preserved, even to such blunders as *essensually* for *essentially.* These things belong to the character of the time no less than the style of the writing itself.

Another little book, entitled 'An Account of the Life and Writings of Spinosa' &c. (London, 1720, 8vo. *Bibliogr.* no. 105) is a servile abridgment of this translation, pp. 1-27, followed by an epitome of the Tractatus Theologico-politicus, pp. 28-96.

THE

L I F E

OF

B E N E D I C T

DE

S P I N O S A

Written by *John Colerus,* Minister
of the Lutheran Church, at the
Hague.

Done out of French

LONDON

Printed by *D. L.* And Sold by *Benj. Bragg,*
at the *Raven* in *Pater-Noster Row,* 1706.

THE LIFE OF *B. DE SPINOSA*.

SPINOSA, that Philosopher, whose name makes so great noise in the World, was originally a *Jew.* His parents, a little while after his birth, named him *Baruch.* But having afterwards forsaken *Judaism,* he changed his Name, and call'd himself *Benedict* in his Writings, and in the Letters which he subscrib'd. He was Born at *Amsterdam* the 24th of *November,* in the Year 1632. What is commonly said, that he was Poor and of a very mean Extraction, is not true. His Father, a *Portuguese Jew,* was in very good Circumstances, and a Merchant at *Amsterdam,* where he lived upon the *Burgwal,* in a good House near the Old *Portuguese* Synagogue. Besides, his civil and handsome behaviour, his Relations, who lived at ease, and what was left to him by his Father and Mother, prove that his Extraction, as well as his Education, was above that of the Common People. *Samuel Carceris,* a *Portuguese Jew,* married the Youngest of his two Sisters. The name of the Eldest was *Rebeckah,* and that of the Youngest *Miriam,* whose Son *Daniel Carceris,* Nephew to *Benedict de Spinosa,* declared himself one of his Heirs after his Decease: As it appears by an Act past before *Libertus Loef,* a Notary, the 30th of *March* 1677, in the form of a Procuration directed to *Henry Vander Spyck,* in whose House *Spinosa* Lodged when he died.

Spinosa's *first Studies.*

Spinosa shewed from his Childhood, and in his younger years, that Nature had not been unkind to him. His quick fancy, and his ready and penetrating Wit were easily perceived. Because he had a great Mind to learn the *Latin* Tongue, they gave him at first a *German* Master. But afterwards in order to perfect himself in that Language, he made use of the famous *Francis Vanden Ende,* who taught it then in *Amsterdam,* and practis'd Physick at the same time: That Man taught with good Success and a great Reputation; so that the Richest Merchants of that City intrusted him with the instruction of their Children, before they had found out that he taught his Scholars something else besides *Latin.* For it was discovered at last, that he sowed the

first Seeds of Atheism in the Minds of those Young Boys. This is
a matter of fact, which I cou'd prove, if there was any necessity
for it, by the Testimony of several honest Gentlemen, who are
still living, and some of whom have been Elders of the *Lutheran*
Church at *Amsterdam.* Those good men bless every day the
Memory of their Parents, who took care in due time to remove
them from the School of so pernicious and so impious a Master.

Vanden Ende had an only Daughter, who understood the
Latin Tongue, as well as Musick, so perfectly, that she was able
to teach her Fathers Scholars in his absence. *Spinosa* having often occasion to see and speak to her, grew in Love with her, and
he has often confest that he design'd to marry her. She was none
of the most Beautiful, but she had a great deal of Wit, a great
Capacity and a jovial Humour, which wrought upon the Heart of
Spinosa, as well as upon another Scholar of *Vanden Ende,* whose
name was *Kerkering,* a Native of *Hamburgh.* The latter did soon
perceive that he had a Rival, and grew Jealous of him. This
moved him to redouble his care, and his attendance upon his
Mistress: which he did with good success: But a Neck-lace of
Pearls, of the value of two or three hundred Pistoles, which he
had before presented to that Young Woman, did without doubt
contribute to win her Affection. She therefore promised to Marry
him: Which she did faithfully perform, when the Sieur *Kerkering*
had abjured the *Lutheran* Religion, which he protest, and embraced the *Roman Catholick.* See the preface of *Kortholt de tribus Impostoribus,* of the 2nd Edition.

As for *Vanden Ende,* being too well known in *Holland,*
to find any Employment there, he was obliged to look for it
somewhere else. He went into *France,* where he had a Tragical
end, after he had maintained himself for some years with what he
got by practising Physick. Some say that he was Condemn'd to
be hanged, and Executed, for having attempted upon the *Dauphin's* Life; but others, who knew him particularly in *France,*
own indeed that he was hanged, but they give another reason for
it. They say that *Vanden Ende* endeavour'd to cause an Insurrec-
tion in one of the Provinces of *France,* the Inhabitants whereof
hoped by that means to be restored to their Ancient Priviledges;
and that he designed thereby to free the United Provinces from
the oppression they were under, by giving so much work to the
King of *France* in his own Country, as to oblige him to keep a

great part of his Forces in that Kingdom. That in order to facili-
tate the Execution of that design, some Ships were fitted out, but
that they arrived too late. However it be, *Vanden Ende* was executed, but if he had attempted upon the *Dauphin's* Life, 'tis
likely that he wou'd have expiated his crime in another manner,
and by a more rigorous Punishment.

He applies Himself to the Study of Divinity, and then to Natural Philosophy.

Spinosa having learn'd the *Latin* Tongue well, applied
himself to the Study of Divinity for some years. In the mean time
his Wit and Judgment encreased every day: So that finding himself more disposed to enquire into Natural Causes, he gave over
Divinity, and betook himself altogether to the Study of Natural
Philosophy. He did for a long time deliberate about the choice he
shou'd make of a Master, whose Writing might serve him as a
Guide in his design. At last, having light upon the Works of *Descartes,* he read them greedily; and afterwards he often declared
that he had all his Philosophical Knowledge from him. He was
charmed with that Maxim of *Descartes,* Which says, *That nothing ought to be admitted as True, but what has been proved by
good and solid Reasons.* From whence he drew this Consequence, that the ridiculous Doctrine and Principles of the *Rabbins* cou'd not be admitted by a Man of Sense; because they are
only built upon the Authority of the *Rabbins* themselves, and
because what they teach, does not proceed from God, as they
pretend without any ground for it, and without the least appearance of Reason.

From that time he began to be very much reserved
amongst the *Jewish* Doctors, whom he shunned as much as he
cou'd: He was seldom seen in their Synagogues, whither he went
only perfunctorily, which exasperated them against him to the
highest degree; for they did not doubt but that he wou'd soon
leave them, and make himself a Christian. Yet, to speak the
truth, he never embraced Christianity, nor received the Holy
Baptism: And tho he had frequent conversations with some
learn'd *Mennonites,* as well as with the most eminent Divines of
other Christian Sects, yet he never declared for, nor protest himself to be a Member of any of them.

Francis Halma says, in the Account of *Spinosa,* which he published in *Dutch,*[302] that the *Jews* offered him a Pension a little while before his Desertion, to engage him to remain amongst 'em, and to appear now and then in their Synagogues. This *Spinosa* himself affirmed several times to the Sieur *Vander Spyck,* his Landlord, and to some other Persons; adding, that the Pension, which the *Rabbins* design'd to give him, amounted to 1000 Florins. But he protested at the same time, that if they had offered him ten times as much, he wou'd not have accepted of it, nor frequented their Assemblies out of such a motive; because he was not a Hypocrite, and minded nothing but Truth. Monsieur *Bayle* tells us, That he happen'd one day to be assaulted by a *Jew,* as he was coming out of the Playhouse, who wounded him in the Face with a Knife, and that *Spinosa* knew that the *Jew* design'd to kill him, tho his wound was not dangerous. But *Spinosa's* Landlord and his Wife, who are still living, give me quite another account of it. They had it from *Spinosa* himself, who did often tell them, that one evening as he was coming out of the Old *Portuguese* Synagogue, he saw a Man by him with a Dagger in his Hand; whereupon standing upon his guard, and going backwards, he avoided the blow, which reached no farther than his Cloaths. He kept still the Coat that was run thro' with the Dagger, as a Memorial of that event. Afterwards, not thinking himself to be safe at *Amsterdam,* he resolved to retire somewhere else with the first opportunity. Besides, he was desirous to go on with his Studies and Physical Meditations in a quiet Retreat.

He was excommunicated by the Jews.

HE had no sooner left the Communion of the *Jews,* but they prosecuted him Juridically according to their Ecclesiastical Laws, and Excommunicated him. He himself did very often own that he was Excommunicated by them, and declared, that from that time he broke all Friendship and Correspondence with them. Some *Jews* of *Amsterdam,* who knew *Spinosa* very well, have also confirmed to me the truth of that fact, adding, that the Sentence of Excommunication was publickly pronounced by the Old

---

[302] [This was a translation from Bayle's *Dictionary,* as Colerus himself afterwards says.]

Man *Chacham Abuabh, a Rabbin* of great Reputation amongst 'em. I have desired in vain the Sons of that old *Rabbin* to communicate that Sentence to me; they answered me, that they could not find it amongst the Papers of their Father, but I cou'd easily perceive that they had no mind to impart it to me.[303]

Spinosa learns a Trade or a Mechanical Art.

THE Law and the antient *Jewish* Doctors do expressly say, that it is not enough for a man to be learned, but that he ought besides to learn a Profession or a Mechanical Art, that it may be a help to him in case of necessity, and that he may get wherewith to maintain himself. This *Rabbin Gamaliel* does positively say in the Treatise of the *Talmuel Pirke avoth* Chap. 2. where he teaches, that the study of the Law is a very desirable thing, when it is attended with a Profession or a Mechanical Art: For, says he, a continual application to those two exercises keeps a Man from doing Evil, and makes him forget it; and every Learned Man who neglects to learn a Profession, will at last turn a loose Man. And *Rabbi Jehuda* adds, that every Man, who does not take care that his children shou'd learn a Trade, does the same thing as if he taught them how to become High-way-men.

Spinosa being well versed in the Study of the Law, and of the Customs of the Ancients, was not ignorant of those Maxims, and did not forget them, tho he was separated from the *Jews,* and excommunicated by them. Because they are wise and reasonable Maxims he made a good use of 'em, and learned a Mechanical Art before he embraced a quiet and a retir'd Life, as he was resolv'd to do. He learned therefore to make Glasses for Telescopes, and for some other uses, and succeeded so well therein, that People came to him from all Parts to buy them; which did sufficiently afford him wherewith to live and maintain himself. A considerable number of those Glasses, which he had polished, were found in his Cabinet after his death, and sold

---

[303] Colerus proceeds to discuss the Jewish law and practice of excommunication, and inserts a form communicated to him by Surenhusius. The shorter form actually used in Spinoza's case, and first made known by Van Vloten, has already been given in the text, p. 46 above. A revised version of that set out by Colerus may be seen in G. H. Lewes's *Hist. of Philosophy,* ii. 165 (3rd ed.).

pretty dear, as it appears by the Register of the Publick Cryer, who was present at the Sale of his Goods.

After he had perfected himself in that Art, he apply'd himself to Drawing, which he learn'd of himself, and he cou'd draw a Head very well with Ink, or with a Coal. I have in my Hands a whole Book of such Draughts, amongst which there are some Heads of several considerable Persons, who were known to him, or who had occasion to visit him. Among those Draughts I find in the 4th Sheet a Fisherman having only his Shirt on, with a Net on his Right Shoulder, whose Attitude is very much like that of *Massanello*[304] the famous Head of the Rebels of *Naples,* as it appears by History, and by his Cuts.[305] Which gives me occasion to add, that Mr. *Vander Spyck,* at whose House *Spinosa* lodged when he died, has assured me, that the Draught of that Fisherman did perfectly resemble *Spinosa,* and that he had certainly drawn himself. I need not mention the considerable Persons, whose Heads are likewise to be found in this Book, amongst his other Draughts.

Thus he was able to maintain himself with the work of his Hands, and to mind his Study, as he design'd to do. So that having no occasion to stay longer in *Amsterdam,* he left it, and took Lodgings in the House of one of his Acquaintance, who lived upon the Road from *Amsterdam* to *Anwerkerke.* He spent his time there in studying, and working his Glasses. When they were polished, his Friends took care to send for them, to sell 'em, and to remit his Money to him.

He went to live at **Rynsburg,** *afterwards at* **Voorburg,** *and at last at the* **Hague.**

IN the year 1664 *Spinosa* left that place, and retired to *Rynsburg* near *Leyden,* where he spent all the Winter, and then he went to *Voorburg,* a league from the *Hague,* as he himself says, in his 30th Letter written to *Peter Balling.*[306] He lived there, as I am informed, three or four years; during which time, he got a great many Friends at the *Hague,* who were all distinguisht by

---

[304] *Sic.*

[305] Fr. 'comme il est représenté dans l'Histoire et en Taille-douce.'

[306] Misprinted *Ralling* in the English version.

their Quality, or by Civil and Military Employments. They were often in his Company, and took a great delight in hearing him discourse. It was at their request that he settl'd himself at the *Hague* at last, where he boarded at first upon the *Veerkaay,* at a Widow's whose Name was *Van Velden,* in the same House where I lodge at present. The Room wherein I study, at the further end of the House backward, two pair of Stairs, is the same where he lay, and where he did work and study. He wou'd very often have his Meat brought into that Room, where he kept sometimes two or three days, without seeing any Body. But being sensible that he spent a little too much for his Boarding, he took a Room upon the *Pavilioengracht,* behind my House, at Mr. *Henry Vander Spyck's,* whom I have often mention'd, where he took care to furnish himself with Meat and Drink, and where he lived a very retired Life, according to his fancy.

He was very Sober, and very Frugal.

IT is scarce credible how sober and frugal he was all the time. Not that he was reduced to so great a Poverty, as not to be able to spend more, if he had been willing; he had Friends enough, who offered him their Purses, and all manner of assistance: But he was naturally very sober, and could be satisfied with little; and he did not care that People shou'd think that he had lived, even but once, at the expence of other Men. What I say about his Sobriety and good Husbandry, may be prov'd by several small Reckonings, which have been found amongst his Papers after his death. It appears by them, that he lived a whole day upon a Milk-soop done with Butter, which amounted to three pence, and upon a Pot of Beer of three half pence. Another day he eat nothing but Gruel done with Raisins and Butter, and that Dish cost him fourpence half penny. There are but two half pints of Wine at most for one Month to be found amongst those Reckonings, and tho he was often invited to eat with his Friends, he chose rather to live upon what he had at home, tho it were never so little, than to sit down at a good Table at the expence of another Man.

Thus he spent the remaining part of his Life in the House of his last Landlord, which was somewhat above five years and a half. He was very careful to cast up his Accounts every Quarter;

which he did, that he might spend neither more nor less than what he could spend every year. And he would say sometimes to the people of the House, that he was like the Serpent, who forms a Circle with his Tail in his Mouth; to denote that he had nothing left at the years end. He added, that he design'd to lay up no more Money than what would be necessary for him to have a decent Burying; and that, as his Parents had left him nothing, so his Heirs and Relations should not expect to get much by his Death.

His Person, and his way of Dressing himself.

As for his Person, his Size, and the features of his Face, there are still many people at the *Hague,* who saw and knew him particularly. He was of a middle size, he had good features in his Face, the Skin somewhat black, black curl'd Hair, long Eyebrows, and of the same Colour, so that one might easily know by his Looks that he was descended from *Portuguese Jews.* As for his Cloaths, he was very careless of 'em, and they were not better than those of the meanest Citizen. One of the most eminent Councellors of State went to see him, and found him in a very slovenly Morning-Gown, whereupon the Councellor blam'd him for it, and offer'd him another. *Spinosa* answer'd him, that a Man was never the better for having a finer Gown. To which he added, *It is unreasonable to wrap up things of little or no value in a precious Cover.*[307]

His Manners, his Conversation, and his Uninterestedness.

IF he was very frugal in his way of living, his Conversation was also very sweet and easy. He knew admirably well how to be

---

[307] But see the *Treatise of God and Man,* part ii. cap. 12, where Spinoza says that it is fit for us to take notice of men's common feelings and prejudices, and that sometimes we are even bound to abridge our otherwise lawful freedom: thus it is wrong to wear costly apparel for mere show and selfish pride: 'but if a man sees that his wisdom, whereby he might profit his neighbours, is despised and trodden under foot because he is ill clad, then he does well to furnish himself (from desire to help his neighbours) with such clothing as offends them not.' We may therefore believe Lucas when he tells us that Spinoza, so far from being habitually careless of his appearance, was scrupulously neat: 'il ne sortoit jamais qu'on ne vit paroître en ses habits ce qui distingue d'ordinaire un honnête Homme d'un Pédant.'

master of his Passions: He was never seen very melancholy, nor very merry. He had the command of his Anger, and if at any time he was uneasy in his mind, it did not appear outwardly; or if he happen'd to express his grief by some gestures, or by some words, he never fail'd to retire immediately, for fear of doing an unbecoming thing. He was besides, very courteous and obliging, he would very often discourse with his Landlady, especially when she lay in, and with the people of the House, when they happen'd to be sick or afflicted; he never fail'd then to confort[308] 'em, and exhort them to bear with Patience those Evils, which God assigned to them as a Lot. He put the Children in mind of going often to Church, and taught them to be obedient and dutiful to their Parents. When the people of the House came from Church, he wou'd often ask them what they had learn'd, and what they cou'd remember of the Sermon. He had a great esteem for Dr. *Cordes,* my Predecessor; who was a learned and good natured Man, and of an exemplary Life, which gave occasion to *Spinosa* to praise him very often. Nay, he went sometimes to hear him preach, and he esteem'd particularly his learned way of explaining the Scripture, and the solid applications he made of it. He advised at the same time his Landlord and the People of the House, not to miss any Sermon of so excellent a Preacher.

It happen'd one day, that his Landlady ask'd him whether he believed, she cou'd be saved in the Religion she profest: He answered, *Your Religion is a good one, you need not look for another, nor doubt that you may be saved in it, provided, whilst you apply yourself to Piety, you live at the same time a peaceable and quiet Life.*

When he staid at home, he was troublesome to no Body; he spent the greatest part of his time quietly in his own Chamber. When he happen'd to be tired by having applyed himself too much to his Philosophical Meditations, he went down Stairs to refresh himself, and discoursed with the people of the House about any thing, that might afford Matter for an ordinary Conversation, and even about trifles. He also took Pleasure in smoaking a Pipe of Tobacco; or, when he had a mind to divert himself somewhat longer, he look'd for some Spiders, and made 'em fight together, or he threw some Flies into the Cobweb, and

---

[308] *Sic.*

was so well pleased with that Battel, that he wou'd sometimes break into Laughter. He observed also, with a Microscope, the different parts of the smallest Insects, from whence he drew such Consequences as seem'd to him to agree best with his Discoveries.

He was no lover of Money, as I have said, and he was very well contented to live from Hand to Mouth. *Simon de Vries* of *Amsterdam,* who expresses a great love for him, in the 26th Letter, and calls him his most faithful Friend, *Amice integerime,*[309] presented him one day, with a summ of two thousand Florins, to enable him to live a more easie Life; but *Spinosa,* in the presence of his Landlord, desired to be excused from accepting that Money, under pretence that he wanted nothing, and that if he received so much Money, it wou'd infallibly divert him from his Studies and Occupations.

The same *Simon de Vries* being like to die, and having no Wife nor Children, design'd to make him his general Heir; but *Spinosa* wou'd never consent to it, and told him, that he shou'd not think to leave his Estate to any Body but to his Brother, who lived at *Schiedam,* seeing he was his nearest Relation, and natural Heir.

This was executed as he proposed it; but it was upon condition, that the Brother and Heir of *Simon de Vries* shou'd pay to *Spinosa* a sufficient Annuity for his maintenance; and that Clause was likewise faithfully executed. But that which is particular, is, that an Annuity of 500 Florins was offered to *Spinosa* by virtue of that Clause, which he would not accept, because he found it too considerable, so that he reduced it to 300 Florins. That Annuity was regularly paid him during his Life; and the same *de Vries* of *Schiedam* took care after his death to pay to Mr. *Vander Spyck* what *Spinosa* owed him, as it appears by the Letter of *John Rieuwertz,* Printer at *Amsterdam,* who was employed in that Affair. It is dated the 6th of March, 1678,[310] and directed to *Vander Spyck* himself.

Another instance of the Uninterestedness of *Spinosa,* is what past after the death of his Father. His Father's Succession was to be divided between him and his Sisters, to which they

---

[309] *Sic.*
[310] A mistake for 1677?

were condemned in Law, tho they had left no Stone unturn'd to exclude him from it. Yet instead of dividing that Succession, he gave them his share, and kept only for himself a good Bed, with its furniture.

He was known to several Persons of great Consideration.

Spinosa had no sooner published some of his Works, but he grew very famous in the World, amongst the most considerable Persons, who look'd upon him as a Man of a noble Genius, and a great Philosopher. Monsieur *Stoupe,* Lieutenant-Collonel of a Regiment of *Swissers,* in the service of the King of *France,* commanded in the City of *Utrecht* in 1673; he had been before Minister of the *Walloon Church,*[311] in *London,* during the Civil Wars of *England* in *Cromwel's* time; he was made afterwards a Brigadeer, and was killed at the Battel of *Steenkirke.* Whilst he was at *Utrecht,* he writ a Book entituled, *The Religion of the* Dutch, wherein he upbraids the Reformed Divines, amongst other things, for neglecting to confute or answer a Book, which was published under their Eyes, in the year 1670, entituled *Tractatus Theologico-Politicus,* whereof *Spinosa* owned himself to be the Author, in his nineteenth Letter. This is what Monsieur *Stoupe* says.[312] But the famous *Braunius,* Professor of the University of *Groningen,* shewed the contrary in his Answer to Monsieur *Stoupe's* Book: And indeed so many Books published against that abominable Treatise, do evidently shew that Monsieur *Stoupe* was mistaken. At that very time he writ several Letters to *Spinoza,* from whom he received several Answers; and at last he desired him to repair to *Utrecht* at a certain time. Monsieur *Stoupe* was so much the more desirous that he shou'd come thither, because the Prince of *Condé,* who took then possession of the Government of *Utrecht,* had a great mind to discourse with *Spinosa:* And it was confidently reported that his Highness was so well disposed to recommend him to the King, that he hoped to obtain easily a Pension for him, provided he wou'd be willing to dedicate one of his Books to his Majesty. He received

---

[311] 'Ministre de la Savoie.'

[312] Extracts from his book are given in Paulus's ed. of Spinoza's works, vol. ii p. 670.

that Letter with a Passport, and set out from the *Hague* a little while after he had received it. *Francis Halma* says, in his *Dutch* Account of *Spinosa,*[313] that he paid a Visit to the Prince of *Conde* with whom he had several Conversations for several days, and with some other Persons of note, particularly with Lieutenant Colonel *Stoupe*. But *Vander Spyck* and his Wife, in whose House he did lodge, and who are still living, have assured me, that he told them positively at his return, that he cou'd not see the Prince of *Conde,* because he set out from *Utrecht* some days before he arrived there. But that in the discourse he had with Monsieur *Stoupe,* that Officer had assured him, that he wou'd willingly use his Interest for him, and that he should not doubt to obtain a Pension[314] from the King's Liberality, at his recommendation. *Spinosa* added that, because he did not design to dedicate any Book to the King of *France,* he had refused the offer that was made him, with all the civility he was capable of.

  After his return, the Mob at the *Hague* were extreamly incensed against him, they look'd upon him as a Spy, and whispered in one anothers Ears, that they ought to kill so dangerous a Man, who treated, without doubt, of State affairs, keeping so publick a Correspondance with the Enemies. *Spinosa's* Landlord was alarm'd at it, and was afraid, not without reason, that the Mob wou'd break into the House, and perhaps plunder it, and then drag *Spinosa* out of it: But *Spinosa* put him in heart again, and remov'd his fears as well as he could. *Fear nothing,* said he to him, *upon my account, I can easily justify myself: There are People enough, and even some of the most considerable Persons of the State, who know very well what put me upon that Journey. But however, as soon as the Mob make the least noise at your Door, I'll go and meet'em, tho' they were to treat me, as they treated poor Messieurs* de Wit. *I am a good Republican, and I always aimed at the Glory and Welfare of the State.*

  In that same year *Charles Lewis,* Elector Palatine, of glorious Memory, being informed of the capacity of that great Philosopher, was desirous that he shou'd come to *Heydelberg* to teach Philosophy there, knowing nothing, without doubt, of the

---

[313] Fr. 'La Vie de notre Philosophe, qu'il a traduite et extraite du Dictionnaire de Mr. Bayle.'

[314] *The King of* France *gave at that time Pensions to all learned Men, especially to the Strangers, who presented or dedicated some Books to him.*

Venom concealed in his Breast, and which was more openly manifested afterwards. His Electoral Highness ordered the famous Dr. *Fabritius, Professor* of Divinity, a good philosopher, and one of his Councellors, to propose it to *Spinosa.* He offered him in the Prince's Name, with that Professorship, a full Liberty of Reasoning according to his Principles, as he shou'd think fit, *cum amplissima Philosophandi libertate.* But that Offer was attended with a Condition, which *Spinosa* did not like at all. For tho' the Liberty granted to him was never so great, yet he was not allowed in any manner whatsoever to make use of it, to the prejudice of the Religion established by the Laws: As it appears by Dr. *Fabritius's* Letter dated from *Heydelberg* the 16th of *February.* See *Spinosa's Opera Posthuma* Epist. 53. pag. 561. He is honoured in that Letter, with the Title of most Acute and most Famous Philosopher, *Philosophe acutissime ac celeberrime.*

This was a Mine, to which he easily gave Vent, if I may be allowed to use such an Expression: He perceived the difficulty, or rather the impossibility of reasoning according to his Principles, without advancing anything that shou'd be contrary to the established Religion. He return'd an Answer to Dr. *Fabritius* the 30th of *March* 1673, and refused civilly the Professorship that was offered him. He told him that *The instruction of young Men wou'd prove an Obstacle to his own Studies, and that he never had the thoughts of embracing such a Profession.* But this was a meer pretence, and he does plainly enough discover his inward thoughts by the following words. "Besides, (says he "to the Doctor) I consider that you don't tell me within what "bounds that liberty of Philosophizing must be confined, that I "may not publickly disturb the established Religion. *Cogito deinde me nescire quibus limitibus libertas illa Philosophandi intercludi debeat, ne videar publice Stabilitam Religionem perturbare velle.* See his *Posthumous* Works, pag. 563 Epist. 54.

His Writings, and his Opinions.

As for his works, there are some, which are ascribed to him, but it is not certain that he is the Author of 'em: Some are lost, or at least are not to be found, others are Printed and exposed to every Body's view.

Monsieur *Bayle* tells us in his *Historical* and *Critical Dictionary,* that *Spinosa* writ an Apology in *Spanish* for his leaving the Synagogue; but that it was never Printed. He adds, that *Spinosa* inserted several things in it, which were found afterwards in his *Tractatus Theologico-Politicus:* But I have not been able to hear any thing concerning that Apology; tho in my enquiries about it I have consulted some Persons, who were familiarly acquainted with him, and who are alive still.

He published in the year 1664, *Descartes*'s Principles of Philosophy Geometrically demonstrated: *Renati Descartes principiorum Philosophiæ pars prima et secunda more Geometrico demonstratæ;* which were soon followed by his Metaphysical Meditations, *Cogitata Metaphysica:* and had he gone no farther, he might have preserved to this day, the deserved Reputation of a Wise and Learned Philosopher. In the year 1665 there came out a little Book in *Twelves* entituled, *Lucii Antistii Constantis de Jure Ecclesiasticorum. Alethopoli apud Caium Valerium pennatum.* The author of that Book endeavours to prove that the Spiritual and Political Right, which the Clergy ascribe to themselves, and which is ascribed to them by others, does not belong to them in the least; that Clergy-men abuse it in a Profane manner, and that all their Authority depends upon that of the Magistrates or Soveraigns, who are in the place of God, in the Cities and Commonwealths wherein the Clergy have established themselves: And therefore, that the Ecclesiasticks ought not to take upon themselves to teach their own Religion, but that which the Magistrates order 'em to Preach. All that Doctrine is built upon the Principles, which *Hobbes* made use of in his *Leviathan.* Monsieur *Bayle* tells us, that the Style, Principles and Design of *Antistius's* Book were like that of *Spinosa,* which is entituled, *Tractatus Theologico-Politicus;* but this does not prove that *Spinosa* was the Author of it. Tho' the first Book came out just at the same time that *Spinosa* began to write his; and tho' the *Tractatus Theologico-Politicus* was published soon after; yet it is not a proof neither, that the one was the fore-runner of the other. It may very well be, that two Men will undertake to write and advance the same impious things; and tho' their Writings shou'd come out much about the same time, it cou'd not be inferred from thence, that they were written by one and the same Author. *Spinosa* himself being asked by a Person of great Consideration, whether he was the Author of the first Treatise, denied it positively; I have it from very good Hands. The *Latin* of those two Books, the Style, and the Expressions are not so like neither, as 'tis pretended: The former expresses himself with a profound respect, when he speaks of God: he calls him often *Deum ter Optimum Maximum.* But I find no such Expressions in any part of the writings of *Spinosa.*

Several Learned Men have assured me, that the impious Book Printed in 1666 in *Quarto,* and entituled, *The Holy Scripture explained by Philosophy: Philosophia sacræ Scripturæ interpres,* and the above-mentioned Treatise were both written by one and the same author, *viz. L. M.* and tho the thing seems to me very likely, yet I leave it to the judgment of those who may be better informed.

It was in the year 1670 that *Spinosa* published his *Tractatus Theologico-Politicus.* He who translated it into *Dutch,* thought fit to entitle it, *The judicious and political Divine; De Regtzenninge*[315] *Theologant, of Godgeleerde Staatkunde. Spinosa* does plainly say that he is the Author of it in his 19th Letter, directed to Mr. *Oldenburgh:* He desires him in that same Letter, to send him the Objections, which Learned Men raised against his Book; for he design'd then to get it Re-printed, and to add some Remarks to it. If we believe the Title Page of that Book, it was Printed at *Hamburg,* by *Henry Conrad.* But it is certain that the Magistrates, and the Reverend Ministers of *Hamburg* had never permitted, that so many impious things shou'd have been Printed and publickly sold in their City.

There is no doubt but that Book was Printed at *Amsterdam* by *Christopher Conrad.* Being sent for to *Amsterdam* in 1679 for some Business, *Conrad* himself brought me some copies of that Treatise, and presented me with them, not knowing that it was a very pernicious Book.

The *Dutch* Translator was also pleased to honour the City of *Bremen* with so noble a Production: as if his Translation had come from the Press of *Hans Jurgel Vander Weyl,* in the year 1694. But what is said of those Impressions of *Bremen* and *Hamburg* is equally false: and they would have met with the same difficulties in either of those Towns, if they had undertaken

---

[315] *Sic.*

to Print and Publish such Books therein. *Philopater,* whom we have already mentioned, does openly say in the continuation of his Life,pag. 232, that old *John Hendrikzen, Glasemaker,* whom I knew very well, was the Translator of that Book: and he assures us at the same time, that he had likewise Translated into *Dutch* the Posthumous Works of *Spinosa,* Published in 1677. He values and extols so much that Treatise of *Spiniosa,* that one would think the World never saw the like. The Author, or at least the Printer, of the continuation of *Philopater's* Life, *Aard Wolsgryk,* heretofore a Bookseller at *Amsterdam* in the corner of *Rosmaryn-Steeg,* was punish'd for his Insolence, as he deserv'd, and confin'd to the House of Correction, to which he was condemn'd for some years. I wish, with all my heart, he may have repented of his fault during the stay he made in that place; I hope he came out of it with a better mind, and that he was in such a disposition, when I saw him here (at the *Hague)* last Summer, whither he came to be paid for some Books, which he had Printed heretofore, and deliver'd to the Booksellers of this Town.

To return to Spinosa and his *Tractatus Theologico-Politicus,* I shall say what I think of it, after I have set down the judgment, which two famous Authors made of it, one whereof was of the *Confession of Ausburg,*[316] and the other *Reformed.* The first is *Spitzelius,* who speaks of it thus, in his Treatise entituled *Infelix Literator*[317] p. 347. "That impious author *(Spinosa)* "blinded by a prodigious presumption, was so impudent and so "full of Impiety, as to maintain that Prophecies were only "grounded upon the fancy of the Prophets; and that the Prophets "and the Apostles wrote naturally according to their own light "and knowledge, without any Revelation or Order from God: "That they accommodated Religion, as well as they cou'd, to the "Genius of those who lived at that time, and established it upon "such Principles as were then well known, and commonly "received. *Irreligiosissimus*[318] *Author stupenda sui fidentia plane fascinatus, eo progressus impudentiæ et impietatis fuit ut prophetiam dependisse dixerit a fallaci imaginatione prophetarum, eosque pariter ac Apostolos non ex Revelatione et*

---

[316] *Sic.*
[317] Van der Linde, *Bibliogr.* no. 358, *n.*
[318] *Sic.*

Divino mandate Scripsisse, sed tantum ex ipsorummet naturali judicio; accommodavisse insuper Religionem, quo ad fieri potuit, hominum sui temporis ingenio, illamque fundamentis tum temporis maxime notis et acceptis super œdificasse. Spinosa pretends in his *Tractatus Theologico-Politicus,* that the same Method may and ought to be observed still for explaining the Holy Scripture; for he maintains, amongst other things, that, *as the Scripture, when it was first published, was fitted to the established opinions, and to the capacity of the People, so every Body is free to expound it according to his Knowledge, and make it agree with his own opinions.*

If this was true, good Lord! What respect cou'd we have for the Scripture? How cou'd we maintain that it is Divinely inspired? That it is a sure and firm Prophecy; that the Holy Men, who are the Authors of it, spoke and wrote by God's order, and by the inspiration of the Holy Spirit; that the same Scripture is most certainly true, and that it gives a certain Testimony of its Truth to our Consciences; and lastly, that it is a Judge, whose Decisions ought to be the constant and unvariable Rule of our Thoughts, of our Faith, and of our Lives. If what *Spinosa* affirms were true, one might indeed very well say, that the Bible is a Wax-Nose, which may be turned and shaped at one's will; a Glass, thro' which every Body may exactly see what pleases his fancy; a Fool's Cap, which may be turned and fitted at one's pleasure a hundred several ways. The Lord confound thee, Satan, and stop thy mouth!

Spitzelius is not contented to say what he thinks of that pernicious Book; but he adds to the judgment he made of it, that of Mr *de Manseveld* heretofore Professor at *Utrecht,* who speaks of it thus, in a Book Printed at *Amsterdam,* in 1674. *My opinion is, that that Treatise ought to be buried for ever in an œternal oblivion: Tractatum hunc ad œternas damnandum tenebras, &c.* Which is very judiciously said; seeing that Wicked Book does altogether overthrow the Christian Religion, by depriving the Sacred Writings of the Authority, on which it is solely grounded and established.

The second Testimony I shall produce is, that of Mr. *William van Blyenburg* of *Dordrect,*[319] who kept a long corre-

---

[319] *Sic.*

spondence with *Spinosa,* and who in his 31st Letter to him (See *Spinosa's* Posthumous Works pag. 476) says, speaking of himself, that he had embraced no Profession, and that he lived by an honest Trade, *Liber sum nulli adstrictus professioni, honestis mercaturis me alo.* That Merchant, who is a learned Man, in the Preface of a Book entituled, *The truth of the Christian Religion,* Printed at *Leyden,* in 1674, gives his judgment about the Treatise of *Spinosa* in these words. *It is a Book,* says he, *full of curious, but abominable discoveries, the Learning and Inquiries whereof must needs have been fetched from Hell. Every Christian, nay, every Man of Sense, ought to abhor such a Book. The Author endeavours to overthrow the Christian Religion, and baffle all our hopes, which are grounded upon it: In the room whereof he introduces Atheism, or at most, a Natural Religion forged according to the humour or interests of the Soveraigns. The wicked shall be restrained only by the fear of Punishment; but a Man of no Conscience, who neither fears the Executioner nor the Laws, may attempt anything to satisfy himself,* &c.

I must add, that I have read that Book of *Spinosa* with application from the beginning to the end; but I protest at the same time before God, that I have found no solid arguments in it, nor anything that cou'd shake, in the least, my belief of the Gospel. Instead of solid reasons, it contains meer suppositions, and what we call in the School, *petitiones principii.* The things which the Author advances, are given for Proofs, which being denied and rejected, the remaining part of his Treatise will be found to contain nothing but Lies and Blasphemies. Did he think that the World wou'd believe him blindly upon his word, and that he was not obliged to give good reasons and good proofs for what he advanced?

Lastly, several Writings, which *Spinosa* left after his death were Printed in 1677, in which year he also died. They are called his Posthumous Works, *Opera Posthuma.* These three Letters B. D. S. are to be found in the Title of the Book, which contains five several works. The first, is a Treatise of Morals demonstrated Geometrically, *Ethica more Geometrico demonstrata.* The second, is about Politicks. The third, treats of the Understanding, and of the means of rectifying it, *De emendatione Intellectus.* The fourth, is a Collection of Letters, and Answers to them, *Epistolæ & Responsiones.* The fifth, is an

Abridgement of the *Hebrew* Grammar, *Compendium Grammatices Linguæ* Hebrææ. The Printer's name and the place wherein that Book was Printed, are not mention'd in the Title-page; which shews that the Person who published it, did not care to be known. But Mr. *Vander Spyck, Spinosa's* Landlord, who is alive still, tells me that *Spinosa* ordered, that immediately after his death, his Desk, which contained his Letters and Papers, shou'd be sent to *John Rieuwertzen,* a Printer at *Amsterdam:* Which *Vander Spyck* did not fail to perform according to his Will. And *John Rieuwertzen* acknowledged that he had received that Desk, as it appears by his Answer dated from *Amsterdam* the 25th of March, 1677. He adds towards the latter part of his Letter, that *The Relations of* Spinosa *wou'd fain know to whom it was directed, because they fancied that it was full of Money and that they wou'd not fail to enquire about it of the Waterman, who had been intrusted with it. But,* says he, *if the Packets, that are sent hither by water, are not registred at the* Hague, *I don't see how they can be informed about it, and indeed it is better they shou'd know nothing of it,* &c. He ends his Letter with those words, and it does clearly appear by that Letter, to whom we are beholden for so abominable a Production.

     Several Learned Men have already sufficiently discovered the impious Doctrines contained in those Posthumous Works, and have given notice to every Body to beware of 'em. I shall only add some few things to what has been said by them. The Treatise of Morals begins with some Difinitions[320] or Descriptions of the Deity. Who would not think at first, considering so fine a beginning, that he is reading a Christian Philosopher? All those Difinitions are fine, especially the sixth, wherein *Spinosa* says, that *God is an infinite Being; that is, a Substance, which contains in it self an infinity of Attributes, every one whereof represents and expresses an Eternal and infinite Substance.* But when we enquire more narrowly into his Opinions, we find that the God of *Spinosa* is a meer Phantom, an imaginary God, who is nothing less than God. And therefore the words of the Apostle, *Tit.* 1. 16, concerning impious Men, may be very well applied to that Philosopher: *They profess that they know God, but in Works they deny him.* What *David* says of ungodly

---

[320] *Sic.*

Men *Psalm* 14. 1. does likewise suit him: *The Fool has said in his Heart, there is no God.* This is the true Opinion of *Spinosa,* whatever he might say. He takes the liberty to use the word *God,* and to take it in a sense unknown to all Christians. This he confesses himself in his 21st Letter to Mr. *Oldenburg: I acknowledge,* says he, *that I have a notion of God and Nature, very different from that of the Modern Christians. I believe that God is the* Immanent, *and not the* Transient *Cause of all things: Deum rerum omnium Causam immanentem, non vero transeuntem statuo.* And to confirm his Opinion, he alledges these Words of St *Paul; In him we live, and move, and have our Being.* Act. 17. 28.

In order to understand him, we must consider that a *Transient Cause* is, that[321] the Productions whereof are external, or out of it self; as a Man, who throws a Stone into the Air, or a Carpenter, who builds a House: Whereas the *Jmmanent Cause* acts inwardly, and is confined within itself, without acting outwardly. Thus when a Man's Soul thinks of, or desires something, it is or remains in that thought or desire, without going out of it, and is the immanent Cause thereof. In the same manner, the God of *Spinosa* is the Cause of the Universe wherein he is, and he is not beyond it. But because the Universe has some bounds, it wou'd follow that God is a limited and finite Being. And tho he says that God is infinite, and comprehends an infinity of Perfections; he must needs play with the words *Eternal* and *Infinite,* seeing he cannot understand by them a Being, which did subsist before Time was, and before any other Being was created, but he calls that infinite, wherein the Humane Understanding can neither find an End, nor any Bounds: For he thinks the Productions of God are so numerous, that Man, with all the strength of his Mind, cannot conceive any Bounds in them. Besides, they are so solid, and so well settled and connected one with another, that they shall last for ever.

Nevertheless, he says, in his 21st Letter, that they were in the wrong, who charged him with asserting that God and Matter, wherein God Acts, are but one and the same thing. But after all, he can't forbear confessing, that Matter is a thing es-

---

[321] According to modern practice the sense would require the comma to be after *that.*

sential to the Deity, who is and works only in Matter, that is, in the Universe. The God of *Spinosa* is therefore nothing else but Nature, infinite, but yet corporeal and material, taken in general, and with all its Modifications. For he supposes that there are two Eternal Properties in God, *cogitatio & extensio,* Thinking and Extension: By the first of those Properties, God is contain'd in the Universe; by the second, he is the Universe itself, and both joyn'd together make up what he calls God.

As far as I am able to understand *Spinosa,* the dispute between us Christians and him runs upon this, *viz.* Whether the true God be an Eternal Substance, different and distinct from the Universe, and from the whole Nature, and whether by a free Act of his Will he produc'd the World, and all Creatures out of nothing; or whether the Universe, and all the Beings it comprehends, do essensually[322] belong to the Nature of God, being considered as a Substance, whose Thought and Extension are infinite? *Spinosa* maintains the last proposition. The *Antispinosa* of *L.*[323] *Vittichius,* pag. 18. and seq. may be consulted. Thus he owns indeed, that God is the general Cause of all things; but he pretends, that God produces 'em necessarily without freedom and choice, and without consulting his Will. In like manner, everything that happens in the World, Good or Evil, Virtue or Vice, Sin or good Works, does necessarily proceed from him; and consequently there ought to be no Judgment, no Punishment, no Resurrection, no Salvation, no Damnation. For if it were so, that imaginary God wou'd Punish and Reward his own Work, as a Child does his Baby.[324] Is it not the most pernicious Atheism that ever was seen in the World? And therefore Mr. *Burmanus,*[325] a Reformed Minister, at *Enkhuysen* calls *Spinosa,* with great Reason, the most impious Atheist, that ever liv'd upon the Face of the Earth.

I don't design to examine here all the impious and absurd Doctrines of *Spinosa;* I have mention'd some of the most important only to inspire the Christian Reader with the aversion

---

[322] *Sic.*

[323] *Sic,* an error for Ch. (Christopher), as rightly given in the original and the French. *(Bibliogr.* 384, often confounded with James Wittichius, cf. 254, *n).*

[324] *i.e.* doll.

[325] *Bibliogr.* 492.

and horror he ought to have for such pernicious Opinions. But I must not forget to say, that it does plainly appear by the second part of his *Ethicks,* that he makes the Soul and Body but one Being, the Properties whereof are, as he expresses it, Thinking and Extension; for he explains himself in that Manner, pag. 40. "When I speak of the Body, I mean only a Mode, which "expresses the Essence of God in a certain and precise manner, "as he is considered under the notion of an extended thing. *Per corpus intelligo modum qui Dei essentiam, quatenus ut res extensa consideratur, certo & determinato modo ex-primit.* As for the Soul, which is, and acts in the Body, it is only another Modification or manner of being, produced by Nature, or manifested by Thought: It is not a Spirit, or a particular Substance no more than the Body, but a Modification, which expresses the Essence of God, as he manifests himself, Acts and Works by Thought. Did ever any Body hear any such abominations among Christians! At that rate God cou'd neither Punish the Soul nor the Body, unless he would Punish and Destroy himself. Towards the latter part of his 21st Letter, he overthrows the great Mystery of Godliness, as we find it expressed 1. *Tim.* 3. 16. by maintaining that the Incarnation of the Son of God is nothing else but the Eternal Wisdom, which having appeared in all things, particularly in our Hearts and Souls, was at last manifested in an extraordinary manner in *Jesus Christ:* he says a little lower, that some Churches indeed add to it, that God made himself a Man; but says he, *I have declared in express terms, that I don't know what they mean by it. Quod quædam Ecclesiæ his addant, quod Deus naturam humanam assumpserit, monui expresse me quid dicant nescire, &c.* He goes on, and says, That Doctrine seems to me to be as strange, as if any one shou'd teach that a Circle has taken the nature of a Triangle or of a Square. Which gives him occasion towards the latter part of his 23rd Letter, to explain the famous passage of St *John The Word was made Flesh* Chap. i. 14. by a way of speaking very common amongst the Eastern Nations, and to render it thus, God has manifested himself in Jesus Christ, in a most particular manner.

I have shewn plainly, and in a few words, in my Sermon, how in his 23rd and 24th Letters, he endeavours to destroy the Mystery of the Resurrection of Jesus Christ, which is a Capital Doctrine amongst us, and the ground of our Hopes and Comfort.

I need not spend more time in setting down the other impious Doctrines, which he teaches.

Some Writings of Spinosa, which have not been Printed.

HE, ho took care to publish the Posthumous Works of *Spinosa,* reckons amongst the Writings of that Author, which have not been Printed, a Treatise concerning the Rain-Bow. I know some Men of great note in this Town, (at the *Hague)* who have seen and read that Treatise; but they did not advise *Spinosa* to publish it: Which perhaps gave him some trouble, and made him resolve to burn it half a year before he died, as I have been informed by the people of the House, where he lived.[326] He had also begun a Translation of the Old Testament into *Dutch,* about which, he often discoursed with some Men learned in the Languages, and enquired into the Explications which the Christians give to several Passages. He had finished the five Books of *Moses,* a great while ago, when some few days before he died he burnt the whole Work in his Chamber.

Several Authors confute his Works.

HIS works were scarce published, but God raised to his Glory, and for the defence of the Christian Religion, several Champions who confuted them with all the Success they cou'd hope for. Dr. *Theoph. Spitzelius* names two of 'em in his Book entituled *Infelix Literator, viz. Francis Kuyper* of *Rotterdam,* whose Book printed in the same Town, in the year 1676, is entituled *Arcana Atheismi revelata,* &c. *The profound Misteries of Atheism discovered.*[327] The second is, *Regnier de Mansveld* Professor, at *Utrecht,* who in the year 1674 Printed in the same place a Book upon the same Subject.[328]

The next year 1675, a Confutation of the same Treatise of *Spinosa,* entituled, *Enervatio Tractatus Theologico-Politici,*[329] came out of the Press *of Isaac Nœranus:* It was written by *John Bredenburg,* whose Father had been Elder of the Lutheran

---

[326] See p. 46 above.
[327] *Bibliogr.* 365.
[328] *Bibliogr.* 363.
[329] *Bibliogr.* 208.

Church at *Rotterdam. George Mathias Konig* was pleased in his Bibliotheque of ancient and modern Authors, pag. 770, to call him a certain Weaver of *Rotterdam, Textorem quendam Rotterodamensem.* If he exercised such a Mechanical Art, I am sure that no Man of his Profession did ever shew so much ability, or produced such a Work; for he does Geometrically demonstrate in that Book, and in a clear and unanswerable manner, that Nature neither is, nor can be God himself, as *Spinosa* pretends. Being not very well skill'd in the *Latin* Tongue, he was obliged to write his Book in *Dutch,* and to make use of another Man's hand to Translate it into *Latin.* Which he did, as he himself says in the Preface to his Book, to the end, that *Spinosa,* who was still alive, might have no excuse or pretence, in case he made no reply to it.

Nevertheless, I don't find that all the Arguments of that Learned Man are convincing. Besides, he seems to incline to *Socinianism* in some parts of his Book. This is at least the judgment I make of it, and I believe it does not differ in that respect from the judgment of knowing Men, to whom I leave the decision of it. However, it is certain, that *Francis Kuyper* and *Bredenburg* published several Writings one against another, and that *Kuyper* in his accusations against his Adversary, pretended to no less than to convince him of Atheism.

In the year 1676, *Lambert Veldhuis* of *Utrecht,* published a Book, entituled, *Tractatus Moralis de Naturali pudore, & dignitate hominis.*[330] He overthrows, in that Treatise, the Principles whereby *Spinosa* pretends to prove, that all the Good or Evil, which Men do, is produc'd by a Superior and necessary operation of God or Nature. I have already mention'd *William Van Bleyenburg,* a Merchant of *Dordrecht,* who enter'd into the List in the year 1674,[331] and refuted the impious Book of *Spinosa,* entitul'd, *Tractatus Theologico-Politicus.* I cannot forbear comparing him with the Merchant, whom our Saviour speaks of, *Mat.* XIII. 45, 46. Seeing he does not present us with worldly and perishable Riches, by the publishing of his Book, but with a Treasure of an infinite value, and which shall never perish. It were to be wish'd, that there were many such Merchants upon the Exchanges of *Amsterdam* and *Rotterdam.*

---

[330] *Bibliogr.* 358, *n.*
[331] *Bibliogr.* 364.

Our Divines of the Confession of *Augsburg* have also distinguisht themselves amongst those, who have refuted the impious Doctrine of *Spinosa*. His *Tractatus Theologico-Politicus* was scarce come out, but they took Pen in hand and wrote against him. We may name first Dr *Musœus,* Professor of Divinity, at *Jena,* a Man of a great Genius, and who perhaps had not his like in his time. During the Life of *Spinosa, viz.* in the year 1704, he publish'd a Dissertation of twelve Sheets, entitul'd, *Tractatus Theologico-Politicus ad Veritatis Lumen examinaius.*[332] "The Theological and Political Treatise examin'd by the "Light of Reason and Truth. He declares, pag. 2, 3. his aversion and horror for such an impious Production, and expresses it in these words, *Jure merito quis dubitet, num ex illis, quos ipse Dœmon ad humana divinaque jura pervertenda magno numero conduxit, repertus fuerit, qui in iis depravandis operosior fuerit quam hic Impostor, magno Ecclesœ malo & Reipublicœ detrimento natus.* "One may very well doubt, whether, amongst the "many Men, whom the Devil has hir'd to overthrow all Humane "and Divine right, any of 'em has been more busy about it, than "that Impostor, who was born to the great Mischief of Church "and State. He sets down (pag. 5, 6, 7.) with great clearness the Philosophical Expressions of *Spinosa,* he explains those which are capable of a double sense, and shews in what sense *Spinosa* made use of 'em, that one may the better understand him. He shews (pag. 16, § 32) that when *Spinosa* published that Book, he design'd to teach that every Man has the right and liberty of fixing his Belief in point of Religion, and of confining it only to such things as are not above his reach, and which he can comprehend. He had already (pag. 14, § 28) very clearly stated the Question, and shewn wherein *Spinosa* differs from the Christians: And in the same manner he continues to examine that Treatise of *Spinosa,* and confutes every part of it with good and solid Reasons. There is no doubt but *Spinosa* himself read that Book of Dr. *Musœus,* seeing it was found amongst his Papers after his death.

Tho' several Authors writ against the Theological and Political Treatise, as I have already observed; yet none in my Opinion has done it with more Solidity than that Learned Profes-

---

[332] *Bibliogr.* 362.

sor; and my judgment of him is confirmed by that of many others. The Author, who, under the name of *Theodorus Securus,* published a small Treatise, entituled, *Origo Atheismi,* says in another little Book, entituled, *Prudentia Theologica.* "I do very "much wonder that the Dissertation of Dr. *Musæus* shou'd be so "scarce, and so little known here in *Holland.* That learned "Divine, who writ upon so important a Subject, shou'd have "more justice done him; for he has certainly had a belter Success "than any other. Mr. *Fullerus, (in continuatione Bibliothecæ Universalis* &c.) expresses himself thus, speaking of Dr. Musæus: "That most famous Divine of *Jena* has refuted the "pernicious Book of *Spinosa* with his usual solidity and learning. "*Celeberrimus ille Jenensium Theologus Joh.* Musæus Spinosæ *pestilentissimum foetum acutissimis,*[333] *queis solet, telis confodit.*

The same Author does also mention *Frederic Rapoltus,* Professor of Divinity, at *Leipsick,* who in a Speech which he pronounced when he took Possession of his Professorship, did likewise refute the Doctrine of *Spinosa.* I have read his Speech, and I find that he has confuted him but indirectly, and without naming him: It is entituled, *Oratio contra Naturalistas, habita ipsis Kalendis Junii ann.* 1670, and it is to be found in the Theological Works of *Rappoltus* tom. 1. pag. 1386 and Seq. published by Dr. *John Benedict Carpzovius,* and Printed at *Leipsick* in 1692. Dr. *J. Conrad Durrius,* Professor at *Altorf,* followed the same Plan in a Speech,[334] which I have not read, but I have heard it highly commended.

Monsieur *Aubert de Verse* published in 1681 a Book, entituled, *The impious Man convinced, or a Dissertation against* Spinosa, *wherein the Grounds of his Atheism are confuted.*[335] In 1687 *Peter Yvon,* a Kinsman and a Disciple of *Labadie,* and Minister of those of his Sect at *Wiewerden* in *Friseland,* writ a Treatise against *Spinosa* which he published under this Title, *Impiety Vanquished,* &c.[336] In the Supplement to *Moreri's* Dictionary, in the Article of *Spinosa,* there is a Treatise mentioned, entituled, *de concordia Rationis & Fidei,* written by Monsieur

---

[333] The printing of this in the original is almost a curiosity; it gives Spinosa, *pestilentissimum, accutissimis.*

[334] *Bibliogr.* 358, *n.*

[335] *Bibliogr.* 301. The name should be de Versé.

[336] *Bibliogr.* 368, 369 (Latin and French edd.).

Huet:[337] That Book was Reprinted at *Leipsick* in 1692, and the *Journalists* of that City gave a good Abstract of it, (see *Acta Erudit. an.* 1695, pag. 395) wherein the Doctrine of *Spinosa* is set down with great clearness, and refuted with great Force and Learning. The Learned Mr. *Simon*[338] and Mr. *de la Motte,*[339] Minister of the *Savoy* in *London,* have both of 'em writ upon the same subject: I have seen the Works of those two Authors, but I don't understand *French* enough to judge of 'em. Mr. *Peter Poiret* who lives now at *Reinsburg* near *Leyden,* published a Treatise against *Spinosa* in the second Edition of his Book, *De Deo, anima, & malo:* That Treatise is entituled, *Fundamenta Atheismi eversa, sive specimen absurditatis Spinosianæ.*[340] It is a work which very well deserves to be read with attention.

The last Work, I shall mention, is that of Mr *Wittichius,* Professor at *Leyden,* which was Printed in 1690, after the death of the Author, with this Title, *Christophori Wittichii Professoris Leidensis Anti-* Spinosa, *sive Examen Ethices* B. de Spinosa.[341] It was sometime after translated into *Dutch;* and Printed at *Amsterdam* by *Wasbergen.*[342] 'Tis no Wonder to see that great Man defamed, and his Reputation stained after his death, in such a Book as the *Continuation of the Life of* Philopater. It is said in that Book, that Mr. *Wittichius* was an excellent Philosopher, and a great Friend of *Spinosa,* that he kept correspondence and had a great many private Conversations with him; in a word, that they were both of the same Opinion. That Mr. *Wittichius* writ against the Ethicks of *Spinosa,* for fear of being reputed a *Spinosist,* and that his Confutation was Printed after his death only, that he might not lose his Honour, and the Reputation of an Orthodox Christian. These are the calumnies, which that insolent Author has advanced: I don't know from whence he had 'em, nor upon what appearance of Truth he can build so many Lies. How came he to know that those two Philosophers kept such strict a Correspondence together, that they saw and writ so often to one another? We don't find any Letter of *Spinosa* to *Wittichius,* nor of

---

[337] *Bibliogr.* 358, *n*
[338] *Quære.*
[339] *Bibliogr.* 358, *n.*
[340] *Bibliogr.* 382.
[341] *Bibliogr.* 384, 385.
[342] *Bibliogr.* 384, 385.

Wittichius to *Spinosa* among the Letters of that Author, which
have been Printed; and there is none neither among those which
remain to be Printed: So that we have all the reason in the World
to believe, that this strict Correspondence, and the Letters which
they writ to one another, are a meer fiction of that Calumniator. I
confess, I never had occasion to speak to Mr. *Wittichius;* but I
am pretty well acquainted with Mr. *Zimmerman,* his Nephew,
who is now Minister of the Church of *England,* and who lived
with his Uncle the latter part of his Life. What he told me upon
that Subject, is altogether contrary to what has been Published by
the Author of *Philopater's* Life:[343] Nay, he shew'd me a Writing,
which his Uncle had dictated to him, wherein the Opinions of
Spinosa are both well explained and confuted. What can one desire more for his justification, than the last Work which he writ?
There we see what he believed, and there he makes, as it were, a
Confession of his Faith before he died. Will any Man, that has
any sense of Religion, be so bold as to think and even to publish,
that it was all meer Hypocrisy, that he did it only that he might
go to Church, and to salve appearances, and avoid being accounted an Impious Man and a Libertine?

If any such thing cou'd be inferred, when there has been
some Correspondence between two Persons; I shou'd not find
my self very safe; and few Ministers wou'd be secure from the
Tongues of Calumniators, seeing it is sometimes impossible for
us to avoid all manner of converse with some Persons, whose
Belief is none of the most Orthodox.

I shall willingly mention *William Deurhof,* of *Amsterdam,* and I name him with all the distinction he deserves. That
Professor has always vigorously assaulted the Opinions of *Spinosa* in all his Works, but especially in his Lectures of Divinity.[344] Mr. *Francis Halma* does him justice in his *Dutch* account
of *Spinosa;*[345] when he says, that he has refuted the Opinions of
that Philosopher with so much solidity, that none of his Partisans
durst hitherto vye strength with him. He adds, that that subtil
Writer, is able still to confute the calumnies of *Philopater's* Life,
and to stop his mouth.

---

[343] *Bibliogr.* 72-76.
[344] *Bibliogr.* 190-207, see 194, n., where Dr. van der Linde retracts
his former opinion as to Deurhof's Spinozist tendencies.
[345] *Bibliogr.* 70, 71.

I shall say but one word of two famous Authors, and I'll put 'em together, tho' they are now set one against the other. The first is Mr *Bayle,* so well known in the Common-wealth of Learning, that I need not make his *Encomium* in this place. The second, is Mr *Jaquelot* heretofore Minister of the *French* Church at the *Hague,* and now Chaplain to the King of *Prussia.* They made both of 'em learned and solid Remarks on the Life, Writings, and Opinions of *Spinosa,* which have been Translated into *Dutch* by *Francis Halma,* a Bookseller at *Amsterdam,* and a Scholar. He has added to his Translation, a Preface, and some judicious Remarks upon the Continuation of *Philopater's* Life; which deserve to be read.

There is no need to mention here some Writers, who have very lately opposed the Doctrine of *Spinosa,* upon account of a Book, entituled, *Hemel op Aarden, Paradice on Earth,* written by Mr *van Leenhoff,* a Reformed Minister of *Zwol,* wherein 'tis pretended that he builds upon the same foundations with *Spinosa.* Those things are too fresh, and too well known to insist upon 'em: I therefore proceed to mention the Death of that famous Atheist.

Of the last Sickness, and Death of Spinosa.

THERE has been so many various and false Reports about the Death of *Spinosa,* that 'tis a wonder how some understanding Men came to acquaint the Publick with it upon *Hear-says,* without taking care to be better informed of what they published. One may find a Pattern of those falsehoods in the *Menagiana,* Printed at Amsterdam in 1695, where the Author expresses himself thus.[346]

"I have been told that *Spinosa* died of the fear he was in, "of being committed to the *Bastille.* He came into *France* at the "desire of two Persons of Quality, who had a mind to see him. "Mr. *de Pompone* had notice of it, and being a Minister, very "zealous for Religion, he did not think fit to permit that *Spinosa* "shou'd live in *France,* where he might do a great deal of "Mischief; and in order to prevent it, he resolv'd to send him to "the *Bastille. Spinosa* having had notice of it, made his escape in

---

[346] *Bibliogr.* 98.

"a Fryar's Habit; but I will not warrant this last Circumstance. "That which is certain, is, that I have been told by several "people, that he was a little Man, and of a yellowish complexion, "and that he had an ill Look, and bore a Character of "Reprobation in his Face.

There is not one word of truth in this Account; for it is certain, that *Spinosa* was never in *France:* And tho some Persons of great note endeavoured to have him there,[347] as he himself confest to his Landlords, yet he assured them, at the same time, that he hoped he wou'd never be so great a Fool as to do such a thing. One may also easily judge from what I shall say hereafter, that it is altogether false that he died of Fear. Wherefore I shall set down the Circumstances of his Death without partiality, and I shall advance nothing without proving it; which I can the more easily do, because he died, and was buried here at the *Hague.*

Spinosa was a Man of a very weak Constitution, unhealthy and lean, and had been troubled with a *Pthysick* above twenty years, which oblig'd him to keep a strict course of Dyet, and to be extreamly sober in his Meat and Drink. Nevertheless, his Landlord, and the people of the House did not believe that he was so near his end, even a little while before he died, and they had not the least thought of it. For the 22nd[348] of *February,* which happen'd to be then the Saturday before the last week of the Carnaval, his Landlord and his Wife went to the Sermon which is preach'd in our Church, to dispose every Body to receive the Communion, which is administred the next day according to a Custom established amongst us. The Landlord being come from Church at four a Clock, or thereabouts, *Spinosa* went down Stairs, and had a pretty long Conversation with him, which did particularly run upon the Sermon; and having taken a Pipe of Tobacco, he retired into his Chamber, which was forwards, and went to Bed betimes. Upon *Sunday* Morning before Churchtime, he went down Stairs again, and discoursed with his Landlord and his Wife. He had sent for a Physitian from *Amsterdam,* whose Name I shall only express by these two Letters, *L. M.* That Phisitian ordered 'em to boil an old Cock immediately, that *Spinosa* might take some Broth about noon, which he did, and

---

[347] Probably on the occasion of his visit to the French camp in 1672.
[348] It should be 20th. Colerus corrects himself afterwards, *ad fin.*

eat some of the Meat with a good Stomach, when his Landlord and his Wife came from Church. In the afternoon the Physitian *L. M.* staid alone with *Spinosa,* the people of the House being returned to Church. But as they were coming from Church, they were very much surprized to hear, that *Spinosa* had expired about three a Clock, in the presence of that Physitian, who that very Evening returned to *Amsterdam* by the Night-boat, without taking any care of the Deceased. He was more willing to dispense himself from that Duty, because immediately after the Death of *Spinosa* he had taken a Ducatoon and a little Money, which the Deceased had left upon the Table, and a Knife with a Silver Handle; and so retired with his Booty.

The particularities of his Sickness and Death have been variously reported, and have occasioned several Contestations. 'Tis said, 1st, That during his Sickness he took the necessary Precautions to avoid being visited by those whose Sight wou'd have been troublesome to him. 2dly, That he spoke once and even several times these words, *O God have mercy upon me miserable Sinner.* 3dly, That they heard him often sigh, when he pronounced the Name of God. Which gave occasion to those, who were present, to ask him, whether he believed, at last, the Existence of a God, whose judgment he had great Reason to fear after his death? And that he answered 'em, that he had dropt that word out of Custom. 'Tis said, 4thly, That he kept by him some Juice of *Mandrake* ready at hand which he made use of, when he perceived he was a dying, that he drew the Curtains of his Bed afterwards, and then lost his Senses, fell into a profound Sleep, and departed this Life in that manner. 5thly, That he had given express orders to let no Body come into his Room, when he shou'd be near his End: And likewise, that finding he was a dying, he call'd for his Landlady, and desired her to suffer no Minister to come to him; because he was willing to die peaceably and without disputing, &c.

I have carefully enquired into the truth of all those things, and ask'd several times his Landlord and his Landlady, who are alive still, what they knew of it: But they answered me, at all times, that they knew nothing of it, and were perswaded that all those Circumstances were meer Lies. For he never forbad them to admit any body into his Room, that had a mind to see him. Besides, when he was a dying, there was no body in his

Chamber but the Physitian of *Amsterdam;* whom I have mentioned. No body heard the words, which 'tis said, he spoke, *O God, have mercy upon me miserable Sinner:* Nor is it likely that they shou'd come out of his mouth, seeing he did not think he was so near his Death, and the people of the House had not the least suspicion of it. He did not keep his Bed during his sickness; for the very day that he died, he went down Stairs, as I have observed: He lay forwards[349] in a Bed made according to the fashion of the Country, which they call *Bedstead.* His Landlady, and the people of the House know nothing of his ordering to send away the Ministers, that shou'd come to see him, or of his invocating the Name of God during his Sickness. Nay, they believe the contrary, because ever since he began to be in a languishing condition, he always exprest, in all his sufferings, a truly *Stoical* constancy; even so as to reprove others, when they happened to complain, and to shew in their Sicknesses little Courage or too great a Sensibility.

Lastly, as for the Juice of *Mandrake,* which, 'tis said, he made use of when he was a dying, which made him lose his Senses; it is also a circumstance altogether unknown to the people of the House. And yet they us'd to prepare every thing he wanted for his Meat and Drink, and the Remedies which he took from time to time. Nor is that Drug mention'd in the Apothecary's Bill, who was the same to whom the Physitian of *Amsterdam* sent for the Remedies, which *Spinosa* wanted the last days of his Life.

Spinosa being dead, his Landlord took care of his Burial. *John Rieuwertz,* a Printer at *Amsterdam,* desired him to do it, and promised him, at the same time, that he shou'd be paid for all the charges he should be at, and past his word for it. The Letter which he wrote to him upon that Subject is dated from *Amsterdam* the 6th of *March* 1678.[350] He does not forget to speak of that Friend of *Schiedam,* whom I have mentioned, who to shew how dear and precious the memory of *Spinosa* was to him, paid exactly to *Vander Spyck,* all that he cou'd pretend from his late Lodger. The Money was at the same time remitted to him, as *Rieuwertz* himself had received it by the order of his Friend.

---

[349] Sa chambre étoit celle de devant.
[350] A mistake of the French version for 1677? cp. p. 403 above.

As they were making everything ready for the Burial of *Spinosa,* one *Schroder,* an Apothecary, made a Protestation against it, pretending to be paid for some Medicines wherewith he had furnished the Deceased during his Sickness. His Bill amounted to sixteen Florins and two pence. I find in it some Tincture of Saffron, some Balsam, some Powders, &c. but there is no Opium nor *Mandrake* mentioned therein. The Protestation was immediately taken off, and the Bill paid by Mr. *Vander Spyck.*

The dead Body was carried to the Grave in the New Church upon the *Spuy,* the 25th of February, being attended by many Illustrious Persons and followed by six Coaches. The Burial being over, the particular Friends or Neighbours, were treated with some Bottles of Wine, according to the custom of the Country, in the House where the Deceased lodged.

I shall observe by the bye, that the Barber of *Spinosa* brought in after his Death, a Bill exprest in these words: "Mr "*Spinosa, of Blessed Memory,*[351] owes to *Abraham Kervel,* for "having shaved him the last Quarter, the summ of one Florin and "eighteen Pence. The Man, who invited his Friends to his Burial, two Ironmongers, and the Mercer, who furnished the Mourning Gloves, made him the same Complement in their Bills.

If they had known what were the Principles of *Spinosa* in point of Religion; 'tis likely that they would not have made use of the word *Blessed:* Or perhaps they used that word according to Custom, which permits, sometimes, the abuse of such Expressions, even with respect to those, who die in despair, or in a final Impenitence.

Spinosa being buried, his Landlord caused the Inventory of his Goods to be made. The Notary he made use of, brought in a Bill, in this form: *William van Hove, Notary, for having made the Inventory of the Goods and Effects of the late Sieur* Benedict de Spinosa. His Bill amounts to seventeen Florins and eight pence, which he acknowledges to have received the 14th of *November, 1677.*

Rebekah of Spinosa, Sister of the Deceased, declared her self his Heir. But because she refused to pay, in the first place,

---

[351] Fr. 'Mr. Spinosa de bienheureuse mémoire;' in original 'Spinoza Zaliger.'

the charges of the Burial, and some Debts wherewith the Succession was clogged; Mr. *Vander Spyck* sent to her at *Amsterdam,* and summoned her to do it, by *Robert Schmeding,* who carried his Letter of Attorny drawn up and signed by *Libretus Loef* the 30th of *March,* 1677. But, before she paid any thing, she had a mind to know, whether the Debts and Charges being paid, she might get something by her Brother's Inheritance. Whilst she was deliberating about it, *Vander Spyck* was authoriz'd by Law, to make a publick Sale of the Goods in question; which was executed; and the Money arising from the sale being deposited in the usual place, the Sister of *Spinosa* made an Attachment of it. But perceiving that after the payment of the Charges and Debts, there wou'd be little or nothing at all left, she desisted from her pretentions. The Attorny, *John Lukkats,* who served *Vander Spyck* in that Affair, brought him a Bill of thirty three Florins and sixteen pence, for which he gave his Receipt the 1st of *June,* 1678. The Sale of the said Goods was made here (at the *Hague)* the 4th of *November,* 1677, by *Rykus van Stralen,* a sworn Cryer, as it appears by his Account, bearing the same Date.

One needs only cast one's Eyes upon that Account, to perceive that it was the Inventory of a true Philosopher: It contains only some small Books, some Cuts, some pieces of polished Glass, some Instruments to polish them, &c.

It appears likewise, by his Cloaths, how good a Husband he was. A Camlet Cloak, and a pair of Breeches were sold for twenty one Florins and fourteen pence, another grey Cloak, twelve Florins and fourteen pence, four Sheets, six Florins and eight pence, seven Shirts, nine Florins and six pence, one Bed fiveteen Florins, nineteen Bands, one Florin and eleven pence, five Handkerchiefs, twelve pence, two red Curtains, a Counterpain, and a little Blanket, six Florins: And all his Plate, consisted of one Pair of Silver-Buckles, which were sold, two Florins. The whole Sale of the Goods amounted to four hundred Florins and thirteen Pence; and the charges of the Sale being deducted, there remained three hundred ninety Florins and fourteen pence.

These are all the particulars I cou'd learn about the Life and Death of *Spinosa:* He was forty four years, two months and twenty seven days old, when he died; which happen'd the 21st of *February,* 1677, and he was buried the 25th of the same month.

FINIS

APPENDIX B

Ordinance of July 19, 1674, condemning the 'Tractatus Theologico-politicus'

The following is the text of the ordinance condemning the *Tractatus Theologico-Politicus*. That of June 25, 1678, condemning the *Opera Posthuma*, is to be found at p. 525 of the same book; but inasmuch as it is also reprinted in Van der Linde's 'Bibliografie,' no. 24, it is not given here. I have not thought it needful to add a translation.

Groot Placaet Boeck (in's Graven Hage, 1683) 3de Deel, p. 523

Placaet van den Hove van Hollandt tegen de Sociniaensche Boecken Leviathan en andere. In date den negenthienden July, 1674

Wilhem Hendrick, by der gratien Godes Prince van Orange ende Nassau, Grave van Catzenellebogen, Vianden, Diest, Lingen, Mœurs, Buyren, Leerdam, &c... Midtsgaders den Præsident ende Raeden over Hollandt ende West-Vrieslandt: Alsoo Wy in ervaringe komen, dat t'zedert eenigen tijdt herwaerts verscheyde Sociniaensche ende andere schadelijcke Boecken, met den Druck zijn gemeen gemaeckt, ende noch dagelijcx werden gedivulgeert ende verkocht, als daer zijn de Boecken genaemt *de Leviathan, Bibliotheca Fratrum Polonorum, quos unitarios vocant, Philosophia Sacræ Scripturæ interpres:* als mede *Tractatus Theologico Politicus,* ende dat Wy naer examinatie van den inhouden van dien bevinden, niet alleen dat de selve renverseren de Leere van de ware Christelijcke Gereformeerde Religie, nemaer oock overvloeyen van alle lasteringen tegens Godt, ende syne Eygenschappen, ende des selfs aenbiddelijcke Drie Eenigheydt, tegens de Godtheydt Jesu Christi, ende syne Ware voldoeninge; midtsgaders de fondamentele Hooft-Poincten van de voorschreve Ware Christelijcke Religie, ende in effecte d'authoriteyt van de Heylige Schrifture, t'eenemael soo veel in haer is in vilipendie, en de swacke ende niet wel gefondeerde gemoederen in twijfelinge trachten te brengen, alles directelijck jegens iterative Resolutien ende Placaten van den Lande daer jegens ge-emaneert. Soo 1ST, Dat wy tot voorkominge van dit schadelijck Vergift, ende om soo veel mogelijck te beletten,dat daer door niemand en moge werden misleyt, hebben geoordeelt van Onsen plicht de voorsz. Boecken te verklaren soodanigh als voorsz. is, ende te decrieren voor Gods-lasterlijcke en Ziel-verdeffelijcke Boecken, vol van ongefondeerde en dangereuse stellingen en grouwelen, tot naedeel van de Ware Religie ende Kerchendienst. Verliedende dien-volgende als noch by desen allen ende een yegelijcken, de selve of dier-gelijcke te Drucken, divulgeeren ofte verkoopen, op Auctien ofte andersints, op peyne by de Placaten van den Lande, ende specialijck dat van den ne-genthienden September 1653, daer toe ghestatueert: Lastende een yeder die dit aengaet, hem daer na te reguleren, ende dat de-sen sal worden gepubliceert en alomme geaffigeert, daer het be-hoort, ende in gelijcke saecken te geschieden gebruyckelijck is. Gegeven onde het Zegel van Justicie hier onder opgedruckt, op den negenthienden Julij, 1674. Onder stondt, In kennisse van My. Was gheteeckent,

AD. POTS.

APPENDIX C

Letters not contained in Spinoza's published works

1. Prof. Land has recently discovered that the Dutch originals of two of Spinoza's letters to Blyenbergh were printed in an old periodical *(Boekzaal der geleerde Werreld)* as long ago as 1705. One of these (Ep. 32 in Latin version), had been lost sight of ever since. The other (Ep. 38) had meanwhile been recovered by Dr. van Vloten and printed in his *Supplementum.* The final paragraph of Ep. 32 was omitted in the Latin version of the *Opera Posthuma,* but is not without interest, as it shows conclusively that Spinoza wrote Dutch with difficulty and regarded it as a foreign language.[352] This portion is here reprinted from Prof. Land's paper 'Over de eerste uitgaven der brieven van Spinoza,' Amsterdam, 1879: —

Dit is myn Heer al wat ik nu weet by te brenge om U. E. op sijn vraag te aantwoorde. nu wensch ik niet hooger, als dat het U. E. mocht voldoen. doch indien U. E. noch swaarigheyt vint; so versoek ik dat ik die ook mach weeten, om te sien, of ik die sow konnen wegh neemen. U. E. hoeft van sijn kant niet te schroomen, maar so lang hem dunkt niet voldaan te syn, so heb ik niet liever als de reeden daar van te weete, op dat eindelyk de waarheit mocht blyke. ik wenschte wel dat ik in de taal, waar mee ik op gebrocht ben, mocht schryven. ik sow mogelyk myn gedaghte beeter konnen uytdrukke, doch U. E. gelieft het so voor goet te neemen, en selfs de fouten verbeetren. en my te houwe voor

U. E. toegeneege Vrient

En Dienar

B. DE SPINOZA

Op de Lange bogart den 5 Januari 1665

Ik zal op dese boogart een drie a vier weeke noch

---

[352] This throws great doubt on the account given by Colerus of his projected Dutch translation of the Old Testament, p. 415, above. The same statement is made in the 'Catalogue des ouvrages de Mr de Spinosa' at the end of the Life by Lucas.

blyven, en dan meen ik weer nae voorburgh te gaan. ik geloof dat ik voor die tyt aantwoord van U E sal krygen. indien de afairen het niet toe en laate, so gelieft U E na voorburgh te schryve, met dit opschrift, te bestellen in de kerk laan ten huyse van meester daniël tydeman de schilder.

Translation

This, Sir, is all I can now contribute to answering your question, and I have no higher wish than that it may satisfy you. But in case you still find any difficulty, I beg you to let me know of that also, to see if I may be able to remove it. You have nothing to fear on your side, but so long as you are not satisfied, I like nothing better than to be informed of your reasons, so that finally the truth may appear. I could have wished to write in the tongue in which I have been brought up. I should perhaps have been able to express my thoughts better. But be pleased to take it as it is, amend the mistakes yourself, and believe me,

Your sincere Friend
and Servant
B. DE SPINOSA.

Lange Boogart (Long Orchard, Amsterdam)
the 5th January, 1665.

I shall stay here three or four weeks more, and then I think of going back to Voorburg. I believe I shall get your answer before that time. If business prevent it, be pleased to write to Voorburg, addressed to be delivered in the Church lane at the house of Mr. Daniel Tydeman, painter.

2. The following autograph letter of Spinoza is preserved in Victor Cousin's library at the Sorbonne. It was seen in Cousin's lifetime by Saisset, who gave a translation in his *Œuvres de Spinoza* (2nd ed. vol iii. *ad fin.*) but did not publish the original or even mention in what language it was written. The Latin text is now printed for the first time. How the MS. came into Cousin's possession is no longer known, but there is no reason to doubt its authenticity. Being dated as well as signed, the document seems to be the letter actually sent, not a draft retained by Spinoza. It is written on one leaf, 21˙1 x 16˙2 centimetres. The letter and signature closely agree with other known specimens of Spinoza's writing, and are very neat and clear.

The following signs are used to represent the state of the MS. Italics denote interlineations: small capitals, writing interlined over a complete cancellation: square brackets, that the bracketed words or letters are cancelled by drawing a line through but remain legible.

Do. Ludovico Majero S.P.D. B. de Spinoza.

Amice suavissime

Præfationem, quam mihi per amicum nostrum de Vries misisti, en tibi per eundem remitto. Pauca, ut ipse videbis, in margine notavi. sed adhuc pauca supersunt, quæ tibi per literas significare consultius duxi. Nempe 1. ubi pag. 4 [ubi] lectorem mones, quâ ocasione[353] primam partem composuerim, vellem ut simul ibi, aut ubi placuerit, etiam moneres me eam intra duas hebdomadas composuisse. hoc enim præmonito nemo putabit, hæc adeo clare proponi, ut [si] quæ clarius explicari non possent, adeoque verbulo uno, aut altero,[354] quod forte hic illic obscurum ofendent,[355] non hærebunt. 2°. vellem moneres me multa alio modo quam a Cartesio demonstrata sunt demonstrare, non ut Cartesium corrigam, sed tantum, ut meum ordinem melius retineam, et numerum axiomatum non ita a*u*gerem. et hac etiam de causa multa, quæ a Cartesio nuda sine ulla demonstratione proponuntur, demonstrare, et alia, quæ cartesius [o]missa fecit, addere debuisse. denique enixissime te rogare volo, amice charissime, ut illa, quæ in fine scripsisti, in ilium homunculum missa faceres, [et] ipsaque prorsus deleres. Et quamvis ad hoc te rogandum multæ moveant rationes, unam tantum reddam, vellem enim, ut omnes sibi facile persuadere possint, hæc in omnium hominum gratiam evulgari, teque in hoc libello edendo solo veritatis propagandæ desiderio teneri, teque adeo maxime curare, ut hoc opusculum omnibus gratum sit, hominesque ad veræ philosophiæ studium benevole, atque benigne invitARE omniumque utilitati studere. quod facile unusquisque credet, ubi neminem lædi videbit. nec aliquid proponi, quod alicui offendiculo esse

---

[353] *Sic.*

[354] The last letter is an *o* altered to *i*, or *i* altered to *o,* it is difficult to say which: *uno aut altero* makes a good and classical construction: *uni aut alteri* would possibly not be wrong, but there is very little authority for the dative governed by *haereo* in this sense.

[355] *Sic.*

potest. quod si tamen postea vir iste, aut alius suum malevolum animum ostendere velit: tum ejus vitam, et mores non sine applausu depingere poteris. peto igitur, ut eousque expectare non graveris, teque exorare sinas, et me tibi addictissimum credas, atque

> omni studio tuum
> B. de Spinoza.

Voorburgi 3 augusti 1663.

Written across on inner margin:

amicus de Vries hæc secum ferre promisserat,[356] sed quia nescit quando ad vos reversurus est, per alium mitto.

On the back of the leaf:

his tibi simul mitto partem scholii prop. 27. partis 2. sicut pagina 75 incipit, ut ipsum typographo tradas, et denuo imprimatur.

Hæc quæ *hic* mitto debent necessario denuo imprimi et [quamvis] 14 vel 15 regulæ addi debent, quæ commode possunt intertexi.

The preface in question in this letter is that written by Meyer for the 'Principles of Cartesian Philosophy'(see p. 48 above). Spinoza's directions were faithfully carried out. I can offer no definite suggestion as to who the *homunculus* may have been: presumably it was some stubborn opponent of philosophy in general and the new Cartesian doctrines in particular, who had already been engaged in controversy with Meyer.

The quarrel cannot have been with Spinoza, who at that time had published nothing.

Translation

Dear Friend, — The preface you sent me by our friend De Vries I now send back to you by the same hand. Some few things, as you will see, I have marked in the margin; but yet a few remain, which I have judged it better to mention to you by letter. First, where on page 4 you give the reader to know on what occasion I composed the first part; I would have you likewise explain there, or where you please, that I composed it within a fortnight. For when this is explained none will suppose

---

[356] *Sic.*

the exposition to be so clear as that it cannot be bettered, and so they will not stick at obscurities in this and that phrase on which they may chance to stumble. Secondly, I would have you explain that when I prove many points otherwise than they be proved by Descartes, 'tis not to amend Descartes, but the better to preserve my order, and not to multiply axioms overmuch: and that for this same reason I prove many things which by Descartes are barely alleged without any proof, and must needs add other matters which Descartes let alone. Lastly, I will earnestly beseech you, as my especial friend, to let be everything you have written towards the end against that creature, and wholly strike it out. And though many reasons determine me to this request, I will give but one. I would fain have all men readily believe that these matters are published for the common profit of the world, and that your sole motive in bringing out the book is the love of spreading the truth; and that it is accordingly all your study to make the work acceptable to all, to bid men with all courtesy to the pursuit of genuine philosophy, and to consult their common advantage. Which every man will be ready to think when he sees that no one is attacked, nor anything advanced where any man can find the least offence. Notwithstanding, if afterwards the person you know of, or any other, be minded to display his ill will, then you may portray his life and character, and gain applause by it. So I ask that you will not refuse to be patient thus far, and suffer yourself to be entreated, and believe me wholly bounden to you, and

Yours with all affection,

B. DE SPINOZA.

Voorburg, Aug. 3, 1663.

Our friend De Vries had promised to take this with him; but seeing he knows not when he will return to you, I send it by another hand.

Along with this I send you part of the scholium to prop. 27, part 2, where page 75 begins, that you may hand it to the printer to be reprinted.

This matter I send you must of necessity be reprinted, and 14 or 15 lines added, which may easily be inserted.

APPENDIX D

Circular of the Spinoza Committee

AT the beginning of 1876 the following circular was issued in Dutch, English, French, and German by the Committee formed in Holland for the erection of a statue to Spinoza at the Hague

A STATUE TO SPINOZA

The wish expressed among us a short time ago and assented to from many sides, to see a statue of Spinoza arise at the Hague, must find an echo in many minds as the February of 1877, the bicentenary of his death, is drawing near. We have accordingly resolved to combine for its realization, and to invite the co-operation of foreigners as well as of our own countrymen.

While Germany has for many years contemplated the bronze statue of Kant at Königsberg, Holland should no longer be deprived of that of Spinoza, who was born and bred on her ground, and who breathed and thought in her atmosphere. She has honoured her painting in Rembrandt, her poetry in Vondel, her love of liberty in William of Orange, her naval glory in De Ruyter, her literary culture in Erasmus, her medical science in Boerhaave, and she now seeks to add to their bronze statues that of the philosopher, whose writings — too long and too often misunderstood — have proved replete with life-giving wisdom for many countries and for many times.

Unlike Kant at Königsberg, Spinoza had no academical chair at his disposal, nor did he draw around him a circle of private pupils, but from his humble apartment on the Paviljoensgracht at the Hague, where he spent the last ten or twelve years of his short life, he communicated the ripe productions of his mind to humanity at large. From there he drew the attention of contemporaries and of posterity to the nature of man's material and moral existence, and to the conditions of his bodily and spiritual welfare. At the Hague therefore his statue ought to find a place, by preference in sight of that house on the peaceful spot (still remembered as a canal) which by its quiet surroundings is well worthy of the calm thinker.

We are rejoiced, though scarcely surprised, that so many distinguished men of science and letters in different countries have at once expressed their willingness to join with us in the accomplishment of this design. They have understood that Spinoza is not merely a Dutch but also a world-wide name, and that his memory deserves to be gratefully honoured wherever civilization extends. We confidently leave to their care the promotion of our object in their respective countries, and we trust that their encouraging example may stimulate our and Spinoza's countrymen to more strenuous exertion.

We ask the support not only of the students of philosophy who can appreciate his subtle and far-reaching thought, but also of all those who honour that courageous striving for truth and for intellectual liberty in which his moral greatness consists.

The Hague, January 1876.

The Spinoza-Committee:

M. D. Count VAN LIMBURG STIRUM, Honorary Chairman, *The Hague.*

Dr. M. F. A. G. CAMPBELL, Chairman, *The Hague.*

Dr. H. J. BETZ, Secretary, *The Hague.*

Dr. A. WM. JACOBSON, Treasurer, *The Hague.*[357]

Prof. J. BOSSCHA, *The Hague.*

Prof. J. P. N. LAND, *Leiden.*

Dr. A. VAN DER LINDE, *Arnhem.*

MART. NIJHOFF, *The Hague.*

Dr. A. VAN OVEN, *Dordrecht.*

L. PINCOFFS, *Rotterdam.*

Dr. J. RUTGERS, *The Hague.*

Dr. T. J. STIELTJES, *Rotterdam.*

Prof. B. J. STOKVIS, *Amsterdam.*

Dr. J. VAN VLOTEN, *Bloemendaal.*[358]

Dr. J. E. DE VRIJ, *The Hague.*

I add the Dutch text, as being the original.

---

[357] Since retired.
[358] Became Treasurer on Mr. Jacobson's retirement.

EEN STANDBEELD VOOR SPINOZA.

De wensch, vóór korten tijd openlijk ten onzent geuit, en al aanstonds van verschillende zijden beaamd en toegejuicht, om eerlang in den Haag een standbeeld voor SPINOZA te zien verrijzen, moet, bij het naderen van den tweehonderdsten jaardag zijns overlijdens in Februari 1877, in veler gemoed te luider weêrklank vinden. Dit bracht ons tot het besluit, de handen tot zijn vervulling ineen te slaan, en ook anderen, buiten en binnen's land, tot krachtdadige meêwerking uit te noodigen.

Ziet Duitschland reeds sedert jaren zijn KANT in brons te Koningsbergen prijken, Nederland mag den op zijn boden geboren en getogen, en zijn dampkring ademenden en denkenden SPINOZA niet langer derven. Zijn schilderkunst heeft het in REMBRANDT, zijn dichtkunst in VONDEL, zijn vrijheidszin in WILLEM VAN ORANJE, zijn zeeroem in DE RUITER, zijn geletterde beschaving in ERASMUS, zijn medische wetenschap in BOERHAAVE gehuldigd: het voege thans aan hunne bronzen beelden dat van den wijsgeer toe, die voor landgenoot en vreemden van zijnen en later tijd in zijn te lang en te vaak miskende geschriften zoo levenwekkende wijsheid boekte.

Had hij daartoe niet — als KANT te Koningsbergen — een akademischen leerstoel ter beschikking, — in den Haag, waar hij de laatste tien of twaalf jaren van zijn kortstondig leven doorbracht, heeft hij, van zijn kleine woonvertrek aan de Paviljoensgracht uit, tot geen grooter of kleiner tal van scholieren, maar, in zijn rijpste denkgewrochten, tot de gansche menschheid gesproken. Van dáár maakte hij tijdgenoot en nakomeling op aard en wezen opmerkzaam van 's menschen stoffelijk en zedelijk bestaan, en op de voorwaarden van zijn welstand naar lichaam en geest. In dien Haag moet dan ook dat standbeeld, liefst in 't gezicht van dat woonvertrek, op de sedert gedempte stille gracht een plaats vinden, door haar kalme omgeving den kalmen rustigen denker ten volle waardig.

Het verheugt ons, al behoefde 't ons waarlijk niet te bevreemden, voor de verwezenlijking van dat denkbeeld al aanstonds den vollen bijval en welkome toezegging hunner medewerking erlangd te hebben van zooveel uitheemsche mannen van wetenschap, als zich, blijkens hun onderschreven namen, voor verschillende landen bij ons hebben aangesloten.

SPINOZA toch is geen uitsluitend Nederlandsche, hij is tevens een wereldgrootheid, wiens nagedachtenis door de gansche beschaafde wereld dankbaar moet worden gevierd. Dat hebben die mannen begrepen, en terwijl wij daarom ook vertrouwend aan hunne zorg de bevordering van ons plan in hun verschillende woonstreken overlaten, meenen wij te mogen verwachten, dat hun opwekkelijk voorbeeld onze en SPINOZA'S landgenooten tot des te volvaardiger meêwerking zal aanlokken.

Wij verwachten haar niet enkel van de beoefenaars der wijsbegeerte, die SPINOZA'S vernuft en denkkracht roemen, maar van allen, die het moedig streven naar waarheid, en het voorstaan der vrijheid van denken eeren, waarin zijne zedelijke grootheid gelegen is.

's Gravenhage, Januari 1876.

The following persons gave their support as honorary or corresponding members of the Committee. In some cases local subcommittees were also formed, and in this country the London Committee issued a somewhat abridged and modified version of the circular.

Argentine Republic

Dr. D. F. SARMIENTO
Prof. H. WEYENBERGH

Austria

Prof. AD. BEER
Graf CORONINI
Dr. ED. SÜSS
Dr. J. UNGER

Batavia (Dutch East Indies)

Dr. F. H. BAUER
Mr. L. W. C. v. D. BERG
Dr. P. A. BERGSMA
P. v. DIJK
W. P. GROENEVELDT
Mr. T. H. DER KINDEREN

Belgium.

J. DE GEYTER

Prof. J. F. HEREMANS
Prof. F. LAURENT
Dr. A. WILLEMS

France

Prof. CLAUDE BERNARD[1359]
Prof. M. BERTHELOT
Prof. AD. FRANCK
Prof. PAUL JANET
Dr. LOUIS J. KOENIGSWARTER
Dr. E. LITTRÉ
E. RENAN
JULES SIMON
Prof. H. TAINE

Germany

Dr. BERTHOLD AUERBACH
Prof. J. BERGMANN

[1359] Since deceased.

Prof. KUNO FISCHER
Prof. H. HELMHOLTZ
Prof. M. LAZARUS
Prof. C. v. PRANTL
Prof. C. SCHAARSCHMIDT
Prof. CHR. SIGWART
Prof. H. v. SYBEL
Prof. ED. ZELLER

Great Britain and Ireland

MATTHEW ARNOLD, Esq.
Prof. A. BAIN
Sir B. C. BRODIE, Bart
Prof. BRYCE
Prof. W. K. CLIFFORD[360]
Prof. G. CROOM ROBERTSON
M. E. GRANT DUFF, Esq., M.P.
T. H. FARRER, Esq.
J. FOWLER, Esq.
J. A. FROUDE, Esq.
Hon. Mr. Justice GROVE
Prof. T. H. HUXLEY
Prof. B. JOWETT, Master of
        Ballio Coll., Oxford
W. E. H. LECKY, Esq.
G. H. LEWES, Esq.[361]
REV. J. P. MAHAFFY
Sir LOUIS MALLET, C. B.
Rev. Prof. MARKS
Rev. JAMES MARTINEAU
Prof. MAX MÜLLER
F. POLLOCK, Esq.
The Hon. RODEN NOEL
Lord ARTHUR RUSSELL, M.P.
SHADWORTH H. HODGSON, Esq.
HERBERT SPENCER, Esq.
W. SPOTTISWOODE, Esq.[362]

J. HUTCHISON STIRLING, Esq.
JAMES SULLY, Esq.
Principal TULLOCH
Prof. J. TYNDALL

Italy

Prof. A. DE GUBERNATIS
Prof. J. MOLESCHOTT
Prof. A. VERA

Russia

J. ADDENS
Prof. W. BOLIN
Prof. J. J. W. LAGUS
Prof. G. TEICHMÜLLER

Sweden

Prof. S. RIBBING, Upsala

Switzerland

Prof. C. HEBLER, Bern

United States

Prof. E. L. YOUMANS, New-York

---

[360] Since deceased.
[361] Since deceased.
[362] President of the Royal Society.

TABLE SHOWING SPINOZA'S POSITION IN THE HISTORY OF PHILOSOPHY.

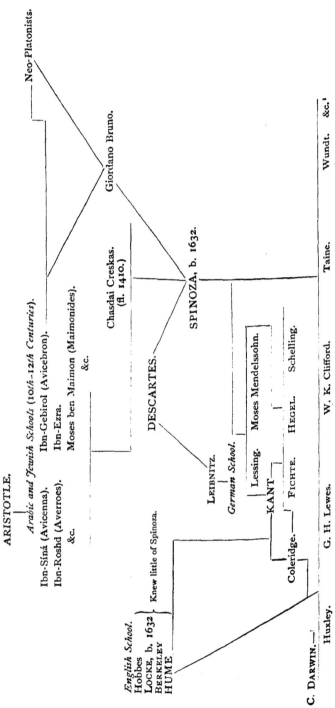

¹ This line does not profess to be a list of modern psychologists of the scientific school, but only to give some representative names of such as have certainly or probably been also students of Spinoza.